Southern Africa in the 1980s

Southern Africa in the 1980s

Edited by

Olajide Aluko
Professor of International Relations, University of Ife

and

Timothy M. Shaw
Professor of Political Science, Dalhousie University

London
GEORGE ALLEN & UNWIN
Boston   Sydney

© George Allen & Unwin (Publishers) Ltd, 1985.
This book is copyright under the Berne Convention. No reproduction without permission. All rights reserved.

George Allen & Unwin (Publishers) Ltd,
40 Museum Street, London WC1A 1LU, UK

George Allen & Unwin (Publishers) Ltd,
Park Lane, Hemel Hempstead, Herts HP2 4TE, UK

Allen & Unwin, Inc.,
Fifty Cross Street, Winchester, Mass. 01890, USA

George Allen & Unwin Australia Pty Ltd,
8 Napier Street, North Sydney, NSW 2060, Australia

First published in 1985.

British Library Cataloguing in Publication Data

Southern Africa in the 1980s.
1. Africa, Southern – Foreign relations
– 1975–
I. Aluko, Olajide   II. Shaw, Timothy M.
327.68   DT746
ISBN 0-04-320169-5

Library of Congress Cataloging in Publication Data
Main entry under title:
Southern Africa in the 1980s.
Includes index.
1. Africa, Southern – Politics and government – 1975-
– Addresses, essays, lectures. 2. Africa, Southern – Foreign relations
–1975– – Addresses, essays, lectures. 3. Africa, Southern – Economic
conditions – 1975– – Addresses, essays, lectures. 4. Africa, Southern
– Strategic aspects – Addresses, essays, lectures.
I. Aluko, Olajide.   II. Shaw, Timothy M.
DT746.S585   1985   968.06'3   84-18544
ISBN 0-04-320169-5 (alk. paper)

Set in 11 on 12 point Times by Fotographics (Bedford) Ltd
and printed in Great Britain by Mackays of Chatham

Preface

This collection marks another stage in the further development of (1) the liberation of the peoples of Southern Africa, and (2) the maturation of the Department of International Relations at Ife, both of which have progressed markedly in the first half of the 1980s. It results from a very successful international conference on 'Southern Africa in the eighties' held on the Ife campus in mid-December 1980. That meeting, including the participation of several international scholars, was made possible by generous grants from the Federal Government of Nigeria, the Ford Foundation and the university authorities. Both the conference arrangements and the preparation of this manuscript were advanced by the unfailing activities of Dr Sola Ojo and Dr Amadu Sesay of the Department of International Relations. And our roles as editors were greatly facilitated, as always, by our outstanding secretaries: 'Tunde Akibu at Ife and Doris Boyle at Dalhousie. It is a pleasure to acknowledge the assistance, support and friendship of such fine people, which is, ultimately, what liberation – political and personal – is all about.

The preparation, presentation and revision of the papers on which this volume is based took place prior to two major events at the end of 1983 and start of 1984: the Buhari *coup* in Nigeria on New Year's Eve 1983 and the Nkomati Accord between South Africa and Mozambique in March 1984. Despite the short-term impacts of these and related events – such as the foreign exchange crisis in Nigeria and three-year drought in Southern Africa – the longer-term analyses proposed here remain valid.

Olajide Aluko, Ife
Timothy M. Shaw, Dalhousie
March 1983

Contents

Introduction

OLAJIDE ALUKO and
TIMOTHY M. SHAW

If the early 1960s were the years of Black Africa because of the rapid rate of decolonisation which resulted from the rise of nationalist parties, then the early 1980s are likely to be the years of Southern Africa because of the series of successes which the liberation movements have scored against the remaining racist regimes. The log-jam along the Zambesi River broke decisively with the Portuguese coup of 1974 following a decade of apparent immobility after Zambia's independence in 1964. But the causes of that metropolitan coup lay in the guerrilla struggles in Portugal's African colonies – Angola, Guinea-Bissau and Mozambique – which had been in progress since the early 1960s because this colonial power refused to accept the inevitability of decolonisation. And independence in Guinea-Bissau (1974), Mozambique (1975) and Angola (1975) was followed by a stunning nationalist victory in Zimbabwe: after fifteen years of UDI, guerrilla struggle and endless diplomacy, Robert Mugabe's ZANU(PF) won the April 1980 election. Following Mozambique, Angola and Zimbabwe, Africa's attentions and resources are now concentrated on Namibia.

(1) From Continuity to Change

The early 1980s symbolise, then, a dramatic shift in the balance of forces in Southern Africa from apparently entrenched white power to increasingly ascendant black power. Assuming that Namibia is free under an internationally acceptable and recognised formula before 1985, the decade 1975–85 will come to mark the turning-point between racism and multiracialism, minority rule and majority rule, individual accumulation and collective development. Thereafter, once Africa has regrouped its diplomatic and strategic forces, it will be ready for the final assault on the white-ruled redoubt – South Africa itself. Despite scepticism early in the 1960s and 1970s, the continent may yet be free before the end of the twentieth century.

This volume is both timely and significant, therefore, because it advances (*a*) analysis of the new situation in Southern Africa as the region digests the manifold implications of the birth of Zimbabwe, and (*b*) analysis of this situation by African as well as non-African scholars. The timeliness of the conference from which this collection results is a tribute both to the tenacity and courage of the freedom-fighters who relentlessly and in the face of seemingly insuperable odds undermine colonial and settler rule, as well as to the foresight of the organisers who set the mechanics for such an international meeting into action well before the catalytic Lancaster House talks and elections. The result, happily, is significant because it presents a set of essentially Afrocentric views on the current history and future direction of Southern Africa.[1] Hopefully timeliness and significance will combine to make this book a notable one, one of which the conference sponsors – particularly the Ford Foundation – can be proud.

The distinctive quality of this collection lies, then, in its contemporary approach to past, present and future conditions and relations in Southern Africa; its underlying theme is change and continuity in regional affairs, continental concerns and global factors. To be sure, certain conservative forces persist, especially at the global level, but their salience declines inexorably as more progressive interests come to determine the direction and rate of change within the region itself.

(2) From Global to Regional Determinants

To be sure, Southern Africa remains an international 'subsystem' because of its continuing incorporation into patterns of world trade, production and communication. Nevertheless, recent shifts within the region mark the commencement of the process of redefining Southern Africa's extraregional relations.[2] To this extent – at present, admittedly, more aspiration than actuality – the subsystem is beginning to look to itself rather than to foreign sources for new opportunities through which to develop. The potential for greater regional autonomy is considerably enhanced, even without the freedom of South Africa, because of the creation of Zimbabwe (see Chapters 5 and 9).

So the primary message of this collection, as of the conference proceedings on which it is based, is that Southern Africa has begun to achieve more autonomy in design and direction than ever before – the prospects for which will grow in both conception and content as Namibia and South Africa are liberated. The most distinct sign of this mood of optimism and opportunity is the formation of the Southern African Development Co-ordination Conference (SADCC), an expanded grouping – with economic and infrastructural rather than political or strategic focus – centred on the six front line states. The ten SADCC members (that is, those of the region without Namibia or South Africa), with their headquarters in Gaberones, Botswana, are determined to disengage from and still confront the white redoubt, while increasing their own multilateral interactions. Together SADCC and the front line states advance movement towards collective self-reliance and towards collective confrontation.

The continuing transition from the FLS to SADCC marks a further step in the development of Africa's continental foreign policy towards the decolonisation of the Southern African subsystem. Initially the Organisation of African Unity (OAU) and then its Liberation Committee were the primary institutions to articulate and advance the continent's interests (see Chapter 2) with Nigeria as a special observer (see Chapter 3). Now the front line states (FLS), with their strategic and diplomatic thrust, are joined by SADCC, with its economic and infrastructural focus. Together these two are both compatible and reinforcing: SADCC plots the regional co-operation that enables the FLS to challenge racist rule. Collective self-reliance in production and exchange serves to erode the constraints that South Africa's established regional dominance has sought to perpetuate as a means to divert the attention and energy of the front line states away from the liberation movement (see Chapter 13).

If one result of the successful execution of FLS/SADCC strategy has been to make the OAU somewhat marginal in regional affairs, then another has been to reduce the salience of extraregional actors (see Part 2). Of course, Southern Africa remains a subsystem, very much affected by broader global trends and events. None the less, the impact of the great powers and major non-state interests like multinational corporations has begun to decline as (*a*) the African states in the region come together and reduce their vulnerability to such intrusive pressures, and (*b*) South Africa increasingly excludes itself from the Western world, the tendency towards conservative governments among the advanced industrialised states notwithstanding.

Despite the revival of the Cold War between Reagan's America and the Soviet Union and the accompanying renewal of the arms race, interimperial rivalries and economic difficulties divert superpower attention away from Southern Africa. For a variety of reasons Europe is increasingly distancing itself from the USA on African issues, despite Mrs Thatcher's conservative coalition with Reagan; the combination of Mitterand's socialist government in France and the anti-nuclear movement throughout Europe will perpetuate this direction. If the USA has difficulties with Europe and Japan, so does the USSR with China and with parts of Eastern Europe. Moreover, the general mood in the North is mercantilist and isolationist rather than interventionist. Therefore, although Southern Africa will feature on Cold War and conference agendas, many pressures will be channelled into the region through the major protagonists – the FLS and South Africa – rather than being applied on the subsystem directly. Multilateral 'contact-group' shuttle diplomacy between these two protagonists is symptomatic of external influence becoming both more indirect and more marginal.

(3) Towards the End of the Century and of the Conflict

If, then, the primary contemporary features of Southern Africa are (*a*) the rise of the liberation movement, and (*b*) decline of extraregional influence, the next twenty years are likely to see a continuity in this trend towards change. Despite ambiguities in the FLS/SADCC groupings and in the OAU, and despite contradictions in great power and corporate strategies (see Part 2, and Chapter 12), the inexorable tendency is towards change; that is, towards majority rule in Namibia and South Africa and towards greater autocentricity in the region as political and economic liberation advance.

Clearly, the crucial factor in the rate and character of change in the future as in the past is South Africa, the regional power (see Chapter 14). Just as a decade elapsed between the independence of Zambia and that of its neighbour, Mozambique, so there may be something of a hiatus between the liberation of Namibia and that of South Africa. While the outcome is unlikely to be either rapid or clean, however, the result is inevitable. But as indicated in Part 4, any number of diversions may arise, especially if the liberation process is protracted.

The postponement of freedom in Namibia and South Africa complicates progress towards collective self-reliance and perpetuates the region's vulnerability to external pressures. Nevertheless, the primary determinants are, as already suggested, likely to be regional: the liberation movements and the FLS/SADCC, along with African interests inside the two territories such as workers, peasants and the unemployed.

The contradictions of apartheid are relentless and unavoidable, despite the Afrikaner regime's continuing attempts to increase its security and authority. Moves towards corporatism or neo-fascism are indicative of settler vulnerability rather than capabilities.[3] As Africa comes to concentrate on Namibia and South Africa, so its strategy will continue to become more appropriate, forceful and sophisticated. For just as the last twenty years reveal a dramatic evolution in OAU/FLS tactics, so the next twenty will be characterised by continued development. To be sure, there will be setbacks and disappointments. But it is no longer wildly fanciful to assert that victory is certain; such is the measure of progress since 1974.

Notes: Introduction

1 By contrast, see the essentially Eurocentric and great power focus of other new publications: Richard E. Bissell and Chester A. Crocker (eds), *South Africa into the 1980s* (Boulder, Colo: Westview Press, 1979); L. H. Gann and Peter Duignan, *South Africa: War, Revolution or Peace?* (Stanford, Calif.: Hoover Institution, 1978); and John Seiler (ed.), *Southern Africa since the Portuguese Coup* (Boulder, Colo: Westview Press, 1980).

2 For one reasonably enlightened attempt to respond to such changes, regrettably one that the present American administration will obviously not consider, see *South Africa: Time Running Out. The Report of the Study Commission on US Policy toward Southern Africa* (Berkeley, Calif.: University of California Press, 1981).

3 See the rather revealing and pessimistic survey on South Africa, Simon Jenkins, 'The survival ethic', *The Economist*, 19 September 1981, facing p. 60: 'There is growing evidence in South Africa that the logic of Afrikaner control will soon require a new phase of concentration of power. Under such a phase a pseudo-parliament, a semi-free press and considerable freedom of speech may all be treated as expendable relics of an essentially English liberal conscience. They are not required by neo-apartheid. If they impede a new authoritarian regime, they will be removed (Survey p. 16).'

PART ONE

Black Africa and Southern Africa

1

The OAU and Southern Africa

ADEKUNLE AJALA

The part played by and the impact of the OAU on the ongoing attempts to solve the problem of Southern Africa are examined in this chapter. The first section gives a historical sketch of (*a*) the problem of Southern Africa within the context of pan-Africanism before the OAU was founded, and (*b*) the efforts the Organisation has made to deal with the issue from 1963 to the end of the Dialogue debate in 1971. The second section examines (*a*) OAU efforts to unite the different liberation movements in each of the territories of Southern Africa, and (*b*) OAU involvement in post-Portuguese coup developments. Finally, the OAU's future role in efforts to solve the remaining parts of the problem of Southern Africa is assessed.

(1) Southern Africa before and after the OAU, to 1971

The OAU emerged in 1963 as the culmination of pan-African efforts (*a*) to liberate the entire continent from the clutches of imperialism and the yoke of colonialism, (*b*) to unite the emerging independent states and (*c*) to create an atmosphere of brotherliness throughout the continent which would enable the new states to join forces to fight poverty, ignorance and disease with a view to improving the standard of living of all Africans irrespective of sex, religion, or race. By the time the OAU was founded the problems of colonialism, racial discrimination and apartheid were several decades old. As a result, the problem of Southern Africa always came up for discussions at pan-African gatherings. For instance, the first Pan-African Conference in London, in 1900, sent a 'petition to Queen Victoria through the British Government complaining about the treatment of Africans in both South Africa and

Rhodesia'.[1] When in the early 1960s Africa was divided into the Brazzaville, Casablanca and Monrovia groups, the only issue on which they all agreed was the need to end colonialism, racial discrimination and the apartheid system in Southern Africa. It, therefore, did not come as a surprise when at the 1963 summit which founded the OAU, the most important unifying factor was the joint African effort to tackle the problem of Southern Africa.[2] This unanimity of purpose led to the adoption of certain special resolutions at the summit, the principal ones of which concerned themselves with decolonisation, apartheid and racial discrimination.

These resolutions spelt out in great detail not only the OAU's stand on decolonisation, racial discrimination and apartheid, but how the Organisation would tackle the problem. After reaffirming that it is the duty of all African independent states to support dependent people in Africa in their struggle for freedom and independence, the summit called on the colonial powers to take all necessary measures for granting independence to their colonies in accordance with the United Nations (UN) Declaration on the Granting of Independence to Colonial Countries and Peoples.[3] It requested all African states to break off diplomatic and consular relations with Portugal and South Africa because of their continued colonial policies. Also it asked for an effective boycott of the foreign trade of both countries by prohibiting the import of goods from them, closing African ports and airports to their ships and planes, and forbidding the planes of the two countries to overfly the territories of all African states. After appealing to all national liberation movements to co-ordinate their efforts by establishing common action fronts so as to strengthen the effectiveness of their struggle and the rational use of the concerted assistance given them, it established in Dar es Salaam a Liberation Committee responsible (*a*) for harmonising the assistance from African states, and (*b*) for managing a special fund to be set up for that purpose. Furthermore, it agreed to provide the liberation movements free transit and set up a body of volunteers who might render assistance to the movements. The summit also agreed to set up 'a fund for concerted financial assistance to the anti-apartheid movement in South Africa'. It decided to grant scholarships, offer educational facilities and also explore the possibilities of employment in African government services to refugees from South Africa. Furthermore, it appealed to all governments which still had diplomatic, consular and economic relations with South Africa to break off those relations. Finally, the summit sent a delegation of African foreign ministers to put the African point of view to the Security Council. The effects of this unanimous African decision were immediately felt not only at the UN, but throughout the world.

The OAU stand helped to further strengthen the worldwide campaign inside and outside the UN against apartheid. Besides, African states and other non-aligned countries mounted increased diplomatic pressure on the Western powers to (a) comply with the UN arms embargo on South Africa, and (b) cease all activities which enhanced the economic and military potential of the Pretoria regime. Furthermore, the compliance of many African states with the directives contained in the above resolutions helped to raise the morale of the liberation movement. But in spite of all these apparently encouraging developments, the recalcitrants of Southern Africa – South Africa, Portugal and the minority regime in Southern Rhodesia – continued with their policies. This led the OAU administrative secretary-general, Diallo Telli, to declare at the 1964 OAU summit in Cairo that the offensive 'did not have the slightest effect on the regimes' in Southern Africa and also conclude that 'all avenues for peaceful and legal means to alleviate the intolerable conditions have been progressively eliminated by the South African government'.[4] This meeting repeated the call for a boycott of South African goods and also appealed to South Africa's major trading partners to co-operate with it. However, a Council of Ministers' resolution which called on 'all oil-producing countries to cease as a matter of urgency their supply of oil and petrol products to South Africa'[5] did not receive the summit's approval.

This refusal to endorse the Council's resolution on the use of the oil weapon (see Chapter 12) was the first manifestation of backtracking by some OAU members. By the end of 1964 it had also become increasingly clear that in spite of their declarations to the contrary, many African countries were themselves still trading with South Africa, while South African vessels enjoyed the facilities of African ports, and South African Airways were not only overflying some African territorial space, but also using some African airports.[6] It was, however, Rhodesia's Unilateral Declaration of Independence (UDI) that clearly demonstrated the OAU members' inconsistency and prevarication.

UDI had been on the cards even before the OAU was founded. That was why the 1963 summit called on Britain 'not to transfer the powers and attributes of sovereignty to a minority government imposed on African peoples by the use of force and under cover of racial discrimination'. The second session of the OAU Council of Ministers in February 1964 not only called on Britain to find an immediate solution to 'the explosive political situation in Southern Rhodesia', but also recommended to 'Member States of the OAU to reconsider their diplomatic and other relations with Britain should the British government ignore [their call]'.[7] The Council's third session in July 1964 recommended, *inter alia*, that 'African states [should] take a vigorous stand against a Declaration of Independence of Southern Rhodesia by a European minority government and pledge themselves to take appropriate measures, including the recognition and support of an African nationalist government in exile should such an eventuality arise'.[8] Similar rituals took place in March,[9] June[10] and October 1965.[11] The latter resolution specifically recommended the following measures to the Assembly of Heads of State: (*a*) to reconsider all political, economic, diplomatic and financial relations with the government of the United Kingdom in the event of UDI; (*b*) to use all possible means, including force, to prevent UDI; (*c*) to give immediate assistance to the people of Southern Rhodesia in order to bring about majority rule in the country; and (*d*) to appoint a special committee to work out all forms of assistance to Rhodesia.

In his opening address to the October 1965 summit President Nkrumah warned that if UDI was declared, 'the OAU will take whatever steps are necessary'. Although this drew an emotional response, the resolution adopted by the summit was moderate in tone; it did not endorse the recommendation of the Council. Instead it placed responsibility squarely on Britain and urged her to use force to prevent UDI. It also called on the UN to do everything possible to prevent such a declaration. However, it did set up a special committee on Southern Rhodesia and also prepared a plan of action in case Britain granted negotiated independence to a minority regime in the colony. This plan envisaged (*a*) refusal to recognise such a government; (*b*) recognition of a Zimbabwean government-in-exile; (*c*) the holding of an emergency meeting of the OAU Council of Ministers with a view to involving the UN more directly in Rhodesia; (*d*) reconsideration of relations with Britain; and (*e*) the equating of the white minority regime in Rhodesia with that in South Africa.[12]

UDI was formally declared by the minority regime under Ian

Smith about three weeks later on 15 November. Although all the OAU members were unanimous in condemning this illegal declaration, they were divided as to how it could be brought to an end. At this juncture a meeting of the proposed special committee was immediately convened in Dar es Salaam. With the OAU administrative secretary-general present, this committee decided to recommend to the Council of Ministers a resolution committing all African states to a diplomatic boycott of Britain if she failed to crush the rebellion.

An extraordinary session of the Council of Ministers was convened at Addis Ababa on 3–5 December 1965 to tackle the crisis. The Council decided on a strongly worded resolution[13] that all OAU member-states 'should bring into immediate effect a complete blockade against Southern Rhodesia' under a minority racist regime. It also declared 'that if the United Kingdom does not crush the rebellion and restore law and order, and thereby prepare the way for majority rule in Southern Rhodesia by 15 December 1965, the Member States of the OAU shall sever diplomatic relations on that date with the United Kingdom'. But when the decision was made known, many African governments panicked and tried to wriggle out of it. In the end only nine of the thirty-six complied with the resolution.

Why did the OAU members let the Organisation down? Many of them depended on Britain for material, technical and financial assistance which they badly needed for their development programmes; awareness of this limitation forced many OAU member-states not to comply with these resolutions. This factor also led to the adoption of the Lusaka Manifesto (discussed below) and to the general belief that the OAU was a toothless bulldog.

While the OAU was trying to repair its battered image over the Rhodesian crisis, the Organisation was beset with another range of problems. Foremost among these was the spate of coups that swept the continent. The impression created by these military interventions and the disastrous consequences of the Nigerian civil war was that the African still needed more time to be able to rule himself properly. Although the Africans did their very best to disprove this assertion,[14] the white minority regimes of Southern Africa capitalised on it. While this psychological warfare was going on, South Africa, as the undisputed leader of the white redoubts, embarked on measures to prop up the regimes in Rhodesia and the Portuguese colonies as well as make inroads into the pan-

African united front. The easiest prey in this battle to win over Black Africa was Malawi.

Before the end of 1966, Malawi started secret contacts with the South African regime in an effort to secure a loan for her development projects including the building of a new capital. As soon as there were indications that the aid would be forthcoming, Malawi started to attack openly the OAU policy on apartheid. The immediate outcome of this was the signing of a trade agreement between Malawi and South Africa in March 1967. This was quickly followed by South African financial and material aid for installing strong radio transmitters in Malawi. The day before the OAU summit began in Kinshasa, Malawi established diplomatic relations with the apartheid regime. Shortly afterwards, South Africa offered to contribute substantially towards the building of Malawi's new capital at Lilongwe. In addition, the South African Industrial Development Corporation offered Malawi a loan to build a railway linking Malawi with northern Mozambique. Dazzled by Malawi's 'achievement' many African countries showed keen interest in following in Malawi's footsteps. Many of these countries received encouragement from foreign powers, especially France in its bid to widen the already-cracking walls of African unity. This played a not insignificant role in the subsequent dialogue issue.[15]

President Houphouet-Boigny of the Ivory Coast formally launched the dialogue issue at a press conference on 6 November 1970. He was promptly supported by the leaders of the Central African Republic, Dahomey, Gabon, Ghana, Lesotho, Madagascar, Malawi, Niger, Swaziland and Upper Volta. 'Dialogue Club' members contended (a) that the African states lacked both the military and the economic resources to challenge South Africa successfully; (b) that the trade embargo against South Africa was bound to fail since powerful non-African powers such as the USA, Britain, France, the Federal Republic of Germany and Japan have maintained their trading links with South Africa, and many African states themselves could not afford not to do so; and (c) that the efforts of the national liberation movements have so far not been encouraging enough to warrant pinning all hope on them. They, therefore, believed that if the independent African states engaged in a dialogue with the South African regime – that is, diplomatic contacts and exchanges – the desired objective of changing apartheid might be achieved.

Opponents of such a line of action maintained that there could be no meaningful dialogue which was not based on respect for human equality and dignity as stipulated in the Lusaka Manifesto. The dialogue issue generated a lot of debate until it was finally dealt with at Addis Ababa in June 1971. A Declaration on the Question of Dialogue[16] was endorsed by twenty-eight states, with Ivory Coast leading Gabon, Lesotho, Malagasy, Malawi and Mauritius to oppose, while Benin (Dahomey), Togo and Upper Volta abstained.

This anti-dialogue declaration reiterated the commitment of OAU members to the principles of the Charter and went on to state that the Lusaka Manifesto was the only basis for solving the problem of Southern Africa. It rejected the idea of any dialogue with South Africa, unless it was designed 'solely to obtain for the enslaved people of South Africa their legitimate and inherent rights and the elimination of apartheid'. It further stated that if there was going to be any form of dialogue at all, it must 'be commenced only between the minority racist regime of South Africa and the people they are oppressing, exploiting and suppressing'. The declaration maintained that 'the proposal for a dialogue between the independent African states and the racist regime of South Africa is a manoeuvre by that regime and its allies to divide African states, confuse world public opinion, relieve South Africa from international ostracism and isolation and obtain an acceptance of the *status quo* in Southern Africa'. As such, it made it absolutely clear that 'there exists no basis for a meaningful dialogue with the minority racist regime of South Africa'. Finally, it reaffirmed the OAU's 'determination to continue to render and increase its assistance to the liberation movements until victory is achieved' and decreed that henceforth any action by any African state on the problem of Southern Africa must be undertaken (*a*) within the framework of the OAU, and (*b*) in full consultation with the liberation movements of the territories concerned.

The decision of the OAU on the dialogue issue had an immense impact on the morale of the freedom-fighters. This, in turn, encouraged the OAU Liberation Committee to call for increased assistance to the movements, resulting in the intensification of the armed struggle, especially in the Portuguese colonies. Besides, it strengthened the hands of the leaders of the African National Council, who were by then engaged in mobilising African opinion against the Home–Smith proposals to end the Rhodesian rebellion. But more importantly it strengthened the OAU's hand in repeating its call for worldwide action against South Africa. As a sequel to this the OAU originated the idea of the OAU–UN Conference on the problems of Southern Africa which took place in Oslo in April 1973.[17] Because of these developments, the remnants of the Dialogue Club fell totally apart in the following year and the issue was not even mentioned during the subsequent OAU summit held at Rabat in June 1972.

(2)   The OAU and the Liberation Movement

The liberation of each colony is primarily the responsibility of the liberation movements of the colony concerned. The OAU Liberation Committee was established to co-ordinate all assistance from African states and also to manage the special fund set up for the liberation struggle. In order to strengthen their effectiveness efforts have been made to unite all liberation movements in territories having more than one movement. With the exception of Mozambique where FRELIMO was the only liberation movement, the OAU was faced at one time or the other with the problem of trying to unify the movements in Angola, Namibia, Rhodesia and South Africa. With the exception of Namibia where SWAPO became recognised as the sole legitimate and authentic representative of the Namibian people, no tangible measure of success was achieved by the OAU.

The OAU's failure can be ascribed to two main factors. The first centred on the preference accorded different liberation movements by different OAU member-states. A typical example was the Angolan case, where Zaire initially succeeded in getting OAU recognition for the FLNA and in discrediting the MPLA. Meanwhile, some radical states became the champions of the MPLA. Therefore, an agreement brought about in 1966 by the OAU between the two movements only achieved paper unity. These two movements, as well as UNITA, engaged in a bitter struggle when the Portuguese suddenly declared Angola independent without handing over power to any constituted authority.

The fact that most of the assistance received by the liberation movements were not channelled through the OAU made it difficult for the Organisation to unite these movements. Although most of this assistance came from the socialist countries, Sino-Soviet rivalry largely determines who gets what and from where. Rhodesia is a classic example of this situation: ZANU had always received assistance from China, while Russia remained ZAPU's chief benefactor. As a result, all efforts to unite both movements in the Patriotic Front failed.[18] This apparent failure to unite the liberation movements coupled with the spate of coups in Africa and their attendant problems led the states near the theatres of the liberation struggle to embark upon a series of 'good neighbourliness' meetings.

The OAU's poor performance over the Rhodesian crisis and the limited economic, political and military capabilities of the Southern African states caused second thoughts among the leaders of East and Central Africa on how best the Southern African problem could be tackled. The outcome of this exercise was the Lusaka Manifesto of April 1969. Although the manifesto sought to reaffirm the previous OAU stand on Southern Africa, it went on to explain the objectives of its signatories in Southern Africa which they claimed 'stem from our commitment to the principle of human equality'. The manifesto continued:

> To talk of the liberation of Africa is . . . to say two things: First, that the peoples in the territories still under colonial rule shall be free to determine for themselves their own institutions of self-government. Secondly, that the individuals in Southern Africa shall be freed from an environment poisoned by the propaganda of racialism, and given an opportunity to be men – not white men, brown men, yellow men or black men.

These objectives were, of course, not new. The new element was that:

> We would prefer to negotiate rather than destroy, to talk rather than kill. We do not advocate violence; we advocate an end to the violence against human dignity which is now being perpetrated by the oppressors of Africa. If peaceful progress to emancipation were possible, or if changed circumstances were to make it possible in the future, we would urge our brothers in the resistance movements to use peaceful methods of struggle even at the cost of some compromise on the timing of change.

This position was subsequently endorsed by both the OAU and the UN.

Reactions to the manifesto were mixed. The liberation movements felt somewhat betrayed and pushed into a compromising posture with the regimes they were fighting. So they ignored the manifesto. The Western press, on the other hand, interpreted this as Africa's abandonment of the armed struggle. More seriously, the Western powers saw it as a sign of weakness which should be exploited to the full. Some of them cajoled certain African leaders into advocating a policy of dialogue with South Africa, while the British Conservative Party made it an election pledge to resume the sale of arms to the South African regime whenever it came back into power. And following its victory at the June 1970 general election Edward Heath, the new British Prime Minister, immediately announced that the new government was willing to break the UN embargo on the sales of arms to South Africa. The OAU sent a delegation under the leadership of President Kaunda not only to persuade the British government to alter its decision, but also to plead with other Western powers to adhere strictly to the UN arms embargo. The mission was a failure.[19]

The humiliation suffered by the OAU delegation, as well as the petulant behaviour of Prime Minister Heath at the 1971 Singapore Commonwealth meeting, contributed in no small measure to the rejection of dialogue at the 1971 OAU summit. The OAU must have come to the conclusion that the Western powers would never abandon their kith and kin in Southern Africa, especially as their economic interests were also at stake. This awareness was reflected in the deliberations of the Organisation during the Rabat Summit in June 1972. Most of the meeting was devoted to decolonisation with particular reference to the Portuguese colonies. Besides, the summit adopted a much more radical stand on the issue of Southern Africa: the special liberation fund was to be increased by 50 per cent; representatives of the liberation movements were to be granted the right to speak at the meetings of the Council of Ministers on all matters concerning the liberation struggle, as well as the right to attend the closed sessions of the assembly; and the membership of the Liberation Committee was also increased. For the first time member-states were called upon to give all necessary assistance to those states which might be attacked by the white minority regimes because of their involvement in the liberation struggle. Finally, the summit approved the setting up of a special committee to examine ways and means to tackle the problem of Southern Africa. The committee's recommendations were unanimously adopted by the 21st session of the Liberation Committee at Accra in January 1973 as the Accra Declaration.

The Accra Declaration reaffirmed the determination of the OAU to make the second decade of the Organisation a decade of the armed struggle; it stressed the need to enhance its capacity to respond effectively to the urgent needs of the next stage of the liberation struggle. It also asserted that while the responsibilities of carrying on the armed struggle rested with the liberation movements, its intensification depended on the availability of appropriate resources at their disposal. African states were expected to (a) pay their outstanding dues to the Special Fund immediately; (b) provide additional material and financial assistance to the liberation movements; (c) provide training facilities for the cadres of the liberation movements in conformity with their needs and requirements; and (d) be ready for collective military and economic assistance to any member-state which might become the victim of aggression from Portugal, Rhodesia, or South Africa.

The Accra Declaration made it clear that the OAU was not happy with the dissension and bickering within the liberation movements and was firmly resolved to grant recognition and assistance in future only to the 'fronts' which were politically and militarily united and could provide evidence of effective operation within their country. More significantly, the OAU agreed to accord priority to the liberation of Portuguese colonies and accordingly decided to give the largest portion of its assistance to liberation movements in those territories.[20]

By this time there were favourable reports about the liberation struggle in the Portuguese territories as well as in Rhodesia. In Rhodesia the north-eastern region was almost virtually under the control of the liberation forces. The situation in the Portuguese territories was so favourable that the executive secretary of the Liberation Committee, Major Hashim I. Mbita, was able to travel extensively in the liberated areas in Guinea and Mozambique. As a sequel to the intensification of the armed struggle the Portuguese dictator, Caetano, agreed to certain changes in the Constitution of Portugal, which included the possibility of the so-called 'overseas provinces' looking forward to some kind of identity of their own and eventual recognition as 'autonomous states'.[21] However, financial, military and administrative control was to remain in Lisbon. The freedom-fighters responded with increased firepower, and the already-devastated Portuguese economy continued its downward trend. Discontent among the populace and the armed forces worsened, thus paving the way for the Portuguese coup of 24 April 1974.

The OAU had cause to be delighted over the overthrow of Portuguese fascism. The white redoubt was in total disarray as the other two partners of the unholy trio began to think seriously how to mend fences with Black Africa. For the OAU, however, the most immediate concern was how to arrange the transfer of power to the indigenous population which had been waging a war of independence since 1961. Meanwhile, the Portuguese government let it be known that Guinea-Bissau's independence would be recognised on 9 September 1974. The dates for the other territories were: Mozambique, 25 June 1975; Cape Verde, 5 July 1975; and São Tomé and Principe, 12 July 1975. Because of the peculiar situation in Angola where three apparently irreconcilable liberation movements were in existence, the independence date was not announced until 5 January–11 November 1975.

Meanwhile, South Africa let it be known in Lusaka that it was prepared to renew the contacts which had been broken off after Vorster's indiscretion over the exchange of correspondence between him and President Kaunda. After several exploratory talks between representatives of both countries, Vorster delivered a speech in the South African Senate in which he advocated a peaceful solution to the problems in Southern Africa as the cost of continued confrontation was 'too high to contemplate'.[22] A few days later Kaunda hailed Vorster's speech as 'the voice of reason'.[23] Thus began so-called 'détente' in Southern Africa. But when it appeared to many OAU member-states and the liberation movements that the front line states which were directly involved in the exercise were going too far, an extraordinary session was convened in Dar es Salaam in April 1975 to deal solely with the new developments.

The Dar es Salaam meeting was very stormy. The front line states in general, and Zambia in particular, came under fire.[24] The Zambian Foreign Minister, Vernon Mwaanga, had the unenviable task of not only defending the policy of his country and the front line states, but also of holding a brief for the South African regime. At the end of the meeting the Dar es Salaam Declaration on Southern Africa was adopted.

According to that Declaration, Africa's real enemy in Rhodesia, Namibia, or South Africa itself is 'the South African government and the power which it wields'. The Declaration then made it absolutely clear that 'there is nothing for free Africa to talk about to the leaders of the apartheid regime in connection with their policies in South Africa', but it left the door open for negotiations on Rhodesia and Namibia as long as the objective of majority rule before independence in those territories was not compromised:

> The OAU would support all efforts made by the Zimbabwe nationalists to win independence by peaceful means. This may mean the holding of a constitutional conference where the nationalist forces will negotiate with the Smith regime. If that takes place, the OAU has the duty to do everything possible to assist the success of such negotiations, in constant consultation with the nationalists until and unless the Zimbabwean nationalists themselves are convinced that talks with Smith have failed. In this event, the freedom fighters will have to intensify the armed struggle with the material, financial and diplomatic assistance of independent Africa.[25]

On Namibia it declared:

> While South Africa remains unwilling to carry out effective decolonisation, Africa as a whole, and all African states, should refrain from any contact with South Africa over the details of its administration of Namibia, or over any plans for the fragmentation of the territory. Instead we must put our full weight behind the demand that South Africa complies with UN Resolutions on Namibia, and we should seek to ensure that all other UN member states observe these resolutions. In the absence of South African agreement to decolonise, Africa must help SWAPO to intensify the armed struggle in Namibia, and support the nationalist movement in every possible way.

Finally, the Declaration made clear that free Africa would never acquiesce in the denial of human equality and human dignity as represented by the apartheid philosophy and system. Africa would continue to urge the world community to ostracise the South African state. And OAU member-states would not only maintain the economic, political and cultural boycott of the republic, but would also seek to extend it.

The Declaration put a check on Zambia's unbridled enthusiasm for peace at all costs, as well as on its undisguised preference for Nkomo. It also made it clear to the South African authorities that free Africa would never abandon its declared policy to bring about majority rule in South Africa itself. It mandated the front line states to go ahead with any meaningful negotiations over Rhodesia with the consent of, and in close collaboration with, the Zimbabwean liberation movements. However, the OAU Liberation Committee must also be involved in all phases of such negotiations.

The Organisation's role in the final stages of Angola's independence struggle is another pointer in the direction of OAU involvement in mediating between and uniting diverse liberation forces. The most significant aspect of this involvement in the last stages of the Angolan independence struggle was the fact that despite foreign manoeuvres and intervention, arm-twisting and financial inducements, the Organisation overcame the initial dilly-dallying of some of its members and finally came round to accord recognition to the government formed by the most dedicated and most capable liberation movement: the MPLA.

Conclusion

In assessing the role of the OAU in decolonisation and in the eradication of racial discrimination and apartheid in Southern Africa one major factor must be borne in mind, that the Organisation can only go as far as its members want it to go. Besides, OAU members are weak both economically and militarily. Furthermore, they pursue different developmental modes. All these factors prevented the Organisation from any drastic or radical decisions which would win the support of most of its members. This situation has made it difficult for the Organisation to be as effective as it should be.

Nevertheless, the OAU has caused change in Southern Africa: it has spearheaded a worldwide campaign against the minority regimes of the area; and it has given the lead in moving many anti-colonial forces in the Third World, and in certain European countries, from moderation to greater militancy. The breaking off of diplomatic relations with Portugal, South Africa and Rhodesia by Third World nations was largely due to its efforts. It has employed diplomacy to muster financial and material support for African liberation struggles.

The OAU will continue with this strategy until independence is achieved in Namibia and the apartheid system in South Africa is abolished. It will now accord priority to the Namibian independence issue. It is then, and only then, that it will be able to work out a new and much more effective strategy for solving the South African problem. In the meantime the OAU will continue to uphold its policy of non-recognition for the so-called 'independence' of the Bantustans.

Notes: Chapter 1

1   A. Ajala, *Pan-Africanism: Evolution, Progress and Prospects* (London: Deutsch, 1973), p. 4.
2   See the speeches made by the different African leaders at the Addis Ababa Summit, 1963, published by the Publications and Foreign Language Press Department, Ministry of Information, Addis Ababa, Ethiopia, 1963.
3   UN General Assembly Resolution 1514 (XV), 14 December 1960.
4   Cited in A. Ajala, 'Conflict and cooperation in Southern Africa', in Timothy Shaw and Sola Ojo (eds), *Africa and the International Political System* (Washington, DC: University Press of America, 1981), pp. 226–68.
5   CM/Res. 31(III).
6   Z. Cervenka, *The Unfinished Quest for Unity: Africa and the OAU* (New York: Africana, 1977), p. 113.
7   CM/Res. 14(II).
8   CM/Res. 33(III).
9   ECM/Res. 50(V).
10 ECM/Res. (V) and ECM/Res. 11(V).
11 CM/Res. 62(V).
12 Ajala, *Pan-Africanism*, op. cit., pp. 221–4.
13 ECM/Res. 13(IV).
14 African students in Europe (especially West Germany in 1966–7) held demonstrations against apartheid and called for the banning of a film called *Africa Addio*, shot on behalf of the South African regime to discredit the entire black race.
15 For accounts of the Dialogue debate, see Colin Legum, 'Dialogue: the great debate', in Colin Legum (ed.), *Africa Contemporary Record. Vol. 4, 1971–72* (London: Rex Collings, 1972), pp. 466–82; and Z. Cervenka, 'The Organisation of African Unity and the policy of "detente" in Southern Africa', *Verfassung und Recht Ubersee* (Hamburg), 3–4 (1975), pp. 372–5.
16 CM/St. 5(XVIII). On the Dialogue debate, see Legum, 'Dialogue: the great debate', op. cit.
17 For the proceedings of the Oslo Conference of April 1973, see Olav Stokke and Carl Widstrand (eds), *Southern Africa: UN–OAU Conference, 9–14 April 1973* (Uppsala: Scandinavian Institute for African Studies, 1973), Vols I and II. Another such major conference was the UN/OAU World Conference for Action against Apartheid, Lagos, Nigeria, 22–26 August 1977.
18 It was much easier for liberation movements from different territories receiving assistance from the same external source to work together. That explains why the ANC of South Africa once formed an alliance with ZAPU of Rhodesia, while both PAC (South Africa) and ZANU (Rhodesia) had a loose working arrangement.
19 Sam C. Nolutshungu, *South Africa in Africa: A Study of Ideology and Foreign Policy* (Manchester: Manchester University Press, 1975), pp. 247–50; and Isebill V. Gruhn, 'British arms sales to South Africa: the limits of African diplomacy', *Studies in Race and Nations. Vol. 3, 1971–72* (Denver, Colo: University of Denver Press, 1972).
20 For the proceedings of the session and the Declaration, see *Africa Research Bulletin*, vol. 10, no. 1 (January 1973), pp. 2714–15.

21   Basil Davidson, Joe Slovo and Anthony R. Wilkinson, *Southern Africa: The New Politics of Revolution* (Harmondsworth: Penguin, 1976), p. 77.
22   South African Senate debates, 23 October 1974; *Eastern Province Herald, Star* and *Rand Daily Mail*, 24 October 1974; and *To the Point*, 1 November 1974.
23   For the full text of President Kaunda's response, see 'Southern Africa: a time for change', address by His Excellency the President, Dr K. D. Kaunda, on occasion of conferment of LL D degree, University of Zambia, Lusaka, 24 October 1974.
24   For the proceedings of the Dar es Salaam meeting, see Colin Legum, *Vorster's Gamble for Africa: How the Search for Peace Failed* (London: Rex Collings, 1976), pp. 16–22; and Douglas G. Anglin, 'Zambia and Southern Africa detente', *International Journal*, vol. XXX, no. 3 (Summer 1975), pp. 494–500.
25   ECM/St. 15 IX.

2
The Roles of the Front Line States in Southern Africa

AMADU SESAY

This chapter, as its title suggests, utilises the concept of role as developed by Kal J. Holsti: national role conceptions can help to explain the foreign policy behaviour of states in the international system. Holsti has defined such national role conceptions as: 'the policy-makers' own definitions of the general kinds of decisions, commitments, rules and actions suitable to their state, and of the functions, if any, their state should perform on a continuing basis in the international system or in a subordinate regional system.'[1] He has also convincingly argued that 'there are reasons for assuming that the role performance (decisions and actions) of governments may be explained primarily by reference to the policy-makers' own perceptions of the nation's role in a region, or in the international system as a whole'. This analysis is supported by Evan Luard, who has argued that 'within international society . . . the relationships in which nations engage represent sets of mutual expectations concerning behaviour, rights and obligations'[2] which define the roles which every state must fulfil in the system. In short, decision-makers pay significant attention to universally accepted norms of interstate behaviour in the formulation and execution of their countries' foreign policies.

In this chapter 'role' refers to a 'coherent set of "norms" of behaviour which are thought', by policy-makers, to have some binding character in their interactions with state as well as non-state actors in the international system. In his framework of analysis Holsti has identified two major sources of national role conceptions: domestic, and external. These also include location, ideology, system structure and general legal commitments.

Introduction: National Roles and Conceptions and the Front Line States

Holsti's role framework of analysis could be usefully employed to study the foreign policies of the front line states towards Southern Africa in 1974–80. First, it would provide us with the tools for explaining the foreign policy decisions and actions of the five states. This could enhance our comprehension and appreciation of the various policies pursued by the front line states in the subregion in general and the liberation struggle in Rhodesia/Zimbabwe (used interchangeably for the period up to April 1980) in particular. Secondly, the concept is dynamic in terms of employing a traditional linkage perspective. In this regard it can assist greatly in the identification and evaluation of the potency of the factors (sources) of the roles of the 'front-liners'. In brief, the framework provides a context within which we can describe and explain the foreign policies of the front line *entente*.

The rest of the chapter is divided into four sections. Section 1 examines the impact of the Portuguese coup on Southern Africa. Section 2 looks at the responses of the blacks to the strategic weakness of the minority regimes in the region following the coup. Section 3 is concerned with the identification of the various roles which the FLS has played in the region since 1974. Section 4, in conclusion, examines the role of the FLS in Southern Africa in the 1980s in the light of Zimbabwe's independence.

(1)   The Impact of the Portuguese Coup on Southern Africa

The coup in Portugal on 25 April 1974 had a traumatic impact on the regional politics and strategic balance in Southern Africa. The sudden collapse of the 500-year-old Portuguese empire in Africa took every observer by surprise, including black and white Southern Africans. Occasioned by the increasingly bitter wars in Angola, Guinea-Bissau and Mozambique as well as by the attendant high costs – both human and financial – the coup upset previous assumptions and strategies of whites as well as blacks; previous scenarios about the region were discarded. For instance, American policy as set out in the secret National Security Memorandum 39 of Henry Kissinger was turned upside-down.[3] The revolution 'introduced not only a new element of universality but also of fluidity in a situation of stubborn rigidity', and called for radically different policies and new strategies from all those involved in the Southern African conflict – whites, blacks, and their respective supporters and sympathisers.

For the blacks inside and outside of Southern Africa, the new balance of power weakened the strategic position of the minority whites and offered the best opportunity to press on with the liberation process. And in accordance with the Organisation of African Unity's strategy of selective liberation, after 1974 all efforts and attention were concentrated on Southern Rhodesia, the most exposed of all the minority regimes. As for the whites in the subregion, their military and economic vulnerability compelled them to buy time, at least, to consolidate their defences or to bring about changes in the political and economic status quo which would guarantee them a future place in Africa. (Again, this was particularly true for the beleaguered Rhodesian regime of Ian Smith.)

In very broad terms, then, the impact of changes in governmental machinery and personnel in Portugal on the Southern African situation was fourfold. First, the morale of the freedom-fighters in Rhodesia and Namibia was boosted tremendously. With the formal independence of Mozambique and Angola, prospects for Rhodesia's independence became much more promising. The illegal regime in Rhodesia was particularly hit by the fall of the Portuguese empire in Africa. Economically the Smith regime, most of whose exports went through Mozambican ports, became highly vulnerable to economic sanctions by its newly independent neighbour. Strategically the coup added some 500 kilometres to Rhodesia's already-wide defence perimeter; the north-eastern frontier became particularly vulnerable to nationalist guerrilla attacks and incursions. A lot of pressure was exerted on the illegal regime and the West to seek a peaceful solution to the conflict.

Secondly, the independence of the former Portuguese colonies also had economic and military implications for the apartheid regime. Its hitherto unreachable defences in Namibia were exposed to nationalist attacks from Angola. It now became possible and practicable for SWAPO to establish rear bases in Angola from which to attack South African forces and defence systems in Namibia. In brief, the South African *cordon sanitaire* was shattered for good.

Thirdly, the coup led to the total collapse of the triple and unholy *entente* between Portugal, Rhodesia and South Africa:

'The weakened white front' which resulted, 'brought reappraisals in Western capitals about their (Western) policies in the area'.[4] For Rhodesia especially, the Western response was to seek ways and means of returning the territory to legality which would ensure a permanent if less privileged place for the whites in the country. And finally, fourthly, the coup had a 'demonstration effect' on the nationalists in the neighbouring minority-ruled territories. They concluded that, if guerrilla war could bring independence to Angola and Mozambique, it could also ensure their own freedom in the future. Thus, while pressing for the intensification of the liberation wars, the blacks were also optimistic that the Prime Ministers of Rhodesia and South Africa would see the writing on the wall and agree to majority rule for the territory. In fact, the peaceful resolution of the Southern African conflicts was in the interest of all the parties concerned.

For landlocked Zambia, independence in Rhodesia would reduce its dependence on its northern neighbours for both imports and exports. Moreover, the end of the guerrilla war would enable Zambia to concentrate on its own economic development and other socio-political problems which had been neglected in the past.[5] In the case of Botswana a peaceful conclusion of the Rhodesian conflict would radically reduce its dependence on South Africa. Trade, political and cultural links with the blacks to the north would accordingly be facilitated. Finally, Gaberones would be freed of its Rhodesian refugees.[6] An end to the conflict in Rhodesia would also benefit Mozambique, terminating more than a decade of liberation wars which had led to the dislocation and neglect of the national economy.

South Africa needed a peaceful settlement in Rhodesia for both economic and military reasons. First, Pretoria needed to be on talking terms with the radical regimes in Angola and Mozambique: this would discourage these regimes, especially that in Maputo, from harbouring ANC guerrillas. Secondly, South Africa relied on Mozambique for power supply from the Cabora Bassa dam; and also needed ports in Maputo and elsewhere in the country for both imports and exports, to ease its already-congested ports. And thirdly, there were the thousands of migrant workers from Mozambique who provided cheap labour for the mines in the republic. It was thus in the interest of South Africa to have stable, 'friendly' regimes to the north and east. This overall interest of the Pretoria regime gave rise to the so-called 'wind of change' speech of

John Vorster in late 1974. The ultimate goal, it seemed, was to arrest the deteriorating security situation and black–white confrontation in the region. Section 2 examines the responses of the blacks.

(2) The Emergence of the Front Line States

Although Black Africa was not in 1974 prepared for the collapse of the Portuguese empire in the continent, nevertheless, the African responses to the political, military and diplomatic challenges posed by the coup were swift. This is because, since the mid-1960s, there had been regular meetings of East and Central African states: Botswana, Tanzania, Uganda, Zambia and Zaire.[7] These meetings gave birth to what later became known as the front line states – Botswana, Tanzania and Zambia since 1974 (later joined by Mozambique in 1975, and Angola in 1976). These states act as a caucus on Southern African affairs both inside and outside the continent, and they were unanimous in their overriding objective in the area: an internationally acceptable majority rule in Rhodesia, and in South Africa and Namibia. In pursuing this objective the front line states were prepared to pay a price in the name of African liberation. Coupled with their advantage of proximity to the theatre of conflict and close contact with the freedom-fighters, they wielded tremendous influence over the OAU as well as the various liberation movements on almost all issues affecting the region's liberation struggle. They helped to co-ordinate the efforts of the liberation movements, the OAU and other friendly states, to enhance the capability of the freedom-fighters. And finally, in carrying out all their functions *vis-à-vis* the liberation movements and the whites in the subregion the front line states had the backing and support of the UN.

But despite their unanimity over the major goal of liberation in Southern Africa, it would be wrong to conclude that the front-liners were a monolithic bloc. On the contrary, they could be categorised into various ideological shades and leanings. On the one hand Mozambique and Angola both styled themselves as Marxist-Leninist regimes, on the other Botswana and Zambia pursued state capitalism. Tanzania, meanwhile, is dedicated to what Timothy Shaw has called a 'transformationist'[8] system, based on policies of self-reliance. Such differences in economic, ideological and social patterns (not forgetting of course the personalities of their leaderships) led to various preferences within the FLS in their support for the liberation movements. Thus, while Botswana and Zambia leaned towards the moderate Joshua Nkomo faction of the Patriotic Front, the rest of the front line *entente* preferred the more radical wing led by Robert Mugabe. The front line states also pursued different policies during the Angolan civil war: Tanzania and Mozambique supported the MPLA, but Zambia gave tacit support to UNITA and advocated a government of national unity consistent with its national interest. Besides these ideological differences, many Zambians perceived that Tanzania was using their dependence on ports in Dar es Salaam and related road and rail facilities to exploit them economically. This, according to Zambians, explains the lukewarm attitude of the Tanzanian leadership towards Kaunda's decision to reopen the border with Rhodesia in 1977.[9]

Again, there was a clear dichotomy between some sub-regional and continental goals of the FLS and their own domestic objectives. Without going into great detail, the more obvious ones are: first, that they were fighting minority regimes with whom some of their number were actively doing business. Secondly, that some of the front line states, themselves capitalists, were trying to topple the obvious outposts of capitalism and subimperialism in Southern Africa. And thirdly, that while all the front-liners were concerned with peace, security and rapid economic development at home, their strong support for the liberation movements opened their territories to 'retaliatory' military action by the minority regimes.

Despite the above contradictions, there was agreement among the front line states on what their immediate goal should be: the liberation of the minority-governed areas; and the front line Five were convinced that the installation of a popular and 'genuine' black government in Salisbury would have positive impact on interstate and international relations in the subregion in general.

The rest of this chapter is devoted to the identification and explanation of the various roles which the front-liners have played in Southern Africa with particular reference to the Zimbabwean conflict. In conclusion I attempt to project the role of the FLS in the region in the 1980s in the light of Zimbabwe's independence under Robert Mugabe.

(3)   The Roles of the Front Line States in Southern Africa

For the purposes of this analysis four broad but interrelated roles can be identified.[10] These roles are: (*a*) the continental/pan-Africanist; (*b*) the internationalist (some of the front line states have referred to their internationalist duty); (*c*) the legitimist/unifying; and (*d*) the bridge-building/intermediary. There are, however, gradations of role performance along the active–passive spectrum. Moreover, role is in part determined by the resources available to the states in the region:

> Central and Southern Africa are passing through the worst crises in our history . . . The new situation is more critical and dangerous than any time before . . . the future of Central and Southern Africa is bound up with the future of our nation. (President Kenneth Kaunda)[11]

> We belong in Southern Africa and it would be unrealistic of us to attempt to sever our Southern African connections completely. Our very survival as a nation requires that we maintain some connection with our neighbours. (Sir Seretse Khama)[12]

Among domestic and external influences, geographic proximity has been a major determinant of role for the FLS in Southern Africa: the closeness of the Five to the theatre of conflict has, of course, made it difficult for them to shy away from events in neighbouring territories. Other than Tanzania, the front line states have had contiguous borders with one or more of the minority regimes, and the ongoing liberation wars have affected them more directly than any other African states. Their economic, social and political lives have been seriously debilitated by pre-emptive attack and 'hot pursuits' by the racists.[13]

The FLS has also been guided by its own national ideology and philosophies. In Tanzania, for example, the ruling Tanganyika African National Union (TANU) stated in unambiguous terms that 'the responsibility of the party is to lead the masses in the effort to safeguard national independence and to advance the liberation of Africa', and TANU itself is regarded as a 'liberation movement'.[14] Thus, Tanzania's role in Southern Africa can be explained in part by reference to its national ideology and political philosophy; at home the party and government are striving for equality irrespective of colour, religion, or race. It would be hypocritical to espouse such lofty aims and ideals at home while pursuing a nonchalant policy towards Southern Africa. Like all of the front line states, Tanzania has a significant settler population: whites, Indians and Arabs; and in the light of this mixed community any policy other than that of racial equality would be disastrous for the country. Once such a policy was adopted at home, it was logical for the government to extend it to foreign policy.[15]

Similar reasons can be found for the role of other front-liners. Zambia's policies in the region are, above all, a matter of principle: President Kaunda has a personal antipathy to violence both as a devout Christian and humanist. Humanism – the country's national ideology – is centred on man, the pivot of all state activity. This belief in the centrality of the individual in the nation's activity, and his consequent sanctity, is reflected in the President's 'open tears' at the sight of human suffering. The ideology of Zambia's ruling United National Independence Party (UNIP) is the basis of all government policy and activity both at home and abroad; hence, it is very strongly believed that 'independence for Southern Africa is good for humanity'.

As for Mozambique, its independence in 1975 was the culmination of many years of liberation war against Portugal. During this struggle the territory received immense moral and material assistance from the entire continent. Having thus secured freedom through the 'barrel of a gun' Mozambique felt obliged to help other minority-ruled areas achieve freedom. But this task and commitment is made much easier by the country's Marxist-Leninist ideology which is both anti-racist and anti-colonial. Among the major tasks of FRELIMO, the national party, is the building of a strong socialist state and the pursuit of a 'vigorous anti-imperialist solidarity with all progressive forces in the world'.[16] President Machel singled out liberation as one of the country's main objectives in Africa, saying that everything would be done to assist the 'liberation struggle of all peoples, and in particular the peoples of Southern Africa'.

The front line states have also been guided in their policies by the perceptions of their policy-makers. Zambian leaders, for example, believed that their country was the main target of the triple alliance of Portugal, Rhodesia and South Africa. In particular, they feared that their state might be the prime pawn of South African apartheid, whose objective is 'either the incorporation of this landlocked but strategic state into South

Africa's orbit, or its destruction'.[17] Consequently, they believe that Zambia's safety will not be assured until apartheid in South Africa is brought to an end and independence secured for other minority white-governed areas.

Continental Role

The subscription of the front line *entente* to the OAU Charter has significantly influenced its attitudes and policy towards the liberation of Southern Africa. Hence, documents like the Lusaka Manifesto set out the broad outlines of the African position on the issue of minority rule. Africa's stand towards South Africa 'involves a rejection of racialism'. Black Africa 'believes that all people who have made their home in the countries of Southern Africa are Africans, regardless of the colour of their skins'.[18] Moreover, the manifesto advocated two options with regard to the liberation of the region: peaceful negotiation, but violence is promised 'if progress is blocked by the actions of those at present in the states of Southern Africa.' Finally, the obligations of every African state were set out in the 1975 Dar es Salaam Declaration. This stated categorically that the main objective was

> independence on the basis of majority rule. This can be achieved either peacefully or by violent means. Either way, Africa will give its unqualified support to the freedom fighters led by their nationalist movement – the African National Council.[19]

Many of the front line states see their roles in Southern Africa as a continuation of pan-African ideals. As strong believers in the objectives and obligation of continental unity, they would be shirking their duty if they did not pursue the goals of the OAU in the region.[20] President Kaunda said in 1975, for instance, that 'whatever contacts have taken place between Tanzania, Mozambique's Frelimo, Botswana and Zambia and . . . the minority regimes led by Vorster . . . have been based entirely on the [Lusaka] Manifesto'.[21] Accordingly, the five states pursued dialogue with the settler regimes when it was thought that such an approach would lead to a peaceful solution of the conflict in Rhodesia; but they also utilised the military alternative when the 'talks' were seen to be unproductive. This 'talk and fight' approach, in fact, pervaded the whole process of 'détente' in Southern Africa after 1974.

Besides such prescriptions, the front-liners have also based their policies on their perception of what other African states expect of them in the region. This constraint was underscored by one of the aides to the late President Seretse Khama. He was explaining his country's rejection of repeated offers of South African financial assistance.'We don't think', he said, 'it would be good for our reputation with other African countries to be going hat in hand to an apartheid government. We very much care about our reputation [in Africa].'[22]

Most of the statements indicating the various roles of the front line states have been made by Zambian officials. This, in part, is due to the special situation of their state: landlocked and dependent on minority regimes for trade and communications. Zambia was also the state most hit by the war in Rhodesia. Therefore, the conflict in Southern Africa is central to Zambian foreign policy. Zambian officials have interpreted their country's role in the region in various ways. In one of his numerous statements on the crisis in the area Vernon Mwaanga said in 1975: 'the Portuguese have bombed our villages, killed our people, destroyed our properties, but as long as liberation movements were engaged in a genuine war against the enemy, no sacrifice is too high for Zambia to pay in the name of Africa.'[23] Implicit in this statement is this: the FLS were by virtue of their strategic location and commitment to the liberation struggle merely performing a function which the rest of Africa could not do. In other words, they were discharging their continental or pan-African duties. Thus, Mwaanga told delegates at Dar es Salaam in 1975 that Africa should have a clear set of priorities with regard to the liberation of Southern Africa:

> let us have a very clear understanding of the means we have for implementing whatever strategy or declaration we choose to adopt. Zambia pledges to give the best we have to support it in the name and interests of the peoples of Africa.[24]

Finally, the front line states have sometimes perceived their roles in the region as a duty or obligation owed the rest of the continent for its assistance during their own struggle for political liberation; there exists what can be called a 'debt syndrome'. Again, no one has stated this position more clearly than Kaunda himself shortly after his country became independent in 1964: 'I say to our brothers of South Africa or Rhodesia and of the Portuguese territories . . . we do not forget you in the day of our triumph.'[25]

A combination of factors, both domestic and external, has shaped significantly the continental role of the front-liners in South Africa. The overwhelming perception seems to be, then, that membership in the OAU carries with it some duties and obligations as well as expectations from others. This involves not only acting on behalf of the Organisation, as in regard to Rhodesia, but also the conscious pursuit and promotion of the continent's objectives and goals *vis-à-vis* the minority-ruled areas and the liberation movements.

Internationalist Role

Implicit in the actions of the FLS is the strong perception that what it is fighting for in Southern Africa has also been prescribed by the international community. The front-liners believe that their policies are based on the principles and universally accepted rules of state behaviour – both domestic and external – as set out in the UN Charter and other relevant documents and conference declarations. Thus, apartheid in South Africa and UDI in Southern Rhodesia – both of which were condemned by the world body in various documents – are anathema to almost all other states. Moreover, such 'illegal' policies and behaviour have also made the minority regimes international 'outcasts' and 'pariahs'. It is accordingly the duty of every member-state to ensure that culprits are pressured into legality; as soon as the outcasts meet the universal requirements of state behaviour, they will be admitted back into the international community. Thus, Rhodesia/Zimbabwe was accepted by every member of the world system, including South Africa, soon after the April 1980 elections had led to its return to legality and 'accepted' behaviour.

The implications of the above reasoning is that: UDI was illegal and was accordingly condemned by the world community through the United Nations. The UN also decided to impose sanctions against the Smith regime in Salisbury in order to get it to comply with internationally accepted norms. Thus, actions by member-states which could help to restore legality in the territory were considered to be in line with world opinion and perfectly legitimate. The front line states took a number of measures which were aimed at reinforcing the UN decisions. Rhodesia was boycotted, politically and diplomatically. Zambia and Mozambique closed their borders with the rebel regime in conformity with UN resolution and campaigned actively for a total ostracism. Interestingly enough, Machel justified the imposition of sanctions by his country against Rhodesia in 1976 as being 'in accordance with UN resolutions'. And in welcoming this border closure Nyerere had this to say: 'by imposing total sanctions Mozambique has once again demonstrated its determination to fulfil its internationalist obligations.'[26] However, such a general 'internationalist' duty for Mozambique also converged with its 'proletariat internationalism', which is anti-imperialist, anti-colonialist and anti-racist. Mozambique is thus ideally placed to play such an internationalist role in Southern Africa.

But for Zambia which, as already noted, practises state capitalism, its internationalist duty stemmed mainly from total support for the UN, as well as a principled commitment to the liberation struggle. Zambian commitment to UN ideals is evident in the country's independence date – 24 October – which is also United Nations Day. This as Philip Morgan has rightly pointed out, 'symbolised not only one further step in the process of decolonisation in Africa but also the beginning of a series of setbacks of white power in Southern Africa'.[27] The Zambian leadership has itself been very outspoken about its internationalist commitments in Southern Africa. The government made it clear in 1974, for instance, that it was 'committed to the UN General Assembly Resolution (1960) on decolonisation. Southern Africa is not our problem alone. It is an international problem and Zambia is a member of the international community'.[28]

Besides the legal invocation towards the subregion in general, and in particular towards the liberation movements, the front-liners have occasionally invoked the moral opprobrium associated with such policies as colonialism and racism. The Angolan Minister of Defence, Henrique Carreira, for instance, told graduates of the All Arms Officers' School in 1979 that 'Angola will do its internationalist duty and give full support for the legitimate struggle by the South West Africa People's Organisation (SWAPO)'.[29] The demonology associated with the minority regimes in Southern Africa was succinctly put by Khama in 1973, when defending his country's decision to support a UN resolution which acknowledged the legitimacy of the armed struggle in Southern Africa. 'The Botswana government', he said, 'has always condemned the denial on the part of the regimes of white ruled areas of Africa of the rights of their black citizens to self-determination and equality ... government has always recognised the right of the black citizens of these countries to achieve their full human rights'.[30] This statement cuts across the objectives of the United Nations in Southern Africa. In that respect the government of Botswana was merely echoing the UN Charter in discharging its internationalist role in the area.

Legitimist/Unifier Role

The perceptions underlying this role by the front line states are somewhat similar to those discussed above. If the policies of minority regimes in Southern Africa are against international norms and principles of state and interstate behaviour, then any moves which African states may take individually and collectively to end such regimes would seem to be legitimate. The front-liners have undertaken measures which have legitimised not only their own policies in the region, but also the activities of the freedom-fighters. This role sometimes leads directly to measures designed to unify and thus strengthen the fighting muscle of the liberation movements: by recognising certain factions within the struggle as the 'sole' or 'only genuine' representatives of the peoples of territories under minority regimes the front-liners have accorded 'legitimacy' and respectability to those particular factions.

But such legitimacy has sometimes been conferred without the prior knowledge of either the OAU or the UN, although both organisations none the less have accepted such decisions and policies. One reason for this apparently overwhelming influence of the front line *entente* is that the OAU to a large extent handed the initiative to them so far as Southern Africa is concerned. In turn, this situation gave the five states a more authoritative voice in the liberation struggle than any other group of African states. From 1974 up to the independence of Zimbabwe in 1980 the FLS collectively embarked upon political, diplomatic and strategic policies which were intended to both unify and legitimise various factions within each territorial liberation movement.

For over a decade the OAU tried in vain to unify the rival liberation movements in Zimbabwe under one parent body. The infighting and political assassinations in the movements had seriously debilitated their fighting capability and adversely affected the morale of the men in the field. However, after a series of meetings, the front line presidents, especially Kaunda and Nyerere, succeeded in December 1974 in unifying all splinter-groups in Zimbabwe in an umbrella organisation – the African National Council (ANC) – under the leadership of Bishop Abel Muzorewa. This unity was short-lived, but while it lasted full legitimacy was accorded to the ANC. And when three years later the ANC collapsed under the weight of political assassination and power struggles, the front-liners once again stepped in. This time, they recognised the break-away factions led by Joshua Nkomo and Robert Mugabe – ZAPU and ZANU respectively – under the parent organisation: the Patriotic Front.

The withdrawal of 'legitimacy' from the ANC had serious consequences for the peace process in Zimbabwe. The decision to 'give full political, material and diplomatic support to the Patriotic Front' during the Geneva recess, in effect, sealed the fate of the British peace initiative. By this decision the front line presidents not only isolated Sithole and Muzorewa from the peace process, but also made it 'illegitimate' for any actor to deal with them in any way. By the same token any settlement reached with the two leaders was also illegitimate and unacceptable to the rest of the continent and the front line states in particular. As the Geneva chairman, Ivor Richard, prophetically recognised: 'that decision by the Front Line States would make his task impossible.' The Geneva conference was never reconvened, demonstrating the tremendous influence of the front-liners over events in the region. But not only that; even the separate and so-called internal settlement between Smith on the one hand, and Muzorewa and Sithole on the other, was unacceptable and 'illegitimate' in so far as the front line states were concerned. Accordingly, no other actor – state or non-state – recognised it apart from South Africa. UN-imposed sanctions were never lifted and the guerrilla war continued unabated until April 1980 when the Lancaster House talks led to formal independence for the territory.

The FLS, on behalf of Africa, put forward conditions which had to be satisfied before any legitimate settlement of the conflict in Zimbabwe could be achieved. One such condition of the front line states was that any agreement must ensure majority rule under a government led by the Patriotic Front. This position was emphasised by Kaunda in 1977, soon after the front line states had accepted the Patriotic Front as the sole representative of the people of Zimbabwe. He told the OAU's Liberation Committee:

let Mr. Smith and the whole world know this. No agreement will end the war in Rhodesia without the fullest participation and consent of the Patriotic Front and its fighting forces . . . any attempt to exclude the nationalist forces under the Patriotic Front will end in civil war.[31]

This basic FLS position held until 1980 when the Patriotic Front negotiated with Britain and Ian Smith the modalities of legal independence for the rebel territory. Before then, Rhodesia remained an international outcast, a 'pariah' state.

A final example of the legitimising and unifying role of the FLS is taken from the attempts by 'third parties' to settle the conflict around the conference table: the so-called Anglo-American initiative of 1976. When America and Britain put forward their peace package for Rhodesia, the move had the initial support of all Africa including the front line states and Nigeria's Olusegun Obasanjo. However, when it became apparent that Smith was not prepared to lead the country towards genuine majority black rule, the front line states withdrew their support for the initiative as did the OAU and Nigeria. At a meeting in Lusaka in September 1976 they rejected Smith's interpretation of the Anglo-American proposals, which they said were 'tantamount to legalising the colonialist and racial structures of power in the colony'.[32] Accordingly, they pronounced the initiative 'dead'. And their alternative – the intensification of the guerrilla war – was accepted by the rest of the world system as the only effective way of pressurising Smith and South Africa into bringing about a genuine settlement in Rhodesia.

Ironically the legitimising and unifying role of the front line Five has sometimes led to friction between them and some OAU states. Many OAU members saw the front-liners as an alternative centre of power, and thus a threat to the Organisation's authority in an important area to which they devoted political, material and financial resources. While they recognised the crucial role of the *entente* in Southern Africa, nevertheless they wanted the OAU to exercise some control over the Five. However, the front line *entente* was by and large able to get its way on almost all matters relating to the liberation of Rhodesia/Zimbabwe in particular, and Southern Africa in general.

Bridge-building/Intermediary Role
According to Kenneth Grundy, bridge-building in the Southern African context refers to 'the activities carried on by the black states in Southern Africa with the object of seeking to expand proper, if not friendly, dialogue and perhaps relations

between, at present distrustful poles of white and black Africa'.[33] While I acknowledge such an African role, bridge-building in the context of this chapter includes 'third-party' roles sometimes played by the front line states in various peace processes such as the Geneva conference and the Anglo-American initiative.

Before I examine some of the FLS bridge-building activities, it is worth noting that the effectiveness of the role is directly related to their cohesiveness and also to the absence of any rival 'club' or bloc of states either in the continent or elsewhere. While their strategic proximity made it futile for any state to bypass them in the peace process, it gave them substantial veto powers over the nature and even the pace of any peace moves in the region.

One example of the bridge-building exercise is the so-called détente or dialogue exercise which started shortly after the Portuguese coup in 1974. It is unnecessary to go into the details of the process here. I will therefore highlight only the major developments in the bridge-building process. The whole détente exercise started shortly after the then South African Prime Minister, John Vorster, made his 'wind of change' speech in October 1974. Vorster acknowledged that there was an urgent need for Southern Africa to 'make a choice between peace on the one hand or an escalation of strife on the other'. He concluded that the 'toll of major confrontation [between blacks and whites] will be high, too high for Southern Africa to pay'. The obvious conciliatory tone of the speech provoked a swift response from the Zambian president, who described it as the 'voice of reason for which Africa and the rest of the world had been waiting'.[34] This verbal exchange produced an optimism, shared by blacks and whites – both within and outside Africa – that 'doomsday' scenarios for the region would after all never come true. Both black and white South Africans seemed anxious to reach a negotiated settlement of the issues dividing them. The most obvious starting-point was Rhodesia, the weakest link in the chain of minority regimes in the region.

After a series of shuttle-diplomatic moves undertaken on the one hand by Mark Chona, President Kaunda's special envoy, and on the other his counterparts from South Africa and Rhodesia, an agreement was reached in November 1974. Nkomo and Sithole were released from detention by Smith to participate in subsequent peace talks. This détente initiative reached its zenith on 10 December that year, when the Lusaka Accords were signed by white and black Rhodesians.[35] This was followed by the Pretoria agreement which set out the modalities for the return of Rhodesia to legality: (*a*) a formal declaration of intent by the Smith government, (*b*) talks which would pave the way for a mixed nationalist government and (*c*) a new Zimbabwean constitution which would eventually lead the territory to legal independence, international recognition and the end of sanctions.[36] The details were to be worked out at a formal conference at Victoria Falls in 1975.

That this conference was held at all in August 1975 was due in no small measure to the presence and determination of both Vorster and Kaunda. But even so these leaders were merely acting as bridge-builders. This role was stressed by Kaunda in his speech at the Falls: 'we want you to be the bridge that brings us all together. Mr. Vorster and I are only messengers.'[37]

It is clear from this cursory examination of the détente process in 1974–5 that the role of the FLS was that of a go-between between the whites and blacks. But there is one important difference between such a role and that identified by Grundy's bridge-building scenario in the opening quotation of this section of the chapter. Only blacks could provide the crucial link between the two antagonistic groups; and as this example has illustrated, both blacks and whites worked hand in hand in the peace initiatives on Rhodesia beginning in 1974. Besides Victoria Falls, which was a local assignment, the same black–white coalition was apparent at the Geneva Conference in 1977 and the Lancaster House talks.

(4) Conclusion: the Front Line States and Southern Africa in the 1980s

I have argued above that the concept of role is a useful tool for the study of African foreign policy in general, and the foreign policies of the front line states towards Southern Africa in particular. I identified two broad sources of their national roles, domestic and external, and four roles which the front line Five have played in the region: the continental, internationalist, legitimising and, finally, bridge-building roles. This concluding section of the chapter presents a number of scenarios with regard to possible roles for the FLS in Southern Africa in the 1980s.

Two basic factors must be taken into consideration in describing these roles. The first factor is that the number of front line states is bound to increase to six now that Zimbabwe is independent (see Chapters 4 and 6). Given time, the new Zimbabwe will join the ranks of the other front-liners in their efforts to secure majority rule in Namibia. Robert Mugabe, Zimbabwe's new Prime Minister, has already put his country solidly behind the liberation struggle in the region:

> We have a moral and political obligation to the people of Namibia and of South Africa. We uphold the right of Namibians to fight for their liberation . . . similarly we uphold the right of the people of South Africa to establish a democratic system in their country. We will assist if we can . . . at international forums where we hope to play an active part in obtaining the objectives of liberation in those countries.[38]

I have quoted this statement, one of Mugabe's first public pronouncements on liberation in Southern Africa, because it gives a clear indication of what Zimbabwe's role in the area will be in the future: a strong and virile Zimbabwe will join hands with the original front-liners and bring about the liberation of Namibia and South Africa.

This leads to a second factor: with Zimbabwe now out of the way, the efforts of the OAU and the front line states will now be concentrated upon Namibia, in accordance with Africa's strategy of selective liberation of minority and colonial territories (see Chapter 1). But such a development has serious implications for the roles of the front-liners in the decades ahead. The long distance (and absence of territorial contiguity) of Namibia and the front line states, besides Angola, may have a taming effect. While the front-liners continue to support liberation in the territory, the majority may no longer be prepared to take the sort of risks which they took over Zimbabwe: all, except Angola, will now have more time to concentrate on domestic socio-political and economic development.

Zambia, for instance, will no doubt devote most of its energies to economic reconstruction and social issues, for the first time since independence in 1964. Zambia is a capitalist state, and Shaw rightly points out that state capitalism in that country has 'resulted . . . in the emergence of a new class . . . that may come to see its own interests as being different from, and perhaps superior to, those of the country as a whole . . . and given such an orientation, it may come to favour stability rather than change in Southern Africa'.[39] The possibility of such an orientation by the new class in Zambia was demonstrated in the late 1970s over the border closure with Rhodesia and what the elites then saw as an overemphasis on external affairs to the detriment and neglect of domestic issues.[40] The major objective of leaders in the future may, therefore, be economic reconstruction, cheaper imports, reliable routes for both imports and exports, and improved living standards. It is with such motives in mind that Zambia has tried to link up with Malawi and Mozambique. And with the independence of Zimbabwe, the southern route may become more attractive to Zambian imports and exports in the 1980s. In short, I envisage a less forward political and diplomatic role for Zambia in the region in the future.

Tanzania likewise, although it will continue to play a leading role in the liberation struggle, will have a different role from that played in Rhodesia, or for that matter in Angola and Mozambique. The main reason is geographic: Tanzania is now 'a very far-away country' in so far as the liberation struggles in Namibia and South Africa are concerned. This distance makes it impossible for Dar es Salaam to offer bases to SWAPO freedom-fighters, even if it wanted to do so. Nevertheless, the presence of the Liberation Committee's headquarters in Dar es Salaam, and of its Tanzanian executive secretary-general, may yet ensure a continuous and prominent role for the country on liberation issues.

Botswana's role in the liberation struggle had always been peripheral, due mainly to its encirclement by the minority regimes and its overwhelming economic dependence on apartheid South Africa. Its influence has thus been mainly political, diplomatic and humanitarian. This country will continue to provide such services in the future, especially in respect of South Africa; but it may not provide bases to ANC nationalist guerrillas in view of this extreme vulnerability to economic and military coercion by South Africa.

Mozambique's position is rather different from that of Botswana. Like Tanzania, it will play a leading role in the liberation of the remaining minority territories. With time and given a strong economic and military situation, Mozambique may provide military rear-bases to ANC freedom-fighters from the republic. Its support for Namibia will, however, be largely diplomatic and confined to the format of FLS and OAU strategies in the area. Again, the major constraint here is the physical distance between Mozambique and Namibia. This conclusion also takes into consideration Mozambique's present substantial trade and economic links with South Africa which any government in Maputo would not, at least for the time being, want to jeopardise.

Angola appears to be the only member which is ideally situated to play a forward and 'practical' role in the anti-minority regime campaign in the subregion, and Namibia in particular. It is the only country which provides rear-bases to SWAPO freedom-fighters, and as with Zambia and Mozambique in the Rhodesia situation, it continues to fulfil this role despite frequent military raids and 'occupations' by the apartheid forces of South Africa. Its support will continue until legal independence is achieved in the territory under a government acceptable to the majority of African states.

The front line states will devote more time in the future to economic relations – both bilateral and multilateral – in the region. The emphasis will be on economic liberation/integration, on the attempt to devise alternative economic linkages in the subregion and so decrease dependence on apartheid South Africa. Such an objective, as a Tanzanian official has said, is to create a network of political, economic and transport as well as communications linkages among the independent states in the subregion. A policy of self-reliance by the black states would also mark another vital step in the worldwide isolation of the republic.

These analyses and scenarios are supported by the Zambian official, who pointed out that with the legal independence of Zimbabwe, the front-liners would now turn their attention to regional economic integration. The rationale, it would seem, is to wage a psychological war against the racist government in Pretoria. A viable regional economic community in Southern Africa would also fall neatly within the OAU's goal of setting up an African Common Market by the year 2000. The initiative in that regard was first taken in April 1980 by the nine African states meeting in Lusaka.[41] Their main goal was to find practical ways of ending their economic dependence on South Africa. (A second meeting was held in Maputo in November 1980.) It is too early yet to evaluate the impact of these moves on the subregion generally, and on South Africa especially. One thing that is significant, none the less, is that, with the encouraging presence of the 'satellite' states of Lesotho and Swaziland, this pair have undoubtedly gained a greater sense of security and 'belonging' than ever before. In the long run they may be able to disengage, albeit slowly, from the racists' economic encirclement.

The pace of change within South Africa, or for that matter

progress towards independence for Namibia, must depend on a number of global and subsystemic factors. First, is the attitude of the conservative administration of Ronald Reagan: if Washington decided to embrace the apartheid regime in Pretoria, changes in the republic and the securing of Namibia's independence would be much more difficult to achieve. Close links between the USA and South Africa would make it easier for the latter to resist African and international pressure to effect change in the country's racial policy. Overt or covert support for the republic by Washington may, however, also provoke Soviet interest or intervention in the area.

A viable and prosperous regional economic community in Southern Africa would put tremendous pressure on South Africa both economically and politically. Pretoria would lose most, if not all, of its traditional markets in the region and cheap labour for its mines. And with increasing urban-guerrilla activities in future by the ANC, there are bound to be significant demands for domestic reform in the country in the 1980s from the major Western powers, as well as Africa's traditional friends – the socialist states – for the liberation movement. Whatever the case might be, and whatever happens in Washington, Moscow, or London and other world capitals, or within the subregion itself, the roles of the front line states in Southern Africa in the 1980s will not be the same as those of the 1970s.

Notes: Chapter 2

1 For more details on Holsti's framework, see his long piece: 'National role conceptions in the study of foreign policy', *International Studies Quarterly*, vol. 14, no. 3 (September 1970), pp. 233–309.
2 E. Luard, *Types of International Society* (New York: The Free Press, 1976), p. 259.
3 See *Africa* (London), no. 44 (April 1975), p. 29.
4 See Colin Legum (ed.), *Africa Contemporary Record 1974/75* (London: Rex Collings, 1975), Vol. 7, pp. 43–4.
5 Personal discussions with an official of the Zambian High Commission, Lagos, October 1980.
6 For details on the impact of the liberation wars on the front line states, see *The Front Line States: The Burden of the Liberation Struggle* (London: Commonwealth Secretariat, n.d.).
7 Uganda pulled out after the Amin coup in 1971 and Zaire's Mobutu withdrew in 1975.
8 For more details, see T. Shaw, 'Political economy of Zambia and the future of Southern Africa', public lecture, Nigerian Institute of International Affairs, Lagos, February 1980, p. 6.

9   Personal discussions with Zambian High Commission official in Lagos.
10   The roles were determined by reading the speeches of the leaders of the front line states; however, because of limited time and other constraints, the exercise was not as comprehensive as that undertaken by Holsti.
11   Quoted in Shaw, op. cit., p. 1.
12   Quoted in Legum, op. cit., p. B363.
13   For more details on the damages to property and lives in the FLS, see *The Front Line States*, op. cit.
14   See 'TANU guidelines on guarding, consolidating and advancing the revolution of Tanzania, and of Africa (*Mwongozo*)', *African Review*, vol. 1, no. 4 (April 1972), pp. 1, 2. The name of the new party in Tanzania after the merger with that in Zanzibar is Chama Cha Mapinduzi.
15   Personal discussions with an official of Tanzanian High Commission, Lagos, October 1980.
16   See Robert D'A. Henderson, 'Principles and practice in Mozambique's foreign policy', *World Today*, vol. 34, no. 7 (July 1978), p. 281.
17   *Zambia 1964–74* (Lusaka: Government Printer, n.d.), p. 9.
18   *Africa*, no. 42 (February 1975), p. 7.
19   *Africa*, no. 45 (May 1975), p. 18.
20   But I must emphasise here that such ideals are sometimes overwhelmed by idiosyncratic factors. For instance, the maverick attitude of Malawi.
21   *Africa*, no. 42 (February 1975), p. 10.
22   Quoted in K. W. Grundy, *Confrontation and Accommodation in Southern Africa* (Berkeley, Calif.: University of California Press, 1973), p. 137.
23   Quoted by Dunstan W. Kamana, 'Zambia', in Douglas G. Anglin, Timothy M. Shaw and Carl G. Widstrand (eds), *Conflict and Change in Southern Africa* (Washington, DC: University Press of America, 1978), p. 46.
24   *Africa*, no. 45 (May 1975), p. 20.
25   Quoted by Kamana, op. cit., p. 35.
26   *Africa Research Bulletin Economic Series*, 15 February–14 March 1976, p. 3803.
27   Gwendolen Carter and Patrick O'Meara (eds), *Southern Africa: The Continuing Crisis* (Bloomington, Ind.: Indiana University Press, 1979), pp. 205–6.
28   See *Zambia in Brief* (Lusaka: Government Printer, n.d.) for more details.
29   *New Nigerian* (Kaduna), 27 September 1978.
30   Legum, op. cit., p. B363.
31   *Africa Diary* (New Delhi), 12–18 March 1977.
32   *Africa Diary*, 14–20 October 1976.
33   Grundy, op. cit., p. 119.
34   *Africa*, no. 51 (October 1975), p. 16; *The Times* (London), 4 November 1974; and *Guardian* (London), 4 April 1975.
35   *The Times*, 12 December 1974.
36   *The Times*, 26 April 1974.
37   *The Times*, 26 April 1975.
38   *Africa*, no. 104 (April 1980), p. 17.
39   Shaw, op. cit., p. 5.
40   Personal discussions with Zambian official.
41   The nine states are: Angola, Botswana, Lesotho, Malawi, Mozambique, Swaziland, Tanzania, Zambia and Zimbabwe.

3

Nigeria, Namibia and Southern Africa

OLAJIDE ALUKO

Nigeria has always been against the existence of the racist white-supremacist regimes in Southern Africa. Recently, however, Nigeria has brought greater urgency to this policy. At Niamey, Niger Republic, early in 1980 President Shehu Shagari declared that his government would take all measures to ensure the speedy independence of Namibia. At the OAU summit meeting early in July 1980 he said that 'Namibia must be independent next year [that is, 1981]'.[1] He reaffirmed support for the liberation movements in Namibia and South Africa, adding with regard to the former that her 'independence without Walvis Bay is a sham'.[2] In his address to the UN General Assembly on 6 October 1980 President Shagari condemned the continued illegal occupation of Namibia by South Africa, and pledged that Nigeria would 'continue to assist, encourage and support that struggle (for independence in Namibia, and the elimination of apartheid system in South Africa) with all our might and resources'.[3] He added that the termination of apartheid and racism in South Africa is the challenge of the decade.[4] In the following month he said that Nigeria was prepared to start an arms race with South Africa if Pretoria continues its arms build-up.[5]

From all this one must wonder why the 'new' ferocity and urgency in policies towards South Africa and Namibia by the Nigerian government. Two reasons are plausible: first, that the Nigerian government did not want the enthusiasm for de-colonisation and the elimination of apartheid abroad after the independence of Zimbabwe, in April 1980, to be lost. Secondly, that the rhetoric has been designed largely to galvanise public opinion behind the federal government at home.

Certainly, more fundamental questions have to be asked about the country's policy towards the white-supremacist regimes. First, what are the objectives of Nigeria in Namibia and South Africa? Secondly, what is the nature of Nigerian interests in Southern Africa? Thirdly, what is the capability of Nigeria to attain these objectives? Fourthly, what are the circumstances of Namibia and South Africa? Fifthly, what are the past and present strategies of Nigeria towards South Africa, and what have been the results? And sixthly, what are the possible policy options for Nigeria towards the white-controlled areas of Southern Africa in the 1980s?

(1)   Objectives

It is easier to say something about the objectives of Nigeria in Namibia and in South Africa than the precise nature of its interest in them. The objectives are broadly similar to those of the OAU. These are: the eradication of apartheid and racism in South Africa, and the attainment of majority rule and independence in Namibia.[6]

(2)   Nature of Interests

As indicated above, it is difficult to write about the nature of Nigerian interests in Namibia and South Africa. However, one can deduce something from the various speeches of Nigerian leaders. Broadly speaking these interests can be grouped into three: security, racial and economic. I will examine each of them briefly.

Security Consideration
The participation of the white-supremacist regimes on the side of Biafra during the civil war (1967–70) brought home to the Nigerian leaders that these governments posed a dangerous threat to the security and survival of Nigeria as a united country. As Dr Okoi Arikpo, then Commissioner for External Affairs, said early in 1970, the first bomb dropped on Lagos was manufactured in Rhodesia (now Zimbabwe) under Ian Smith.[7] The South African government also provided moral, material and military support for the Biafrans. There has been no doubt among Nigerian leaders after the civil war that the white minority regimes will continue to pose a threat to the

independence, sovereignty and territorial integrity of their country as long as they exist. As General Gowon put it at the OAU summit in September 1970 at Addis Ababa: 'We know from experience that in opposing colonialism and racialism in Angola, Mozambique, Guinea-Bissau, Zimbabwe, Namibia and South Africa, we are serving the cause of our own freedom and independence.'[8] In his address to the Assembly of Heads of State and Government in June 1971 Gowon re-emphasised this link between Nigeria's security and the independence and freedom of Southern Africa. He declared in a speech that bore a Nkrumahist strain that:

> The forces which impede the freedom and independence of Africa and which at the same time seek to undermine our achievements remain very formidable . . . They will never leave us alone to develop our natural and human resources to our advantage. They will forever want us to waste our time and energy in negative pursuits.[9]

All subsequent Nigerian leaders have shared this view. General Murtala Muhammed described the invasion of Angola by South Africa with the tacit support of some Western powers as 'a conspiracy against our continent'.[10] Indeed, the Adedeji Report on foreign policy said in 1976 that the expansion of South African military capabilities and the extension of this into African countries and oceans must be seen as 'a threat to Nigeria's security'.[11] The dangers and threats posed to Nigeria by South Africa may have been exaggerated by various Nigerian leaders, but there is no doubt that the authorities in Pretoria will exploit any opportunity to weaken and destabilise the most populous, and potentially most powerful, black country in the world. This is understandable, given the posture of Nigeria on the question of apartheid, separate development and racism in Southern Africa, and the fact that the greatest potential threat to South Africa is black nationalism rather than international communism.

Racial Factor
The question of race in shaping Nigeria's attitude to the white-supremacist regimes is relatively new. Under the Balewa government the country took a moral attitude to apartheid and racism in Southern Africa. However, the experience of the civil war in which the majority of black people inside and outside Africa supported the federal government while the majority of

the white population in North America and Western Europe were either indifferent or hostile to Lagos, brought an element of black solidarity to the planning, policy and pronouncements of Nigerian leaders.

Under General Gowon this element was hardly visible. It was not that the Gowon government did not promote the concept of black solidarity. It was just that it went about this in a discreet, skilful manner. Under the Muhammed/Obasanjo regime it was raised to an important aspect of public policy and, indeed, the Adedeji Report proposed that one of the objectives of the country's external policy should be the defence and promotion of the rights and interests of all black people within and outside Africa.

The Shagari government has given greater emphasis to this concept of black solidarity than ever before. In his maiden address to the National Assembly on 16 October 1979 President Shagari declared that one of his foreign policy objectives would be to promote the interests of 'all black people throughout the world'.[12] He has continued to repeat this commitment: at the UN General Assembly on 6 October 1980 the president stated that 'the destiny of Nigeria is inextricably linked with the fortunes of all countries of Africa and all the peoples of African descent abroad'.[13]

Given the fact that Nigeria is the largest black country in the world with a population of nearly 80 million, and given its relative wealth, it is understandable that it should champion the cause of blacks in Africa, especially in Namibia and South Africa. But to make the interests of all black people throughout the world an important foreign policy objective is to engage in an illusion; indeed, it is an exercise in futility. Not only are the interests of black peoples in Africa, let alone outside the continent, diverse, Nigeria simply does not possess the capacity to advance this type of nebulous policy.

Admittedly the pursuit of such a dynamic and vigorous foreign policy requires ideals, those of racial solidarity or the universalist ideology of the pan-negro movement, of capitalism or communism, but a country that seeks to pursue such a policy must have the appropriate muscle to move it forward. Furthermore, charity is believed to begin at home: the Nigerian government is supported and financed by the taxpayer, to serve the interests of the country and its people. All other interests are secondary. Moreover, such ideals must first take firm root in the country wishing to propagate them in the rest of the world. In the case of Nigeria questions of ethnic rivalry, jealousy and hatred are far from being resolved. All this must necessarily weaken the ability of the government to advance the cause of black solidarity abroad.

Despite this argument, however, the federal government has succeeded by using slogans redolent of enslavement of black people in Southern Africa, and the exploitation and oppression of blacks elsewhere, to whip up greater support among the Nigerian intelligentsia. This could be seen in the setting up of a liberation fund in the early 1970s by the Afro-Asian Solidarity Organisation with the encouragement of the Gowon government, and also the establishment of the Southern African Relief Fund later in the 1970s. The success of these strategies must not be overstressed. For they were effected under the military regime during which time the country was under emergency laws and regulations.

Economic Interest

Economic interest has hardly featured in the pronouncements of Nigerian leaders on South Africa and Namibia. While Nigeria has banned all economic and commercial ties with the racist regimes, the leaders of the country – especially those in business and government – are anxious to promote economic and trade ties with these territories once they come under black majority rule. For instance, in the future Nigeria will sell oil to these territories, she will get access to fish off the coast of Namibia and buy industrial goods from South Africa.

All this remains for the indeterminate future. In the meantime Nigerian leaders have been silent about their economic interests in those territories under the white-supremacist regimes. In actual fact, when after a trip to the front line states, Chief Adeyemi Lawson, the then President of the Nigerian Chamber of Commerce, Industry, Mines and Agriculture, in 1978, advocated the striking of economic and commercial ties with South Africa on the ground that the Nigerian government was ignoring the economic interest of Nigeria abroad, the weight of public opinion was critical of his stand.[14] Although the then federal military government replied to deny that it was working against the country's foreign economic well-being, the official ban on economic, commercial and technical ties with these supremacist regimes was not lifted. Whatever goods come from South Africa – and they must be quite negligible – are shipped to Nigeria illegally, just as some Nigerian crude oil gets to South Africa through third parties. What all this tends to show is that despite the confrontation between Lagos and Pretoria over apartheid, racism and what the United Nations has described as the mass violation of human rights, there has been some move, though unofficial, by both sides towards developing economic and commercial ties. Once their sharp disagreement on political, diplomatic and security levels is resolved, one can expect the establishment of substantial economic links between the two countries.

(3)   Nigeria's Capability

The capability of Nigeria to make South Africa comply with her objectives and interests in Namibia and the apartheid republic itself is very limited. While the concept of capability is difficult to define precisely – involving as it does tangible and intangible elements[15] – I will concentrate only on three salient elements of Nigeria's capability: economic, military and political.

Economic Capability

The economic capability of the country is potentially great. With a population of about 80 million, covering an area of about 356,669 square miles, it is not only big in size and population, it is also rich in agricultural and mineral resources. Agricultural products include cocoa, palm oil, ground nuts, logs, cotton, rubber and coffee; mineral resources include tin, columbite, tantalite, wolfram, gold, lead-zinc, limestone, clay, kaolin, marble, coal, uranium, lignite, natural gas and crude oil. However, apart from the crude oil industry, very few of these resources have been mobilised let alone developed.

While since the mid-1970s the country has been producing an average of 2 million barrels of crude oil a day, other sectors of the economy have declined. Agricultural production has sharply declined since the late 1970s and the country has had to spend an annual average of ₦1,700 million or about 13 per cent[16] of its total imports on food. While in the 1970s, and even during the civil war, agricultural output was so good that Nigeria was able not only to feed its population, but also to export to other African and extra-African countries, the situation has been reversed since the mid-1970s. Apart from heavy dependence on food imports now, there have been some occasional food shortages.

Manufacturing industry is in its infancy, contributing less

than 6·5 per cent of GDP in 1979. The level of technological development is very low. Although crude oil contributed about 80 per cent of federal government revenue and over 92 per cent of foreign exchange earnings in 1980, in the 1979–80 fiscal year oil revenue accounted for ₦9·9 billion of the total federal revenue of ₦11·8 billion.[17] Although oil, with recent increases in prices, has enabled the country to build up its external reserves to over ₦5 billion in October 1980, the overall economic position has not become very strong. For if the oil market were to glut and prices were to go down as was the case in 1977–8, the country would face a severe balance of payments deficit, as it did in 1976–9. In fact, the balance of payment surplus of ₦1·53 billion[18] recorded in October 1980 was largely due to the high prices of oil following the crisis in Iran, and subsequently the Gulf War between Iran and Iraq.

Moreover, despite the oil boom, the country has been borrowing money from abroad since 1977. In the 1981 budget proposals presented to the National Assembly by President Shagari on 24 November 1980 there was provision for an external loan of ₦1·522 billion.[19] The value of such loans is likely to be higher during the coming years with the launching of the fourth national plan, 1981–6.[20]

Per capita income has been about $400 a year; and in 1978 GDP was estimated at $35 billion. The economy remains predominantly a colonial one, depending on the export of primary products and the import of finished goods. In almost every sense the economy is still underdeveloped. Given this, the capacity of the economy to support an active policy in Southern Africa is really very small.

Military Capability
The military capability of the country is very low, especially when compared with that of any of the great powers. Although the size of the Nigerian armed forces put at 146,000 by *The Military Balance 1980/81* is more than adequate for the needs of the country, they are ill-equipped. While the army has recently acquired some light tanks, it does not have a mechanised battalion. The navy, consisting of about 4,500 men, does not have a single destroyer or a submarine; neither has it a single minesweeper. The airforce, with 6,000 men and women, has only twenty-one combat aircraft; it has only six medium-range C-130H transport aircraft. It does not possess any modern bombers or a fighter squadron.[21] Although the country spent about 8 per cent of GDP on defence (that is,

about $2·67 billion) during the 1977–8 fiscal year, about 90 per cent of this, according to Lt-General T. Y. Danjuma, the former Chief of Defence Staff, was spent on salaries and personal emoluments. Even though defence expenditure has been rising under the civilian administration (for example, the recurrent budget for the defence rose from ₦489,396,300 in 1980 to ₦725,136,450 in 1981), only a small fraction of this has gone on the acquisition of modern weapons.

The level of military technology in the armed forces is very low. Most of the weapons used by the armed forces are imported from the developed countries. Although a defence factory exists in Kaduna for the production of light arms, very little seems to have come out of it. For in April 1980 the Defence Minister, Professor Iya Abubaker, told the press that arrangements to manufacture arms locally had reached an advanced stage.[22]

It is difficult to talk about morale, leadership, or training within the armed forces because of the secrecy that surround them. No doubt some training of the armed forces is going on, but it is difficult to say how important the military leadership considers training to be.[23] If we cannot talk of the quality of leadership and morale within the armed forces, we can certainly talk of their mobility. Given the poor, outdated equipment available to them, they are not a mobile force. They could not seriously support and engage in any active operation outside Nigeria's borders which involved supplying the army by land, sea, or air, as the Chad débâcle in 1979 proved. In relation to the question of Namibia and South Africa, then, Nigeria's military capability[24] is extremely limited, if not non-existent.

Political Capability
Although the country now seems more united than during the First Republic and the Constitution vests the conduct and control of external relations and defence matters in the federal government, the Shagari administration's control of these is not nearly absolute, unlike that of its military predecessors. To mention a few constraints: the 1979 Constitution restricts federal power in some foreign policy matters. Under section 5(3)(a) the president cannot declare war on another country without the approval of a resolution of both Houses of the National Assembly in joint session. Furthermore, under section 5(3)(b) the president cannot send any member of the armed forces on combat duty outside Nigeria without the

approval of the Senate. Under section 12(1) no treaty between Nigeria and any other country can come into force unless the National Assembly has enacted such a treaty to law. And under section 74(2) no money can be spent by the president from the Consolidated Revenue Fund without the authorisation of the National Assembly; it was under this provision that the Assembly queried the ₦10 million independence grant to Zimbabwe by the president. Finally, appointments of heads of diplomatic missions have to be ratified by the Senate before they become valid (section 157(4)).

Apart from these constitutional restrictions, the federal Cabinet has consisted of a coalition of two rather different parties, the National Party of Nigeria (NPN) and the Nigerian People's Party (NPP). While the president is NPN, his Minister of External Affairs, Professor Ishaya Audu, is an NPP man. This sometimes creates difficulties in the formulation of foreign policy, especially on Southern Africa. The most notable case to date was the minister's statement opposing the use of force to change the status quo in South Africa as this might be 'counter-productive'.[25] This is diametrically opposed to the known and public position of the president on South Africa. Whether this was due to the minister's better appreciation and understanding of the circumstances of South Africa is unclear. But whatever the reason, one would have expected him to have co-ordinated his policy and position with those of the president to avoid creating the impression of sharp divisions in policy on South Africa within the government.

Apart from the constitutional constraints dealt with above, there are some political constraints. Nigeria has since October 1979 had a uniquely awkward political arrangement in which five different political parties control different states in the federation. While the federal coalition parties control nine states, the other three parties control ten. All these reflect the diversity in culture, history, tradition and perhaps religion within the country. While constitutionally the conduct of external affairs and defence matters are the exclusive responsibility of the federal government, the government cannot but tread cautiously abroad lest its political opponents seize on its adventurism to undermine its position within the country. Indeed, Ambassador Gabriel Ijewere has stated that even under the military the vast diversity in the country dictated caution and moderation in foreign policy.[26] Thus, we can see that the political muscle of the country to play a vigorous role abroad, especially in Southern Africa, is small.

(4)   The Circumstances of Namibia and South Africa

The first important circumstance of these target territories is their sheer geographical distance from Nigeria: the nearest point of either to Nigeria is over 4,000 miles, creating enormous logistical problems for Nigeria if her armed troops engaged South Africa in combat. At present the Nigerian armed forces lack the capacity to operate at such a distance, while South Africa which has illegally occupied Namibia and maintained apartheid in the republic, is the industrial giant of Southern Africa. Her economic and military capability is enormous.

Militarily South Africa is strong. While it has only 86,050 men[27] and women in the armed forces – the South African Defence Force (SADF) – it can quickly mobilise about half a million people in the Citizen Force and the reservists.[28] Apart from sheer size, the army is mobile and well equipped with modern weapons. These include two mechanised brigades, an armoured and parachute brigade, and a missile regiment; the SADF also has over 200 Centurion tanks[29] and other types of modern tank. It has over 1,600 AML Eland MKIV armoured cars, and 230 scout cars; it is also equipped with long-range guns and mortars, such as the 155-mm and 120-mm types.

Likewise, the navy is well equipped. Although the navy has about 4,750 men and women, it has a reserve 10,000 Citizen Force. It is equipped with frigates, minesweepers and different classes of submarine; some of the naval boats carry surface-to-surface missiles (SSMs). The airforce, consisting of 10,300 people (with a reserve 25,000 Citizen Force), is well equipped with 204 combat aircraft.[30] Among its strike-command aircraft are Canberra bombers, Buccaneer and Mirage jet fighters. Among its maritime command are two squadrons – one with seven Shackleton Mr-3s, and one with eighteen Piaggio P-166s. Its transport command includes medium-range military aircraft such as C-130H, and long-range such as the Transall C-1602.[31] It is said that the South African airforce has the capability to strike targets as far as Zaire and beyond.

Very little is published about the nuclear capability of South Africa. None the less, it is believed in many world capitals that South Africa has got the bomb. In September 1979 a nuclear device was exploded in the Indian Ocean which was widely thought to have been detonated by Pretoria. Although South Africa denied this, political analysts like Robert Jaster believed that it was South Africa that was responsible for the test.[32] Indeed, Jaster added that the South African authorities would not hesitate to use tactical nuclear weapons against an invasion of Namibia by conventional troops operating from the southern part of Angola.[33]

Another important aspect of the military capability of South Africa is that the level of military technology in the republic is very high. While South Africa still obtains some equipment from abroad, she is almost self-sufficient in the production of arms and ammunition, and other types of equipment including missiles, electronics and even maritime assault vessels for her armed forces. Fighters, helicopters and light-strike aircraft are being produced under French and Italian licences.

The economic capability of South Africa is enormous: GDP in 1979 was estimated at $54·3 billion. Although a population of about 28 million in 1980 is just about a third of that of Nigeria, the country is rich in strategic mineral and industrial resources. South Africa alone has 68 per cent of total gold reserves outside the Soviet Union and is also the largest producer of industrial diamonds outside the communist world. In addition, the country has other minerals such as copper, coal, iron, phosphate, zinc and lead. Because of the sharp increases in the gold price in the world market over the past few years, South Africa has made substantial profits. As a result, the balance of payments has been in surplus since the 1970s. The chances that this trend will continue for the foreseeable future are high. South Africa also has strategic goods such as uranium, columbite and chrome.

Furthermore, the agricultural capacity of the country is great. Pretoria exports food to neighbouring states including Botswana, Lesotho and Swaziland, and to Kenya, Mozambique, Zambia and Zaire. Industrial technology in the apartheid republic has advanced greatly; oil is being produced from coal in order to reduce its dependence on the outside world for its oil requirements.

Western capital – direct and indirect investment – has been involved on a massive scale in the exploitation of the mineral, industrial and agricultural resources of South Africa. Partly as a result of the low cost of unskilled labour in the republic, almost all the companies – mostly subsidiaries of some Western multinational corporations – have succeeded in maximising their profit beyond what obtains in any other part of the world. As a result of all these factors, South Africa has recorded the highest rate of growth in the world since 1945.[34]

Much of what is said above is also true of Namibia. Despite the Namib and Kalahari deserts, Namibia is rich in agricultural and mineral resources. Because of the special breed of sheep farmed in Namibia, that territory is the world's largest supplier of Karakul sheep, whose tightly curled, glossy fur is sent abroad to be made into coats for the luxury trade. Apart from this, it is the world's second largest supplier (after South Africa) of gem diamonds.[35] Other mineral resources include phosphate, zinc, tin, vanadium, petroleum and uranium. The territory also has a thriving fishing industry, especially in pilchard and lobster. As in South Africa, most of the firms operating in Namibia are either South African or Western-owned. For instance, the major mining companies in the territory include Consolidated Diamond Mines, a subsidiary of De Beers Consolidated Mines, the Tsumeb Corporation owned by American Metal Climax, Newmont Mines Corporation and the South West African Co.

Another relevant circumstance of Namibia is her international character, having been first a mandated territory under the League of Nations from 1922 with South Africa as the mandatory power. Not only has South Africa refused to transfer it to the UN as a trust territory under chapters XI and XII of the UN Charter, it has extended apartheid and racial segregation to the territory. South Africa now has about 50,000 troops in Namibia with heavy, modern equipment. In addition to the military bases maintained on Namibian territory, South Africa has an extensive naval base at Simonstown outside Cape Town.

Despite the Security Council declaration in 1966 that South Africa's continued occupation of Namibia was illegal, Pretoria has continued to defy the UN. Indeed, in 1977 South Africa went ahead to annex Walvis Bay, which is the only deep-water harbour in Namibia, as an integral part of South Africa.

While South Africa is sovereign and independent, it practises a unique form of institutionalised racism: apartheid. Since 1945 the UN has in different ways tried to make the South African government change this system without avail. South Africa has been able to defy the world largely because of the support – economic, technological and military – of the major Western powers, including the USA.

(5)   Nigeria's Attempts at Changing the Status Quo

From the above it is clear that the capability of Nigeria to take any direct measure against South Africa and Namibia in order to attain her objectives and interests in both territories is minimal. Although some Nigerian leaders have been saying that oil should be used as a weapon against South Africa, this is out of the question because Nigeria's oil does not go directly to South Africa. None the less, Nigeria has tried to apply pressure on South Africa indirectly, by assisting the liberation movements and aiding the immediate neighbours of the apartheid regime, and by propaganda and conference diplomacy.

Since the establishment of the OAU Liberation Committee Special Fund in 1963 Nigeria has contributed generously to it. And since the end of the civil war in 1970 Nigeria has not only increased her contributions to the Liberation Committee Fund, but has also provided direct material, military, financial and moral aid to the leading liberation movements of the territories: the African National Congress (ANC), the Pan-African Congress (PAC) and the South West Africa People's Organisation (SWAPO). These liberation movements have also been allowed to open offices in Lagos and some of the members receive military training in Nigeria.[36] Scholarships have also been offered for study in various institutions in Nigeria.

Despite all this, Nigeria has not been impressed with the performance of the ANC and PAC. In 1977 the Nigerian government decided to recognise a 'third force' in South Africa,[37] the South African Youth Revolutionary Council (SAYRCO) led by Khotso Seathlolo. The government believes that it is the type of youth found in SAYRCO which shook South Africa with the Soweto uprising of 1976, and which could really threaten and undermine the existence of apartheid. Thus, it has been providing military aid, including military training, to SAYRCO. In addition, Nigeria co-ordinates the training of SAYRCO fighters with the Palestinian Liberation Organisation (PLO). SAYRCO has its headquarters in Lagos and its members enjoy diplomatic immunity, just like the representatives of other liberation movements.

Nigeria also provides material, military and moral aid to SWAPO.[38] Indeed, since the independence of Zimbabwe, Nigeria has stepped up her material support: clothing, relief supplies, drugs, food, watches and arms are supplied to SWAPO, from Lagos through Rwanda, at least once a week by Nigerian military transport planes.

It is difficult to assess the effect of SWAPO operations against the racist forces. The People's Liberation Army of Namibia (PLAN), the military wing of SWAPO, has claimed a series of successes against the South West African territorial forces and claims to control about half of the territory.[39] Many of these claims have been exaggerated for propaganda purposes; however, the strengthening of the size of weapons of the South African forces in Namibia, especially since the independence of Zimbabwe, would seem to suggest an intensification of the guerrilla war by PLAN.

On the propaganda field the Nigerian government has been trying to publicise the evils of apartheid, separate development and racism on different platforms. The external service of the Federal Radio Corporation beams regularly to Southern Africa. But this is hardly effective, for the transmitter is of poor quality and its broadcasts are rarely audible in places like Maputo or Salisbury. Moreover, the South African government jams Nigerian broadcasts to prevent any of them from reaching a South African audience.[40]

At home the federal government has encouraged the publication of anti-apartheid newspapers as well as the formation of anti-apartheid organisations. The most notable of these is the National Committee on the Dissemination of Information on the Evils of Apartheid. The hosting of the UN Action Conference on Apartheid, in August 1977, in Lagos was part of the propaganda war against South Africa. Again, the setting up of the South African Relief Fund by the government in 1977 was to raise money for the liberation movements and to mobilise public opinion for their cause within Nigeria. The results of this activity on South Africa, if any, must have been minimal. For there has been no fundamental change in either the apartheid republic or in Namibia. In actual fact, in some cases the plight of the blacks has grown worse since Soweto.

At different international conferences Nigeria has been active in mobilising international opinion against South Africa. Indeed, at the Commonwealth Prime Ministers' meeting of March 1961, Sir Abubakar Tafawa Balewa, then Prime Minister, was the most vocal critic of South Africa. All subsequent Nigerian leaders have followed this trend with increased vigour in some cases. It was Gowon who spear-headed the anti-dialogue proposal in 1970–1; and at the OAU summit meeting in June 1971 he succeeded in getting the support of over two-thirds of heads of state against any dialogue with Pretoria. Nigeria has continued to champion the anti-apartheid crusade at the UN General Assembly and at Security Council meetings. In fact, the main reason why Nigeria sought and got the non-permanent seat on the Security Council in October 1977 was to be in a position from where it could influence developments in Southern Africa, especially Zimbabwe, Namibia and South Africa.

The immediate objective of Nigeria's campaign against South Africa is to isolate her diplomatically, economically, militarily and culturally. While some success has been recorded in areas such as sport and the UN conferences, it has not been possible to isolate South Africa in military, economic, financial, technological or even cultural fields. This is understandable. To be able to do so would require either the total consent of all members of the international community or a practically impossible effective siege of South Africa by air, sea and land.

In order to isolate South Africa economically the Obasanjo government tried to introduce measures making it impossible for any firms operating in South Africa to make new contracts or even do business in Nigeria. The government promised to set up an economic intelligence unit to monitor the activities of all multinationals, operating both in Nigeria and in South Africa, with a view to taking appropriate steps against them. But because of the heavy involvement of the multinational corporations in the Nigerian economy, there was very little the government could do. Apart from the assets of Barclays Bank, nationalised in 1978 because of the indiscretion of its chairman, and those of British Petroleum in 1979, no other important foreign firm has been taken over. Indeed, many multinational giants – such as the Standard Bank, ICI, Shell, Texaco, Gulf, PANAM and UTA, to name a few – that operate in Nigeria have continued to expand their activities in South Africa.

Despite the efforts of Nigeria, the armour of apartheid has remained undented. And whatever cosmetic changes have been made by South Africa have been more in response to critical opinions in Western capitals, especially to the rather truculent insistence on human rights by President Carter during the first two years of his administration. Pretoria continues with its apartheid policy and new Bantustans such as Ciskei are being prepared for pseudo-independence. Political and economic rights are still denied to the majority black population. In military terms South Africa has now become a more formidable power than it was in the 1960s. As Peter

Calvocoressi stated recently,

> in the sixties South Africa was nervous about her position in Southern Africa, but by the end of the seventies much had changed. South Africa sustained Smith's rebellion almost single-handed. It ended its acute dependence on foreign oil . . . It is getting its way in Namibia where only a few years ago, it feared the establishment of a hostile state.[41]

Not only has Pretoria defied the United Nations over its refusal to implement Security Council Resolutions 385 and 435 on the transitional arrangement for the independence of Namibia, but the UN secretary-general's delegation that went to Pretoria, in October 1980, over Namibia was virtually snubbed by the Botha government. Pretoria is going ahead with its plans to foist a puppet regime on that territory, led by the Democratic Turnhalle Alliance (DTA). The SWAPO leadership believes that the Botha government may even go further to make the DTA declare UDI. This is doubtful, however. From the experience of Smith's UDI, Pretoria knows that such 'independence' would not be recognised by the rest of the world. What is more likely is that the Botha government will play for time, and in the meantime will work to weaken SWAPO and destabilise Angola and other neighbouring states that give sanctuary to the freedom-fighters. The landslide victory of Reagan in the US presidential elections of November 1980 gave Pretoria comfort. But nothing can permanently halt the march of history. What can Nigeria do to hasten this process in the 1980s?

(6) Policy Options in the 1980s

Writing about the future is a risky venture. But in some real sense the future is a function of the past and the present. So Nigerian policy towards South Africa and Namibia for the rest of this decade will be a reflection of her past and present policies.

Given the size and population, and the economic and military potential of Nigeria, it cannot easily retreat from the struggle against apartheid, against serfdom and against the mass violation of fundamental human rights in South Africa and Namibia. Therefore, in the 1980s it will have to continue to intensify its material, military, moral and diplomatic support for the liberation movements in these territories.

However, Nigeria has to supplement past policies with new ones if any significant impact is to be made on South Africa. First, it must be fully recognised in Lagos that South Africa can only be toppled by military force.[42] If Nigeria cannot send troops directly to Namibia, it must be ready to assist Angola with men and materials to defend the southern border with Namibia. This will help the Angolan government to flush out the remnants of UNITA rebels to strengthen the base of operation of SWAPO fighters. This certainly cannot be done until the capability of the Nigerian armed forces is improved.

South Africa has a nuclear capability, and the Nigerian government now seems determined on developing its own nuclear device, despite the controversy this has generated over cost. But given effective management, it is argued, the production of a bomb will not harm the country's economy. Countries which are economically poorer than Nigeria, such as India and Pakistan, now have a nuclear capability; and in the case of India the total cost of producing a device including the cost of plutonium and the preparation of a test site was put, in 1974, at only $400,000.[43] Even while making allowance for inflation since then, the cost of producing something similar in Nigeria is estimated to be less than $2 million. The purpose of such an acquisition is to signal Pretoria that Nigeria cannot be subjected to political blackmail by apartheid bombs.

At the UN General Assembly Nigeria should try to work for a new strategy; and with skilful diplomacy among Third World members, work out a proposal for a Uniting for Peace resolution over Namibia. It must be accompanied by a military preparedness by a number of countries, including Nigeria. Such a proposal needs proper planning and co-ordination, but were it attainable South Africa's position in Namibia would become threatened and untenable.

Furthermore, the Nigerian government must be prepared to take tougher measures against any of the Western powers that are insensitive to Nigerian opinion on apartheid and the continued illegal occupation of Namibia. It must be made clear to the great powers that Nigeria's opposition to apartheid is not negotiable. During the last two years of the Obasanjo regime the country became too much identified with US interests in Southern Africa. This position has not been helped by the fact that the present Nigerian government does not profess 'socialism'. While this has caused some Western countries to take Nigeria for granted over apartheid, it has made her suspect in the eyes of the freedom-fighters.[44]

Finally, Nigeria in the 1980s must work in close concert with the front line states and the OAU over policies to be adopted. For instance, for nearly two years until July 1980, only Nigeria among the OAU member-states recognised the PAC faction led by Leballo.[45] Until now only Nigeria has supported SAYRCO – which none of the front line states recognises. Yet the support of these states is critical to the success of any of the liberation movements. Nigeria should now try to make SAYRCO acceptable to the front line states not as a rival to the ANC and PAC, but as a partner in the common struggle.

If Nigeria is able to adopt the above policy options, then it will have done much towards achieving its objectives in Namibia and South Africa. The ability to follow any of these options will, however, depend on the capacity of the federal government to ensure political stability, economic prosperity and social progress at home: if the government succeeds in meeting these domestic imperatives, it can justifiably be hoped that Namibia will be independent before the end of the decade. Although South Africa will be exposed on all fronts, the elimination of apartheid in the republic may take a much longer period.

Notes: Chapter 3

1   Address by President Alhaji Shehu Shagari of Nigeria to OAU Assembly of Heads of State and Government, Freetown, Sierra Leone, 1–4 July 1980.
2   ibid.
3   Address by President Shagari of Nigeria to 35th Session of the UN General Assembly, 6 October 1980.
4   ibid.
5   *Daily Sketch* (Ibadan), 26 November 1980.
6   See 'OAU Lomé Declaration on a new strategy for the liberation of Namibia and the elimination of apartheid and racial segregation in South Africa', Paper PL/DEC/32 (II/43.80/Rev. 1 1980).
7   *Daily Times* (Lagos), 17 March 1970.
8   'Long live African unity', text of statement by Major-General Yakubu Gowon at 7th OAU Assembly of Heads of State and Government, 4 September 1970.
9   For full text of this address, see *Morning Post* (Lagos), 25 June 1971.
10   Text of address to OAU summit extraordinary session, Addis Ababa, Ethiopia, 11 January 1976.
11   *Report of the Committee on the Review of Nigeria's Foreign Policy including Economic and Technical Cooperation under the Chairmanship of Professor A. Adedeji* (Lagos: Government Printer, May 1976).
12   President Shagari's address to meeting of National Assembly, 16 October 1979.

13 President Shagari's address to 35th session of the UN General Assembly, 6 October 1980.
14 See *Daily Sketch*, 17 August 1978.
15 For details, see Charles O. Lerche and Abdul Said, *Concepts of International Politics*, 2nd edn (Englewood Cliffs, NJ: Prentice-Hall, 1970), pp. 59–77; and Theodore A. Couloumbis and James H. Wolfe, *Introduction to International Relations* (Englewood Cliffs, NJ: Prentice-Hall, 1978), pp. 56–73.
16 *West Africa* (London), 15 September 1980.
17 *New Nigerian* (Kaduna), 20 March 1980.
18 *Daily Times*, 27 November 1980.
19 *New Nigerian*, 25 November 1980.
20 President Shagari speculated that this would likely happen with the launching of the ₦40 billion development plan in 1981.
21 International Institute for Strategic Studies, *The Military Balance 1980/81* (London: IISS, 1979), p. 53.
22 *New Nigerian*, 19 April 1980.
23 Of the ten army officers originally nominated for training in the Department of International Relations, University of Ife, during the 1980–1 session, about half were not released for the programme.
24 It is interesting to note that, despite the increased expenditure on defence since the 1970s, the military capability of the country is now lower than in the mid-1970s.
25 *Punch* (Lagos), 9 December 1980.
26 For details, see Gabriel O. Ijewere, *Two Decades of Independence in Nigeria with Special Reference to Nigeria in International Relations: Text of Paper Presented on the Occasion of the 20th Independence Anniversary of the Federal Republic of Nigeria* (Lagos: Ministry of External Affairs, September 1980).
27 *The Military Balance 1980/81*, op. cit., pp. 54–5.
28 Gwendolen M. Carter, *Which Way is South Africa Going?* (Bloomington, Ind.: Indiana University Press, 1980), p. 114.
29 *The Military Balance 1980/81*, op. cit., pp. 54–5.
30 But an American military expert Dr Sean Gervasi said that South Africa in reality has over 625 combat aircraft.
31 *The Military Balance 1980/81*, op. cit., pp. 54–5.
32 Robert S. Jaster, *South Africa's Narrowing Security Options* (London: IISS, 1980), p. 47.
33 ibid., p. 45.
34 Colin Legum, *The Western Crisis over Southern Africa* (London: Africana, 1979), p. v.
35 United Nations, *Namibia: A Trust Betrayed* (New York: UN Secretariat, 1974).
36 Interview, November 1980.
37 Alaba Ogunsanwo, *The Nigerian Military and Foreign Policy 1975–79: Processes, Principles, Performance and Contradictions*, Research Monograph No. 45 (Princeton, NJ: Princeton University Press, 1980).
38 Interview, September 1980.
39 See, for example, *SWAPO – Information and Comment: War Communiqué* (Luanda: SWAPO Information Office, 1 September 1980); and the official organ of SWAPO, *Namibia Today*, vol. 4, no. 2 (1980).

40   During the writer's visit to Southern Africa in August–September 1980 Nigeria Radio could not be picked up in most of the Southern African countries, except Zambia at night.

41   *Sunday Times* (London), 9 March 1980.

42   The Adedeji Committee recommended this in 1976; a similar view was expressed in *West Africa*, 3 November 1980.

43   J. A. Camilleri, 'The myth of the peaceful atom', *Millennium*, vol. 6, no. 2 (Autumn 1977), p. 115.

44   The writer witnessed the sixteenth anniversary celebrations of SWAPO in Dar es Salaam in August 1980, where SWAPO dancers wore dresses sewn from materials provided by Nigeria, yet sang heartily in praise of the socialist countries – the USSR, East Germany and Cuba – without mentioning Nigeria at all.

45   *Punch* (Lagos), 13 August 1980.

4
Zaire and Southern Africa

THOMAS M. CALLAGHY

> Foreign policy must be flexible; yesterday's enemy can be tomorrow's ally, while yesterday's ally may be the adversary of tomorrow.

> The expression 'neither rightist, nor leftist, not even centrist', is self-explanatory . . . Zaire's diplomacy is based on realism. It serves its national interests while seeking harmony with those of others . . . According to its interests, it follows the appropriate path and does not burden itself with vague principles. (Umba di Lutete, Foreign Minister of Zaire, in a speech in Washington, DC, 9 October 1978)

This chapter will portray and analyse Zaire's relations with South Africa and its recent apparent attempts to alter these relations by playing a major role in Southern African affairs.

Zaire under its presidential monarch, Mobutu Sese Seko, has what I have characterised elsewhere to be an absolutist regime.[1] It is a conservative and corrupt authoritarian regime of limited capabilities which greatly exploits its own people while preaching revolutionary transformation. The 'presidential monarch' creates and uses an administrative monarchy with mixed patrimonial power and glory. The sovereignty of this early modern state is proclaimed by and embodied in the person of the president, who exercises almost unlimited personal discretion. He manifests a will to dominate and a desire for unity, obedience and glory both internally and externally. This absolutist regime exhibits little concern for the welfare of its people, who are subjects not citizens,[2] but enormous concern for the power and wealth of those who control the state. The major preoccupations of the ruling elite are the classic ones of state formation and self-interest, and the principal modes of operation are those of the *raison d'état* including the flexibility mentioned in the opening quotation.

The nature of Zaire's relations with South Africa and its role in Southern Africa generally can be explained in large part by two main variables: (1) Zaire's strategic situation and structural position in the political economy of Southern Africa specifically,[3] and of the world more generally; and (2) the nature of the Mobutu regime and the way it discerns its interests.

Given these two variables, the regime has periodically perceived a coincidence of partially autonomous political, strategic and economic interests between itself and the South African government and established mutually convenient relations with it. This is not to say that these interests are identical, nor that both states occupy similar positions in the international or regional systems or that one is completely dependent on or the 'puppet' of the other. Both states have acted in a relatively autonomous fashion, mutually 'using' each other to protect perceived state, race and class interests. Rather than being fully dependent on South Africa as a subsystem imperialist power, Mobutu has been able to a certain extent to manipulate it (along with the USA and most recently France and other Western states, banks and international organisations) to protect his personal, state and class interests. This has been possible because of the nature of conflict and co-operation in the international system and because of a complex and partially shifting, but relatively stable, interpenetration of interests between the major state organisational and class actors.[4] In pursuing his perceived interests President Mobutu has readily and creatively used classic notions of statecraft and the *raison d'état*, first so elegantly elaborated by Machiavelli and Guicciardini. It appears these notions are becoming more salient in behaviour, if not in rhetoric, in African interstate relations: and this trend is likely to continue as the African state system develops further.[5]

Some relationships and role elements are primarily the result of one or the other of the factors listed above; some are a distinct mixture of the two. Zaire's dependence on the South African rail system is an example of a relationship determined primarily by a structural factor, that is, the closure of the Benguela railroad. The inordinate size of Zaire's non-essential trade with South Africa is an instance of a relationship primarily determined by the nature of the regime. And some relationships or conditions determined in large part by structural factors can be greatly aggravated by the nature of the regime. This is particularly true of Zaire's current severe economic, fiscal and infrastructural crises.

In this chapter the following topics will be examined in turn: (1) Zaire's view of South Africa; (2) South Africa's view of Zaire; (3) economic relations and investment; (4) economic relations and trade; (5) Angola; (6) Shaba I and II; (7) Zaire in Southern Africa after Shaba II; and (8) the future.

(1) Zaire's View of South Africa: the Rhetoric of a Janus-Faced Regime

Public vilification and quiet co-operation constitute the main elements of an amazingly consistent pattern in Zaire's relations with South Africa. Zaire periodically condemns South Africa at the UN and the OAU, and in Mobutu's speeches and the local press, for its race policies and its meddling in the affairs of other states in Southern Africa.

A small but revealing example of this hypocrisy came in December 1973. The Zairian regime publicly agreed to terminate a relationship with the South African-operated International Red Locust Control Service because of apartheid practices, but privately asked South Africa not to withdraw its aeroplanes, equipment and experts.[6]

The rhetoric of condemnation becomes most intense when President Mobutu is seeking personal glory and prestige by attempting to assume a Third World or African leadership role, and it gets toned down when the regime becomes more dependent on external actors for assistance due to internal or external crises.

President Mobutu initiated a bid for 'radical' leadership in 1973 with his visit to China and a scathing speech attacking South Africa at the UN in October. In this call to arms Mobutu sketched a major role for Zaire (and himself, of course) in Southern Africa:

> Today, while we have political, economic, and social stability, we cannot feel happy at home while our brothers of Angola, of Mozambique, of Zimbabwe, of South Africa, and of Namibia are yet held under the yoke of the Portuguese colonialists, British settlers, and South African racists . . . Did not Frantz Fanon say that Africa has the form of a pistol, whose trigger is

placed in Zaire? ... The sons and daughters of Zaire have mandated me to tell you that, henceforward, all of Zaire is mobilised to confront the racists and the colonialists of Southern Africa. Zaire stands ready to assume its full responsibilities, with our finger on the trigger of Frantz Fanon's revolver of Africa.[7]

Unfortunately for President Mobutu, the stability he spoke of above quickly disintegrated both internally and on Zaire's borders, rudely shattering his hopes for continental leadership. Although partly self-induced and partly structural in nature, the vast difficulties that Mobutu confronted by mid-1975 eventually dictated a much lower profile in regard to South Africa and liberation issues, led to actions during the Angolan civil war which severely damaged his reputation and increased his dependence on important Western powers. As will be shown later, the Angolan civil war initiated substantially closer political, military and economic ties with South Africa, many of which still exist, some in strengthened form. The 'radical' phase died quickly and brutally.

An event during the Angolan civil war vividly illustrates the depths of the hypocrisy of the Zairian regime in its stance towards South Africa. After South African military supplies and advisers had been used by Zairian units inside Angola, Zaire condemned South Africa's intervention in Angola at the UN in December 1975 in the following terms:

The Assembly must condemn apartheid; the Assembly must condemn South African interference in Angola. Even if South Africa were not carrying out its hateful policy of apartheid, its conduct could not but evoke the disapproval of this Assembly. The direct intervention of South African forces in Angola must be condemned – not principally because it is a manifestation of South Africa's determination to dominate and to practice racism, but because that intervention violates the principle of non-intervention in the internal affairs of another state.[8]

This same month, however, Zaire also opposed South Africa's expulsion from the UN. This was part of a larger pattern of voting at the UN on anti-apartheid, anti-South African resolutions. Generally Zaire votes in favour of these resolutions, but it also abstains on certain issues. Abstentions were not infrequent before 1970, diminishing during the brief 'radical' phase, only to emerge again as Zaire's internal and external crises compounded themselves after 1975. After

Shaba I, for example, Zaire voted in December 1977 in favour of ten anti-South African resolutions, but did not vote on two others. One condemned Israel for its collaboration with South Africa; the other condemned all military and nuclear collaboration with South Africa, focusing on France, the UK and the USA. A similar pattern emerged in January 1979, less than a year after Shaba II and with the 'pan-African' military force still in Shaba, but this time Zaire also abstained on a resolution condemning all economic co-operation with South Africa. By then, of course, Zaire's trade with South Africa had become quite substantial.

Another important characteristic of Zaire's public approach towards South Africa is a constant denial of *all* dealings with Pretoria. In 1977 after Shaba I, for example, Umba di Lutete, then Foreign Minister, stated that 'Zaire has been accused for a long time of receiving help from South Africa. It is absolutely untrue'. The aim, he went on, is to discredit Zaire in order to justify aggression: 'What Zaire has often been accused of is that some private corporations take advantage of the lack of control in our country and trade with South Africa, but Zaire cannot be accused – not the official government – of trading with or getting help from South Africa. This is utterly false.'[9] Contrast this with Tanzania and Zambia who have publicly admitted that of necessity they are forced to trade with South Africa to a certain degree. Zaire, on the other hand, continually denies *all* contact.

By 1978 the Zairian press was still periodically publishing anti-South African material, such as a series of articles by Michael Savage on the nature of apartheid in the weekly magazine *Zaire*. These were published 'in order to sensitise public opinion about the crimes of apartheid'.[10] The condemnation of South Africa by state officials was, however, more attenuated:

> Turning now to South Africa, Zaire considers it to be a multi-racial, independent state. The whites, blacks, and others who live there are all true natives. Therefore, there can be no question of expelling the whites, of throwing them into the ocean. They are citizens of that country, which they made prosperous, as are the blacks and the coloureds. But we neither accept nor tolerate white minority rule over the majority.[11]

Most recently, at a time when Mobutu may again be seeking a continental leadership role or at least a 'progressive' image, the tone has intensified once more. During his July visit to Luanda this year Mobutu condemned the 'reactionary and imperialist' incursions of Angola by the 'fascist Pretoria regime'. The joint communiqué issued about the meeting discussed the 'criminal attacks by the racist South African regime' on Angola. President Mobutu voiced 'his strong repudiation of the attacks on the PRA by the racist South African armed forces and called for their immediate withdrawal'; expressed Zaire's 'support for and solidarity with the oppressed people of Namibia and their vanguard, SWAPO, who are the victims of colonial exploitation and racist oppression by the hateful apartheid regime'; and condemned Pretoria's apartheid policies and reiterated 'support for the heroic struggle being waged by the South African people' as Zaire had always done![12] And all this while maintaining, if not actually increasing, ties with UNITA.

Since Zaire has never *publicly* supported South Africa, it is consistent that the regime has always *publicly* rejected all dialogue and détente offers. Zaire signed the Lusaka Manifesto of 1969. It also engaged in vigorous anti-dialogue lobbying at the January 1971 OCAMM meeting in Ndjamena and supported the anti-dialogue resolution at the June 1971 OAU summit meeting.[13] Early in 1971, at a press conference in Senegal, Mobutu said that a dialogue with South Africa was not desirable until South African leaders held a dialogue with their own black population.[14] A tangible result of this position and Mobutu's efforts during the 'radical' phase was the invitation by Tanzania and Zambia to be part of the so-called Mulungushi Club on Southern African issues in 1973–4.[15]

By 1975 this 'radical' image had evaporated and rumours began to circulate that Zaire was engaging in an 'underground' dialogue with South Africa as the situation in Angola became more tense.[16] One report had Prime Minister Vorster trying to set up an interview with Mobutu; another had a Zairian minister visiting Pretoria in April 1975.[17] In August 1975 the Johannesburg *Star* reported government-to-government contact between Zaire and South Africa and announced that the latter had left the 'hawks' and joined the 'doves'.[18]

During 1975–6 Eschel Rhoodie reportedly flew to Kinshasa three times to see Mobutu about setting up a front magazine (a sort of *Time* for West Africa) to be published and distributed from Paris to Zaire, Chad, Gabon, Ivory Coast, Cameroon and Senegal by Rhoodie's department. It was to have a conservative pro-Mobutu view of West African politics and would support

South Africa in a 'subtle' way. Mobutu was to raise £1·5 million for the project, but he failed to do so and may have had second thoughts about the idea.[19]

In 1978 several South African commentators portrayed Zaire as a supporter of détente, but Zaire vehemently denied it. Mulder reportedly had plans to expand contacts with Zaire that were set back by the breaking of the scandal that bears his name.[20] All this time the rhetoric of the regime continued.

(2) South Africa's View of Zaire: a Well-Developed Case of Schizophrenia

South Africa's view of Zaire is typical of its complex, condescending and ambivalent attitudes towards Black Africa in general. South Africa sees Zaire as a brutal, authoritarian state led by a ruthless, shrewd Machiavellian prince with delusions of personal glory. One South African writer called President Mobutu 'one of the most formidable and fascinating demagogues that black Africa has produced – and one of the richest and most deliberately glamorous'.[21] As the incarnation of the state, he is portrayed as having vast ambitions for Zaire and for himself. Mobutu's desire to be a leading African statesman is seen as the cause of his periodic rabid anti-South African tirades. These are forgiven, however, because of his 'pragmatic' informal dealings with South Africa, especially the 'readily evident' trade patterns. In Zaire 'the gap between reality and ideal remains irreconcilable'.[22] According to the South African view, human rights, democracy and freedom of the press are all non-existent in Zaire although constantly proclaimed in incessant propaganda. Right after Shaba II, *To The Point* published a highly critical view of Mobutu which stressed the ongoing disintegration of Zaire under his rule.[23]

Mobutu is generally given credit for returning order to Zaire, but his regime is seen as typical of the poor economic perform-ance of African regimes in large part due to the 'passive and change-resistant nature of African society'.[24] This economic failure is seen to stem more from a lack of will and capability than from neo-colonial exploitation. One South African publication points to Zaire as a prime example of the general trend of 'disastrous economic performances characterised by low productivity, bad management, corruption and lack of discipline'.[25] This is especially true for the agricultural sector. The Zairian state is also characterised by bureaucratic inefficiency and massive corruption which in great part explained the disastrous results of 'Zairianization'. Kinshasa 'learnt the hard lesson that indigenisation and nationalisation can only work within a limited sphere of government control'.[26] Some South African commentators referred to the Zairianization measures as 'socialist policies' (as if a non-socialist parastatal sector were not possible!). The failure of these policies is frequently pointed out along with the lesson that Africans are just as likely to exploit their people as foreigners. 'De-Zairianization' was seen as a necessity as is white assistance: 'Zaire without the skills and ability of the white man would be a Zaire taking a three century leap backwards.'[27] This need is seen to be reflected in the current IMF-mandated supervision of the Zairian state and the economy in its progressive decline. These general trends lead South African commentators to believe that Zaire and other African states like it, will have to rely increasingly on South African trade and assistance and that this dependence will somehow lead to political acceptance.

On the other side of this schizophrenic case Zaire is viewed as a reasonable, moderate, capitalistic and anti-communist country. Despite his periodic public rantings against South Africa, Mobutu is viewed as a friend, an ideological and strategic ally, as witnessed by actions during the Angolan civil war, the failure to vote to expel South Africa from the UN in 1975 and Zaire's role as an important trading partner. Mobutu is given credit for keeping the country together, despite its 'rampant tribalism', and for condemning Soviet, Cuban and East German expansionism on the continent. Zaire is portrayed as a potential economic giant with minerals crucial to the defence of the West.[28] For its own strategic purposes South Africa wants to keep Zaire moderate, capitalist and anti-communist. It is seen as a key state, especially since Moscow 'is striving to throw a Red girdle across the African midriff'.[29] In this regard South Africa has sought to co-operate and assist Zaire to the fullest extent possible.

(3) Economic Relations: Investment

The major source of South African investment in Zaire is through the Anglo-American Corporation headed by Harry Oppenheimer. This vast multinational corporation, directly and through its complex holdings in De Beers, Société

Générale de Belgique, Union Minière du Haut Katanga and Tanganyika Concessions, has played a key role in the 'Cape-to-Katanga' mining complex. De Beers has controlled the sale of all diamonds in Zaire, although smuggling is common. President Mobutu profits directly from diamond sales. The frontman for Anglo-American in Zaire is Mobutu's long-time friend and business partner, Maurice Templesman. He brought together investors from the USA, France, Japan and South Africa to form Société Minière de Tenge-Fungurume (SMTF) to exploit copper and cobalt deposits. A South African firm headed by Harry Oppenheimer, Charter Consolidated, has a 28 per cent share in SMTF. It is an investment that has yet to pay off, however, as the project was suspended in 1976 primarily due to the depressed price of copper and logistical problems resulting in the progressive disintegration of Zaire's current severe debt crisis through holdings in Banque de Paris et des Pays Bas, Rothschilds, Morgan Grenfell, First National City Bank and Morgan Guaranty. In 1971 an Afrikaner businessman, Anton Rupert, created a multi-national Bank for the Development of Equatorial and Southern Africa (Edesa) which was to raise European finance for South African investment in Africa. Zaire was mentioned as a key focus, but nothing much appears to have come of it.

(4) Economic Relations: Trade

It has been a widespread belief in South Africa that black-ruled states need trade with South Africa, and that this trade will lead to greater co-operation, interdependence, even closer political ties and eventually to acceptance of South Africa as it is now.[30] Because of the poor performance of most African economies in the last several years, and their economic, debt and agricultural crises in particular, this belief has been reinforced and is reflected in the grander versions of the 'constellation of states' concept. Many South Africans believe that they can help Black Africa develop, especially since South Africa is already the 'centre' or 'north' of the regional economy of Southern Africa. Trade with the rest of Africa has become important for South Africa, but it has not lessened its political isolation. Many South African commentators point to the need for internal reform before trade can increase dramatically and have an effect on political isolation. G. M. E. Leistner, a leading writer on this issue, also asserts that expanded economic co-operation with Black Africa depends on keeping the Soviets out of Africa, particularly Southern Africa.[31]

Zaire has long been an important but quasi-clandestine trading partner for South Africa. Formal trade and consular relations existed before independence. Trade was quietly maintained after independence and has increased considerably since the Angolan civil war with the closing of the Benguela railroad and Zaire's subsequent economic and fiscal crises. The politico-commercial elite has had to trade with South Africa to a certain degree, but it has increased the level of trade considerably beyond the minimum. Unlike the situation in other African countries, trade ties with South Africa do not appear to trouble the Zairian elite very much. These are conservative, authoritarian, pragmatic and money-oriented individuals. The regime has made no real effort to reduce its economic dependence on South Africa as Zambia has, for example. This is clearly related to the nature of the Mobutu regime. While publicly denying it, this regime has systematically and blatantly violated OAU and UN pro-scriptions on trade with South Africa and Rhodesia before it became independent.

Major items imported from South Africa have included mining equipment (and technical and support services), coal, dynamite, sulphuric acid, building equipment, electrical machinery, chemicals, general manufactured goods, car parts, oil, steel, transportation equipment, pharmaceuticals, maize, meat, canned goods, fish (including one-fifth of Namibia's output of pilchards), fruit, sugar and luxury goods. Most of these imports go to Shaba province and Kinshasa. Food, especially maize, is an important and growing item due to the continuing decline in Zairian food production. One estimate puts Shaba's imports of maize from Zimbabwe and South Africa at between one-half and two-thirds of Shaba's yearly needs. The figure for the region is now about 130,000 ton a year. Yellow corn is sent to Zimbabwe from South Africa, and Zimbabwe sends white corn to Shaba. Jean Rymenam reported in *Le Monde Diplomatique* that by early 1977 Zaire was spending about one-third of its foreign exchange earnings on food imports.[32] As agricultural output drops in many African countries, South Africans become more convinced that they can become the major food suppliers for Africa. Even Tanzania is now importing South African maize in large quantities.

As the economic situation continues to worsen Zaire relies

more heavily on the sometimes cheaper and more readily available South African goods. This is especially true, since until quite recently the South Africans have been quite free with credit. The current economic and fiscal crunch in Zaire will, of course, limit the degree to which this trade can increase.

Trade statistics are very hard to acquire, since South Africa does not break them down by country. What figures are available may not accurately reflect the real level or direction of trade because of the practices of third-party trade, double-invoicing and clandestine (unreported) trade.[33] The IMF does publish trade statistics, however, which yield interesting findings. Recorded Zairian imports from South Africa have risen from $12·7 million in 1972 to $130·8 million for 1979, or an increase of more than eight times. In 1973 these imports accounted for 2 per cent of total imports. The figures for the subsequent years are: 1974, 3·9 per cent; 1975, 4·5 per cent; 1976, 7·23 per cent; 1977, 8·45 per cent; 1978, 9·96 per cent; and 1979, 9·2 per cent. This is a steady percentage increase during 1973–8, with a slight decline (but quantitative increase) for 1979. During the same period Zairian exports to South Africa have steadily declined from $1 million in 1972 to $0·1 million in 1979. Zaire's $130·8 million in imports from South Africa in 1979 accounted for 21·2 per cent of South Africa's exports to Africa. By contrast, during the 1973–9 period Zambia's imports from South Africa declined from $62·8 million in 1973 to $43·9 million in 1979, and in 1978 they had gone down to $39·9 million. This constitutes a decline from 11·8 per cent to 5·8 per cent. In 1979 Zambia accounted for only 7·1 per cent of South Africa's exports to Africa.[34]

Much of the food and luxury-goods trade with South Africa is carried out by members of Mobutu's 'presidential family' (Litho, Bemba, Moleka, Singa, Nendaka, Lukusa, and others). This flagrant violation of OAU and UN proscriptions of trade was dramatically demonstrated to other African states in November 1979 when a chartered air-cargo plane reportedly carrying Rhodesian beef for Litho was shot down over Mozambique.[35] The common practice is to send planes directly to South Africa or to use South African chartered aircraft which often land at Kinshasa or Lubumbashi at night. This trade with South African businessmen often involves elaborate kickback schemes under which the South Africans invoice high and the Bank of Zaire pays the difference in foreign exchange directly into the accounts of the Zairian 'entrepreneurs'. These individuals also trade with Europe, but they can frequently get better credit terms from the South Africans. The South African government itself has, according to some reports, supplied credit or credit guarantees for these transactions. Much of this trade goes completely unrecorded.

Zaire's dependence on South Africa increased greatly when the Benguela railroad was cut on 10 August 1975 during the early days of the Angolan civil war. In 1973 Zaire shipped out 624,100 ton of copper, manganese ore, cobalt and bulk zinc exports on the Benguela and shipped in 246,600 ton of imports. The problem was further compounded on 3 March 1976, when the rail route through Rhodesia to the Mozambique port of Beira was cut because the Rhodesia–Mozambique border was closed. Between April 1976 and April 1977 265,000 ton of copper was shipped out through Rhodesia to South African ports. By June 1977 the monthly average stabilised at about 24,000 ton. Only 1,400 ton were being shipped out via the Tazara railway a month. The Zairians have consistently preferred the South African route, because of its high efficiency and better facilities and despite its higher cost. South African rails have also been used heavily for imports and not just for goods from South Africa and Rhodesia. The *Guardian* reported in February 1980 that 30,000 ton of imports a month were coming into Zaire from South Africa. Currently about half of Zaire's copper is going out by rail through the South African port of East London. Most of the rest is going out by the tortuous national route to Matadi.[36]

Since Zaire's second reconciliation with Angola in 1978, efforts have been made to open the Benguela railroad. It is now technically open as of September 1981, but very little actually goes out or in because UNITA can cut it practically at will. A series of efforts are now being taken, which are described later in the chapter, to alleviate or lessen Zaire's dependence on the South African rail network, but the likelihood of being able to significantly do so within the next five or ten years is slim unless there is a resolution to the continuing conflict in Angola.

As already noted, there are air links between Zaire and South Africa. After the closure of the Benguela railroad, the Zairians asked Safair, a South African air firm with strong government ties, to fly food into Zaire. In May 1975 Pranay Gupte reported in the *New York Times* that 'almost every night South African-operated planes loaded with cobalt, diamonds and coffee take off for undetermined destinations from Kinshasa' and that the flights go unrecorded. On 31 July 1980 the South African

Minister of Transport announced in Pretoria that negotiations were going on to establish regular, formal cargo flights between South Africa and Zaire. The flights would be made by South African Airlines' pool partners and charters. Cargo flights between Johannesburg and Kinshasa by Air Zaire may also be established according to this report.[37]

The South African government has been underwriting to a certain degree this ongoing and growing trade relationship. In mid-October 1975 a representative of the semi-official Credit Guarantee Corporation (CGIC) reportedly visited Zaire with a group of South African businessmen. The intent evidently was to increase food exports to Zaire, but the Zairians denied the whole thing. It was also reported that a government-to-government loan of R8 million to cover food imports was extended and that the CGIC was arranging considerably larger credits for Zaire. The South African Industrial Development Corporation (IDC) also supposedly negotiated a R6·7 million six-month credit to two Zairian food importers. In 1978 it was reported that the IDC had again extended R20 million in credits for food imports and that the CGIC had granted credits for Zairian imports of steel and pharmaceuticals. Then Zaire began to default on payments, and South African banks began refusing to confirm letters of credit from Zairian importers even with a central bank guarantee. They also refused to supply new credit until outstanding amounts had been paid. Evidently, Zairian merchants are still able to buy on credit at the moment.

The South Africans have vaguely mentioned Zaire as a possible member of a greater constellation of states in Southern Africa. The Prime Minister has stated on more than one occasion that such a constellation might jut 'into the mineral-rich Shaba province of Zaire'. The likelihood of any type of formal arrangement is very small indeed, and the South Africans now seem to realise that. Instead, they are talking about 'concentrating on the "inner constellation".'[38] The formal trade ties between the two countries will continue, however, and the size of these trade relations will in large part depend on the health of the domestic Zairian economy and the international prices for copper, cobalt, diamonds, coffee, and so on.

(5) Angola: a Mutual Zairian and South African Disaster

The civil war touched off in Angola by the *coup d'état* in Portugal, in April 1974, severely shook both Zaire and South

Africa, dramatically affecting their respective strategic/ military situations and the substance, if not the rhetoric, of their foreign policies. It also profoundly altered the relationship between them.

Major new actors were now operating in Southern Africa, thereby confirming many of South Africa's worst fears. In fact, from its point of view, this new situation vindicated its long-held view about the nature of Soviet aims in Africa which had been so frequently scoffed at by Western governments and commentators over the years. South Africa believed that the goal of the Soviet Union was to isolate it, destroying its *cordon sanitaire* by, as Prime Minister Vorster put it, 'creating a string of Marxist states across Africa', by threatening its and the West's crucial sea lanes, by taking control of mineral supplies crucial to the West, and by showing South Africa and the West to be unreliable allies.[39] According to some South African commentators, the Soviets also wanted to diminish Chinese influence in Southern Africa. Vorster likewise felt that Soviet influence in Angola could have a destabilising effect on neighbouring territories – particularly Rhodesia and Namibia, but also possibly on Zaire and Zambia. Zaire was viewed as being basically anti-communist, despite Mobutu's recent efforts to portray himself as a radical Third World statesman. South Africa believed it was acting in the interests of these countries in particular and of Africa in general by helping to resist Soviet encroachment, by combating Soviet imperialism and its 'Red impis'. A few South African commentators also claim that South Africa wanted to show itself to be a reliable détente partner while providing its worth to the West by protecting its interests in Southern Africa generally, but also specifically in Zaire and Zambia. After all, the South Africans claim that the road to London, Paris and Washington goes through Africa.[40]

As Mozambique shows, however, South Africa is willing to work with a Marxist state or at least tolerate it as long as it is not seen to be a destabilising force. South Africa greatly miscalculated the public support it would get from all quarters by its intervention. Rather than furthering détente policies and strengthening its overall position, South Africa's intervention killed détente, or at least drove it underground, and weakened South Africa's international position. In fact, as we have already seen, even Zaire publicly condemned South Africa's intervention in Angola.

Despite this public condemnation, however, South Africa's

reactivated anti-communism coincided almost directly with Mobutu's perceived interests, fears and basic orientation. He feared a communist-supported regime in Angola; he feared the threat of the Katangans still operating in Angola; he was concerned over the fate of the Benguela railroad, and he feared for his own imperialistic designs in Cabinda. The new relationship with South Africa created by the Angolan crisis did not seriously offend Mobutu, given his absolutist orientation to statehood and the authoritarian and conservative nature of his regime. It did, however, pose severe image problems for him, and the overall stakes of the crisis were very large indeed.

Mobutu had long supported the FNLA, and the South Africans had developed ties with it via Daniel Chipenda who met with BOSS officials in May and July 1975. Mobutu most likely knew of and approved these contacts. UNITA in particular needed help, and Savimbi asked for South African assistance after reportedly consulting with Mobutu, Kaunda and Houphouet-Boigny. Kaunda has denied this, as has Mobutu, but much less convincingly. As the crisis continued, Mobutu established much closer ties with UNITA. He also tried to get the USA, France (successfully) and China (unsuccessfully) to intervene.[41]

Very clear intelligence and co-ordination linkages were developed between Zaire, the USA, South Africa and to a lesser extent France during the Angolan crisis. Some of these linkages survived the civil war, and some still remain. John Stockwell notes that CIA and BOSS officials met regularly in Kinshasa; that the South Africans picked up American supplies flown to Kinshasa and transported them to Silva Porto; that South Africa provided advisers, supplies and artillery pieces, and the soldiers to man them for the joint FNLA/Zairian column in the north to which Zaire had committed two battalions; and that the South Africans even wanted to fly a task force into Southern Zaire in order to attack Texeirada Sousa.[42] Some FNLA troops also fought alongside South African and UNITA forces in the south. Zaire, of course, also funnelled arms to the FNLA and acted as a conduit for American assistance to UNITA and South Africa. Finally, when the situation became desperate in late 1975, Zaire insistently urged South Africa not to pull out, but to no avail.

(6) Shaba I and II: Precipitative Crises

In conjunction with Soviet and Cuban activities in Angola, the invasions of Shaba province by Katangan rebels from Angola in 1977 and again in 1978 intensely reactivated and validated longstanding South African notions about communist expansion in Africa and the threat this poses to Western interests generally. We have already seen that Prime Minister Vorster predicted that one of the most serious possibilities resulting from a Soviet/Cuban-assisted MPLA victory might be direct territorial threats to Zaire and Zambia.[43] The South African assessment of this general situation had only a limited impact on the Carter administration, but it may have a greater impact on a Reagan administration.

Generally the South Africans viewed the Shaba invasions as evidence of Marxist, particularly Soviet, designs on Africa, and more specifically as examples of Soviet/Cuban imperialism – the ultimate aim and prize of which is South Africa itself. P. W. Botha referred to the Shaba invasions 'as clear evidence of a global communist strategy to conquer the whole of Southern Africa, seize its wealth and control the Cape sea route'.[44] He went on to assert that the aim was to eliminate moderate black leaders and regimes and that the West must stop this enslavement of Africa by Marxism. The Soviets after all were striking at Eurafrica, according to the South Africans, using Lenin's strategy of hitting Europe and America through Africa – the soft underbelly.[45]

This is particularly true in their minds in regard to crucial minerals which the Soviets want to deny to the West. In the context of Zaire, cobalt is the key element.[46] More narrowly, this low-risk Soviet-designed invasion furthered Soviet consolidation in Angola and threatened both Chinese and American interests.[47] One South African commentator sums up the general view of these 'proxy wars' by asserting that the Cuban and East German-trained Katangan rebels

> were attempting to depose the pro-Western government in Zaire. These incursions clearly demonstrated Soviet determination to exploit irredentist, tribal and/or ethnic issues and to disrupt the political and territorial integrity of African states if this should serve Moscow's interests. A pro-Moscow regime in Zaire would boost Soviet expansionism in Africa to a considerable degree.

He also stresses that the Soviets have selected Africa as 'the crucial battleground to break the political deadlock with U.S.A. and gain the upperhand in the continuing struggle for world domination'.[48] In regard to other African states, the South Africans felt a victory in Zaire would reinforce the view that the Soviets are the wave of the future.

Surprise and pleasure were the two principal South African reactions to Western moves to support the Mobutu regime. Vorster expressed satisfaction at the turn of events and congratulated the West for at last 'waking up to the threat of Marxism in Africa'.[49] All commentators extended particular praise to the French for what was seen as their dynamic and rapid response. Both official and unofficial figures expressed considerable support for the French idea of a permanent African security force, in part because it showed a change in Western attitudes. One South African noted that 'for once the West did not drag its heels and under French initiative repelled an anti-status quo adventure that would have had extremely serious consequences if it had been successful'. He also noted that even the USA provided some assistance.[50]

Characteristically, but unrealistically, the two Shaba invasions revived old hopes that so-called moderate states would join with South Africa to resist Marxist expansionism. The South African belief that the communist threat is 'indivisible' and requires co-operation between states in Southern Africa leads them to *expect* such co-operation.[51] Although President Mobutu publicly assessed the Shaba invasions in much the same terms as the South Africans and used similar justifications in appealing for Western aid, this does not mean that he is willing to enter into any sort of public and formal alliance with South Africa. This type of thinking on the part of the South Africans is reflected in several versions of the 'constellation of states' idea and is as unrealistic as all of its predecessor grand concepts.[52] This clearly does not mean, however, that secret assistance is not desired by some states or not offered by South Africa.

Certainly, South Africa played no major role in repelling the two invasions of Shaba province, but there were persistent reports during Shaba I in 1977 that a high BOSS official clandestinely visited Kinshasa to negotiate secret assistance to Zaire in the form of fuel, food and credits. Some saw this as a natural extension of a longstanding policy of behind-the-scenes South African support of the Mobutu regime that had reached intense levels during the Angolan civil war.[53] Without much doubt, many of these ties had been maintained. There was most likely a sharing of intelligence information as South African intelligence officers turn up periodically in Kinshasa. There is a reliable but unconfirmed report that an informal South African adviser has been in Kinshasa for a number of years and that he was a good deal of help to the Mobutu regime during both invasions of Shaba province.

(7) Zaire in Southern Africa after Shaba II: Rehabilitation and a New Radicalism?

The second invasion of Shaba in 1978 came as a real shock to Mobutu and his regime. A combination of a finally recognised need to deal systematically with surrounding states and Southern Africa generally, foreign pressure, and a rapidly disintegrating internal situation led, in late 1978, to a series of moves that now can be seen as a major reorientation or rapprochement with neighbours and the other black-ruled states of Southern Africa.

These moves are prime examples of the flexibility of approach in Zaire's foreign policy (some might call it a lack of firm principles). On the whole, Zaire's relations with its Southern African neighbours are now quite respectable. Tensions and suspicions remain, however, and Zaire is being kept on the margin of the action as it was by the front line states over Zimbabwe and Namibia. Mobutu's frustration at this time is enormous. He would again like to be seen as a respectable member of 'progressive' Africa. But Nyerere still distrusts him intensely, the Angolans have suspicions over continuing ties with UNITA and relations with Zambia follow their normal roller-coaster course under a modicum of decorum – the most recent aggravation being the attempted coup in Zambia, in October 1980, in which the South Africans and dissident Zairians have been implicated by the Zambians. Mobutu was not invited to Zimbabwe's independence celebrations, although Mugabe did attend a later meeting in Lubumbashi. There are also countertrends such as the continually increasing trade relations with South Africa which go way beyond necessity, recent rumours of increased ties with and activity on behalf of UNITA, increasingly close ties with the West, especially France, and potentially with a Reagan administration in the USA, and support within Africa for Morocco over the Western Sahara and Mobutu's handling of the Zimbabwe situation. Zaire has a clear-cut reputation for unprincipled flexibility and volatility and vacillating, two-faced rhetoric in its foreign policy. This reputation is reinforced by the way the regime treats its own subjects, by its current severe economic, fiscal, political and social crises, and by the dependence on Western powers generated by these crises. Only some of this can be explained by the fluidity of the Southern African regional state system; much of it can be explained by the nature of the regime and the characteristics of its presidential monarch. Mobutu has always and will continue to hedge his bets. It is in the nature of his statecraft, and this breeds suspicion and caution on the part of other states in the region.

The first major move in this reorientation was a real, substantive reconciliation with Angola. In early 1978 relations were still bad as Angola consistently charged both Zaire and South Africa with committing aggression against it. By June representatives of five Western powers were strongly urging Mobutu to come to terms with the MPLA government. By the middle of July a major agreement had been worked out to normalise relations, control their respective borders and resident rebels, exchange refugees and reopen the Benguela railroad. A variety of co-operation agreements were also signed. In August Neto paid a rousing visit to Kinshasa, and Mobutu travelled to Luanda in October. The two core elements of this pragmatic agreement were the pledges of non-aggression and control of rebels and the reopening of the Benguela railroad. Compliance with the first part has been amazingly good, despite suspicions that Mobutu has not fully cut his ties with UNITA. Opening the Benguela railway has proved to be much more difficult. It is clearly not yet fully operational, and the South Africans do not find it in their interest to encourage Savimbi to show restraint. The current situation is a burden for Angola and reinforces the dependence of Mobutu on South African rail facilities. On the other hand, the situation has also forced and/or allowed Mobutu to co-operate more with his neighbours.

Basically the reconciliation has worked well and, despite some lower-level sabotage on both sides, has survived the transition to dos Santos very nicely. The agreement was widely hailed in Africa and gave Mobutu a badly needed boost. The Tanzanian *Daily News* commented that 'the restoration of normal neighbourly relations between Zaire and Angola is a move in the right direction. Both countries need peace to develop in their different ways . . . African unity is not only an ideal worth striving for, it is also an instrument in the struggle against exploitation and under-development. In unity lies our strength'.[54] This diplomatic coup set the stage for Mobutu to make broader moves including rapprochement with the Soviets, the Cubans and the East Germans. In turn, these began to refurbish his image.

Eventually these actions even led to a partial thaw in relations between Nyerere and Mobutu. The latter headed a large Zairian delegation which visited Arusha on 31 May–1 June 1979. A permanent co-operation commission was agreed to and the 'fascist' Idi Amin was castigated.[55] Mobutu also had talks with Kaunda in Lusaka. Two weeks later President Neto again paid a visit to Kinshasa. Southern African détente without South Africa was further strengthened and broadened in mid-October 1979, when presidents Mobutu, dos Santos and Kaunda met at Ndola and signed a mutual non-aggression pact and a series of economic co-operation agreements focusing on transportation and communications problems. Subsequently Zaire expelled Holden Roberto from Zaire and banned all Angolan opposition leaders, and Angola sent Nathaniel Mbumba and forty other FNIC leaders to Guinea-Bissau. In February 1980 Nguza Karl-i-Bond further broadened contacts in a series of meetings in Tanzania, Zambia and Mozambique.[56]

Zaire's rehabilitation is still not fully accepted, however. This has been made clear by the exclusion of Zaire from a major Southern African initiative. After a preliminary meeting of the front line states in Arusha in July 1979,[57] a major Southern African Development Co-ordination Conference (SADCC) was held in Lusaka on 1 April 1980 attended by the leaders of nine Southern African states: Tanzania, Zambia, Mozambique, Zimbabwe, Angola, Malawi, Swaziland, Botswana and Lesotho. The intent appears to be the creation of a sort of 'counter constellation of states' which would seek to lessen dependence of the nine countries on South Africa by increasing interstate economic ties and creating an alternative transportation and communications grid. South Africa's much ballyhooed hopes for a constellation of states of its own was rendered obsolete by the nature of the settlement in Zimbabwe. Instead this settlement has permitted an initiative like the Lusaka one.

Structurally Zaire is clearly part of Southern Africa, certainly as much so as Tanzania, for example, and logically Zaire should be included in such an enterprise. But Zaire was not invited, and it was Mobutu who had a fit of pique. He desperately wants to be included and not just for economic reasons, but for political and personal reasons as well. As a result, he has been systematically attempting to further refurbish his 'progressive image' while using transportation issues as his substantive wedge into this effort. The regularity and vehemence of his anti-Pretoria rhetoric has increased again, and Zaire is once more active in OAU Liberation Committee work and in anti-apartheid efforts at the UN. But memories are long. Feeling left out of earlier moves by the front lines states, in regard to Zimbabwe, Mobutu had attacked them in March 1977 for seeking 'to divide Africa . . . In fact, we are now watching the birth of a restricted club, a club where hypocrisy is the only slogan'.[58] He also accused some of them of trading with South Africa and even of receiving loans, thereby benefiting from apartheid! The hypocrisy was clearly with Mobutu, however, as the trade with South Africa by the front line states was openly declared and accepted by the OAU as essential and no such loans existed. As was pointed out earlier, this is not the case for Zaire.

The front line presidents are well aware that Zaire is structurally part of the Southern African complex and have, therefore, not excluded Zaire completely. They have simply proceeded cautiously with Zaire for primarily political reasons, while Mobutu for his part has sought to use his transportation card to get into the game. For example, the transportation ministers of Zambia, Angola and Zaire met in Lubumbashi in April 1980 after the Lusaka meeting to discuss transportation issues, and then on 20 June 1980 presidents Kaunda, Machel and Mugabe met with Mobutu in Lubumbashi to discuss ways of diminishing rail dependence on South Africa, especially by using upgraded Mozambique facilities. They established a ministerial committee outside the SADCC structure to follow up these matters. This committee met and signed a co-operation agreement in Maputo on 10 July. This meeting came right after the one, also in Maputo, of the Transportation and Communications Commission in Southern Africa created by the Lusaka SADCC meeting. Zaire is not a member of the commission, but it was 'allowed' to join the discussions.

In the process of these refurbishing efforts Mobutu has visited Mozambique, and presidents Nyerere, Machel and dos Santos have all briefly visited Kinshasa either in conjunction with the 1980 OAU meeting or Zaire's 30 June independence celebrations. Then on 3 July Mobutu paid a 'friendly working visit' to Luanda where he vehemently condemned apartheid,

South Africa's illegal occupation of Namibia, and the 'attacks on Angola by the racist South African armed forces'.[59] President Mobutu may slowly be making some progress. Zaire attended the 2nd Southern African Development Co-ordination Conference in Maputo, in November, as an observer, and its application for membership may be approved at the next summit meeting.[60] In the meantime the hope of this is a very sophisticated way of keeping President Mobutu in line.

(8)   Concluding Remarks: the Future

Lastly, what about the future? This must be discussed in two parts. The first assumes that President Mobutu stays in power. Given this assumption, past patterns are likely to be maintained in general – flexibility and sudden shifts in orientation and action; two-faced dealings with regard to South Africa; attempts to play a larger role in Southern Africa for reasons of glory, power, or statecraft; and continued dependence on and manipulation of Western powers' international organisations, and private banks, for support while attempting to cope with a disastrous internal situation. In short, the interests and methods of absolutist statecraft will remain dominant.

But what if this internal situation fully disintegrates and/or a change of regime is attempted, whatever the means and whatever the ideological position or patron–client ties of the group? The likelihood of a peaceful and orderly change of regime is, in my mind, slim. The army is weak and disorganised as are the internal and external oppositions in all their factional glory. The possibility of full-scale territorial and political disintegration should not be easily dismissed. If such disintegration occurs and major upheaval results, outside intervention of just about every kind is highly possible. All major regional (including South African), continental and international actors would seek to affect the outcome. The impact on political stability and economic performance in the entire central and southern portions of the continent would be dramatic and probably very costly for all involved.

Finally, in regard to Zaire and South Africa specifically, it is hoped that both governments will choose to take better care of their own populations. The outlook in both cases, however, is not sanguine.

Notes: Chapter 4

1 See Thomas M. Callaghy, 'State formation and absolutism in comparative perspective: seventeenth-century France and Mobutu Sese Seko's Zaire', PhD dissertation, University of California, Berkeley, California, USA, 1979).

2 See Thomas M. Callaghy, 'State–subject communication in Zaire: domination and the concept of domain consensus', *Journal of Modern African Studies*, vol. XVIII, no. 3 (September 1980), pp. 469–92.

3 For Southern Africa considered as a regional subsystem, see: Kenneth Grundy, *Confrontation and Accommodation in Southern Africa: The Limits of Independence* (Berkeley, Calif.: University of California Press, 1973); Timothy M. Shaw, 'Southern Africa: co-operation and conflict in an international sub-system', *Journal of Modern African Studies*, vol. 12, no. 4 (1974), pp. 633–55; and Timothy M. Shaw and Kenneth A. Heard (eds), *Cooperation and Conflict in Southern Africa: Papers on a Regional Subsystem* (Washington, DC: University Press of America, 1977).

4 For a somewhat similar perspective from a Marxist viewpoint, see the nuanced and realistic piece by Nzongola-Ntalaja, 'The US, Zaire and Angola', in René Lemarchand (ed.), *American Policy in Southern Africa* (Washington, DC: University Press of America, 1978), pp. 147–69.

5 See Thomas M. Callaghy, 'The rise of the African state', *Problems of Communism*, vol. 29, no. 5 (September–October, 1980), pp. 56–64.

6 John Barratt (ed.), *Accelerated Development in Southern Africa* (New York: St Martin's Press, 1974), p. 568.

7 Quoted in Crawford Young, 'The Portuguese coup and Zaire's Southern Africa policy', in John Seiler (ed.), *Southern Africa since the Portuguese Coup* (Boulder, Colo: Westview Press, 1980), p. 195.

8 UN General Assembly debate, 'South Africa: race problems, apartheid', 8 December 1975.

9 *Africa Report*, vol. 22, no. 4 (July–August 1977), pp. 11–12.

10 *Zaire*, 10 April 1978.

11 Michael A. Samuels (ed.), *Africa and the West* (Boulder, Colo: Westview Press, 1979), p. 80.

12 *AZAP*, 11 July 1980.

13 Yashpal Tandon, 'South Africa and the OAU: the dialogue on the Dialogue issue', *Instant Research on Peace and Violence*, 2 (1972), p. 58. On dialogue and détente generally, see O. Geyser, 'Detente in Southern Africa', *African Affairs*, vol. 75, no. 299 (April 1976), pp. 182–207.

14 *Africa Research Bulletin (ARB)*, 1–28 February 1971, vol. 8, no. 2, p. 2009.

15 Guy Arnold, 'Mobutu picks up the pieces', *African Development* (July 1976), p. 667; and Shaw, 'Southern Africa', op. cit., p. 655.

16 See Thomas A. Marks, 'The Shaba adventure', *Bulletin*, vol. 16, no. 3 (1978), pp. 111–15.

17 'How Black Africa views Pretoria's overtures', *Banker* (September 1975), p. 1101; and *OER: Zaire*, 3 (1975), p. 2.

18 *Star*, 15 August 1975.

19 Reported by 'Muldergate' journalist Kitt Katzin in *Sunday Express*, 10 June 1979 and reprinted in the *Guardian* next day; the veracity of these reports is difficult to ascertain.

20   Colin Legum (ed.), *Africa Contemporary Record 1978–79 (ACR)* (New York: Africana, 1980), p. B916.

21   Al J. Venter, *The Zambezi Salient: Conflict in Southern Africa* (Cape Town: Howard Timmins, 1974), p. 204. On South Africa's general view of black Africa, see three other books by Venter: *Africa Today* (Johannesburg: Macmillan, 1975), *Black Leaders of Southern Africa* (Pretoria: Siesta, 1976) and *Vorster's Africa: Friendship and Frustration* (Johannesburg: Ernest Stanton, 1977).

22   Venter, *The Zambezi Salient*, op. cit., p. 207.

23   *To the Point*, 14 July 1978.

24   G. M. E. Leistner, 'South Africa, Africa and the North–South conflict', *South African Journal of African Affairs*, vol. 8, no. 2 (1978), pp. 49–100; Leistner specifically cites Zaire as an example of this trend.

25   *African Freedom Annual 1978*, p. 31.

26   ibid., p. 30.

27   Venter, *The Zambezi Salient*, op. cit., p. 202.

28   See Cas F. de Villiers (ed.), *Southern Africa: The Politics of Raw Materials*, Conference Report No. 3 (Pretoria: Foreign Affairs Association, 1977): specifically A. J. Cottrell, 'The geo-strategic importance of Southern Africa', pp. 9–18, and J. P. Vanneman, 'Soviet strategy in Central and Southern Africa: the case of Zaire', pp. 34–40.

29   *African Freedom Annual 1979*, p. 104; on the general perception of the communist threat, see C. F. de Villiers, *et al.*, *The Communist Strategy* (Pretoria: Republic of South Africa Department of Information, February 1975); and J. H. Coetzee, 'South Africa and Africa', *South Africa International*, vol. 9, no. 3 (January 1979), pp. 128–39, and 'Communist penetration in Africa', *Bulletin*, vol. 16, no. 2 (1978), pp. 62–9.

30   On this set of attitudes, see the following series of articles by G. M. E. Leistner: 'Southern Africa – today and tomorrow', *Bulletin*, vol. 12, no. 10 (1974), pp. 418–25, 'Southern Africa in transition', *South African Journal of African Affairs*, vol. 5, no. 1 (1975), pp. 5–13, and 'Economic cooperation in Southern Africa', *South Africa International*, vol. 6, no. 1 (July 1975), pp. 35–45.

31   G. M. E. Leistner, 'Economic interdependence', *Bulletin*, vol. 16, no. 9–10 (1978), p. 317.

32   *Le Monde diplomatique*, May 1977.

33   See Adrian Guelke, 'Africa as a market for South African goods', *Journal of Modern African Studies*, vol. 12, no. 1 (1974), pp. 69–88, and 'South Africa's African connection', *African Business* (February 1978), pp. 45–6, 51.

34   International Monetary Fund, *Direction of Trade Yearbook 1980* (Washington, DC: IMF, 1980), pp. 338–9, 402–5.

35   *Africa Confidential*, vol. 20, no. 1, 3 January 1979, and 'Zaire: salvaged but not saved', 9 April 1980; and *ACR 1977–78*, vol. 10, op. cit., p. B603.

36   *Guardian*, 25 February 1980; and Kenneth W. Grundy, 'Economic patterns in the new Southern Africa balance', in Gwendolen M. Carter and Patrick O'Meara (eds), *Southern Africa: The Continuing Crisis* (Bloomington, Ind.: Indiana University Press, 1979), pp. 291–312.

37   *ARB*, vol. 17, no. 7, 15 July–14 August 1980, p. 5602; and *ARB*, vol. 16, no. 3, 15 March–14 April 1979, p. 5048.

38   Information Counselor, 'A bright new constellation', in *Backgrounder*,

January 1980 (Washington, DC: South African Embassy, 1980); and *To the Point*, 7 November 1980, p. 19.

39 See Deon Geldenhuys, *South Africa's Search for Security since the Second World War* (Pretoria: South African Institute of International Affairs, 1978), pp. 10–11; and J. E. Spence, 'South African foreign policy; changing perspectives', *World Today*, vol. 34, no. 11 (November 1978), p. 424.

40 See D. T. Kunert, 'The role of the superpowers in Africa', *South African Journal of Africa Affairs*, vol. 8, no. 2 (1978), pp. 129–33.

41 Robin Hallett, 'The South African intervention in Angola 1975–76', *African Affairs*, vol. 77, no. 308 (July 1978), pp. 347–86; Colin Legum, *After Angola: The War over Southern Africa* (New York: Africana, 1976), pp. 13–14, 32–8; and Douglas G. Anglin and Timothy M. Shaw, *Zambia's Foreign Policy: Studies in Diplomacy and Dependence* (Boulder, Colo: Westview Press, 1979), pp. 332–3, 338. The Zairian opposition has echoed the charges of collusion with South Africa; see Le Comité Zaire, *Zaire: le dossier de la recolonisation* (Paris: L'Harmattan, 1978), pp. 163–8, and 'La CIA et le Zaire' (Antwerp, 31 December 1977), p. 19.

42 John Stockwell, *In Search of Enemies: A CIA Story* (New York: Norton, 1978), pp. 163, 165, 186–7, 209, 213, 218; R. W. Johnson, *How Long Will South Africa Survive?* (New York: Oxford University Press, 1977), pp. 129–71; and Arthur Jay Klinghoffer, *The Angolan War: A Study in Soviet Policy in the Third World* (Boulder, Colo: Westview Press, 1980).

43 Hallett, op. cit., pp. 363–6.

44 Quoted in Spence, op. cit., p. 424.

45 See Basil Hersov, 'Demands of a new era', *South Africa International*, vol. IX, no. 4 (April 1979), pp. 169–85.

46 See de Villiers, *Southern Africa*, op. cit.; P. Janke, 'New perspectives to strategic studies', in ibid., pp. 28–33; see also Thomas A. Marks, 'Communist penetration in Africa', *Bulletin*, vol. 16, no. 2 (1978), pp. 62–9; and Ian Grieg, in *African Freedom Annual 1979*, pp. 73, 104.

47 Vanneman, 'Soviet strategy in central and southern Africa', pp. 34–7.

48 Kunert, op. cit., pp. 129, 132; on South African views about Cuban and East German involvement, see O. F. Nieuwoudt, 'Cuba in Africa', *Bulletin*, vol. 16, no. 2 (1978), pp. 44–8; *African Freedom Annual 1979*, pp. 68, 104; and David Williers, 'Cuba, Angola and the West', *International Affairs Bulletin*, vol. 2, no. 3 (1978), pp. 24–34.

49 Quoted in 'Zaire: global diplomacy', *Africa Confidential*, vol. 19, no. 13 (June 1978).

50 Barnard, in *African Freedom Annual 1979*, p. 93; and *South African Digest*, 15 May 1977, and 29 May 1977; and *To the Point*, 30 June 1978.

51 de Villiers, *The Communist Strategy*, op. cit., p. 140; and Geldenhuys, op. cit., p. 13.

52 On the vagaries of the constellation concept, see Deon Geldenhuys and Denis Venter, 'A constellation of states: regional cooperation in Southern Africa', *International Affairs Bulletin*, vol. 3, no. 3 (December 1979), pp. 36–72; and Deon Geldenhuys, 'The neutral option and subcontinental solidarity', South African Institute of International Affairs, Pretoria, March 1979.

53 *Washington Post*, 9 April 1977.

54 *Daily News* (Tanzania), 17 August 1978.

55   *ARB*, vol. 16, no. 5, 15 May–14 June 1979, p. 5121; this commission was finally established on 24 February 1980.
56   *ARB*, vol. 16, no. 10, 1–31 October 1979, p. 5431.
57   'A constellation of states?' *XRAY: Current Affairs in Southern Africa*, 62 (January–February 1980); and *New African*, 153 (September 1979), pp. 66–7.
58   Radio Kinshasa, quoted in Legum, *The Western Crisis over Southern Africa* (New York: Africana, 1979), p. 21; and on SADCC, see *Africa* 105 (May 1980), pp. 43–4.
59   Radio Luanda, 3 July 1980.
60   *Africa News*, 8 December 1980.

PART TWO

Great Powers and Southern Africa

5
The Soviet Union, Zimbabwe and Southern Africa

JAMES MAYALL

Great events extend our social and political horizons. They also create new opportunities and constraints, primarily for those who are directly caught up in them but also for those whose involvement is more vicarious. We know that something genuinely historic has happened when our expectations alter: what was previously entertained as a utopian dream, is suddenly transformed into the realm of practical politics. The military coup in Portugal in April 1975, which heralded the end of the Portuguese empire in Africa, was just such an event. For many the transfer of power to Robert Mugabe's government in Zimbabwe, in February 1980, was another. In each case not only was a deep-rooted and intractable historical conflict 'resolved', but the form of resolution was widely perceived as having implications for the future. In each case – first, in Mozambique and Angola, and then in Zimbabwe – the achievement of sovereign independent statehood was held both to vindicate the OAU's policy towards the liberation of these countries and to promise the inevitable ultimate success of the same policy in Namibia and the Republic of South Africa.

The Soviet Union, which has long occupied a central place in the demonology of the South African government, and which has conversely been valued by several of the major nationalist movements in Southern Africa for its material and moral support, was the beneficiary of these historic shifts in the Southern African landscape. For since 1963 the Soviet government has given unqualified public support to the African policy – enshrined in the OAU Charter – of confrontation with white power. By contrast, the Western powers, whose public values were in conflict with their material interests in Southern Africa, had attempted to support the objectives of majority rule while refusing to acknowledge the legitimacy of wars of national liberation. In 1974 they paid the price for this equivocation.

Until the Portuguese coup the ambivalence of Western policies had not threatened a major international crisis in Southern Africa. Although Rhodesia's UDI was a constant source of strain in Britain's relations with independent Africa, and to a lesser extent those of the other Western powers also, it had little impact on East–West relations. South African complaints on precisely this score made little or no impression either: no Western government appeared to take seriously the prospect of a Soviet threat to their interests in the region. After the successful Cuban and Soviet intervention in the Angolan civil war, and the failure of Western efforts, however, the British and American governments were forced to admit that they now faced a diplomatic question which was both urgent and complicated. A series of initiatives, starting with Dr Kissinger's 'shuttle diplomacy' in 1975 and culminating with the Lancaster House conference in London, which set the stage for Zimbabwe's independence, tacitly acknowledged that in the absence of a more constructive diplomacy by the Western powers, the Soviet Union was bound to earn substantial dividends at their expense from its historic investment in African nationalism.

From the point of view of Western governments, the question which arose in the aftermath of Zimbabwe's independence was whether, by assisting in the orderly transfer of power to nationalist forces, they had regained the diplomatic initiative from the Soviet Union; or whether, on the contrary, as Soviet theorists would argue, they had merely bowed to the inevitable by recognising, very late in the day, changes in the 'objective' configuration of forces within the region?

Those who argue the former case point to the contrasts rather than the continuities between the events of 1974–5 and those of 1978–80. Whatever the relationship between the events in Portugal and the outcome in Africa, the governments which succeeded to power in Mozambique and Angola did so after fighting prolonged guerrilla wars, and without submitting to the constitutional ritual of democratic elections. One consequence of their success was to raise the stock of those in Africa who argued that *true* independence was only to be achieved through a war of national liberation, since only in that way would the Western-dominated economic and political structure of the colonial state be smashed. On this view, which certainly advanced Soviet interests even if it was unlikely to be endorsed publicly by the Soviet authorities, Western democratic procedures merely served to preserve these structures and therefore had no relevance to African conditions. The fact that FRELIMO and the MPLA declared themselves to be Marxist-Leninist movements; that their leaders subsequently negotiated treaties of friendship and co-operation with the Soviet Union; and that Angola was accepted as an observer by COMECON[1] dramatically symbolised the realignment of forces in Southern Africa.

But if in Angola, the West, and particularly the USA, had forfeited the diplomatic initiative by effectively allying itself with South Africa in an attempt to frustrate the MPLA's victory in the civil war, in Zimbabwe it was the USSR which backed the wrong horse. Although four Cabinet posts were given to the Patriotic Front (ZAPU) led by Joshua Nkomo, a frequent visitor to Moscow whose ZIPRA forces had been trained and armed by the Soviet Union and East Germany, the party which won an overall majority in the elections – Robert Mugabe's ZANU – had never enjoyed close relations with the USSR. It is perfectly true, of course, that the settlement grew out of a war which was fought by both wings of the Patriotic Front with the material and moral support of the communist powers, and not from a process of gradual preparation for self-government and constitutional development. To that extent Britain's brief period of direct rule and the transfer of power according to the familiar pattern of earlier British decolonisations was indeed a ritual, an exercise in deliberate political symbolism. But in an area where it is the legacy of British settlement rather than Portuguese colonialism which must be accommodated, the symbolism of 'due process' may be as potent as its alternative.

Just as the victory of FRELIMO and the MPLA in Mozambique and Angola had both encouraged Zimbabwe's nationalists to pursue a military solution, and released resources for their struggle, so their eventual return to constitutionalism encouraged those who argue that this is the more appropriate model for effecting change in Namibia and in the Republic of South Africa itself. At first sight, however, it is a model which limits the opportunities for the projection of

Soviet influence: if force is to be subordinated to political negotiation, it is in large measure in order to preserve rather than to destroy the economic and social system developed by the colonial state, or at least to allow for its gradual adaptation.

It is not my purpose here to suggest which of these two views – that is, of Southern Africa regained for liberal democracy and the forces of 'moderation', or of the Zimbabwe settlement as a temporary hiatus on the road to the South African revolution and the incorporation of the entire region in the international socialist division of labour – is the most likely to be vindicated by history. As stated here, both outcomes seem fairly improbable; not only is the contrast between the international consequences of Portugal's withdrawal from Africa and of Britain's final essay in African decolonisation dangerously oversimplified in both directions (it is not in reality a simple contest between the forces of passion and those of reason), but the attempt to frame the question in the form of an historic choice often has an avowedly polemical purpose in what is after all a political competition which is far from over. On the other hand, the contrast between the two events does provide a useful reminder of the role of the continent in international politics, and of the danger of assuming that the radicalisation of African politics will inevitably favour the Soviet Union in its global competition with the West. No one foresaw with any accuracy the collapse of Portuguese power in Africa in 1974–5 or its international consequences, and very few – certainly not the Russians – would have predicted a constitutional settlement in Zimbabwe before the Commonwealth Conference in Lusaka in August 1979. The reason was simple: on both occasions most observers, with their own loyalties and prejudices, anxiously scanned the battlefield for evidence that the struggle was going their way and paid inadequate attention to the wider international context in which it was occurring. With the benefit of hindsight, it is clear that any analysis of Soviet policy in Southern Africa must pay due regard not only to the African context, but to the impact on Soviet perceptions and policy of constraints emanating from elsewhere in the international system. I shall return to these wider considerations shortly but since the fortunes of Soviet diplomacy in Southern Africa, like those of the Western powers, are, in the first instance, dependent on the extent to which Soviet and African interests coincide, it is to Soviet perceptions of the Southern African conflict, and to the reception of Soviet policies in Africa, that I turn first.

(1) The African Context: from Analysis to Policy

In one sense the distinction between Soviet perceptions of the global 'correlation of forces' and of the development of African societies is false. Ever since, in the aftermath of the Russian Revolution, Lenin turned his attention to the colonial question, the outside world, in the form of the debate about the strategy and tactics to be adopted in the struggle against world imperialism, has coloured Soviet assessment of African developments.[2] Since the immediate target was the industrial countries of Western Europe which were seen to be threatening the heartland of socialism, namely, the Soviet Union itself, while the ultimate goal was the destruction of the system of capitalism and imperialism which these same countries had created, it followed that the interests of those living under colonial oppression could be regarded as synonymous with, and in practice subordinated to, those of the Soviet state. This basic orientation of Soviet thinking has always made for flexibility in policy; for example, in the period between the two world wars, it led to the 'united from above' strategy (that is, a working alliance between communist and non-communist nationalists) being replaced by the 'united from below' (that is, communist-led revolution) and vice versa whenever this was considered prudent in terms of the Soviet Union's own relations with the capitalist powers.

While this tradition of flexible response has persisted, from the mid-1950s two problems complicated the task of identifying Soviet interests in Africa. The first was the independence of African countries; the second the adoption of the doctrine of peaceful coexistence at the 20th Party Congress in 1956. No longer was it possible to assume that the anti-capitalism of the USSR was necessarily synonymous with the anti-imperialism of independent African governments. And since under the new strategic doctrine nuclear confrontation had to be avoided, it was necessary also to limit the USSR's commitment whenever it seemed to threaten such a confrontation. The policy which was developed as a response to the first of these problems – of concentrating Soviet diplomatic effort and economic assistance on those countries whose leaders had opted for the 'non-capitalist road' to development – was quietly abandoned in the mid-1960s as one after the other the 'progressive' African leaders were toppled from power. The need to temper revolutionary enthusiasm with both pragmatism and caution – the latter because of the dangers of superpower confrontation and the volatility of African politics, the former because the Soviet Union lacked the means of effective military intervention in African affairs[3] – may have been prudent but also revealed Moscow's vulnerability to the criticism, most often advanced from Peking, that the Soviet leadership had abandoned its responsibilities to international socialism.

In Southern Africa, however, the Soviet authorities were able to reconcile their traditional anti-imperialism with the maintenance of correct, even friendly, relations with independent African governments, many of which were strongly anti-communist. According to Vasily Solodonikov, then director of the African Institute of the Soviet Academy of Sciences:

> the Soviet Union's implacable attitude to colonialism and racism stems from the Marxist-Leninist ideology, from the nature of the socialist state. All oppression of man by man, of one nation by another, is alien to this ideology and to the nature of the socialist state.[4]

But while such points were endlessly debated in Sino-Soviet exchanges, in Africa it was not ideology but the framing of the OAU Charter which provided a legitimate basis for Soviet policy in support of the liberation movements.

Except in relation to Southern Africa, the OAU is a traditional diplomatic organization, the underlying principles of which are respect for the sovereignty and territorial integrity of its member-states, non-interference in their domestic affairs and non-alignment. The commitment to liberation and majority rule, however, is absolute. Whatever their own ideological convictions and attitudes towards the Soviet Union (and many of them are deeply equivocal), until the Angolan civil war very few African leaders would have disagreed publicly with Solodonikov's assessment of Western policies towards the South:

> The imperialist forces support and strengthen the racist colonial regimes in order to preserve their control over this rich area of Africa in which they have invested billions of dollars. They also plan to use the military-political bloc of Portugal, South Africa and Rhodesia in striking blows at independent African states.

This was essentially Nkrumah's thesis that the independence

of African states would not be secured until the whole continent was free. In 1963 it was adopted as official OAU policy and provided the basis for the obligation on all OAU members – admittedly often honoured more in the breach than the observance – to provide material assistance to the liberation movements in their struggle with the Portuguese, South African and Rhodesian authorities. In assessing current Soviet policies in Southern Africa and African attitudes towards the Soviet Union it is important to recall that while the Western powers never supported the liberation movements and indeed, until the Geneva Conference on Rhodesia in 1976, barely acknowledged their legitimacy, Soviet and OAU policies on the liberation issue have always run parallel.[5]

Until the Portuguese coup suddenly changed the 'correlation of forces' in the region, the USSR's 'principled' policy in Southern Africa had not carried with it any serious risk of a confrontation with the West. On the one side, while the USA and its allies were not prepared to alienate African opinion to the extent of actively opposing OAU policy, they did not regard the Soviet-backed insurgencies in Southern Africa as a serious threat to their interests: indeed, after 1969 when Henry Kissinger commissioned a special report on Southern Africa from the National Security Council,[6] the US administration concluded that it was only by tacitly co-operating with those in power that there was any hope of promoting desirable (that is, pro-Western) change. On the other side, since the liberation movements had all opted for a protracted guerrilla strategy and looked to the communist powers for training and small arms only, the Soviet commitment to the liberation struggle offered significant diplomatic returns for a relatively modest financial and political outlay. The scale of the Soviet involvement was sufficient to earn them influence with the movements and the gratitude of the OAU but insufficient to threaten Soviet relations with the Western powers in other more important areas, particularly in central Europe and with regard to the stabilisation of strategic weapon systems, or to seriously alarm African governments about the dangers of Soviet penetration.

Viewed from outside, it appears that Soviet policy in Southern Africa may also have been designed to serve two other purposes. The first was to contain Chinese influence. Ever since the Sino-Soviet split had become a public affair in the early 1960s the two communist powers had engaged in a ferocious competition, conducted through their bilateral relations with African states and through the activities of the front organizations such as APSO, to win the diplomatic allegiance of the African countries or at least to discredit the other country in their eyes. This competition was extended early on to the liberation movements. By virtue of being first in the field, and of its superior resources, the Soviet Union was generally able to insist on a position of monopoly patronage for its clients, forcing China to content itself with the less effective, often breakaway movements. There were two exceptions to this generalisation, both of significance for the present analysis. In the case of Mozambique the nationalist party did not split and the Soviet Union had to wait until after independence to consolidate its position against the Chinese, although even then the FRELIMO government succeeded in maintaining friendly relations with both communist powers. In the case of Zimbabwe the Soviet authorities consistently favoured ZAPU on the ground that it was the original nationalist movement from which ZANU subsequently split off, and because the Soviet leaders had developed good working relations with the ZAPU leader, Joshua Nkomo.

With the benefit of hindsight, the Soviet preference for ZAPU may prove to have been a serious miscalculation. But it is also arguable (in the nature of the case hard evidence on such matters is unlikely to be available) that the general policy of outbidding China had already proved substantially successful. In the liberation struggle there are no second prizes. After the Chinese had been forced to withdraw their support for the FNLA in the Angolan civil war, and the South Africans had intervened on behalf of UNITA, the Soviet authorities did not have much to fear from the Chinese argument that Soviet/ Cuban involvement in Southern Africa represented a dangerous threat of social imperialism.

On the other hand, it was always fairly predictable that despite more than a decade of prevarication since UDI, the Western powers would not stand by in the event of a major Soviet initiative in Zimbabwe, if only because Britain still claimed constitutional responsibility for the rebel colony. To the extent that the Soviet authorities were concerned to meet the Chinese challenge to their authority it is also arguable, therefore, that they never seriously expected to replace Western influence in Zimbabwe in the way they were able to do in Mozambique and Angola, where they were actively competing for patronage with the Chinese.

A second purpose of the USSR's Southern Africa policy was to lay the basis of a more stable relationship with friendly

African governments than the one which they attempted to develop with the governments which opted for the 'non-capitalist road' in the early 1960s. The collapse of this policy was followed by major adjustments to Soviet Third World policies, particularly in the economic field. The essence of the new approach was a willingness to do business and maintain friendly relations with all regimes regardless of their ideological complexion. More specifically, from 1971, the Soviet authorities sought to establish a division of labour with developing countries under which trade would be conducted according to the principle of mutual advantage, that is, it would take account as much of the interests and needs of the Soviet state as of the developing countries. Since the policy was a general one, in principle it was directed as much to Southern Africa as to other parts of the Third World. The treaties with Angola and Mozambique, for example, both provide for economic co-operation under the new formula, in addition to which they have negotiated fishery agreements with the Soviet Union. But although it is too early to predict with any confidence the long-term yield of these agreements: their current trade with the centrally planned economies, at between 1 and 2 per cent of their total trade, hardly suggests a very dramatic reorientation of either country's external economy. No doubt trade will grow but, for the most part, it seems Southern Africa is not a natural candidate for the new policy.[7]

This last point is, perhaps, worth emphasising since it has been widely misunderstood. Between them the countries of Southern Africa and the USSR account for a high proportion of both production and known reserves of an important range of strategic raw materials. As a consequence, it is often argued that one motive behind the USSR's Southern African policy is the desire to throttle Western supplies of such materials. It may be so. The evidence for this view, however, is not impressive. It seems reasonable to assume that before the Soviet Union would consider cutting off vital Western supplies (assuming also that it had the capability to do so) one or more of three things would have happened: (*a*) a crisis in East–West relations such that the Soviet authorities were prepared to precipitate a direct confrontation with the West and risk a general war; (*b*) a total disengagement by the Soviet Union and more important by its allies from the Western international economy and, therefore, a willingness to engage in active economic warfare in an effort to bring about its collapse; and/or (*c*) a willingness by the Soviet authorities to purchase South African raw materials themselves, even when these were surplus to their own requirements. None of these contingencies is inconceivable but, despite the deterioration of East–West relations, none seems very likely either. It has been suggested more plausibly that the USSR will find it increasingly difficult to meet the raw-material needs, including oil, of its East European allies and that the incorporation of African 'countries of socialist orientation' into the socialist division of labour will be encouraged as a hedge against such shortages. But if this is the long-term plan, very little appears to have been done so far to implement it. Nor given the development plans and foreign exchange needs of the Southern African countries is it at all easy to see what they could do.

Without a major restructuring of the world economy as a whole, therefore, it seems inevitable that the countries of Southern Africa will continue to be tied economically to the industrial West. No doubt, apart from South Africa, they will welcome the opportunity of diversifying into East European and Soviet markets but a major reorientation is unlikely and from available evidence is *not* a current objective of Soviet foreign policy.

On the contrary in recent years the main emphasis of Soviet economic policy has been on the internationalisation of the Soviet economy, a process which, among other things, leads it to concede the West a legitimate role in the global international division of labour, and more particularly to hold that 'the LDCs keep producing the resources necessary for the functioning of the advanced economies'.[8] From the Soviet point of view, therefore, there is no contradiction between their development of special relationships with Southern African countries and the continuing role of Western corporations in the region. On what ground, Soviet development economists are liable to ask, should the USSR object to Gulf Oil's involvement in the Angolan economy – the company provides over 90 per cent of Angola's foreign exchange from the exploitation of its concession in Cabinda – when the Soviet Union is itself heavily involved in joint ventures with Western corporations? It would be a mistake to assume, however, that the ideological loyalty of Third World governments is a matter of indifference to the Soviet authorities.

It may be, indeed, that pragmatism in foreign economic policy is easier to defend at home because Soviet support for the countries of 'socialist orientation' is not primarily an economic matter – the emphasis of the Soviet aid programme has gradually switched from economic assistance to military aid – and can be represented, therefore, as a revolutionary duty. Although they have provided military assistance to twenty-one African countries,[9] the major transfers in sub-Saharan Africa have been to four – Angola, Ethiopia, Somalia and Mozambique – whose leaders have declared their commitment to Marxism–Leninism. It is true that Soviet writers are careful to distinguish between the 'socialist orientation' of their African allies and genuine socialism, a position which prudently allows for the possibility of reversals such as Moscow experienced in its relations with Somalia in 1977. At the same time it is only with countries that have developed considerable military dependence on the Soviet Union that the Russians have entered into treaty relations. All of these friendship treaties include clauses providing for military operation and consultation in the event of attack, a formula which clearly represents a political commitment, although one which falls deliberately short of a formal alliance. Within this framework, indeed, there is some evidence to suggest that in Southern Africa the Soviet Union has worked out a division of labour with its Warsaw Pact allies, particularly East Germany,[10] designed to share the burden and lower the visibility of the Soviet involvement. Soviet and East German military missions regularly visit Luanda and Maputo, the former to discuss the provision of weaponry and the latter training in its use.

There is no unambiguous answer to the question which these observations raise, namely, about the strength of the Soviet commitment in Southern Africa. The original commitment to support African liberation dates from a time when it presented Soviet leaders with few difficult political decisions and even fewer risks. Anti-colonialism and opposition to racist oppression was at once in keeping with Leninist principles; an easy way of picking up Third World support against the West at the United Nations and elsewhere; a necessary strategy in containing the Chinese challenge to Moscow's leadership of the communist world and influence among the non-aligned; a method ready to hand of reconciling the revolutionary and statist elements in Soviet foreign policy; and finally an obvious way, if not of ensuring, certainly of increasing the chances of Soviet influence over the long term in any new political dispensation in Southern Africa. But the opportunities offered by the collapse of the Portuguese empire required decisions from the Soviet leadership which were both difficult and potentially risky and which were likely to become more so as the Soviet government entered into specific commitments with particular regimes.

Not surprisingly (and indeed with a certain justice), official Soviet pronouncements stress both the continuity and the consistency of Soviet policy in the region. But there is no doubt that since 1976 the Soviet leadership has acknowledged by its actions not only that Soviet prestige is more heavily involved in Southern Africa than before, but that as a consequence decisions which it faces are likely to be increasingly problematic. In other words, for the first time in their Southern African policy they have to face the necessity of reconciling rhetoric with reality.

Two episodes are perhaps worth citing in support of this judgement. The first was the appointment of their leading African expert, Vasily Solodonikov, as ambassador to Zambia after the MPLA victory in the Angolan civil war. Inevitably there was much speculation, some of it wild, about this appointment. Most probably it reflected Zambia's strategic position in the subcontinent, which made it the best possible listening-post, rather than the fear that the Zambians might continue their initial opposition to Soviet involvement with the MPLA into the independence period. Once the Soviet Union had demonstrated its ability to support its allies in Southern Africa, and had entered into treaty relations with them, it had an obvious interest in accurate intelligence particularly since, if Angola and Mozambique were regarded as two battles in a wider war, the next encounters in Rhodesia, Namibia and South Africa would risk a more direct and dangerous encounter with Western interests and/or South African military power.

The second episode suggests that the Soviet leadership is, indeed, wary of such encounters. Among the documents captured in July 1979 by Rhodesian commandoes in their raid on ZAPU headquarters in Lusaka, was a report by a ZAPU mission to the Soviet, East European and Cuban embassies in Dar es Salaam in December 1978. According to this report, a Soviet official, Alexander Sando, told the mission that he saw no reason why the Soviet Union should desert its traditional ally, namely, ZAPU, at so crucial a time in the struggle. No doubt this is what his visitors wanted to hear. But there were apparently implicit conditions to this support:

Sando says that he understands we are now preparing to launch a conventional war against the white racist regime in Rhodesia. He is deeply opposed to such a plan. He feels that we should continue to wage guerrilla warfare until victory. He quoted examples – the Vietnam case. He said we must consider the role South Africa and the West may play in defence of their interests in Rhodesia.[11]

There are obvious difficulties in interpreting evidence of this kind. Not only was it released to the press by one side in the war for its own propaganda purposes, but even assuming its authenticity there is no corroborating evidence that the same advice was being given to ZAPU headquarters by the Soviet embassy in Lusaka. It also raises the question why, if they favoured a protracted guerrilla campaign, the Soviet Union had provided ZIPRA with the heavy armour suited to conventional rather than guerrilla warfare.[12] But since Nkomo did in fact withhold the bulk of his forces and his Soviet armour from the battlefield, the episode at least supports the view that the USSR was reluctant to get deeply embroiled. History, it seems, did not, after all, repeat itself: in Angola the decision was taken to back one side in a three-sided civil war, even though the Soviet authorities must have been aware of the regional loyalties which the other parties – FNLA and UNITA – could command; in Zimbabwe they attempted to persuade ZANU to mend its fences with ZAPU, consistently refused to recognise the extent of ZANU's potential support, and the fact that it was ZANU which had borne the brunt of the fighting, sniped at the Western powers whenever possible in the hope of exposing the ulterior motives behind their diplomacy, but never made any serious attempt to seize the diplomatic initiative from them.

(2) Soviet Perceptions of the Central Balance

Why not? To answer this question we must look beyond Africa to the impact of Soviet policies on the central balance of power with the United States and its allies. This is, of course, as much a matter of perception as of fact. From a Western perspective, at least at first sight, one conclusion about Soviet involvement in Southern Africa seems obvious. As in the past Soviet policy reflects a cautious assessment of what is and is not possible within the prevailing configuration of power or, in Soviet terms, the correlation of forces. In other words, their assessment of Western interests and intentions, particularly those of the USA, remains an all-important determinant of Soviet policy.

In short run this assessment does not appear to be ideologically predetermined. Indeed, the Soviet government apparently has no preconceived view of Western behaviour. Consider, for example, its reaction to three African crises, in Nigeria, Angola and Zimbabwe respectively. During the Nigerian civil war the USSR was careful to avoid committing itself to the federal side until it was clear that the USA would not become involved and that the conflict would not polarise along Cold War lines. Similarly, in Angola where the risks of such polarisation were greater not only did they act in inherently favourable circumstances – they were able to confine themselves largely to a logistic role relying on Cuba to provide the manpower, while the USA was inhibited by domestic opposition and consequently forced to combine covert operations with tacit support for South African military intervention – but even then the Soviet leadership was careful to test American reactions before committing itself irrevocably.[13]

And in Zimbabwe and Namibia, where the risks may plausibly be regarded as greater still, they have been careful to avoid pushing their opposition to US proposals that they should co-operate in seeking negotiated (that is, compromise) solutions to these conflicts[14] to the point of alienating the front line states. For it is the front line presidents (including the presidents of Mozambique and Angola) who have acted as the essential swing-factor in Southern African diplomacy. In the end, because it was their countries which had to bear the economic and human costs of the guerrilla struggle, they put their weight behind a negotiated settlement in Zimbabwe and less successfully (so far, at any rate) in Namibia. As in the Middle East, the very ambiguities of Western interests gave Western governments access to both sides, whereas the Soviet Union had access only to its clients. The Soviet authorities may not like this state of affairs, and would no doubt exploit any opportunity for reversing it, but they evidently appreciate that the support of the African states is an essential prerequisite for their diplomacy and for this reason have not themselves taken specific initiatives to displace Western influence.

But is this conclusion as obvious as it seems? It is tempting to argue that because the Soviet government has shown itself reasonably sensitive to local and great power pressures,

Western and Soviet perceptions of the conflict are essentially the same and that the pseudo-scientific language in which Soviet international analysts are habitually decked out is no more than a veneer over the universal foundations of great power *realpolitik*. But the Soviet conception of an evolving correlation of world forces to which the powers must necessarily adjust is not more or less a term of art than the Western conception of an international system ordered by the manipulation of the balance of power. Much Western concern about Soviet policy in Southern Africa is after all because, in a region which had hitherto been closed to them, the Soviets have acted on their claim to be a global power of equal importance to the USA. In other words, they have not accepted that the international order is primarily a Western concern which can be settled without reference to their interests.

The Western powers have been unwilling to acknowledge that the Soviet Union has *any* legitimate interests in the region because for them the concept of interest is bound up with historical ties and economic dependencies both of which, they maintain, the Soviet Union lacks. Even Henry Kissinger who wished to induce 'responsible' behaviour on the part of the Soviet Union through the mechanism of linkage politics – that is, by offering Moscow the rewards of interdependence – and who certainly hoped to persuade Americans that they could not remake the world in their own image, none the less believed in US primacy even if on a modified scale. It was the United States, not the Soviet Union, which was to offer the rewards and threaten the punishments on the basis of which the new diplomatic structure was to be erected.[15]

It is hardly surprising that this is not how the matter is viewed in Moscow. Whatever Soviet priorities may be (and there can be little doubt, for example, that Southern Africa is much less important than Afghanistan, Iran and Turkey or even the Horn of Africa and the North African littoral of the Mediterranean), the distinction between progressive and reactionary world forces is fundamental to Soviet analysis of world politics. At the present time, as Robert Legvold has noted, the Russians contend that

> the correlation of forces has been radically altered by the dramatic increase in Soviet military power, the continued success of the socialist economies, the growth of the national liberation struggles, and unprecedented convergence of crises in the industrialised capitalist countries and a strengthening of 'democratic' and 'peaceloving' forces within the other camp.[16]

It is this underlying conceptual optimism which colours their long-term view of Southern African developments. Whatever the need for tactical adjustments or retreat – as Legvold also notes, they have a deep respect for the powers of recovery and retaliation of the capitalist West (witness the alleged advice to ZAPU, already quoted) – they believe that 'the spread and entrenchment of the socialist world outlook in Africa undoubtedly marks the beginning of a new, higher stage in the development of the African revolution'.[17] In the end, it seems, world politics are still to be interpreted in terms of a Manichean struggle between the forces of progress and reaction. It is essential to grasp how deep-rooted is this world view because otherwise it is impossible to understand how readily they seem prepared to risk the détente on which, as they themselves admit, their own as well as the West's survival ultimately depends.

Until the term was quietly dropped from public debate in the West after the Soviet invasion of Afghanistan, it was often claimed that détente was indivisible, that the relaxation of tension had to be across the whole front of international relations and not merely confined to the central balance and the stabilisation of strategic weapons. But the Soviet authorities have never accepted that détente had any implications for their Third World policy. Anatoly Gromyko, the current director of the African Institute, has clearly stated the orthodox Soviet view:

> Detente has nothing in common with any artificial preservation of a social status quo. It proceeds from the objective content of the historic process, from inevitability of a struggle for elimination of inequality and exploitation, for recognition of the right of every people to choose at its own discretion the path of political, economic and social development . . . In conditions of detente, the universal recognition of the principle of peaceful coexistence of states with different social systems, imperialism finds it much more difficult to interfere in the internal affairs of developing countries, especially by means of military force.[18]

It seems a fair inference from this conception of the historical process that under détente the Soviet Union and its allies are freer than they were previously to support the self-determination of the 'progressive' forces in Southern Africa. Indeed, after the failures in the early 1960s, they had made certain that they were in a position to exercise such freedom by the development 'of mobile armed forces appropriately trained and equipped' specifically for 'peoples fighting for their freedom and independence against the forces of international reaction and imperialist intervention'.[19]

(3) The Costs and Benefits of Soviet Policy in Southern Africa

From the Soviet point of view the trouble is, of course, that success has its costs as well as its rewards. For while even now the United States, by virtue of its tenuously held world pre-eminence, is able to live in a world of its own conceptual choosing, the Soviet Union, despite its dramatic rise to global power, is not. Western reactions to the projection of Soviet power or influence are always likely, therefore, to expose the asymmetry of the central balance. The success of Soviet intervention in Angola; of subsequent Soviet diplomacy in Mozambique and the massive scale of their involvement in Ethiopia (whether successful or not hardly matters) had the undoubted effect of undermining the superpower détente by calling attention to the conflict over its interpretation in relation to the Third World. As soon as the Western powers found an issue on which to react – and Zimbabwe provided them with one – the Soviet Union was faced with the perennial tension between its strategic commitments and the historical vision on which these were based, and the tactical but overriding necessity not to force the pace where to do so might put at risk Soviet state interests.

In a sense, despite their own role in forcing the breach, Africa posed fewer problems for Moscow when the battle-lines between the progressive forces of liberation and those of reaction were clearly drawn along the Zambezi. As I have already argued, prior to 1974 the scale of their support for the liberation movements did not threaten their relations with the USA, while it provided valuable support for their historical theory of political development and, in their own eyes therefore, for their own view of détente. Soviet Africanists had plausibly assessed that most independent African states were likely to remain socially unstable and politically volatile for the foreseeable future.

Consequently, outside Southern Africa, the Soviet government has opted for a pragmatic policy designed to protect its own state interests and to establish African confidence in doing business with Moscow as with any other power on a normal diplomatic basis. For example, rather than jeopardise a major phosphate deal with Morocco, the Soviet Union apparently gave undertakings that it would not support the activities of the Polisario guerrillas in the former Spanish Sahara, despite the fact that a majority of African states including Angola and Mozambique now support the movement within the OAU. Such evidence that the Soviet Union was prepared to subordinate its revolutionary pretensions to its own national interests not only fitted in with Western perceptions about the nature of Soviet foreign policy, but also supported the quite erroneous view that the doctrine of the indivisibility of détente was accepted, and in the same sense, by both sides.

The independence of Angola and Mozambique strained this convenient distinction between pragmatism north of and principles south of the Zambezi, but did not altogether destroy it. Despite Western hostility to Soviet intervention in Angola from the Soviet point of view, the fact that both the Angolan and Mozambique governments declared their allegiance to Marxism–Leninism while themselves adopting a pragmatic attitude to relations with the non-communist world was a positive gain. The conclusion of treaties of friendship and co-operation with these countries signalled the West that the Soviet Union considered the victory of the liberation movements to have historical significance (and that they themselves had a legitimate interest in their future development), while the fact that Maputo reached its own *modus vivendi* with Pretoria and that Luanda not only came to an accommodation with its pro-Western neighbours, Zaire and Zambia, but itself initiated a modest opening to the West, gave the lie to the description of these countries as little more than Soviet colonies. For some African governments which had previously restricted their dealings with Moscow for fear of getting enmeshed in a great power confrontation, the risks now seemed more equally balanced, or at least not quite so awesome.

In Zimbabwe, however, the tension between pragmatism and principle is not so easily masked. Not only is there no present prospect of a treaty of friendship and co-operation to suggest a degree of dependence on the Soviet Union and to symbolise the legitimacy of Soviet policy, but the new government is fairly openly suspicious of Moscow's intentions. In a message to the Yugoslav people following independence, the new government commended President Tito's courageous challenge to superpower hegemonism – the phrase which is currently used by the Chinese and in the non-aligned movement to indict Soviet power politics as distinct from those of the Western imperialists.[20] According to some accounts, indeed, the Soviet Union was only invited to Zimbabwe's independence celebrations after the personal intervention of Mugabe himself who overruled the ZANU Central Committee on the ground that as a non-aligned country Zimbabwe must pursue an even-handed policy to both superpowers. Even so, the belated decision to allow the opening of a Soviet Embassy in Salisbury required 'certain assurances' from Moscow.

For the moment, at least, the automatic anti-colonial alliance between the liberation movements in Southern Africa and the Soviet Union has been broken. The reason, presumably, is that ZANU(PF) which, as their leaders repeatedly insist, owes nothing to Moscow, wants to be satisfied that disaffected elements within the minority party – ZAPU – will not attempt to use their ties with Moscow to reverse the political settlement.

How long-lasting the estrangement with Zimbabwe is likely to prove and how widely its repercussions will be felt, probably depends as much on what happens in the region as a whole and on how the Western powers react to Southern African developments as on any Soviet initiative. Since the Russians habitually present their policy as one of responding to African needs and requests (and so long as they remain preoccupied with their intervention in Afghanistan and its impact on East–West relations), they are in any case unlikely to make any dramatic moves. Moreover, while in their day-to-day diplomacy their embarrassment at the outcome in Zimbabwe was undoubtedly genuine, one may reasonably doubt how deep it goes or indeed how much ground they have really lost in Southern Africa. It is difficult to speculate intelligently on such matters but three sets of considerations are clearly relevant to any assessment.

(4) Zimbabwe: Pressures for Normalisation

There are, in the first case, factors operating on both sides of the relationship which will doubtless make for reconciliation with Zimbabwe before long, or at least for the normalisation of relations.

For their part, the Soviet authorities have already made it clear that they desire this.[21] The independence of Zimbabwe is undoubtedly regarded in Africa as a vindication of OAU policy in general, and of the front line stewardship of Southern African diplomacy in particular. Since 1963 the Soviet Union has sought to distinguish its own policy from that of the Western powers on the ground that it alone has endorsed the OAU policy in all its aspects. By and large this policy has served them well and they seem unlikely to risk alienating Mozambique and the other front line states by pursuing their partisan support for ZAPU into the independence period particularly since, on all the evidence, they have no immediate ambitions to replace Western involvement in Zimbabwe's economy. Had the war continued, or the elections produced different results, the Soviet Union and its allies might have been in a position to develop the kind of military relationship which constitutes the main prop of their position in Angola and Mozambique. But at present Mugabe's government and the Western powers share an interest in excluding the Soviet Union and its partners from a role in the reconstruction of Zimbabwe's armed forces, the former presumably to forestall a future pro-Soviet, anti-ZANU *coup d'état* and the latter to prevent any further erosion of their influence. This could be reversed in future, however, particularly if conflict within South Africa spills over the border and leads to retaliatory raids by the South African forces. It was precisely such circumstances during the war in Zimbabwe that led President Machel's government in Mozambique to look increasingly to the Soviet Union for heavy armour and to East Germany and Bulgaria for military training. And even President Kaunda was finally persuaded to diversify his military dependence by purchasing MIG fighters.

Rather similar constraints seem likely to influence Mugabe's diplomacy with the USSR. Both his own past treatment by Moscow and his present need to attract foreign investment and reassure private industry about their future will, no doubt, prompt him to take his time in defining Zimbabwe's relationship with the Soviet Union and to proceed with caution even when he has done so. But he has little to gain from letting such considerations harden into permanent antagonism. He was attacked by ZAPU militants for making a mockery out of non-alignment by not establishing diplomatic relations with the Soviet Union promptly.[22] Moreover, against a leader who came to power with a reputation as a militant Marxist-Leninist, the charge that he is 'soft on capitalism' will be an obvious line of attack for his domestic opponents. One inevitable result of the Lancaster House agreement was to raise expectations to a point which almost certainly exceeds his ability to satisfy them. If, none the less, the government is to establish its authority, it will almost certainly require concessions to demands for economic nationalism and redistributive socialism as well as to private industry. Although there is little evidence that the USSR will provide significant aid, there is already considerable doubt as to whether the Western powers will be sufficiently generous. Common prudence would seem to suggest, therefore, that Mugabe should cover his vulnerable flank at home and increase his options for securing assistance from abroad. And the most obvious way of doing so (apart from land distribution) will be to reach an accommodation with Moscow.

(5) Namibia: the Contradictions of Communism

The second set of considerations which is likely to influence the future of Soviet policy in Southern Africa may be called without undue frivolity the contradictions of communism. These are mainly but not solely economic in character. The problem is not that the Russians cannot offer an alternative to the economic dependence of the region or, as they see it, its continuing penetration by the capitalist West. These are realities which they have no option but to accept and indeed, so long as the primacy of the state is assured, they are in favour of economic non-alignment for their Third World allies and even a modest role for the private sector domestically. Since one of their major objectives in pursuing détente was to secure for themselves access to Western markets and technology (they were even accused at the UN of sanctions-busting in order to sell Rhodesian chrome to the USA),[23] it cost them in any case little to make virtue out of necessity. Rather, the problem is how to combine this tolerance of the mixed economy and the constraints imposed upon its Southern African allies by geography and history with an active political strategy aimed at replacing Western influence, since the Soviet government has supported continuation of the military struggle and has been slow to recognise the merits of negotiation. But in both cases the pressures for a negotiated settlement have come not merely from the West, but from the front line states which, by hosting the liberation movements, gained some leverage over them although at the cost of putting their own physical security and economic development at risk.

Namibia provides the clearest example of these contradictory pressures. Because of its huge mineral resources, small population and vast territory, it is difficult to envisage Namibian development proceeding without substantial external assistance. It cannot be excluded that if SWAPO was to secure a military victory in its struggle with South Africa, the Soviet Union and its allies (most probably East Germany) would provide the required capital and technical assistance. But on precedent it seems unlikely. More to the point, even if this was the outcome, there would still remain the question of the disposal of the product. In isolation from a general political upheaval in South Africa, however, it is extremely difficult to foresee SWAPO winning a direct military victory, although perfectly feasible that by progressively raising the financial and human costs of defending the status quo a continued SWAPO insurgency could over the long run contribute to bringing about a crisis of this kind. It is entirely possible that some such calculation underlies the Soviets' support for SWAPO, or rather their visible lack of enthusiasm for the efforts of the Western powers (the contact group) to secure a negotiated settlement. Yet they have not been in a position to prevent SWAPO engaging in these negotiations – in 1978 they abstained in Security Council votes out of respect for 'SWAPO's position and the position of other African states'[24] – nor even to prevent the Angolan government from bringing pressure to bear on Sam Nujoma, the SWAPO leader, to make concessions in the course of the negotiations. While there is no argument between the Soviet Union and the front line states on either the illegality of South Africa's occupation of Namibia or on SWAPO's status as the sole legitimate nationalist party, the African states have an obvious interest in any internationally guaranteed solution which, without sacrificing the principle of majority rule, will reduce the dangers of a general racial war in Southern Africa. For Angola, the problem is particularly acute because not only does its support for SWAPO expose it to military attack by South Africa's forces, but South Africa is able to supply the UNITA rebels across the Namibian border. From the MPLA's point of view, therefore, an independent Namibia would immediately improve Angola's security on two counts: cross-border raids would stop and the 'rebels' would have their major supply-lines cut.

It is sometimes suggested that the Soviet Union has deliberately stiffened SWAPO's will and ability to stand out against a settlement,[25] despite front line efforts, as a means of securing continued Angolan dependence on the Soviet bloc and Cuba. But although it is certainly true that so long as the military conflict continues the Soviet Union is able to extract a useful propaganda advantage at the UN by contrasting the vacillation of the Western powers with its own constant support for African liberation, it is much less certain that they wish to see a major escalation of the Namibian conflict which might lead to a premature confrontation with South African military power, from which they might find it difficult to disassociate themselves. Thus, although in June 1980 in the Security Council's debates on South African raids into Angola the Soviet representative held the Western powers directly responsible and called for 'specific measures in accordance with the UN Charter', Western correspondents who were briefed in Luanda, reported that in engagements between South African and Angolan troops the Cuban forces had been deliberately held back to avoid inflaming the conflict while there was still a prospect of a negotiated settlement. As the liberation struggle is carried closer to South Africa's borders it is likely to become increasingly clear that there is a deep tension between the Soviet Union's declaratory policies and its remaining Southern African commitments.

(6) The Soviet Dilemma in South Africa: Tilting the Balance or the Rules of the Game?

Finally, therefore, some assessment must be made of the Soviet Union's attitude and policies towards South Africa. Namibia has been frequently represented by Soviet spokesmen as a stepping-stone on the way to the final target: South Africa itself. But South Africa has in turn been seen as an integral, if informal, part of the Western alliance whose eventual collapse would do much to tilt the balance in East–West relations, but whose resistance by the same token would be both more formidable and more prolonged than that of the other minority regimes. In South Africa more than in any other part of the continent the historical optimism of the Soviet world view and the practical constraints imposed on Soviet policy by the necessity of peaceful coexistence stand in sharp juxtaposition.

So long as the international struggle against apartheid was very largely confined to the United Nations and similar bodies the problem was not serious. Over the years Soviet spokesmen have been lavish with their condemnation of the South African regime but respectful of its power and convinced that the Western powers would ultimately intervene to prevent its collapse. However, this is a double-edged conviction: it allowed them to exploit Western discomfort and expose Western hypocrisy on the South African question, but it also gave them a good reason for avoiding a premature confrontation with Western interests. Nothing was to be gained from provocation. In this case there is no reason to doubt that the Soviet Union has acted on its own maxim, namely, that revolution cannot be exported and that success requires certain 'objective' conditions be met. The question which now arises is whether they will be able to maintain this position of involved detachment now that all but one of the outer bulwarks of white power have fallen.

Such evidence as is available suggests that while they believe that the 'liberalisation' of the South African system, and the attempt to co-opt a black middle class will in the end undermine rather than strengthen the government's position, they do not expect the rapid momentum of political change in Southern Africa in recent years to be maintained. In this respect Soviet commentators have generally followed those of the West who initially viewed the Soweto riots as a major revolutionary challenge to the government but were subsequently more impressed by the relative ease with which the South African authorities, while shaken, were none the less able to survive the crisis. Like their Western counterparts, Soviet students of South Africa do not have a single view of the likely course of events in the republic or how long the present system is likely to survive.

Meanwhile, both Soviet theoretical perspectives on the relations of the social to the national problem in South Africa – that is, of race to class – and the historical entanglement of the Soviet Union with the African National Congress and the South African Communist Party similarly dictate caution. Although in the 1920s the Comintern alienated much white working-class support by instructing the SACP to press for the creation of a native republic – that is, in effect to go for partition – contemporary Soviet writers generally argue that the struggle in South Africa will grow with the development of class consciousness across racial lines – for example, their response to the black consciousness movement has been relatively cool. Once power has been transferred on the basis of class solidarity, it will then theoretically be possible to resolve the national problem along Soviet lines, that is, by granting cultural autonomy to different groups within a single socialist system. However implausible this scenario may be in practice, it becomes more credible in theory the longer the South African struggle persists, since it depends on the radicalisation of the masses through political education and the development of class rather than group consciousness. But if such a development may seem more probable in South Africa's burgeoning industrial society than in those African countries where the basis of class as opposed to ethnic conflict barely exists – and this *is* the argument – Soviet policy has so far been hamstrung by the absence of an ally within the country with a secure powerbase and, therefore, since its South African allies have to operate clandestinely and mostly in exile by inadequate and inaccurate intelligence.

The contrast with the situation in the rest of Southern Africa is sharp and ironic. The liberation movements in Angola, Mozambique, Zimbabwe and Namibia, which sought and obtained Soviet support, were all able to operate openly from neighbouring countries and to demonstrate the existence of their authority and support (though not always its extent) in their own countries. The Soviet authorities, for their part, were able to approach the liberation struggle encumbered with only minimal ideological and theoretical baggage. Their African experiences in the 1960s had convinced them of the dangers of attempting to base policy on a Marxist analysis of African societies about which in reality they knew little. It is true that they have always justified their support for the liberation struggle with references to Lenin's analysis of imperialism and the colonial question and that they have also carried on their ideological struggle with the Chinese through their African relations. But since their knowledge of African conditions was so slight, what really mattered in these relations was success, not how this was achieved or by whom.

In South Africa, on the other hand, while their basic strategy has been the same – for example, in refusing to recognise the Pan-African Congress (PAC) which promptly turned to China after its break with the African National Congress (ANC) – it is virtually impossible to detach policy from the long history of ideological argument about the development of South African society and the relative roles of the nationalist and communist parties in furthering the revolution. The PAC's break with the ANC was among other things on the race/class issue, and since the early 1960s (when all three movements were proscribed and their leaders either imprisoned or driven into exile) the

ANC and the Southern African Communist Party (SACP), in which whites have traditionally played an important part, have been in alliance. Indeed, in a 'Manifesto for the freedom, independence, national revival and social progress of the peoples of tropical and Southern Africa', published in Moscow in the summer of 1978, this alliance was taken as a model for other African countries.[26] In the sense that the ANC is the oldest nationalist party and SACP the oldest communist party in Africa, and that both have a long history of experience within the underground system of international communist parties and front organisations, there is perhaps nothing odd about this choice. But in the sense that the Soviet Union appears to have preselected its major vehicle for influencing South African developments it may create as many problems as it solves. For while the ANC and SACP have remained loyal to Moscow and are evidently able to maintain a reasonably effective exile organisation, they have had much more difficulty in demonstrating the extent to which they remain a potent political force within South Africa itself.

The Soviet Union now faces the same problem as the independent African states themselves, namely, how best to orchestrate and carry forward the international struggle against apartheid. Although, as the controversy over 'dialogue' demonstrated conclusively in the early 1970s, opposition to South Africa has always been the major unifying factor in the OAU, the strategy of concentrating first on the Portuguese territories, Rhodesia and Namibia was not merely because these were correctly perceived as the weak links in the structure of white power, but because no one really knew what to do about South Africa. The alliance between ZAPU and the ANC and the introduction of ANC units into Rhodesia in 1968 was a tactical error which merely drew the South Africans into the conflict and strengthened the will and capability of the Rhodesian military to resist. Now, once again, the Organisation and the front line states will have to decide on strategy which will both support nationalist forces in South Africa and limit the dangers to themselves. But while it is important to recall the essential identity of interests between African and Soviet positions on the liberation issue, for the Soviet authorities the problem of an appropriate strategy has two additional complexities.

The first of these is how to strengthen the ANC at the expense of its present and future rivals without running into conflict with the OAU, which provides the basis of legitimacy for Soviet policy generally. After the failure of their early efforts, notably in Angola, to unite liberation movements and, failing that, to single out one of these as the official representative of African nationalism, the OAU adopted an even-handed policy of recognising all movements which could demonstrate that they were offering effective resistance in the field. In the South African case the OAU and the United Nations recognise both the ANC and PAC as 'the authentic representatives of the overwhelming majority of the South African people',[27] whereas other organisations which operate legally in the country – for example, Chief Buthelezi's Inkatha Movement – have no such status. In line with their policy of exclusive patronage, wherever possible, the Russians have allegedly attempted to persuade the OAU to designate the ANC as the sole legitimate liberation movement in South Africa, as they did with SWAPO in Namibia and the Patriotic Front in Zimbabwe.[28]

African reluctance to follow this course, it should be said, is not a consequence of the ANC's ties with Moscow, still less does it indicate any general rift between the ANC and the front line states. Rather, it represents a deliberate decision not to attempt to direct the South African struggle from outside at a time when the form that the struggle will take and the ability of the traditional nationalist parties to re-enter the political arena in South Africa has still to be demonstrated. The dramatic strike against the two SASOL plants in June 1980 for which the ANC claimed credit, and the much-publicised tension between the ANC and Inkatha after their earlier flirtation, were presumably intended to demonstrate both to the black population in South Africa and to the outside world that the ANC does have just this ability. The question which has still to be resolved is the kind of support which the front line states, Mozambique and Zimbabwe in particular, will be prepared to give to the ANC and the risks they will be prepared to carry on its behalf. From their restrained behaviour over Namibia and the emphasis that has been placed on regional economic co-operation to lessen their dependence on South Africa, it seems fairly clear that the front line states want a breathing-space; and given their reliance on OAU support and their need to repair their relations with Zimbabwe, this may suit the USSR also.

The second dilemma for Soviet policy is how to maximise the gains of its allies and its own interests without provoking a confrontation with South Africa and/or the Western powers, which would undermine Soviet efforts to normalise great power relations on its own terms after the Afghan crisis and alarm African governments. For although a competition for external patronage, even at the risk of involvement in non-African quarrels, has been a feature of African diplomacy since 1974, African leaders are well aware that the advantages of being able to play one superpower off against the other have to be balanced against the risks to their own independence and precarious political stability, of reactivating the Cold War in Africa.

On the whole the Soviet handling of this dilemma has been fairly successful. On the one side the Soviet authorities have taken every occasion to reiterate the importance they attach to the question of African liberation and their determination not to negotiate with the USA at the expense of their allies. Hence, Brezhnev's refusal to include Southern Africa on the agenda when he met President Carter in Vienna and the uncompromising position which the Russians continue to adopt at the United Nations. On the other, having secured their major objective in terms of East–West relations – namely, to establish their influence alongside that of the West in one of the few regions of international conflict from which they have been traditionally excluded – they have been careful to follow the implicit rules of behaviour which have developed over the years in relations between the nuclear powers.

In a study of these rules of 'controlled competition' in the Middle East, Yair Evron has detected a pattern which at first sight seems to apply equally well to Southern Africa.[29]

> The essence of this pattern is that super powers explicitly or tacitly agree to accept each other's presence in the region. They also recognise that each other's efforts to advance their own interests are unavoidable and should be strongly resisted only if these attempts threaten a brutal and rapid change in the region's balance of power.

Despite Western claims that the Soviet intervention in Angola represented just such a brutal change, their attempts to reverse it lacked credibility, as did Soviet attempts to undermine the Lancaster House settlement in Zimbabwe.

In Southern Africa two other aspects of the superpower relationship as interpreted by Evron are also relevant: they 'tacitly agree to establish communication mechanisms in order to ensure a credible system of mutual expectations' and, by their behaviour, they acknowledge a 'system of tolerance thresholds the crossing of which would result in uncontrolled escalation'. Thus, in 1977–8 the USA apparently acted on Soviet intelligence to deter the South Africans from testing a nuclear device in the Kalahari;[30] while the USSR has so far been careful to avoid arousing Western fears by a rapid influx of military personnel into Angola and Mozambique. Angola continues to depend on the Cuban expeditionary force (and the absence of any similarly legitimate intervention force on the Western side certainly gives the USSR an advantage in the controlled competition) but there are very few Soviet military personnel in Southern Africa, certainly when compared with the numbers in Ethiopia, and by relying on its East European allies the Russians have attempted to be as inconspicuous as possible in their regional diplomacy. Provided that the tolerance threshold is defined clearly enough, therefore, the prospects of avoiding a great-power crisis over South Africa appear at least reasonable. The main danger, however, is probably not that the Soviet Union will cross the threshold of intervention – this seems extremely unlikely – but that because the Western dilemma in support of South Africa is so much more acute than the Soviet one in opposition, the line will not be drawn clearly; and a future South African domestic crisis will involve the outside powers regardless of their efforts to restrain their adversaries and their own behaviour.

South Africa is an inconvenient country for both East and West. There can be no doubt that the existing social and economic organisation is profoundly unjust. The transformation of the existing order and its replacement by a system enjoying the support of all South Africans would certainly constitute a historic event of the kind I sketched in beginning this chapter. But South Africa also continues to defy categorisation. Change is in the air. And optimists certainly detect an expansion of horizons. Whether or not they see a future for the Soviet Union and international socialism in the country depends, of course, on their position as participants in the domestic South African debate about constitutional reform or as members of the underground. But I fear that for many whose involvement is more distant, and possibly more vicarious, the political climate seems dark and threatening and the analogy of Greek tragedy played out in slow motion and modern dress sadly more compelling.

Notes: Chapter 5

1   The treaties were signed in 1977 and 1976 respectively. An agreement of co-operation between the MPLA and CPSU was also signed in October 1976.

2   For the historical background to the Soviet Union's African policies, see Edward T. Wilson, *Russia and Black Africa before World War II* (New York: Africana, 1974).

3   This was the major lesson of the Congo crisis in 1960, when the Soviet government was outmanoeuvred by the United States and was both unwilling and unable to intervene effectively on behalf of Patrice Lumumba and his successors.

4   Vasily G. Solodonikov, 'For the full liquidation and racism in Southern Africa', in Olay Stokke and Carl Widstrand (eds), *Southern Africa: The UN–OAU Conference, Oslo, 9–14 April 1973* (Oslo: Scandinavian Institute of African Studies, 1973), Vol. 2, pp. 53–68.

5   They have not always been without strain, however. The original OAU policy was for all external assistance to the liberation movements to be channelled through the African Liberation Committee (ALC). This proposal was unpopular with the movements, which saw it as an attempt to limit their freedom of action and was in any case ignored from the start by both the Soviet Union and the People's Republic of China.

6   Barry Cohen and Mohamed A. El-Khawas (eds), *The Kissinger Study of South Africa* (Nottingham: Spokesman, 1975).

7   On the new economic policy in the Third World, see R. Loewenthal, *Model or Ally? The Communist Powers and the Developing Countries* (New York: Oxford University Press, 1977), pp. 359–76.

8   Elizabeth Kridl Valkenier, 'The USSR, the Third World and the global economy', *Problems of Communism*, vol. 28, no. 4 (July–August 1979), pp. 17–33.

9   See George T. Yu, 'Sino-Soviet rivalry in Africa', in David E. Albright (ed.), *Africa and International Communism* (London: Praeger, 1980), pp. 168–88.

10 See George A. Glass, 'East Germany in Black Africa, a new special role?', *World Today* (London), vol. 36, no. 8 (August 1980), pp. 305–12.

11 *Guardian*, 3 July 1979.

12 No official inventory of Soviet armour supplied to ZIPRA forces in Zambia is available, but apart from the AK-47 rifles which were used by both guerrilla armies, it is said to have included T-54/55 tanks; 82-mm and possibly 120-mm mortars; 122-mm artillery; RPG-7 anti-tank guns; SAM-7 surface-to-air handheld missiles and thirteen MIG aircraft.

13 See Jiri Valenta, 'Soviet decision-making on the intervention in Angola', and W. Scott Thompson, 'The African–American nexus in Soviet strategy', in Albright, op. cit., pp. 93–117, 189–218.

14 *Guardian*, 13 July 1980.

15 Stanley Hoffman, *Primacy or World Order: American Foreign Policy since the Cold War* (New York: McGraw-Hill, 1978), p. 48.

16 Robert Legvold, 'The nature of Soviet power', *Foreign Affairs*, vol. 56, no. 1 (October 1977), pp. 49–71.

17 Anatoly Gromyko, 'The present stage of the anti-imperialist struggle in Africa', *Social Sciences*, vol. X, no. 4 (1979), pp. 24–38.

18 ibid., pp. 24–38.
19 V. M. Kulish (ed.), *Voyennaya Silai Mezhdunavodnyye ot nosheniya* (Moscow, 1972), p. 136, quoted by David L. Morrison, 'African policies of the USSR and China in 1976', in Colin Legum (ed.), *ACR 1976–7* (New York: Africana, 1977), Vol. 9, pp. 476–83.
20 *Guardian*, 8 May 1980.
21 In his congratulatory message to Prime Minister Mugabe and President Banana, Mr Brezhnev expressed the USSR's willingness to establish ambassadorial relations. But by this time the damage had apparently already been done. During a visit to Zambia before Zimbabwe's independence the Soviet Deputy Foreign Minister, Leonid Illychev, announced the Soviet Union's intention of opening an embassy in Zimbabwe without first consulting the ZANU leadership. Mugabe subsequently invited the USA, China and the USSR to the independence celebrations but refused to allow a visit to Zimbabwe by Illychev before independence.
22 In July 1980 the Finance Minister, Enos Nkala, charged the Soviet Union with supporting one tribal leader and backing disunity in Zimbabwe. A ZAPU spokesman immediately counterattacked with a demand for an immediate exchange of diplomats with Moscow to make credible Zimbabwe's claim to be non-aligned.
23 A Western report to the UN Sanctions Committee, subsequently denied by the USSR, claimed that the Soviet Union had purchased chrome and tobacco from Rhodesia using Swiss front companies in both cases. It was also claimed that the chrome had been purchased at $32 a ton and resold to the USA at $58 a ton.
24 United Nations, *Monthly Chronicle*, vol. XV, no. 8 (August–September 1978). For an analysis of Soviet policy towards Namibia based largely on Soviet sources, see Moris Rothenberg, *The USSR and Africa: New Dimensions of Soviet Global Power* (Miami, Fla.: University of Miami Advanced International Studies Institute, 1980), pp. 199–220.
25 Rothenberg, *The USSR and Africa*, op. cit., p. 219.
26 Quoted in Colin Legum, 'African outlooks towards the USSR', in Albright, op. cit., p. 34.
27 See UN General Assembly Resolution 3161, 1976.
28 When he visited Africa in March 1977 President Podgorny met Nujoma, Nkomo and Oliver Tambo, the leaders of SWAPO, ZAPU and the ANC, together in Lusaka. Soviet pronouncements also frequently link these three movements together; see Rothenberg, op. cit., ch. IX.
29 Yair Evron, 'Great powers' military intervention in the Middle East', in M. Leitenber and G. Sheffer (eds), *Great Power Intervention in the Middle East* (New York: Pergamon, 1979), pp. 17–45.
30 See Robert S. Jaster, *South Africa's Narrowing Security Options*, Adelphi Paper No. 159 (London: IISS, Spring 1980), pp. 45–6.

6

The Strategic Importance of South Africa to the United States: an Appraisal and Policy Analysis

LARRY BOWMAN

Introduction

There are two quite distinct problems that arise when considering South Africa's strategic importance to the United States. The first is in assessing how important South Africa is to the USA. This involves an evaluation of those attributes that would cause us to decide whether South Africa is or is not strategically important. Once this first assessment is made, we come to a second question involving US relations with South Africa. This is whether or not working with the present South African government is an appropriate, expeditious, or necessary means for securing US strategic interests with the republic.

It is critical that we understand that there are two quite different concerns at issue here: the definition of strategic importance in and of itself, and the explicit acceptance that a specific political regime is the protector of those interests. The present South African government and its many friends and allies throughout the Western world (and to some degree their enemies as well) go out of their way to argue that the two are inextricably linked – that secure strategic relations require close ties with the apartheid regime. I will argue that this is not the case.

It will be my intention to explicitly disaggregate these two issues. In the first two sections of this chapter the various arguments for and against South Africa's strategic importance will be adduced. In the final two sections the policy implications – both short and long term – of the various strategic assessments will be considered. Here questions of regime maintenance and regime change will be explicitly analysed.

(1) Arguments in Favour of South Africa's Strategic Importance

There is a vast literature that argues, in one way or another, that South Africa is strategically important to the United States.[1] It is also a point of view that is commonly expressed in political and military circles in the USA, Western Europe and South Africa. Whether or not one believes this to be true depends upon answers to a variety of complex questions: how secure is the present South African government? What are the likely directions of change throughout Southern Africa? What are the objectives of the USSR in this region? What obligations does the USA have to its allies and to other non-communist states? How critical are questions of racial discrimination likely to be in the international politics of the late twentieth century? Many other questions could obviously be added. What is clear is that we are dealing in the realm of assumptions, expectations, hopes and aspirations, none of which are easily tested or confirmed.

There also is no time-tested US strategic doctrine that we can fall back on as a guidepost to current strategic thinking. Indeed, William H. Lewis, a defense planner with long experience on African questions, argues that 'the United States has no overall strategy or conceptual approach to Africa and African problems'.[2] A former chairman of the Joint Chiefs of Staff writes that the USA is now paying for three decades of strategic neglect in the 'crescent of crisis' region. This he attributes to the neglect of visible US military power, naïve assumptions about Soviet goals, and the unwarranted assumptions about the security of US and Western economic interests, regardless of political change.[3] Prime Minister P. W. Botha of South Africa remarked early in 1980 that 'we have convinced ourselves of the lack of total strategy on the part of Western nations'.[4]

Despite this sense of disarray from those who actually make strategic judgements, it seems that four arguments are central to those who believe in South Africa's strategic importance.

(a) It is important geopolitically for the West to maintain control of the sealanes around the Cape of Good Hope.

(b) South Africa is a bulwark against the Soviet/Cuban threat to Southern Africa.

(c) South Africa is the dominant military power in Africa. It may even be a nuclear power. It has bases and facilities that potentially could be extremely useful to the USA and other Western countries if there was a major conventional war in the Middle East or Indian Ocean region. Moreover, South Africa seeks friendly relations with the USA and other Western countries. Therefore, it should be embraced as part of a global coalition of regionally dominant pro-Western powers.

(d) South Africa uniquely possesses key minerals that are increasingly critical to the economies of the industrial democracies. Assuring this continued access is thus seen as a central consideration in any policy formulation towards South Africa.

Each argument requires some elaboration.

The Cape Route Argument
Much has been written about the Cape route in the past decade.[5] The core of the argument is rather simply stated. From the mid-1960s onwards, an ever-higher absolute volume of goods and an ever-higher percentage of imports to the USA and to Western Europe have been borne by sea around the southern tip of the African continent. There are several reasons for this: the overall expansion of world trade and the vast growth of imports, the changed character of world shipping caused by the long closure of the Suez Canal after 1967, the growing use of oil supertankers that are too large to use the Suez Canal in any case, and others.

The key commodity that causes concern about the Cape route is, of course, oil. Geoffrey Kemp has had designed very interesting maps which show the large growth in oil traffic around the Cape, from 0·8 million barrels per day in 1965 to 18 million barrels per day in 1976.[6] In the report of the Study Commission on US Policy toward Southern Africa, published in May 1981, a similar map was prepared which showed the Cape route as the shipping-lane carrying the largest volume of oil traffic in the world.[7] The level of usage of the Cape route is about 2,300 ships per month which includes about 600 oiltankers.[8] This gives a total of over 27,000 ships per year –

about half of which call in South Africa annually; the rest navigate the Cape without stopping.[9] Moreover, it is now estimated that about 65 per cent of Western Europe's oil and 28 per cent of US imported oil travels the Cape route.[10] In addition, some 70 per cent of the strategic raw materials used by NATO are transported via the Cape route.[11] Both figures are likely to grow during the 1980s.

Many strategists look at these figures and see potential danger for the USA and the West. Air Vice-Marshal Stewart Menaul writes, 'Southern Africa is the key to the security of NATO's lines of communications ... and South Africa in particular has the facilities ... to provide the surveillance necessary for the security of European interests'.[12] In the South African Parliament, an MP quotes Lt C. B. McEwan's book, *Lifeline or Strategic Backwater*, which says, 'There can be no doubt that NATO as a whole and especially Western Europe is vulnerable to an interdiction of the Cape Sea Route'.[13] The orientation of Robert J. Hanks to these matters is fully revealed in the title of his book: *The Cape Route: Imperiled Western Lifeline*. Even the Joint Chiefs of Staff are concerned: General George S. Brown has written that

the threat to the Atlantic area is primarily from the Soviet Union maritime forces. Increasing Soviet naval capability to operate along the littoral of Africa has put increasing pressure on our ability to protect important South Atlantic trade routes which provide materials essential to the United States and Western Europe.[14]

Quotes along these lines could easily be multiplied.

For many, South Africa becomes strategically important simply because it sits astride this important shipping-lane. The need to protect the Cape route is taken as a given and the South Africa government is seen as the actor that can best do it. As we shall see, there actually is a considerable international debate over whether the Cape route is, in fact, threatened. For others, however, the fact that the Soviet Union is now active in Southern Africa and the Indian and Atlantic Oceans make the threat self-evident.

South Africa and the Soviet/Cuban Threat
With the success of the liberation movements in Angola, Mozambique and Zimbabwe, and the prospects for change still possible in Namibia in the not distant future, the overall

balance of forces in Southern Africa has been changed from what it was ten, or even five, years ago. The white buffer-states that used to guard South Africa's northern frontiers have collapsed one by one, and the republic stands more exposed than ever before as the last bastion of white minority rule on the continent.

As these important transitions have occurred the USSR and its allies have had opportunity to be of assistance to the liberation movements. Because they do not share the West's apprehension about arming the liberation movements, the USSR and its allies have proved of great assistance in helping the African states achieve independence. This was particularly true in Angola where Soviet material and Cuban troops provided crucial support for the MPLA as it consolidated its rule after the Portuguese withdrew. In Mozambique and Zimbabwe, however, the role played by the Soviet Union was far more modest. The USSR was but one of many nations that supported FRELIMO in Mozambique, and for a long period of time the Chinese were the preferred communist benefactor. In Zimbabwe the ZANU(PF) government of Robert Mugabe practically showed its disdain of the Soviet Union by delaying the granting of diplomatic relations until long after independence.

Certainly, since 1975–6 and the arrival of Soviet advisers and Cuban troops in Angola, there has been growing concern in the USA and the West about the Soviet presence in Southern Africa. Concern that they might become active in the Zimbabwe struggle provided a key impetus for all Anglo-American activity about Zimbabwe in 1976–9. The same fear provides at least a partial explanation for the intense Western diplomatic effort in recent years to find a solution to the Namibian impasse.

There are many ideas associated with the perceived or presumed Soviet threat. One is that if the USSR and its alleged proxies gain access to ports in Mozambique, Angola and other African littoral states, they will be in a position to successfully harass Western shipping and to apply a pincer movement against the oil and raw materials that either come from or go around South Africa. Captain J. M. Brink of the South African navy argues that 'The strangulation of the merchant shipping flow across the South Atlantic by the Russian Navy would have been completely impossible ten years ago. At present this must be considered a viable possibility'.[15] Forebodings of the most extreme nature can easily be found in the Southern African literature. Robert J. Hanks argues that 'the entire Southern Atlantic coast of Africa is not only barred to the West, but is actually a region of Soviet naval and air domination', and that 'it is evident that Western forces operate at a significant, if not fatal, disadvantage along almost 7,000 miles of the Cape Route'.[16]

Looked at more from a landward perspective there is the obvious concern in South Africa about the persistence of Cuban forces in Angola. The solution of the Zimbabwe conflict without external intervention, however, has eased fears about the possibility of Cuban armies stationed across the entire northern frontier of South Africa. None the less, it is clear that much of the concern about the Soviet/Cuban threat is focused on the role that they might play in any eventual conflict in South Africa.

No one can easily foretell just what pressures will be mounted against South Africa in the 1980s, but most serious analysts of the region believe that guerrilla incursions will be a likely component of the struggle. Soviet and Cuban advisers can here play a major role in training guerrillas, even if they do not themselves become directly involved in the conflict. A good bit has been written about Soviet motives and goals in Southern Africa, but there is no consensus in the literature. Dimitri Simes rightly points out that 'there are probably as many lists of Soviet objectives in Africa as there are Western analysts studying them'.[17] He goes on to suggest that the Soviet Union hopes to establish itself as 'an accepted part of the African political terrain', to reduce Western influence wherever possible, to counter Chinese influence and position itself as a champion of the Third World, to support Third World countries in driving up the price of resources sold to the West and to gain military access to Africa whenever possible.[18] Simes acknowledges that it is impossible to clearly define Soviet priorities among these various desires.

As for Cuba, it too has its foreign policy objectives in Africa. Chief among them seem to be the support of ideologically compatible regimes, the promotion of its own position as a militant champion of Third World revolution and the sustaining of its domestic revolutionary *élan*.[19] While there is some overlap here with Soviet goals, it should be acknowledged that Cuban and Soviet motives are not and need not be necessarily aligned for both to be active with respect to Southern Africa.

The South African government has sought to foster fears of a wider Soviet/Cuban involvement in Southern Africa in the hope that its willingness to stand with the West against the USSR would lead to closer strategic relations. Prime Minister P. W. Botha of South Africa has argued that 'today we are witnessing an encircling strategy which is being deployed step by step across the globe',[20] and 'the main object of the onslaught on the Republic of South Africa, under the guidance of the planners in the Kremlin, is to overthrow this state and to create chaos in its stead, so that the Kremlin can establish its hegemony here'.[21] When a Russian soldier was captured by South African forces during its August 1981 invasion of Angola, South African officials could scarcely conceal their glee. General Magnus Malan, South African Minister of Defence, remarked that this proved that the issues of Southern Africa 'have nothing to do with liberation but involve Soviet imperialism'.[22]

The Soviet Union/Cuban argument is particularly appealing for a variety of reasons. From the South African viewpoint, the government has sought for many years to find a rationale for its importance to the West that would defuse the tensions and criticisms associated with its racial policies. This has been hard to do but, as ardent cold warriors, the South African government has long had a direct stake in poor relations between the two superpowers. For those many people in the West who feel that the overall Soviet threat to the West is a more important political concern than any issue of South African domestic politics, the Soviet and Cuban activity in Southern Africa provides a useful rationale for maintaining ties with South Africa.

This view is at least partially shared by the current administration in Washington. In his important 29 August 1981 address, *Regional Strategy for Southern Africa*, Chester A. Crocker, Assistant Secretary of State for African Affairs, stated: 'We are concerned about the influence of the Soviet Union and its surrogates in Africa', and 'the U.S.S.R. and its clients have shown every interest in keeping the pot of regional conflicts boiling'. In this same speech Crocker made a strong defence of the Reagan administration's improved ties with South Africa and noted that 'In South Africa ... it is not our task to choose between white and black ... The Reagan administration has no intention of destabilising South Africa in order to curry favour elsewhere'.[23]

As with the Cape route argument, there is much contention among strategists over the character and quality of the Soviet threat. No one can deny, however, that the South African government has developed an awesome military strength and this itself provides another rationale for its strategic importance.

South Africa as a Regional Power

Some years ago during the heyday of the Nixon administration Samuel Huntington noted that 'regionally dominant powers or "local Leviathans" have begun to emerge'.[24] South Africa was mentioned as the dominant actor in Southern Africa and, in the context of Huntington's argument, the case was made that such powers should be drawn into the Western camp and supported if at all possible.

This idea reflected the orientation of the Nixon Doctrine and was also cental to the National Security Study Memorandum 39, the famous (or infamous) Kissinger study of Southern Africa.[25] Several ideas were pulled together in the Nixon Doctrine which remain prominent in the ongoing argument for South Africa's strategic importance: it is valuable to have friends who are regionally dominant actors, it is important to support countries that are strongly anti-communist and it is extremely valuable to have allies that are strongly committed to spending their own resources for their own defence.

It has become axiomatic to argue that South Africa is the strongest military power on the African continent. From a total of R470 million in 1973–4, South Africa's defence budget has been rapidly increased to R1,972 million estimated for 1979–80.[26] Recent reports indicate that the defence budget for 1981–2 has been increased by another 30–40 per cent.[27] The South African Armaments Manufacturing Corporation (ARMSCOR) produces a vast range of weapons. Despite the mandatory arms embargo voted by the United Nations in November 1977, South Africa already possesses or is capable of manufacturing many advanced weapons systems; it is all but self-sufficient for small arms.[28]

South Africa may also be a nuclear power; if it is not already, most informed observers have little doubt that South Africa could complete a nuclear device in a relatively short period of time. In an outstanding article on this topic Richard Betts flatly asserts: 'With a highly developed nuclear establishment, including unsafeguarded uranium enrichment facilities, Pretoria could build a bomb at any time it wishes.'[29] While there remains confusion and disagreement over whether there were nuclear detonations over the South Atlantic in September

1979 and December 1980, there is no doubt about South Africa's commitment to develop its nuclear facilities.[30] Reports in late 1981 indicated that South Africa had been able to buy sufficient quantities of lightly enriched uranium reactor fuel, so that it could start up its 2,000 megawatt power-station at Koeberg, near Cape Town, in June 1982. Both the Carter and Reagan administrations had been withholding enriched uranium from South Africa in the hope of inducing South Africa to sign the Nuclear Non-proliferation Treaty and to open its nuclear facilities to inspection by the International Atomic Energy Agency.[31]

South Africa also has a strong army and many important military bases and facilities. The Simonstown naval base near Cape Town remains a major facility standing astride the Cape route. There are highly sophisticated intelligence and communications facilities at Silvermine, again near Cape Town. There is a military radar surveillance installation there which can monitor shipping throughout the Southern oceans. One military journalist has noted that the South Africans can chart ship movements 'in an operational arc ranging from the Antarctic to North America and from South America to Bangladesh'. In addition, this electronics gear 'can flash these ship plottings to war rooms in the United States and the United Kingdom in seconds'.[32] There are further South African naval facilities at Saldanha Bay and at Walvis Bay in Namibia on the west coast, and at Richards Bay and Durban on the east coast. And there are operational airfields throughout South Africa itself and as far north as the Caprivi Strip in Namibia, from which strike aircraft can presently operate.

Many strategists, having observed South Africa's armed might, advanced equipment and sophisticated facilities, quickly conclude that South Africa must be supported and accepted as a useful Western ally. Since South Africa has the desire to carry out regional tasks on behalf of the West, it is simply asserted that this would be beneficial to the West in times of hostility or war. All this is made more enticing to some by the fact that 'For at least a decade South Africa has been soliciting Western support by offering its base at Simonstown on the Cape to virtually any Western taker. Four years ago South African authorities showed off their computerized, bomb-resistant, oceanwide ship-monitoring facility at Simonstown like landlords eager to rent their property'.[33] More recently, Prime Minister P. Botha of South Africa remarked about Simonstown that

The dockyard and its sophisticated planning systems is one of the keys to our defence system. It is flexible enough to adapt to the support of ships of other countries interested in the stability and growth of South Africa.[34]

The argument, however, is often made in the most facile way. One searches in vain for serious analyses for just how South Africa would be crucial to the West in wartime. Where would such wars be fought? What would their character be? The assumption that a non-white-dominated South Africa would invariably be the enemy of the West is made far too casually in most of the military literature about the region. In reality it should not be taken as a foregone conclusion that South Africa's military support would invariably be helpful. In any war in Africa, in the Indian Ocean and probably in the Middle East or Persian Gulf regions as well, if South Africa was perceived as being an active Western ally, it would almost certainly help turn many local countries against the Western cause. In a conventional war in Europe perhaps South African manpower and material would be useful to the West, but it is hard to envision how South African support would be crucial. These concerns will need to be kept in mind in assessing South Africa's strategic importance to the West.

South Africa's Mineral Wealth

The final argument for South Africa's importance to the West centres on its impressive mineral wealth and resources. At least since 1973–4 and the emergence of OPEC as a powerful force in the international petroleum trade, there has been a sharp upsurge of concern and interest in the West about access to other non-fuel minerals and metals. Numerous books and studies have been written on this topic.[35] Although their perceptions of strategic importance and their policy perceptions vary widely, all the studies are agreed that South Africa is an impressive world producer of many important minerals – gold, diamonds, antimony, vermiculite, vanadium, chromium, the platinum-group metals, uranium, and manganese, among others. Overall South Africa is the world's fourth largest non-fuel minerals producer.[36]

The US Geological Survey has identified twenty-seven minerals as critical to industrial societies. South Africa has reserves of eleven of these twenty-seven critical minerals and is a significant producer of several of them. In addition, of thirty-one non-critical minerals identified, South Africa exports fifteen, five of them – antimony, asbestos, diamond, fluorspar and vermiculite – in substantial quantity.

The case for South Africa's importance to the USA and the West rests on its major position with respect to critical minerals. Of the twenty-seven, the USA imports seven from South Africa – chromium, manganese, vanadium, the platinum-group metals, gold, copper and coal – as well as two key alloys: ferrochromium and ferromanganese. In as much as coal and copper imports are only a small part of US consumption access to South African supplies are not considered important. As for gold, there is no doubt that supply disruptions would have an impact on world gold prices and international monetary stability. However,

> supplies of gold are not as crucial to the West from a strategic or industrial standpoint. American production, government stockpiles, and the holdings of other developed countries would be sufficient to meet the industrial needs of the Western world for some time.[37]

Table 6.1   *US Dependence on South African Supplies of Four Key Minerals*

Mineral/alloy	Total imports as %age of US consumption (1978–9 average)	Imports from South Africa %age of US imports (1978–9)	%age of US consumption (1978–9)
Chromium:			
ore	100	46	46
ferroalloys	55	72	40
Manganese:			
ore	98	15	15
ferroalloys	71	58*	42*
Vanadium:			
pentoxide	30	72	22
ferroalloys	net exporter	—	—
Platinum-group metals	90	67†	60†

* Includes an estimated amount for ferromanganese imports from France and other countries of ore originating in South Africa.
† Includes an estimated amount for imports from Britain of platinum-group metals originating in South Africa.
Source: US Bureau of Mines, *Minerals Yearbook, 1978–79* (as taken from *South Africa: Time Running Out*, p. 311).

Thus, the case for South Africa's strategic importance to the West with respect to minerals ultimately rests on four commodities: chromium, manganese, vanadium, the platinum-group metals and their alloys. Together they are essential for many important industrial and defence uses.[38] Table 6.1 reveals the extent of US dependency.

Two other issues are also commonly adduced in making the case for South Africa's mineral importance. One is that the USA's allies in Western Europe and Japan are even more dependent than is the USA for imported raw materials from South Africa. In 1977 the members of the European community depended upon South Africa for 49 per cent of their chromium, 44 per cent of ferrochrome, 41 per cent of manganese, 8 per cent of ferromanganese, 18 per cent of platinum-group metals and only a minor percentage of their vanadium. Japan's percentages for chromium, ferrochromium and platinum-group metals were even higher.[39]

Secondly, there are the concerns raised by the fact that for these critical minerals the USSR is usually the other major world producer. Table 6.2 summarises this situation.

Table 6.2 *1979 World Mine Production and Reserves of Four Key Minerals*

Mineral	USA (%)	South Africa (%)	USSR (%)*
Chromium:			
production	—	33·0	24·5
reserves	—	66·4	2·9
Manganese:			
production	—	20·9	45·8
reserves	—	37·2	50·7
Vanadium:			
production	17·6	42·3	27·9
reserves	0·7	49·4	45·9
Platinum-group metals:			
production	0·1	47·5	47·5
reserves	0·1	73·2	25·1

* The USSR production and reserve percentages for chromium and manganese include production and reserve figures for all the Soviet bloc countries.

Source: US Bureau of Mines, *Mineral Commodity Summaries 1980* (as taken from *South Africa: Time Running Out*, p. 312).

Policy-makers look at these figures and perceive two quite distinct problems. One has to do with fear of being beholden to the Soviet Union if South African supplies were to be cut; and secondly, fear of a Soviet/South African cabal over mineral prices and supplies if a regime friendly to the USSR were to emerge in South Africa.

Taking together South Africa's overall mineral production, the West's dependency on a few key minerals and the Soviet Union's position as the primary alternative supplier, it is not surprising that the importance of South African minerals is probably the one most commonly used to explain the strategic importance of South Africa and to justify continued ties with the present government. Early in his administration President Reagan struck this theme during a televised interview with Walter Cronkite when he remarked, 'Can we abandon a country that has stood by us in every war we have fought, a country that is strategically essential to the free world in its production of minerals that we all must have?'[40]

Other spokesmen articulate similar concerns. Chester Crocker has noted that one of the three basic realities around which the current regional strategy is built is the concentration of mineral wealth there: 'The area contains immense deposits of many strategic minerals which are vital to industrial economies like ours.'[41] The Supreme Allied Commander, Atlantic, Admiral Harry D. Train II, in wide-ranging comments on NATO's global responsibilities stated directly that 'we [NATO] are facing a contest for "control of the flow of vital resources"' and he specifically pointed to South Africa's importance in this respect.[42] General Alexander M. Haig, Jr, in remarks made a few months before he was named secretary of state, is reported to have said that 'the era of resource war has arrived'.[43] The Train and Haig remarks echo earlier comments by Sir Neil Cameron of the British defence staff who argued that NATO 'might be obliged to wage peripheral wars to keep its share of the world's resources'.[44]

The policy reasoning that flows out of this type of orientation is fairly straightforward. South Africa has been a reliable trading partner to the USA and its allies for a long time; the present government assures the West that it will keep the minerals flowing to their countries; the West's need for these minerals is demonstrably clear; therefore, we should be at the very least wary of political changes that might jeopardise this security of supply.

As we shall see, however, there are many crucial questions that are not addressed by those who so surely support the present South African government on account of its mineral wealth. When we focus on the policy implications of South Africa's minerals, we consider the likelihood of supply cut-offs both in the short and long term. Alternative sources of supply will have to be considered as well as substitutes. As these questions and others are raised, we will discover broad disagreements about South Africa's strategic importance and surprising evidence that suggests there is little to fear from South African/Soviet Union collaboration.

(2) Arguments Opposing South Africa's Strategic Importance

Although the weight of strategic and military literature seems to suggest that South Africa is strategically important to the United States and its allies, there remain clear counter-arguments. Three can be briefly mentioned.

The No-Policy Perspective

In a lengthy study compiled for the American Enterprise Institute Helen Kitchen termed one orientation towards Africa as the 'no-policy' approach. It draws its support from a diverse body of opinion. Some on the left simply oppose all American private and public activity in Africa on the ground that this activity is inherently counter-revolutionary. Others suggest that Africa as a whole is so weak and unstable that there is no point in trying to shape its future. It is sometimes also suggested that the USA and its allies can get what they want from Africa, regardless of who is in power, simply because of the vast discrepancy between Western power and African needs. This being the case there is very little need to be concerned with the specifics of African political change. There is a general desire here to reduce the global profile of the USA and to free ourselves from concern about Africa.[45]

We Have Interests, but There Is No Threat

A second orientation, focusing more directly on South Africa, suggests that the USA may have interests in the country (especially economic ones), but that there is no serious threat to South Africa and therefore no need for strategic ties. As I will argue more extensively in Section 3, many scholars have called into question the whole notion of Soviet geopolitical momentum either in Africa or anywhere else in the world. In an extensive current article in which 'Trends of Soviet influence around the world from 1945 to 1980' were traced, the *Defence Monitor* concluded that

A comprehensive study of trends of Soviet world influence to 155 countries since World War II does not support perceptions of consistent Soviet advances and devastating U.S. setbacks . . . Starting with influence in 9% of the world's nations in 1945, they peaked at 14% in the late 1950's, and today have influence in 12% of the world's nations.[46]

In Africa the Soviet record is certainly a mixed one in terms of friends won and lost.

With respect to South Africa, many see the Soviet-threat notion as no more than a convenient smokescreen behind which ties with white South Africa are maintained.[47] Former US ambassador to the UN, Andrew Young, and countless others, have maintained that the USA and its West European allies will have no problem in purchasing South African minerals, even if a successor regime takes on a Marxist character. Continuing good Western relations with Angola, Mozambique and Zimbabwe are seen as a case in point. Therefore, there is no need to take the 'threat' too seriously, and no need to promote ties with the current regime.

We Have Interests, but the Current Costs Are Too High

A third orientation again holds that the West does have interests, but to promote those interests via an alliance, or the appearance of an alliance, with the apartheid government of South Africa is unwise. The argument here may take several variations, but the central thread is that given global hostility towards South African racism, any linkages with the present South African government will entail damaging political costs, regionally, continentally and globally (especially within the Third World). As Richard Betts notes,

To many today, long-term strategic interests dictate . . . staying on the good side of black African nationalists. If maintenance of military capabilities in the area is vital, they should be independent, rather than ones requiring South African cooperation.[48]

In this argument, as with the previous two, there is a general apprehension about falling for the propaganda of South Africa and its various allies. By providing a word of caution, and in arguing that South Africa's strategic importance is not that great, they are also intimating that nothing very harmful is going to happen by standing aside from South Africa for a time.

(3)   US Policy towards South Africa: General Implications of Supporting Strategic Ties

There has been a great deal of thinking and writing done on US policy towards South (and Southern) Africa. The focus, assumptions and goals of various analysts vary widely as do their policy prescriptions.[49] The same range of differences can be found among policy-makers. Yet some lines of continuity, however slender, can be found. Nearly all policy analysts in the West agree at some level on the need to bring change to South Africa. Nearly all recognise that apartheid is a political system that is anathema to most of the world, and that there is no likelihood that the international community will relax until the African majority is freed. Having said this, however, the consensus rapidly breaks down. There is little accord over what constitutes appropriate means to induce change in South Africa, and divisions exist over the timeframe in which it is hoped change will be affected. There is little consensus on what priority should be given to affecting change in South Africa, the level of resources to be committed, or what risks should be run. And there is apprehension for the profound potential for violence.

It has become commonplace to comment on the indecisiveness and lack of clarity of US policy towards South Africa. Richard Bissell has rightly noted the unique ability of the USA to pursue contradictory policies simultaneously.[50] William Lewis remarks that 'there are few signs at present that the United States is prepared or is preparing to make clearcut choices'.[51] In one of the more important articles written on US–South African relations in many years Chester A. Crocker sharply criticised US policy towards South Africa under both presidents Nixon and Carter: 'In the past neither U.S. pressure nor U.S. support has been credibly organised, while policy oscillations have done little to engender respect for America's sense of purpose.'[52] Bruce Oudes would like to believe that 'in the 1980s South Africa should be at the cutting edge of America's intellectual interest in the evolving relationship between race and democracy'.[53] But when he views the policy process more carefully, he concludes that 'the chances a constituency of either the Right or Left might lurch policy precipitately and extensively in one direction or the other in the years just ahead appear rather slight'.[54] All of these commentators, and many others who could be mentioned, recognise that American policy vacillates between commitment to human rights and the abhorrence of apartheid; they share a continuing unease about how to induce change and what the likely consequences might be. Thus, indecision.

Despite the rather jaundiced eye of many observers, the USA does try to articulate its interests in and policy towards South Africa. Richard Moose, Assistant Secretary of State for African Affairs under President Carter, described US interests in South Africa as

> Preserving our national consensus on foreign policy goals relating to human rights and human dignity; assuring long-term access to strategic minerals in South Africa and surrounding countries both for our own and our allies' economies and defence; and foreclosing opportunities for expanded Soviet influence that come with protracted violent conflict.[55]

Chester Crocker, who followed Moose as Assistant Secretary of State for Africa, has argued that

> the fundamental goal is the emergence in South Africa of a society with which the United States can pursue its varied interests in a full and friendly relationship, without constraint, embarrassment, or political damage. The nature of the South African political system prevents us from having such a relationship now. That goal will remain elusive in the absence of purposeful, evolutionary change toward a nonracial system.[56]

These general statements of Moose and Crocker – however clear they seem on the surface – still have to be implemented in the context of the real world, forged by the cross-cutting pressures of domestic and international developments. To fully assess the policy choices before us, I will now evaluate the implications of supporting the present South African government in the context of the four arguments presented earlier: protecting the Cape route, stemming the Soviet threat, assuring regional order with South African military might and guaranteeing access to critical minerals.

Protecting the Cape Route: Policy Implications
At one extreme it can easily be argued that if the Cape route is so important, then the USA and its allies should have formal military ties with South Africa. This, however, has not been the case. Britain, which did have formal defence links through the

Simonstown Agreement, broke this arrangement in 1975. Although the USA has maintained a military attaché in its Pretoria embassy, US naval ships have not been allowed to dock in South Africa since 1967. And even France, South Africa's primary arms supplier in the 1970s, has felt the need to draw back from South African defence ties. All three countries, as permanent members of the Security Council, supported the 1977 UN arms embargo.

This drawing back from regular military ties angers the South African government. At one time the communications centre at Silvermine was linked to NATO's IFF system and serviced 'the UN Navy at its Puerto Rico base with full intelligence on constant surveillance of Soviet and other shipping'.[57] In recent years this intelligence connection has been severed and Prime Minister Botha has noted,

> We decided a few years ago that the West no longer wanted us and were avoiding Simonstown. We have erected numerous facilities there and offered them to the West . . . However, the West cannot expect us to protect this sea route for them . . . If the West wants to protect its own interest, it will have to provide for that in its own way.[58]

These angry words of Prime Minister Botha have been reflected in South African defence planning. Deep-sea patrols of the Cape route by South African frigates have largely been abandoned. South African navy chief, Rear-Admiral R. A. Edwards, has noted that 'our navy must, and shall, become a small ship navy'.[59] This defence posture implied that Pretoria's future naval interest would largely be limited to coastal patrols.

If Western countries are unprepared to have formal military relations with South Africa, and South Africa is prepared to forgo many naval patrol activities, it seems plausible to suggest that no one shows much concern about the Cape route, once you go beyond the rhetoric. Yet this is not entirely the case.

There is a substantial body of opinion that argues that 'one of the imperatives of the real power-political world in which we currently live is the necessity to police the globe's sea lanes'.[60] As early as 1970 Lt Commander Beth F. Coye and her associates wrote in the *Naval War College Review* that 'In light of U.S. desire to protect U.S. interests in the Indian Ocean . . . the United States should encourage the nations of the area to operate their forces in a multinational naval capacity. The Navy of the Republic of South Africa should be invited to participate'.[61] A full decade later, during the US election campaign, an adviser to Ronald Reagan, General Daniel Graham, was reported to have suggested in Argentina 'that Mr. Reagan would favour a NATO-like treaty linking the militaristic nations of South America with South Africa'.[62] Nothing formally appears to have been done in this regard, although there have been reports of meetings between US, Argentine and Brazilian military leaders to discuss security questions in the South Atlantic.[63]

Central to all considerations of the Cape route, however, are two political realities – South Africa wants formal ties with the West, but only with the white minority in control. It is the interplay of these two factors that muddies the waters of the Cape route and makes it mandatory for us to carefully separate matters of strategic need from those of white privilege.

The South Africans would like to see NATO scrap the Tropic of Cancer as its southern boundary and embrace South Africa in a wider and more inclusive defence pact. In the early to mid-1970s there was a substantial push in the Military Committee of the North Atlantic Assembly to give South Africa what it wanted. At the full meeting of the North Atlantic Assembly in November 1972 a recommendation was adopted to 'give SACLANT authority to plan for the protection of NATO–Europe's vital shipping lanes in the Indian Ocean and the South Atlantic including surveillance and communications'.[64] In 1976 the NATO parliamentarians again passed a resolution calling on the North Atlantic Council to 'give top priority to increasing the strength of NATO ASW vessels and aircraft and reinforce the authority given to SACLANT with regard to the protection of vital shipping lanes'.[65]

There is really no doubt that NATO has developed contingency plans for the defence of the Cape route. This was confirmed by Dr Joseph Luns, secretary-general of NATO, when he remarked in Cape Town that 'we [NATO] have made contingency plans to defend the Cape Route in time of war'.[66] Admiral Harry D. Train, Supreme Allied Commander, Atlantic, has made similar comments: 'there is no NATO border. There never was the slightest thought in the mind of the drafters [of the NATO Charter] that it [article 6] should prevent collective planning, manoeuvres, or operations South of the Tropic of Cancer.'[67]

All of this pressure for expanded defence ties to defend the Cape route flounders, however, in the face of four realities: direct ties are seen as politically impossible due to South

Africa's racial policies; South Africa's anger towards the West for being ignored cannot readily be translated into Western concern; South Africa has no other potential allies, and few really doubt that it would not support the West in any real crisis; and finally, it is extremely difficult to make a compelling military case for the threat to the Cape route.

It is hard to think of the Cape route as a 'choke-point', once the logistical requirements are considered of somehow blockading the sea between the Cape and Antarctica. Now, obviously, most ships circumventing the Cape pass close to the South African shore and would be most vulnerable there.[68] But the logistical requirements that the Soviet Union would face in positioning its ships for such a blockade, let alone the likely political and military consequences that would quickly ensue, make the whole proposition dubious at best. R. W. Johnson has argued that 'the whole idea of Russian submarines starving the West into submission by a strategy of protracted interdiction or blockade was . . . absurdly nineteenth century in its conception. The very first ship sinking, after all, would constitute a major act of war and the nuclear bombers and missiles would be in the air only a few minutes later'.[69] A very conservative US think-tank, the Institute of Foreign Policy Analysis, presented a major study of the South Atlantic in 1977. It too saw little cause for concern:

> the United States does not face any serious challenge to its naval position in the South Atlantic . . . The near-term scenario for the South Atlantic suggests that there is unlikely to be a crisis that will jeopardize the security of its important sea lanes.[70]

Robert Price has demonstrated in a tightly reasoned argument that not only would a Soviet blockade be politically unlikely, it would also be difficult logistically and technically to carry out off African waters; and it would be strategically untenable given the likely range of military consequences. He asks two key questions: if the Soviet Union wished to interdict Western oil shipments, why would it do so at the Cape? And if the Soviet Union was prepared for a war with the West, why would it want its navy in South African waters? His answers seem to me to thoroughly demolish the Cape route argument. Obviously, if the Soviet Union wished to halt the flow of oil to the West, it could do so far more efficiently by bombing the oilfields or blockading the Straits of Hormuz. Because of their proximity to the Soviet Union, each of these operations could be carried out much more effectively than any operation off the Cape. As for the war that would certainly ensue from any such provocative Soviet behaviour, Price notes that the Soviet Union would need its navy in the North Atlantic and Mediterranean, where it could assist in responding to the nuclear threat posed by US SLBMs (submarine launched ballistic missiles). Any ships based as far away as South African waters could be easily destroyed by US air power.[71] It seems to me, therefore, in a view shared by many others, that there is no credible reason for the Cape route argument alone to be deemed a sufficient basis to build strategic ties with South Africa.

The Soviet Threat: Policy Implications
Even if we agree that a superpower naval confrontation in Southern African waters is unlikely, this does not detract from the legitimate concern that the United States and its allies have about communist influence in the continent. David D. Newsom, Under Secretary of State for Political Affairs during the Carter administration and Nixon's Assistant Secretary of State for Africa in 1969–73, has argued that the presence in Africa of military and civilian personnel from communist states 'represents a threat to our interests and, in our view, to the long-term interests of the African states as well'.[72] The Reagan administration is also obviously concerned about the presence of Soviet, Eastern bloc, and Cuban troops and advisers in the continent.

But how great really is the threat? There are numerous states in Africa – Egypt, the Sudan, Somalia, Guinea, Ghana and Uganda, among others – where the Soviet Union at one time or another has had what was believed to be considerable influence, only to lose it. Recent political changes in Nigeria, Uganda, Equatorial Guinea and the Central African Republic should be seen as positive from both African and Western viewpoints. Today the two countries in Africa which have the preponderance of communist military and civilian personnel – Angola and Ethiopia – are far from being supine puppets of the Soviet Union.[73] Indeed, there is evidence from both countries, and particularly from Angola, that they would like to broaden their ties with Western countries. The continuing refusal of the USA to recognise Angola only serves to induce Angola to remain close to the Soviet Union and Cuba, a result we presumably would wish to avoid. There is a further difficulty for the Soviet-threat argument in the fact that, for the most part, Soviet and communist personnel in Africa are there either at the invitation of legitimate governments or in support of liberation movements formally recognised by the Organisation of African Unity. It may become awkward to lecture African countries for actions they have freely taken.

What, then, motivates Soviet activity in Africa? Newsom argues that 'Soviet motivations are probably a mixture of geopolitical, strategic, and ideological. The Soviet Union's approach continues to be one of seizing opportunities as they arise and relying heavily on military rather than economic assistance to gain their objectives.'[74] Another expert on Soviet policy stresses this opportunistic element. In an extensive analysis of Soviet African policy for *Problems of Communism* David Albright argues that the Soviet Union has 'no grand design' for Africa and they do not really anticipate any ' "genuine" Marxist-Leninist breakthroughs in Africa'. None the less, he expects 'continuing Soviet efforts to take advantage of whatever openings develop'.[75]

These openings will, no doubt, continue to arise from time to time. But there is little evidence to suggest that deepening our strategic ties with South Africa is a sensible way to confront this possibility. John Marcum and Gerald Bender have convincingly argued with respect to Angola that it took a series of US policy errors to open the way for the Soviets and Cubans in Angola, and that it was our complicity with the South African invasion that assured African support for the MPLA and their Soviet/Cuban allies.[76] Marcum notes,

> All disclaimers notwithstanding, the United States fell here into a double trap. In addition to its de facto alliance with South Africa, it also over-reacted to the harsh rhetoric and socialist advocacy of a Marxist-influenced liberation movement by identifying it as the 'enemy' . . . Because of the powerful racial symbolism of South Africa its intervention had a convulsive effect among Africans, overriding anxieties related to Soviet and Cuban intervention.[77]

What is needed, therefore, is a policy focused on African realities rather than one which simply sees Africa through the prism of superpower competition. While it has so far proved impossible for the USA to alter its Angolan policy, errors made there have not been repeated. In particular, US policy towards Zimbabwe, both under Carter and Reagan, has been far more intelligent, sophisticated and successful. The current test on this issue certainly arises in Namibia, where it is too early to know whether a solution acceptable to the international community, South Africa, SWAPO and Angola, not to mention the Namibians and others, can be forged.

The West really has little to fear from directly competing with the Soviet Union on all issues of importance to Africa. Newsom summarises:

> The Soviets do not provide a market for most African goods; they are not part of the world economic system; not members of the IMF; they have no multilateral companies to spread technology; their ruble is not convertible ... On balance, I believe that these policies have resulted in our being in a stronger position *vis-à-vis* the African continent than the Soviet and other communist states have achieved with their MIGs and Kalashnikov-bearing troops.[78]

Unless things in Africa change dramatically in directions not now foreseen, there is little reason to believe that Western strategic ties with South Africa would be helpful for stemming opportunities for Soviet penetration of the continent.[79]

Geostrategic Concerns in Africa: Policy Implications
If there is little to fear from the naval side, and Soviet successes on land seem modest enough, what is left to entice the West into strategic relations with South Africa? The answer is to me the most compelling of those offered in defence of South Africa's strategic importance. It has to do with matters of perception: how do we believe we are doing *vis-à-vis* the Soviet Union? How do others in the world view the trends in our global competition? What is the perceived image of contemporary geopolitical momentum? What would be the consequences if South Africa were to be removed from the Western camp? William Lewis has laid the issue out clearly:

> Perception is important. Detente is not a synonym for alliance or for friendship, but a limited tacit agreement to avoid escalation of differences to a state of war, while continuing to compete for ideological, political, economic, and strategic gain ... But this unfolding pattern confronts us with a choice. How do we perceive Soviet ambition? Do we perceive the spreading of the Soviet presence as a challenge to vital U.S. interests or as part of a natural process in which we both have a role to play and in which our fundamental interests are not threatened? Do we return to the dogma of the past in which power was regarded as a zero-sum game ... or do we search for a basis for

accommodation? The answers to these questions will influence most profoundly how the U.S. evaluates its security interests in Africa ... The answers will also shape decisions on the distribution of resources to friends and allies, and even how we define friends and allies.[80]

In the past decade US policy towards South Africa has vacillated as policy-makers have made different assumptions about the balance of forces in the region and have had different views about the direction of Soviet policy and the appropriate manner by which to counter it. Robert Price has made the very valuable observation that choices in these matters are often made on the basis of what he calls 'intangible aspects of policy formulation' rather than on that of clearly defined tangible interests.[81] Price frankly argues that there are no threats to American security interests in Southern Africa and little cause to worry about threats to our economic interests. He asserts that 'the calculation of these threats [to US resolve and credibility] is based on assumptions that are no longer rooted in the facts of the real world. As such the "threats" are more myth than reality, and the policies developed to respond to them are dangerously "out of sync" with the environment in which they must operate'.[82] Yet he ruefully acknowledges that the need to present an image of resolve and determination may often override tangible interests, and that this 'neo-containment' orientation is 'likely to emerge as the dominant tendency' because 'it is supported by the assumptions of twentieth-century American political culture, and has well-entrenched constituencies in the Executive bureaucracy, the Congress, the defence and intelligence communities, and the public'.[83]

In the policy debates of the past decade those who favour a tough policy towards the Soviet Union in the African context have generally been termed globalists, while those seeking to find African solutions to African problems outside the framework of East–West competition have been termed Africanists; and Helen Kitchen has referred to their respective orientation towards Africa as geostrategic or Afrocentric.[84] Each side has had its notable proponents and victories. Framed by Henry Kissinger the geostrategic orientation dominated the field in the early 1970s. The belief that the white regimes were secure and that the liberation movements had no prospects for success was enshrined in National Security Study Memorandum 39.[85] This policy focus, now almost laughable in retrospect, ignominiously collapsed in the wake of the April

1974 Portuguese coup and the rapid devolution of power to the liberation movements in the former Portuguese colonies.

In 1975 Senator Dick Clark led a bitter but victorious fight in the US Congress to halt both overt and covert US intervention in Angola, and this victory marked the emergence of an Afrocentric orientation in Washington that continued into the first years of the Carter administration. United Nations ambassador Andrew Young, Assistant Secretary of State for African Affairs Richard Moose, Director of the Policy Planning Staff Anthony Lake, and many others, led the way in rebuilding US ties with Nigeria, the front line states and the liberation movements. Vice-President Walter Mondale's 1977 comment with respect to South Africa that 'Every citizen should have the right to vote and every vote should be equally weighted' was seen as the most direct statement ever made by an American official on the changes we desired in South Africa.[86] Yet by 1980, in the wake of the Soviet/Cuban intervention in Ethiopia and the Soviet intervention in Afghanistan, the globalists were in ascendancy once again. David Ottaway noted a mood of 'increasing unease over perceived Soviet and Cuban advances throughout the Third World' and that the USA felt it 'had to draw the line in a stiffened defence of its interests and allies wherever they might be threatened, directly, or indirectly, by the Soviet Union'.[87]

Attitudes towards South Africa are thus altered somewhat depending on the global situation. When the USA wants to show resolve, it tends to be more attracted towards, and less critical of, those who are like-minded. Thus, US policy tended to be somewhat more favourably disposed towards South Africa during the first Nixon administration and the last years of the Carter presidency.

Chester Crocker has articulated the hope that policy towards South Africa could be more steadfast – building a 'fragile centrist consensus' between the 'slick hucksters of the status quo peddling a message of krugerrands, the Cape route, and chrome reserves' on the one side, and those in favour of disinvestment, trade embargoes and possibly revolutionary change on the other.[88] Instead he has introduced a policy of 'constructive engagement' by which he hopes both to work closely with the white South African government and to support change in the direction of non-racialism and power-sharing. Whether the Reagan administration can both rebuild ties with the white government and still remain a credible force for change is, of course, the big question about current policy.

There are political dangers in all of this. William Lewis's admonition that 'the prudent planner would not choose to have the U.S. locked into a dependency relationship with the South African military establishment, if – or when – the Republic becomes a garrison state'[89] seems to be accepted by both geostrategic and Afrocentric theorists. Where there are differences of opinion is in respect to the time South Africa still has to change. Crocker argues that 'the balance of coercive power remains overwhelmingly in favour of the whites'. Since, in his view, this precludes the possibility of any near-term revolutionary change, he believes that at the present there is a 'window of opportunity' to build a 'regional climate conducive to compromise and accommodation'.[90] Those less sanguine about either American motives or white South Africa's interest in change will view 'constructive engagement' as little more than a 1980s replay of Nixon's NSSM-39. In the meantime South Africa will be able to buy time to continue its impressive military build-up which, even if only indirectly supported by Western countries, is generally perceived as a plus for the West in the global balance. What is less easily fitted into this equation of regional muscle and global perceptions of toughness are the costs of regional destabilisation caused by South Africa and the price to the USA for its diplomatic protection of South Africa. Meanwhile, before these bills are tallied, the mineral relationship proceeds apace.

Access to Strategic Minerals: Policy Implications
This final argument for maintaining strategic ties with South Africa is probably the most commonly heard and seemingly the most self-evident of the four. No one really disputes the importance of South African mineral deposits. Once the raw figures are adduced, many jump to the conclusion that South Africa is strategically important and must be supported. A recent US congressional report typifies this line of reasoning. In January 1980 Congressman James D. Santini, chairman of the House of Representatives Subcommittee on Mines and Mining, took a short trip to Southern Africa. On the basis of this twelve-day trip to Zaire, South Africa and Zimbabwe Santini prepared a report in which he called Southern Africa 'the Persian Gulf of minerals' and then went on to 'confirm that the United States and its Western allies are dependent upon South African mineral supplies', and that 'America thus has a vital interest in the survival of South Africa as a Western ally'.[91]

At almost exactly the same time that the Santini Report was

being presented, the Subcommittee on African Affairs of the US Senate was receiving a report on exactly the same topic that it had commissioned from the Congressional Research Service. The key conclusion of this report was that 'South African minerals are of significant, but not critical, importance to the West'.[92]

Three questions seem to dominate the debate about South Africa's mineral importance to the USA. One has to do with the likelihood of a cut-off of mineral supplies from South Africa; the second has to do with the possibility of South Africa and the Soviet Union conspiring as to supply and price of key minerals; finally, there is the question of US and Western vulnerability to the loss of South African minerals in either the short or long term, given the range of alternatives available. Taken in turn, each seems to me to clearly counter the facile reasoning that often underlies the mineral-dependency argument.

In 1980 the South African mining industry generated 67 per cent of South African export earnings, up from 57 per cent in 1979.[93] To say the least mineral exports are vital to the health of the South African economy. Can anyone really foresee the circumstances when *any* South African government would be in a position to forego these massive earnings ($25·6 billion in 1980)? In a short piece, entitled, 'Can Africa afford not to sell minerals?', Robert Price has argued that African countries (South Africa among them) depend on their mineral earnings. If a radical or leftist government were to come to power in South Africa, it would be even more dependent on mineral earnings in as much as it would presumably be seeking to improve the lot of all South Africans. And the hard truth of the mineral world is that only the USA and its Western allies (plus Japan) are likely purchasers of these minerals. Seen in this light Price comments that 'The notion of a resource war is revealed to be a fantasy'.[94]

A second concern has to do with the fear that a liberated South Africa might join with the Soviet Union in a minerals cabal against the West. United States Congressman David Marriott has warned that 'If the Soviet Union in their efforts in southern Africa would team up with those nations in southern Africa we could well have the entire Western World shut down in approximately six months'.[95]

Two quite different arguments seem to me to effectively counter this grim, if not ridiculous, prediction. The first has already been made: it simply does not seem plausible to argue that African states would want to cut off mineral sales; their economies could not stand it and there is no evidence to suggest that the USSR and its allies would step in as alternative buyers. The speed with which Angola and Zimbabwe have sought to stabilise their resource sales to the West underscores this point; would South Africa really be any different? Secondly, it needs to be noted that South Africa and the Soviet Union *already* collaborate on the world minerals market. Several recent reports have revealed that these two countries talk regularly together about the marketing of diamonds, gold and platinum; there are even suggestions that they may move into further collaboration on mining expertise and metals technology.[96] While future projections about these contacts can only be speculative, it can at least be said that a pattern of co-operation with the USSR has been undertaken by apartheid South Africa and it need not await a South African revolution.

Finally, there is the matter of vulnerability to a minerals cut-off, and the industrial and defence problems that could cause. The Rockefeller Foundation-funded Study Commission on US Policy Toward Southern Africa looked at this problem in detail; it also had the benefit of other recent studies.[97] The commission concluded that there were only four minerals – chromium, platinum-group metals, vanadium and manganese – that posed any real problem. The commission carefully reviewed the supply situation with respect to each mineral, but in no case did it foresee a problem that could not be overcome with foresight and planning.[98]

Looking at the overall problem the commission judged that 'stoppages, if they should occur, are likely to be partial, intermittent, and short term'.[99] If this indeed proved to be the case, little difficulty was anticipated; but if minerals were held up for five years or more, it was agreed that larger problems would arise. None the less, several potential actions were suggested which would help alleviate problems if a lengthy stoppage were to occur. These included: increasing stockpiles; developing a national minerals policy and contingency plans; diversifying sources of supply; developing regional transport systems (primarily to help bring out Zimbabwean chrome); and encouraging allies to take similar steps.[100]

Taken together it simply does not seem to me that the Cape route, the Soviet threat, South Africa's military strength and our fears about 'losing' in the region, and the minerals issue, sufficiently make a case for the necessity of building strong strategic relations with the present South African government.

The 'threat' simply is not sufficient – either now or in any international situation that we can foresee. Indeed, support for South Africa, and visible ties with South Africa, is the one thing that will surely turn African opinion against the West and open opportunities for the Soviet Union and its allies to be the champion of African nationalism and the foe of white minority rule. Although African countries disagree on many things, and their regimes vary widely in character and quality, they overwhelmingly share the consensus that racism and minority rule must be eradicated from the continent. Those that will help in this task will be welcomed; those that oppose this goal or prevaricate in their commitment to it will necessarily pay a political price for their lack of concern.

(4)   The Rejection of Strategic Ties and the Issue of Sanctions Against South Africa

There is no way to avoid the observation that there is a gathering international consensus that something must be done about South Africa. Just what should be done, the timeframe in which action should be taken and the means that should be used are the subject of deep and divisive debates within Western countries; and between the socialist bloc and capitalist countries, between the African countries of the Organisation of African Unity and the Western nations.

The crux of these countless debates can be easily described. Nearly all of the world is committed, at least at a rhetorical level, to the idea that South African apartheid is an oppressive and uniquely disgraceful political system. What to do about it is the problem.

For the United States, as for other countries in the West, the South African problem poses a unique set of dilemmas. There is no ignoring certain facts: African countries are committed to the liberation of South African blacks; weapons and training will be made available to all who are prepared to commit themselves to the struggle; and there is little indication that South Africa's white rulers are prepared to compromise in any substantial way in their determination to retain power and resist African majority rule. This is a recipe that can only lead to disastrous conflict.

Moreover, Western countries for the most part acknowledge they have interests in South Africa. They may not find these interests compelling enough to defend white South Africa with arms, but they are important enough to worry them about their economic stake and the domestic consequences of South African developments, and to interest them in the speed and direction of change. What Western nations seek, with increasing desperation and concern, is a means to promote peaceful change that is focused specifically on bettering the economic, social and political situation of the Africans. By so doing, they hope to keep faith with the African people of South Africa and align themselves with the dominant thrust of African opinion, while at the same time preventing a bloody war in which both blacks and whites would suffer greatly.

What are the prospects for bringing reform via evolutionary and incremental means in a situation where few seem interested in compromise? In recent years there has been a remarkable increase in both public and private pressure brought to bear on South Africa; and there has been a marked upsurge in thinking and writing about how to induce change in South Africa.[101]

In the USA the Sullivan Principles have been a first step in drawing US business attention to its labour practices in South Africa. While not compelling companies to do anything they do not wish to do, they have offered a framework within which modest changes have been effected.[102] In Western Europe the European Economic Community has adopted a code of conduct which is a joint business and government effort – albeit voluntary – 'to achieve some social and economic improvements for the blacks of South Africa, and ... to counter criticisms, both international and domestic, of a lack of concern about or even support for apartheid by Western governments and companies'.[103]

Behind these first tentative efforts stand many who seek a far more rapid escalation of economic pressures against South Africa. Martin Bailey has prepared a detailed document for the United Nations Center against Apartheid on oil sanctions. This has become a new focus of international attention following the achievement of the mandatory arms embargo. Bailey argues that

Oil is South Africa's most vulnerable point, and the country's economy would grind to a halt if oil supplies ran out; South Africa could probably only survive for a maximum of two and a half years if all oil imports were cut out; the impact of an oil embargo on the international community, at least in direct costs, would be relatively low; some of South Africa's neighbours (particularly Lesotho) would be severely hit by oil sanctions, but these effects could be cushioned if precautionary measures were taken; and finally, it would be feasible to effectively implement an oil embargo if measures were concentrated on preventing the shipping and transport of oil.[104]

Bailey's analysis mirrors that of Richard C. Porter, who argues in an admittedly tentative way that it is on the import side that sanctions against South Africa are likely to be most effective.[105]

In yet another piece Clyde Ferguson and William R. Cotter have systematically laid out forty-one different steps that the United States could take under a variety of headings (diplomatic, military, refugees and liberation movements, and mild or tough economic steps) to escalate pressure against the South African government. They argue for a 'carefully moderated but vigorous policy to deal with South Africa'. While acknowledging that these pressures will hurt blacks, they suggest that 'they will affect the still-complacent white community most fundamentally. Blacks have little to lose – and they know it'.[106]

How likely is it that the USA and Western Europe will go down the road to comprehensive mandatory sanctions against South Africa? As James Barber and Michael Spicer point out,

> For every argument that favours sanctions another can be found to consider it. One reason for this is that the different sides usually debate from different assumptions, premises, and priorities – covering such fundamental issues as order against revolution, individual right against community rights, and the benefits of economic prosperity as compared with those of political change.[107]

Barber and Spicer acknowledge that there are grave problems for Western countries as they take up the question of sanctions, but they recognise that international pressures are impelling them in the direction of action. They expect that Western policy is likely to be a mix of a carrot-and-stick approach (communication), disengagement and pressure for reform in light of African and Third World pressure. Countries will make their choices on the basis of their own economic needs, the state of the international political and strategic situation, and in light of what is happening in Southern Africa.[108]

As the 1980s begin two orientations dominate the policy discussion about South Africa in the USA. Each has been mentioned previously in this chapter: the notion of 'constructive engagement' with South Africa as enunciated by Chester Crocker and the Reagan administration, and the various proposals put forward in the lengthy Study Commission report. What is interesting and telling about US policy prospects is the extent of agreement between Crocker and the Study Commission.[109] Both seek to find a way to evolutionary change in South Africa; to resist the likelihood or inevitability of a violent solution; and each recognises the limits of American power over the situation, while acknowledging that the USA has a unique role to play. Both support the continuation of the arms embargo and the non-recognition of the 'independent' homelands, but resist pressure for trade sanctions and disinvestment – Crocker does so emphatically, while the Study Commission is prepared to 'limit' new investment.[110]

Crocker's 'constructive engagement' and the Study Commission report differ markedly in one crucial respect. Crocker's entire perspective is rooted fundamentally in his belief that white South African politics 'are demonstrating a degree of fluidity and pragmatism that is without precedent in the past generation'.[111] He believes that Prime Minister Botha and his senior supporters 'have been carrying out the equivalent in Afrikaner nationalist terms of a drawn out coup d'état' with which they will build a political apparatus capable of 'autocratic political change'.[112] Crocker argues that the USA has no alternative but to support Botha since, 'apart from revolution, change can only happen this way'.[113] In the Study Commission's section on support for organisations working for change in South Africa, Prime Minister Botha and the National Party are never mentioned as potential change agents.[114] And Simon Jenkins, writing in *The Economist*, views the same white political structure that Crocker is so hopeful about and comments that the 'South African regime is narrowing rather than widening its political constituency as it endeavours to forestall change'.[115]

Both the Crocker study and the Study Commission report reflect the fact that it is as yet politically impossible to build the domestic coalitions necessary to directly support the liberation movements or to countenance mandatory economic sanctions. In a recent study William Foltz has pointed out that neither elite American constituencies with knowledge of Africa nor the general public favour a rapid escalation of pressures against South Africa.[116] This being the case it is not surprising that policy-makers are tentative about pushing hard for sanctions.

Even if sanctions were implemented, how likely would they be to work? The South African government is sure to be hostile. It can certainly count on finding many allies in Western countries who would be eager to help white South Africa survive. Simon Jenkins has written a lengthy report in which he states that 'the clock of South Africa's history may be at five minutes to midnight, but it seems resolutely stuck there. The horsemen of the apocalypse have grown weary of waiting and have trotted off to Asia and Latin America, a baggage train of media commentators stumbling disappointed behind'.[117] R. W. Johnson answers his question, in *How Long Will South Africa Survive?*, by saying 'The laager is intact and can be defended'.[118]

These sombre assessments do not detract from the need to recognise that both domestic and international constituencies will continue to push for change regardless of the odds. And all of Africa's history since the Second World War suggests that in the long run white minority rule cannot be sustained. Despite the fact that the transition scenario as yet seems unclear, and the exact pace of the escalation of pressures remains negotiable, there can be little doubt that the USA and its major Western allies are reluctantly, but irrevocably, being forced to join the cause of freedom for the Africans of South Africa. In the absence of acceptable alternatives sanctions may become the least costly of the available choices. As John Marcum has suggested,

> It is crucial that the U.S. disassociate itself from the cause of white minority rule and its overt race discrimination in Southern Africa . . . Unless and until South Africa does achieve fundamental internal change, it will remain a magnet for trouble. And it is the kind of trouble that the U.S. should avoid.[119]

And David Ottaway notes that any evidence of support for South Africa 'would serve to alienate most of Africa, including those countries the U.S. has relied on most closely in furthering its economic and political interests'.[120] I share their concerns and believe that the USA must act more expeditiously and intensely to push for fundamental change in South Africa.

Conclusion

In the short term (say, the next five years) there seem to be several givens to the South African situation: African hostility towards South Africa will continue as will its commitment to the liberation struggle; there will be continued ebb and flow in both internal and external actions against the current South African government; there will be ever-more sweeping calls internationally for mandatory action against the Pretoria government; and the crisis will deepen.

American policy is likely to continue to vacillate between the conflicting demands of both domestic and international groups for greater or lesser rhetorical pressure, for implementation of sanctions, for disengagement of investment and trade, or for support of either the South African government or liberation movements. It is to be hoped that we can somehow avoid having to give up our preference for peaceful change, despite the realities of the intensified conflict.

The South African government will not offer us much help. It will continue to resist all calls for reform and change, and it will meet both internal unrest and externally based guerrilla incursions with harsh repression. A policy of regional destabilisation already seems firmly in place. As a counter to this, however, the USA can hope for the development of good and mature relations with Angola, Mozambique, Zimbabwe (and perhaps Namibia) that may ameliorate the fears often expressed about dangers of the increased radicalisation of the region. South Africa's calls for Western support against the communist menace will seem more and more forlorn.

Looking further ahead (say, to the end of the century) one must obviously be more speculative. But it is likely that South Africa's internal conflict will have intensified and probably spread to neighbouring countries. There will be a sharply intensified demand for support for the African majority, and the USA and its Western allies will ultimately have no option but to bite the bullet on disinvestment, oil sanctions and, perhaps, ultimately on the question of a naval blockade of South Africa. We shall have to scurry to catch the African wave of the future that we are so fearful and reluctant to embrace at the present time. This may seem unlikely and far-fetched, but in another decade if the Soviet Union is seen to gain overwhelming influence with the Azanian freedom-fighters, and if American and Western European industrialists still require South African mineral access, then many things could happen.

All that can be ruled out is the possibility of direct military support of the white South African government. The times, and the core American values of freedom and democracy, plus the constraints imposed by a multiracial population, make this choice implausible, regardless of what party is in power. Whatever happens, there is little doubt that strategic relations between the United States and South Africa can only grow as a subject of both domestic debate and international importance for the rest of the twentieth century.

Notes: Chapter 6

An initial draft of this chapter was prepared for and presented to the Study Commission on US Policy toward Southern Africa, October 1980. This version has been considerably revised, expanded and updated to include developments in 1981.

1   See, for example: Richard E. Bissell, 'How strategic is South Africa?', in Richard E. Bissell and Chester A. Crocker (eds), *South Africa into the 1980s* (Boulder, Colo: Westview Press, 1980), pp. 209–31; Christopher Coker, 'South Africa's strategic importance: a re-assessment', *RUSI Journal for Defence Studies*, 124 (December 1979), pp. 22–6; and Michael Samuels, *et al., Implications of Soviet and Cuban Activities in Africa for U.S. Policy* (Washington, DC: Georgetown University Center for Strategic and International Studies, 1979).

2   William H. Lewis, 'How a defence planner looks at Africa', in Helen Kitchen (ed.), *Africa: From Mystery to Maze* (Lexington, Mass.: Lexington, 1976), p. 302.

3   Admiral Thomas H. Moorer and Alvin J. Cottrell, 'The search for US bases in the Indian Ocean: a last chance', *Strategic Review*, vol. 8, no. 2 (Spring 1980), pp. 30–2.

4   *Republic of South Africa House of Assembly Debates*, 21 March 1980, col. 3320.

5   See, for example: *The Cape Route* (London: Royal United Service Institution, 1970); Michael Burrell, 'The Cape route and the oil trade: a problem not yet resolved', *Round Table*, no. 251 (July 1973), pp. 353–61, and 'Simonstown and the Cape sea route', *Africa Institute Bulletin*, vol. 13, no. 2 (1975), pp. 62–5; W. C. J. Van Rensburg, 'Africa and Western lifelines', *Strategic Review*, vol. 6, no. 2 (Spring 1978), pp. 41–50; and Robert J. Hanks, *The Cape Route: Imperiled Western Lifeline* (Cambridge, Mass.: Institute for Foreign Policy Analysis, 1981).

6   Geoffrey Kemp, 'The new strategic map', *Survival*, vol. 19, no. 2 (March–April 1977), pp. 51, 53.

7   *South Africa: Time Running Out*, Report of the Study Commission on US Policy Toward Southern Africa (Berkeley, Calif.: University of California Press, 1981), p. 305.

8   Richard Bissell, 'How strategic is South Africa?', op. cit., p. 215, and 'South Atlantic – new zone of strategic concern?', *South Africa Foundation News* (August 1981), p. 2.

9   *Official Yearbook of the Republic of South Africa* (Pretoria: South African Department of Information, 1977), p. 324.

10 Hanks, op. cit., p. 19; Bissell's figures are somewhat lower, 57 and 20 per cent respectively. See Bissell, 'How strategic is South Africa?', op. cit., p. 215.

11 John Peel, 'The growing threat to freedom and the North Atlantic Alliance', *South Africa International*, vol. 9, no. 2 (October 1978), p. 79. I am grateful to Robert J. Griffiths and his unpublished paper, 'The threat to the Cape sea route: myth or reality?' for this reference.

12 Stewart Menaul, 'The Security of the Southern oceans: Southern Africa the key', *NATO's Fifteen Nations*, vol. 17, no. 2 (April–May, 1972), p. 46.

13 J. T. Albertyn, in *Republic of South Africa House of Assembly Debates*, 24 April 1979, col. 4827.

14 General G. S. Brown, 'Current JCS theatre appraisals: the strategic importance of 7 vital international areas', *Commanders' Digest*, 17 March 1977, p. 21.

15 Captain J. M. Brink, 'The South Atlantic and South African security', *African Institute Bulletin*, vol. 16, no. 2 (1978), pp. 55–6. See also: Patrick Wall (ed.), *The Southern Oceans and the Security of the Free World* (London: Stacey International, 1977); and the articles and general news reports found regularly in the quarterly, *South Africa International*, published by the South Africa Foundation.

16 Hanks, op. cit., p. 65.

17 Dimitri Simes, 'The Soviet offensive in Africa', in Samuels, *et al.*, op. cit., p. 34.

18 Samuels, *et al.*, ibid., pp. 35–7. See also David R. Smock and Norman N. Miller, *Soviet Designs in Africa* (Hanover, NH: American Universities Field Staff Report No. 17, 1980).

19 On Cuban policy, see: Roger Fontaine and Robert Henderson, 'Cuban activities in Africa', in Samuels, *et al.*, op. cit., pp. 43–55; and Abraham F. Lowenthal, 'Cuba's African adventure', *International Security*, vol. 2, no. 1 (Summer 1977), pp. 3–10.

20 *Republic of South Africa House of Assembly Debates*, 21 March 1980, col. 3317.

21 *Republic of South Africa House of Assembly Debates*, 21 March 1980, col. 3321.

22 Humphrey Tyler, 'S. Africa savors news of Russian involvement in Angola', *Christian Science Monitor*, 4 September 1981. A somewhat more balanced view of the situation was provided by David Newsom, a former US Assistant Secretary of State for Africa during 1969–73, in his article 'Russians in Angola – this is news?', *New York Times*, 10 September 1981.

23 Chester A. Crocker, *Regional Strategy for Southern Africa* (Washington, DC: US Bureau of Public Affairs Department of State, 29 August 1981).

24 Samuel P. Huntington, 'After containment: the functions of the military establishment', *Annals*, no. 406 (March 1973), p. 5.

25 Mohamed A. El-Khawas and Barry Cohen (eds), *The Kissinger Study of Southern Africa* (Westport, Conn.: Lawrence Hill, 1976).

26 William Gutteridge, 'South Africa's defence posture', *World Today*, vol. 36, no. 1 (January 1980), p. 26.

27 Simon Jenkins reports in *The Economist*, 19 September 1981, a rise of 30 per cent. The *New York Times* of 13 August 1981 reports a 40 per cent rise in defence spending for 1981–2 to a total of $2·75 billion.

28   A good brief review of the South African arms build-up can be found in Robert S. Jaster, *South Africa's Narrowing Security Options*, Adelphi Paper No. 159 (London: International Institute for Strategic Studies, 1980), pp. 12–17. See also *South Africa: Time Running Out*, op. cit., pp. 233–53; and Caryle Murphy, 'Embargo spurs S. Africa to build weapons industry', *Washington Post*, 7 July 1981.

29   Richard K. Betts, 'A diplomatic bomb for South Africa', *International Security*, vol. 4, no. 2 (Fall 1979), p. 91.

30   On the South African nuclear issue, see: J. E. Spence, 'South Africa and the nuclear option', unpublished dissertation, Leicester University, 1978; Barbara Rogers and Zdenek Cervenka, *The Nuclear Axis: Secret Collaboration between West Germany and South Africa* (New York: New York Times, 1978); Thomas O'Toole, ' "A"-blast was no lightning bolt, panel decides', *Washington Post*, 1 January 1980; Thomas O'Toole and Milton Benjamin, 'Officials hotly debate whether African event was atom blast', *Washington Post*, 17 January 1980; Thomas O'Toole, 'New light cast on sky-flash mystery', *Washington Post*, 30 January 1980; and Walter Sullivan, 'Defence Dept. concludes Dec. 16 flash was meteor, not a nuclear test', *New York Times*, 19 February 1981.

31   See Paul Lewis, 'South Africa secretly obtains uranium fuel, French report', *New York Times*, 14 November 1981; George Lardner, Jr, and Don Oberdorfer, 'China was source of atomic fuel for South Africa, US believes', *Washington Post*, 19 November 1980; and Caryle Murphy, 'S. Africa skirts US efforts to bar nuclear fuel supply', *Washington Post*, 13 November 1981.

32   Robert Poos, 'South Africa: profile on defence policies and armed forces', *Armed Forces Journal International* 110 (June 1973), p. 31; and Rogers and Cervenka, op. cit., p. 102. David Coetzee has noted that 'the statistics of around 20,000 war and merchant ships of 85 states are computerised at Silvermine'. See 'NATO and Pretoria – liaison now public', *New African*, 169 (January 1981), p. 40.

33   Michael T. Kaufman, 'Ports and oil spur naval buildups by US and Soviet', *New York Times*, 20 April 1981.

34   'South Atlantic – new zone of strategic concern?', op. cit., p. 2.

35   Among many studies, see: *Mineral Development in the Eighties: Prospects and Problems* (Washington, DC, and London: British–North American Committee, 1976); W. C. J. Van Rensburg and D. A. Pretorius, *South Africa's Strategic Minerals – Pieces on a Continental Chessboard* (Johannesburg: Valiant, 1977); *White Paper on Defence* (Cape Town, 1977), appendix A, 'South Africa's mineral potential'; 'Mining and Minerals', *South Africa 1979: Official Yearbook of the Republic of South Africa* (Johannesburg: Chris van Rensburg, 1979), pp. 567–94; *Sub-Sahara Africa: Its Role in Critical Mineral Needs of the Western World*, report prepared by Subcommittee on Mines and Mining of Committee on Interior and Insular Affairs, US House of Representatives (Washington, DC: Government Printing Office, 1980); and *Imports of Minerals from South Africa by the United States and the OECD Countries*, prepared for Subcommittee on African Affairs of Committee on Foreign Relations, US Senate, by Congressional Research Service, Library of Congress (Washington, DC: Government Printing Office, 1980).

36   The discussion throughout this section is drawn heavily from *Imports*

of Minerals from South Africa by the United States and the OECD Countries; this is the most thorough, comprehensive and up-to-date analysis of mineral dependency upon South Africa that I have found. It is obvious as well that the Rockefeller Foundation Study Commission report, *South Africa: Time Running Out*, drew heavily on this report in its sections on minerals.

37 *South Africa: Time Running Out*, op. cit., p. 311.

38 Extensive discussions on the primary uses of these minerals can be found in ibid., pp. 310–18; and *Imports of Minerals from South Africa by the United States and the OECD Countries*, op. cit., pp. 9–18.

39 *Imports of Minerals from South Africa by the United States and the OECD Countries*, op. cit., p. 10.

40 Michael Getler, 'America's African dilemma pits anti-communism, human rights', *Washington Post*, 6 March 1981.

41 Crocker, *Regional Strategy for Southern Africa*, op. cit., p. 2.

42 Admiral Harry D. Train, II, 'NATO – global outlook?', *Navy International*, vol. 86, no. 1 (January 1981), p. 11.

43 'USA: Strategic minerals and Africa', *Africa Confidential*, vol. 22, no. 13 (June 1981), p. 1. See also 'South Africa: Persian Gulf of minerals', *Backgrounder*, no. 9 (December 1980), p. 1 (issued by South African Embassy in Washington).

44 'Russia and Africa: the mineral connection', *The Economist*, 9 July 1977.

45 'Options for US policy toward Africa', *AEI Foreign Policy and Defence Review*, vol. 1, no. 1 (1979), pp. 26–7.

46 'Soviet geopolitical momentum: myth or menace?', *Defence Monitor* (January 1980), p. 1. Another book which also attempts to quantify these trends is Ray S. Cline, *World Power Trends and the US – Foreign Policy for the 1980s* (Boulder, Colo: Westview Press, 1980).

47 An early statement of this position can be found in J. E. Spence, *The Strategic Significance of Southern Africa* (London: Royal United Service Institution, 1970). More recently, see the excellent monograph by Robert M. Price, *US Foreign Policy in Sub-Saharan Africa: National Interest and Global Strategy* (Berkeley, Calif.: Institute of International Studies, 1978).

48 Betts, op. cit., p. 102.

49 See, for example: Kenneth Adelman and Gerald J. Bender, 'Conflict in Southern Africa: a debate', *International Security*, vol. 3, no. 2 (Fall 1978), pp. 67–122; George Ball, 'Asking for trouble in South Africa', *Atlantic Monthly* (October 1977), pp. 43–51; Clyde Ferguson and William R. Cotter, 'South Africa – what is to be done', *Foreign Affairs*, vol. 56, no. 2 (January 1978), pp. 253–74; Chester A. Crocker, 'South Africa: strategy for change', *Foreign Affairs*, vol. 59, no. 2 (Winter 1980–1), pp. 323–51; 'Options for US policy toward Africa', op. cit., and *South Africa: Time Running Out*, op. cit.

50 Richard Bissell, 'How strategic is South Africa?', op. cit., p. 229.

51 Lewis, 'How a defence planner looks at Africa', op. cit., p. 303.

52 Crocker, 'South Africa: strategy for change', op. cit., p. 325. This article was published just as Dr Crocker was named Assistant Secretary of State for Africa by President Reagan. It provides a rich source of information on Crocker's thinking about US–South African relations and, not surprisingly, lays out many of the policy orientations that have since been followed.

53   Bruce J. Oudes, 'Evolving American views of South Africa', in Richard E. Bissell and Chester A. Crocker (eds), *South Africa into the 1980s* (Boulder, Colo: Westview Press, 1980), p. 183.

54   ibid., p. 176.

55   *South Africa: US Policy*, Current Policy No. 175 (Washington, DC: US Department of State Bureau of Public Affairs, 30 April 1980).

56   Crocker, 'South Africa: strategy for change', op. cit., p. 324.

57   Carel Birkby, 'Cape sea route', *Africa Institute Bulletin*, vol. 16, no. 2 (1978), p. 50.

58   *Republic of South Africa House of Assembly Debates*, 24 April 1980, col. 4864.

59   'South Atlantic – new zone of strategic concern?', op. cit., p. 2.

60   Rear-Admiral Robert J. Hanks, 'The Indian Ocean negotiations: rocks and shoals', *Strategic Review*, vol. 6, no. 1 (Winter 1978), p. 22. See also Hanks, op. cit.

61   Lt Commander Beth F. Coye, *et al.*, 'An evaluation of US naval presence in the Indian Ocean', *Naval War College Review*, vol. 23, no. 2 (October 1970), p. 46.

62   Warren Hoge, 'Reagan aides, in South America, say he would not favor dictators', *New York Times*, 22 September 1980.

63   Juan de Onis, 'US improving ties to Latin rightists', *New York Times*, 8 March 1981.

64   *Texts Adopted by the North Atlantic Assembly at its Eighteenth Annual Session (Bonn, November 1972)*, as drawn from Sean Gervasi, 'NATO: towards defence co-operation with the white regimes', unpublished dissertation, New York, 1974, p. 20. I have discussed these developments within NATO circles in much greater detail in my 'Strategic planning in Southern Africa: NATO and the South Atlantic', paper presented to 2nd Annual Third World Conference, Omaha, Nebraska, USA, 16 November 1978.

65   *Twenty-second Meeting of the North Atlantic Assembly*, for the use of the Committee on Foreign Relations (Washington, DC: Government Printing Office, 1977), p. 7.

66   'NATO plan to defend Cape's oil route', *Cape Times*, 17 December 1980.

67   Train, op. cit., p. 6.

68   The best discussion of shipping and weather constraints on the Cape route can be found in Hanks, op. cit., pp. 26–43.

69   R. W. Johnson, *How Long Will South Africa Survive?* (New York: Oxford University Press, 1977), p. 213.

70   'US maritime interests in the South Atlantic', Institute for Foreign Policy Analysis, Cambridge, Mass., 1977, Vol. 1, p. xxvi (study undertaken on US Navy contract).

71   Robert M. Price, *US Foreign Policy in Sub-Saharan Africa: National Interest and Global Strategy*, pp. 10–14. Also see my 'African conflict and superpower involvement in the western Indian Ocean', in Larry W. Bowman and Ian Clark (eds), *The Indian Ocean in Global Politics* (Boulder, Colo: Westview Press, 1980), pp. 87–103.

72   *Communism in Africa*, Current Policy No. 99 (Washington, DC: US Department of State Bureau of Public Affairs, 18 October 1979), p. 1.

73   American concern about Soviet activity often leads to the most absurd statements. For instance, Robert Hanks writes in *The Cape Route*: 'The fall of Angola to the Marxists, for example, placed that country's

assets at the exclusive disposal of Moscow', op. cit., p. 64. This comment will no doubt come as a surprise to Gulf, Texaco, and so on.

74 *Communism in Africa*, op. cit., p. 3.
75 David E. Albright, 'The USSR and Africa: Soviet policy', *Problems of Communism*, vol. 27, no. 1 (January–February 1978), pp. 28, 38–9.
76 See: John Marcum, 'Lessons of Angola', *Foreign Affairs*, vol. 54, no. 3 (April 1976), pp. 407–25; Gerald J. Bender, 'Angola, the Cubans and American anxieties', *Foreign Policy*, no. 31 (Summer 1978), pp. 3–30; and Gerald J. Bender, 'Kissinger in Angola: anatomy of a failure', in René Lemarchand (ed.), *American Policy in Southern Africa: The Stakes and the Stance* (Washington, DC: University Press of America, 1978), pp. 65–143.
77 Marcum, op. cit., p. 420.
78 *Communism in Africa*, op. cit., pp. 5–6.
79 Representative Howard Wolpe, chairman of US House of Representatives Subcommittee on Africa, has noted that 'The greatest single threat to U.S. strategic and economic interests in the continent comes from South Africa', and our identification with South Africa 'provides the greatest opportunity for the expansion of Soviet and Cuban influence within the region': Jonathan Harsch, 'African visitors say political issues override need for US agricultural aid', *Christian Science Monitor*, 22 June 1981.
80 Lewis, 'How a defence planner looks at Africa', op. cit., p. 302.
81 Price, op. cit., pp. 6–29 and *passim*, 31.
82 ibid., p. 59.
83 ibid., p. 4.
84 'Options for US policy toward Africa', op. cit., pp. 4–25.
85 Mohamed A. El-Khawas and Barry Cohen (eds), *The Kissinger Study of Southern Africa* (Westport, Conn.: Lawrence Hill, 1976).
86 'The US and Southern Africa', policy statement made by Vice-President Walter Mondale after a meeting with Prime Minister John Vorster in Vienna, 20 May 1977; the text can be found in Colin Legum (ed.), *Africa Contemporary Record, 1977–1978* (New York: Africana, 1979), p. C31.
87 David Ottaway, 'Africa: US policy eclipse', *Foreign Affairs*, vol. 58, no. 3 (1980), p. 657. Richard Deutsch, 'Carter's Africa policy shift', *Africa Report*, vol. 25, no. 3 (May–June 1980), pp. 15–18, provides a somewhat similar analysis.
88 Crocker, 'South Africa: strategy for change', op. cit., pp. 324-5 and *passim*.
89 Lewis, 'How a defense planner looks at Africa', op. cit., p. 295.
90 Crocker, 'South Africa: strategy for change', op. cit., pp. 344–5.
91 *Sub-Sahara Africa: Its Role in Critical Mineral Needs of the Western World*, op. cit., pp. vii and 19–20. In the same vein, Senator Strom Thurmond has called Southern Africa the 'Persian Gulf of minerals' and South Africa its 'Saudi-Arabia': see *Congressional Record*, 5 September 1979.
92 *Imports of Minerals from South Africa by the United States and the OECD Countries*, op. cit., p. xi.
93 'King Solomon's other mines', *The Economist*, 16 May 1981.
94 Robert M. Price, 'Can Africa afford not to sell minerals?', *New York Times*, 18 August 1981.
95 *Imports of Minerals from South Africa by the United States and the OECD Countries*, op. cit., p. x.

96   David Marsh and Bernard Simon, 'Russia's discreet gold chain', *Financial Times*, 31 March 1981; and Caryle Murphy, 'S. Africa and Soviet Union: odd pair on mineral market', *Washington Post*, 4 August 1981.

97   *South Africa: Time Running Out*, op. cit., pp. 310–22, 449–54. See also *Imports of Minerals from South Africa by the United States and the OECD Countries and U.S. Minerals Vulnerability: National Policy Implications*, report prepared by Subcommittee on Mines and Mining of Committee on Interior and Insular Affairs of US House of Representatives, 96/2 (Washington, DC: Government Printing Office, 1980).

98   *South Africa: Time Running Out*, op. cit., pp. 310–18.

99   ibid., p. 450.

100 ibid., pp. 450–4.

101 See, for example: Martin Bailey, *Oil Sanctions: South Africa's Weak Link*, No. 15 (New York: United Nations Center against Apartheid, 1980); James Barber, 'EEC code for South Africa: capitalism as a foreign policy instrument', *World Today*, vol. 36, no. 3 (March 1980), pp. 79–87; James Barber and Michael Spicer, 'Sanctions against South Africa – options for the West', *International Affairs*, vol. 55, no. 3 (July 1979), pp. 385–401; and Clyde Ferguson and William R. Cotter, 'South Africa – what is to be done', *Foreign Affairs*, vol. 56, no. 2 (January 1978), pp. 253–74.

102 Tom Wicker, 'Should American business pull out of South Africa?', *New York Times Magazine*, 3 June 1979, pp. 33, 74.

103 Barber, op. cit., p. 79.

104 Bailey, op. cit., p. 23.

105 R. C. Porter, 'International trade and investment sanctions: potential impact on the South African economy', *Journal of Conflict Resolution*, 23 (December 1979), pp. 579–612.

106 Ferguson and Cotter, op. cit., pp. 269–74.

107 Barber and Spicer, op. cit., pp. 387–8.

108 ibid., pp. 390–401.

109 The Study Commission report was drafted in the name of eleven commissioners: Franklin A. Thomas, president, Ford Foundation; Robert C. Good, president, Denison University; Professor Charles V. Hamilton, Columbia University; Professor Ruth Simms Hamilton, Michigan State University; Alexander Heard, chancellor, Vanderbilt University; Aileen C. Hernandez, urban affairs consultant; Constance Hilliard, international director, Booker T. Washington Foundation; C. Peter McColough, chairman, Xerox Corporation; J. Irwin Miller, chairman, Executive and Finance Committee, Cummins Engine Co.; Alan Pifer, president, Carnegie Corporation; and Howard D. Samuel, president, Industrial Union Department, AFL-CIO. In preparing the report the commissioners were supported by a considerable staff, solicited many outside studies and travelled as a group to South Africa.

110 For the Study Commission recommendations, see in particular ch. 19: 'Policy objectives and actions', in *South Africa: Time Running Out*, op. cit., pp. 410–54; for Crocker's presentation of the policy of constructive engagement, see 'South Africa: strategy for change', op. cit., and *Regional strategy for Southern Africa*, op. cit.

111 Crocker, 'South Africa: strategy for change', op. cit., p. 324.

112 ibid., p. 337.

113 ibid., p. 337.
114 *South Africa: Time Running Out*, op. cit., pp. 440–4.
115 Simon Jenkins, 'South Africa survey', *The Economist*, 19 September 1981.
116 William J. Foltz, *Elite Opinion on United States Policy toward Africa* (New York: Council on Foreign Relations, 1979).
117 Simon Jenkins, 'South Africa: survey', *The Economist*, 21 June 1980, pp. 3–4.
118 R. W. Johnson, op. cit., p. 305.
119 Marcum, op. cit., pp. 423–4.
120 Ottaway, op. cit., p. 658.

7

Britain and Southern Africa

GEOFFREY BERRIDGE

In this chapter I propose to address myself to the following questions:

(1) What shape has British policy towards South Africa assumed since the Conservative government took office in May 1979?
(2) What is the official justification for this policy?
(3) What are the real reasons for this policy?

It is an axiom of British foreign policy that South Africa always has something to look forward to when the Conservative Party returns to power. Thus, shortly after returning to office in 1951, Churchill's administration reversed Attlee's policy by swinging its support behind South Africa's urgent campaign for an increase in the official price of gold,[1] while in 1970 one of the first moves of the new Heath government was to announce (in line with the policy of the Macmillan period) that arms sales to South Africa would be partially restored.

And so it came as no surprise when, in her capacity as standard-bearer of the third Tory restoration of the postwar period, Mrs Thatcher (whose government was installed in May 1979) voiced sentiments in the House of Commons on 15 July 1979 which would have generated euphoria in Pretoria had they not been so predictable. This is what Mrs Thatcher said:

> Within South Africa, as in the outside world, there is a growing recognition that change must come. It is in everyone's interest that change should come without violence. We must work by fostering contact, not by ostracism. We must be ready to acknowledge and welcome progress when it is made, even when it may appear slow and inadequate. We must not drive the South Africans into turning their backs on the world. We need to recognise the immensity and complexity of the problems

they face. We must encourage progress in working out solutions to those problems.[2]

On the following day, 26 July, Mrs Thatcher's new ambassador arrived in Johannesburg and announced that his first priority 'must be to nurture and to improve even further' British–South African relations.[3] And just in case the message had not got through, Mrs Thatcher observed on 18 December 1979 that, in view of the 'real prospect' for settlements in Rhodesia and Namibia and 'welcome initiatives on South African domestic policies', there was a chance 'to make progress towards an ending of the isolation of South Africa in world affairs'.[4] In view of these statements, therefore, it was with good reason that President Viljoen, in his opening statement to the South African Parliament on 1 February 1980, could remark that there were now signs of better international understanding and greater tolerance towards South Africa.

Rhetoric, however, is one thing; fulfilment is usually quite another. Nevertheless, the Conservative government has made good on these promises towards South Africa. As Foreign Secretary in the previous Labour government, David Owen had at least exhorted British businessmen to reduce their involvement in the republic; since the Conservatives returned there has been no evidence of this restraint. On the contrary, it is now British policy to *encourage* new investment in South Africa[5] and to foster British exports to the republic by the provision of financial backing for trade missions from the Overseas Trade Board.[6] In addition, at the end of May 1980 the Secretary of State for Trade, John Nott, reversed previous Labour policy by refusing to publish the names of British companies (thirty-three in all) which were paying starvation-level wages to their black employees in South Africa; as a result, he vitiated the discipline of the EEC code on British companies.[7] And then, as is well known, the Conservative government relaxed the pressure on British sporting bodies to keep their distance from their South African counterparts, as the spirit of the Gleneagles Agreement required.

It is not only, however, in the area of 'low policy' that a new atmosphere of warmth has permeated Anglo–South African relations under Mrs Thatcher's government; this is also true of 'high policy'. Thus, while it is true that Britain joined with the other members of the UN Security Council in a rather innocuous condemnation of South Africa's attack on Zambian territory in April 1980, the British delegate substantially qualified the support which he had given 'with some reluctance' to the Security Council resolution of 13 June 1980 on 'massive repression' in South Africa, and abstained altogether (in company with France and the USA) on the Security Council resolution of 27 June which, *inter alia*, condemned South Africa for 'persistent armed invasions' of Angola. Most recently, Britain has drawn attention to its new attitude by being quite alone in stating reservations to *all* of the thirteen major recommendations made by the Security Council's committee on improving the enforcement of the arms embargo.[8] And finally, on the important question of Namibia, the British member of the Western Five's 'contact group' has happily accepted the snail's pace in negotiations which so clearly suits South Africa's purpose, while London has simultaneously refused to commit itself to sanctions in the event that the negotiations fail.[9]

It is thus clear that on the level of action as well as on that of rhetoric, the Conservative government has set a course in relations with South Africa which is as friendly as will be permitted by binding international agreements (such as the UN arms embargo and the EEC code of conduct) and the need to consider other interests. What is the official justification for this new attitude?

The official justification effectively falls into two parts: first, that close and sympathetic contact is necessary to help to solve the problems of Southern Africa, that is to say, of Namibia and of apartheid in South Africa itself; and secondly, that such contact is necessary to the protection of British interests, specifically, economic and strategic ones. The former is proclaimed from the rooftops; the second tends to be murmured in the lobbies, though less and less guiltily.

As for helping to solve the problems of Southern Africa, the present Conservative view is its traditional one that only persuasion, or diplomacy, will move the National Party government in South Africa to abandon apartheid and grant independence in Namibia. This is so because South Africa is too powerful to be *forced* along these paths and so self-righteous that it would dig in its heels on racial reform if faced with threats; anything other than persuasion, therefore, would not only fail, but be self-defeating. To make persuasion possible contact is the necessary means. Contact, however, can help to solve the particular problem of apartheid in yet another way, at least in so far as this contact consists in continued trade with and investment in South Africa. This, of course, is the argument that such forms of contact foster economic growth in the republic, which is already said to be breaking the artificial shackles of the apartheid system. Finally, in her own contribution to the Conservative refrain on the virtues of contact with South Africa, Mrs Thatcher has offered this as a *reward* for the 'progress' which the Botha regime has already made towards the abolition of apartheid and towards granting independence to Namibia and thus as necessary encouragement to further moves in the same directions.

The second part of the official justification for Britain's South Africa policy – which these days tends to be expressed *sotto voce* – is that British interests of considerable importance are at stake in the republic; Britain cannot go too far in jeopardising the goodwill of Pretoria for fear of endangering them. Attention here is directed, of course, to Britain's still-massive investment stocks in South Africa and to the major outlet which it represents for British exports; and in addition, to the 'strategic' importance of South Africa's mineral production[10] and of its position at a 'choking-point' on one of the world's most important sealanes.

Very little of this official justification can be taken seriously. What can be taken seriously needs to be substantially qualified; and certain additional reasons need to be recorded.

In view of the fact that the increasing refinement of apartheid has coincided with dramatic growth in the South African economy for at least thirty years, and proceeded alongside a policy of external 'persuasion' for at least twenty years, not even the Conservative Party – traditionally regarded with some justice as the 'Stupid Party' – can seriously believe in contact for these reasons any longer. By emphasising South Africa's strength and the 'diehard' character of the Afrikaners in order to justify contact as the route to persuasion and economic growth, the Conservative government is at worst rationalising its actions and at best offering an implicit counsel of despair. What makes us suspect the former is that these arguments are, of course, precisely the ones which are most emphasised by the business communities of both Britain and South Africa. Having said this, however, there is no reason to doubt Mrs Thatcher's sincerity when she says that her policy is in part prompted by a desire to *reward* South Africa for recent changes in domestic policy in particular: because these changes have made it much easier to preserve Britain's links with South Africa and are precisely the sort of adjustments which Macmillan begged Verwoerd to make in 1960 and early 1961 when Britain was trying to make it possible for South Africa to remain within the Commonwealth.

With this final qualification, therefore, the topside of the official justification of Britain's South African policy must be rejected as quite plainly insincere. What, then, are the real reasons behind this policy? It will become clear that these are nearer to the bottomside of the official explanation but also that even this is by no means a wholly accurate or comprehensive account.

At the outset it must be stated quite unequivocally that the principal reason for Mrs Thatcher's friendship towards South Africa in her first twelve months in office was her government's need for South African co-operation in bringing the Rhodesia crisis to a successful conclusion. This had been humiliating Britain for years and it was quite clear that, in the absence of a tangible *quid pro quo* from London, the South Africans would not use their substantial influence with the Smith–Muzorewa regime to get Britain off this hook. Since the independence of Zimbabwe in the spring of 1980, however, this consideration has obviously ceased to be of account and Mrs Thatcher cannot be so anxious for South Africa's help in Namibia since this is not Britain's exclusive responsibility. There remain two principal reasons for Britain's policy of friendship towards South Africa and a variety of subsidiary ones; the latter can be fairly boldly stated and I shall begin by recording them.

There is, in the first place, a particularly principled commitment by the present Conservative government to *laissez-faire* in foreign, as in domestic, economic policy; non-interference in economic relations with South Africa is thus an article of political faith. This reason should not be minimised; this is a very idealistic – some would say fanatical – Conservative government. Secondly, the Conservative government takes encouragement in its South African policy from the pursuit of a broadly similar policy by the other leading West European states and an American administration struggling for life under the shadow of Ronald Reagan which, in turn, is extremely anxious to avoid provoking Pretoria into escalating the proliferation of nuclear weapons. Thirdly, it is clear that the Conservative government shares the now common assumption that white South Africa is going to survive for rather longer than was believed in 1976–7. Fourthly, there is the natural inclination of all Tory governments to do the opposite of what is demanded of them by 'Marxist' intellectuals in such organisations as the Anti-Apartheid Movement and by shrill majorities at the United Nations.[11] And fifthly, the Conservative government clearly believes that first-class public relations and adroit diplomacy on an intergovernmental basis in Black Africa will enable it to get away with it. There is some evidence that it is right in this last assumption and recent publicity about the degree of 'under-the-counter' trade which is going on between South Africa and the black states to the north will only serve to confirm the Conservative government's faith in the 'underlying realism' on which it can rely in Africa.[12]

Although important, these reasons remain largely permissive: what is really pushing the present Conservative government in Britain into a warmer relationship with South Africa is on the one hand a paranoid fear of Soviet expansionism, and on the other a desire to strengthen Britain's share of the South African market. Of these two, the last is in my opinion the most potent, while defence of the first point requires recourse in some measure to the 'stupidity theory' of Conservative policy towards South Africa.

It is absolutely clear that Mrs Thatcher's government is much exercised by what it takes to be the predatory intentions of the Soviet Union throughout the world in general, and Southern Africa in particular. Cuban soldiers, the spread of Marxist regimes and the growing strength of the Soviet fleet in the Indian Ocean all go to make Southern Africa part of the general alarm. It is also difficult to resist the conclusion that Britain has decided that it is necessary to give South Africa as much support as possible in order to prevent the 'loss to the West' of the republic's strategic minerals and controlling position *vis-à-vis* the Cape route. What is not so easy to understand is why it has reached this conclusion.

If the argument is that the National Party regime needs to be propped up to keep South Africa from falling to the communists, it is an argument which hardly makes sense: first, because – 'total onslaught' notwithstanding – the National Party regime can unfortunately look after itself; and secondly, because it is not axiomatic that a black successor regime will be anti-Western. Is this not the 'lesson of Zimbabwe'? If, on the other hand, the argument is that Britain needs to support the National Party as a *quid pro quo* for the guarantee of military and naval assistance in the event of a general war with the Soviet Union, it is an argument which makes even less sense. The reason for this is simple and has been repeated at fairly regular intervals at least since 1951: the National Party regime has no alternative but to guarantee such assistance anyway, since in view of its attitude and in view of its reputation, it will be the Soviet Union's first target in Southern Africa.[13] This is one of the reasons why Verwoerd did not abrogate the Simonstown Agreements when Harold Wilson introduced a total arms ban on South Africa in 1964. No more than Harold Wilson does Mrs Thatcher have to court Pretoria in order to be assured of South African assistance in the event of an East–West shooting war in the Southern oceans or in Southern Africa. But none of this seems to get through.

One is forced to the conclusion, therefore, that Mrs Thatcher's government is obsessed by present dangers to the point of being mesmerised by an apparent rock of anti-communist stability in South Africa; it has absorbed uncritically the view of the South African propaganda machine and of right-wing groups throughout Western Europe and North America that a white-controlled South Africa *has* to be supported in the strategic interests of the West. In short, it is a state of mind which has to be ascribed to assiduous lobbying coupled with a failure of intelligence; one of the brighter Tories realised this in 1970.[14]

Probably more important even than this reason, however, in explaining Britain's present friendship for South Africa is Britain's anxiety to strengthen its export market in South Africa, for here is an interest which is not only more tangible, but also quite unambiguously vulnerable. It is true that South African trade does not loom as large in Britain's overall foreign trade as it used to do in the first half of the postwar period, but there remains no reason to doubt the official statement that 'our bilateral trade with South Africa is not peripheral to our economy. It is of central importance'.[15] In addition, and of psychological importance, the republic is still Britain's second largest market in Africa. In 1979 British exports to South Africa were worth £714 million. In January–August 1980 they were up by 35 per cent in comparison with the same period in the previous year.[16] And yet in 1979 Britain's share of the South African market was only 18 per cent. The competition from West Germany, France, the USA, Japan, and now from Taiwan, is very strong indeed and the British government is obviously correct in its surmise that diplomatic hostility out of step with that of its main rivals would see that share slip even further. Consumer resistance to British goods would mount and major orders from South Africa's huge parastatals would be placed elsewhere – as happened in the earlier periods of Labour government. In short, it is the importance and the vulnerability of Britain's market in South Africa – especially at a time when British exporters are battling with an overvalued pound and the Confederation of British Industry is predicting that exports in general are about to collapse[17] – which is today, as it has always been, the main reason for Britain's South African policy. Investments in the republic are obviously important but, in view of South Africa's political and economic need for a continuing inflow of new capital, invulnerable; consequently, they are diplomatically irrelevant.

Until the Western states *concert* their policy towards South Africa, as they have begun to show a little readiness to do, it will continue to remain extremely easy for the South Africans to trade shares in their import market for political favours; and in a Cold War atmosphere their propaganda machine will continue to have a downhill run. Conservative Britain is peculiarly susceptible to both of these gambits.

Notes: Chapter 7

1 See the author's forthcoming *Economic Power in Anglo-South African Diplomacy* (London: Macmillan, 1981), p. 105.
2 *House of Commons Debates (HCDeb.)* 971, col. 629.
3 *Rand Daily Mail*, 28 July 1979.
4 'The West in the world today', p. 8 (press release, 10 Downing Street); this was a speech given to the Foreign Policy Association in New York.
5 See the statement by the Minister of Trade: *HCDeb.* 967, col. 1389.
6 This was also Labour policy, it is true; but it was with evident pride that the Minister of Trade in the new Conservative government announced on 25 May 1979 that eight trade missions supported by the government had already visited South Africa in the course of 1979 and that another nine were planned: *HCDeb.* 967, col. 1388.
7 See, especially, Adam Raphael in *Observer*, 8 June 1980, and for background James Barber, 'The EEC code for South Africa: capitalism as a foreign policy instrument', *World Today*, vol. 36, no. 3 (March 1980), pp. 79–97.
8 *Anti-Apartheid News*, November 1980.
9 There is a perceptible shift here from the Labour position. Thus, while cautious, the Labour government's position had been that it refused to rule out sanctions (see, for example, *HCDeb.* 959, col. 1826), while the Conservative government's attitude has been that sanctions should not even be mentioned on the ground that such talk might 'undermine the negotiations', *HCDeb.* 967, cols 1386–90, and 980, col. 1318.
10 Chromium, manganese, platinum and vanadium have been singled out for special mention in this connection by the Minister of Trade: *HCDeb.* 967, cols 1386–90.
11 The insensitivity to Third World concerns of the present Conservative government is especially pronounced; witness its attitude to the Brandt Commission report and to the proposed 1981 North–South summit.

12   *Star: International Air Mail Weekly*, 20 September 1980, and 27 September 1980.
13   See, for example, W. Arthur Lewis, Michael Scott, Martin Wight and Colin Legum, *Attitude to Africa* (Harmondsworth: Penguin, 1951); C. and M. Legum, *South Africa: Crisis for the West* (London and Dunmow: Pall Mall Press, 1964); and D. Austin, *Britain and South Africa* (London: Oxford University Press/RIIA, 1966).
14   See Douglas Hurd, *An End to Promises: Sketch of Government, 1970–74* (London: Collins, 1979), pp. 52–3.
15   The Minister of Trade, 25 May 1979, *HCDeb*. 967, col. 1386–90.
16   *British Business*, 10 October 1980, p. 261.
17   *Guardian*, 29 October 1980.

8

The EEC and South Africa

HUMPHREY ASOBIE

Introduction

The policy of the United States towards Southern Africa has often received attention. This is because it is usually assumed that the USA is easily the most important Western actor in the subregion. The significance or role of member-states of the European Community, excepting that of Britain, has not received much attention from analysts. Yet the European Community states are active participants in the decolonisation process of Southern Africa. Three of them – Britain, France and West Germany – form part of the five-member contact group currently involved in seeking a solution to the problem of transition to independence for Namibia. In any case the USA itself tends to regard the whole of ex-colonial and colonial Africa as forming the sphere of influence of Western Europe and therefore gives deference to their views on issues arising on the African continent. Moreover, it seems that since 1976 the European Community states have been trying to work out a common policy on Southern Africa.[1] An examination of the role and attitudes of the West European states towards independence for Namibia and ending white minority rule in South Africa is therefore relevant and useful.

In discussing the relationship between the EEC and Southern Africa two problems arise. The first is theoretical; the second, practical. The theoretical problem concerns the identification of the crucial variables which determine West European behaviour as the issue of decolonisation in Southern Africa. In other words, how does one explain or understand the attitudes of EEC member-states towards Southern Africa. The practical problem flows from the theoretical one: it concerns the appropriate stategy to adopt in solving the twin problems of racism and colonialism in the subregion.

The conventional wisdom is that the strong economic interests which the West European states have in Southern Africa are responsible for their continued support for the status quo in the subregion. So long as these economic ties remain strong and vital to the West, it is argued, the Western powers in general, and the European states in particular, will continue to support the racist regimes in South Africa and Namibia and cannot be persuaded to support any move for fundamental change. The policy recommendation that is then presented, rather illogically, is that the European powers must be persuaded to reduce their economic links with the subregion.

But this viewpoint raises a number of questions. First, if the primary factor determining the behaviour of West European states in the subregion is economic, what evidence is there, from the history of decolonisation in Africa, to show that a transfer of power to black Africans will result in loss of economic benefits to the European states? Secondly, if the choice before the West European powers is simply one between losing their economic benefits in South Africa if they support decolonisation and retaining them if they don't, why should they be expected to yield to mere persuasion to reduce their economic links with South Africa? Thirdly, if one assumes that the European powers recognise that there is also another aspect of the equation involving either losing or retaining their economic benefits in independent Black Africa depending on their stand on the question of decolonisation in Southern Africa, why have they not acted in line with what rational calculation would dictate – namely, to support the decolonisation process and to win the favour of both the present independent black African governments and the future ones in Namibia and South Africa?

On the theoretical level there are two possible answers to these questions. The first is that, as the proponents of the centre–periphery framework of analysis would argue,[2] the critical European actors in Southern Africa today are not states, but non-state actors: that is, Europe-based multi-national corporations (MNCs). And these MNCs though essentially profit-oriented are, as Harry Magdoff has argued, concerned as much (if not more) with the security of sources of strategic raw materials and the need to expand their sphere of operations as with profit maximisation.[3] According to this view, then, racist Southern Africa is attractive to the MNCs and through them EEC member-states not only as outlets for profitable investments, but more importantly, as secure sources of low-cost strategic materials because of cheap labour and phoney 'political stability'.

All this may change with the transfer of power to a Marxist, or even genuinely nationalistic, black-dominated government. It is hardly surprising, then, that the West European powers, seeing the trend in Angola and Mozambique, are not really enthusiastic for a change that could alter favourable investment and trade conditions.

The second possible answer is that the strategic, as distinct from the economic, significance of Southern Africa to the EEC far outweighs other values. In particular, the certainty which the Western powers now seem to have of controlling the crucial Cape route might effervesce with a radical change of regime in South Africa. This explanation, unlike the first, assumes that the significant European actors in Southern Africa are states. These states are concerned more with the alternative naval route around the Cape which links them both to the strategic and contested Indian Ocean and to the important areas of the Arabian Gulf, Asia and the Far East which the West considers crucial for both economic and military/security reasons.

The Nature of EEC Interests in Southern Africa

The starting-point in any discussion of EEC state policies in Southern Africa is to recognise the primacy of their economic interests. Southern Africa is important to West European states primarily because it provides outlets for their manufactured goods; supplies crucial raw materials for their industries; and absorbs a lot of their investment capital.

As a group the EEC is one of the world's greatest trading partners. Its imports in 1975 represented 35·7 per cent of world imports as against 11·4 per cent for the USA and 4·4 per cent for the USSR. And the EEC's exports in the same year represented 36·1 per cent of world exports as against 12·9 per cent for the USA and 4·1 per cent for the USSR. Trade is, in fact, vital for the survival of the EEC member-states for several reasons. First, their economies are strongly export-oriented. For instance, the GNPs of the following EEC member-states are accounted for by exports in the degrees indicated by these percentages: Netherlands, 55·4 per cent; Belgium, 53·5 per cent; Denmark, 33·5 per cent; the United Kingdom, 32 per cent; West Germany, 27·1 per cent; and France, 22·8 per cent.[4] Secondly, the most powerful EEC member-states are also the most industrialised, with a high percentage of their population depending on the sale of manufactured goods, much of it abroad, thereby making their dependence on exports more important than the figures suggest. West Germany's economy, for instance, is founded on industrial power; with 46 per cent of its working population engaged in industry in 1975. France, too, is an important industrial nation in the West, ranking fourth after the USA, Germany and Japan. Moreover, both Germany and France have relatively small populations (compared with the USA and UK, for instance); they are therefore in dire need of external outlets for their finished and semi-processed goods. Generally the economies of EEC member-states would suffer seriously if their export markets are drastically reduced. South Africa and Namibia seem to offer excellent opportunities for the sale of manufactured and industrial goods. At any rate the EEC member-states' exports to this region have been growing in recent years.

Table 8.1   *South Africa–EEC: Direction of Trade (Imports – in US $m.)*

Countries	1969	1971	1973	1975	%age increase 1975–69
Total	2,922·2	4,038·7	4,735·8	7,591·2	160·0
EEC	1,421·7	1,965·6	2,358·5	3,901·5	174·0
West Germany	401·1	572·4	880·3	1,409·2	251·0
France	85·7	146·6	180·9	292·5	241·0
UK	699·4	938·8	908·7	1,493·9	114·0
Italy	118·8	147·3	174·6	275·9	132·0
Belgium	33·5	53·2	79·1	144·3	331·0
Netherlands	58·0	81·7	100·0	192·5	232·0
EEC as %age of total	48·7	48·7	49·8	51·4	
Western Germany as %age of total	13·7	14·2	18·6	18·6	
France as %age of total	2·9	3·6	3·8	3·9	

Source: Julian R. Friedman, *Basic Facts on the Republic of South Africa and the Policy of Apartheid*, New York, United Nations, 1972.

The EEC's exports to South Africa alone (or what amounts to the same thing, South Africa's imports from the EEC) increased by 174 per cent, from $1,421·7 million in 1969 to $3,901·5 million in 1975. The rate of increase was thus greater than that of the total world exports to South Africa which was 160 per cent. The contributions of West Germany and France to this overall increase of world exports to South Africa were substantial. West Germany's exports to South Africa rose by 251 per cent during the period; and France's rose by 241 per cent. Also both countries contributed increasingly more to the world's total exports to South Africa in 1975 than they did in 1969. This means that the EEC countries did not curtail their exports to South Africa in spite of the UN General Assembly Resolution 2054A of December 1965, appealing to the major trading partners of South Africa to end their economic ties with it.[5]

With respect to EEC imports from South Africa (or South Africa's exports to the EEC), the pattern was similar. The EEC's imports from South Africa increased by 296 per cent, from a mere $605·7 million in 1969 to the high figure of $2,400 million in 1975. During this period South Africa's total imports to the world experienced a significant expansion: there was an increase of 143 per cent in 1969–75. But the rate of expansion of the EEC's share of this total was particularly high. For individual EEC countries, however, there was a wide variation. Thus, while Belgium (160 per cent), West Germany (298 per cent) and the Netherlands (261 per cent) recorded substantial increases, others such as the UK (72 per cent) and Italy (37 per cent) recorded much smaller rises. France even recorded a decline in exports to South Africa of 41 per cent (Table 8.2).

Table 8.2   *South Africa–EEC: Direction of Trade (Exports in US $m.)*

Countries	1969	1971	1973	1975	%age increase 1975–69
Total	2,194·2	2,185·8	3,498·2	5,318·2	142
EEC	605·7	997·3	1,819·7	2,400·0	296
West Germany	144·0	154·2	274·5	572·7	298
France	211·7	53·7	99·6	125·2	–41
UK	715·0	585·1	1,012·7	1,228·9	72
Italy	88·3	52·0	114·7	121·0	37
Belgium	11·1	79·7	174·8	188·8	160
Netherlands	31·4	50·9	86·6	113·5	261
EEC as %age of total	27·6	45·6	52·0	45·1	
Western Germany as %age of total	6·6	7·1	7·8	10·8	
France as %age of total	9·6	2·5	2·8	2·4	

Source: As Table 8.1.

Altogether what emerges from the trade figures is that South Africa is of great importance to the EEC. It accounts for 48–51 per cent of the EEC's exports. Equally the EEC has since the 1970s become an important market for South Africa's goods, accounting for 45–52 per cent of its exports. Of the EEC member-countries, it is, first, West Germany, and then the UK, that are the major suppliers of South Africa. France ranks third, having a considerably weaker trade link (see Table 8.3). The major purchasers of South African goods are, first, the UK, and then West Germany. Again, France is not quite so important, it ranks fourth among the EEC countries, trailing behind Belgium. The importance of France to South Africa should, however, not be underrated, for it is a major supplier of arms and ammunition to the apartheid regime. From the 1976 figures, it is clear that the EEC is far more important as a supplier to South Africa than as a purchaser. Conversely, South Africa is of tremendous importance to the EEC as a supplier of vital or strategic raw materials. The dependence is, therefore, reciprocal.

Table 8.3   *Direction of South African Trade (US $m. in 1976)*

Major suppliers	Import		Export	
UK	1,185·3	(17·5%)	1,146·6	(15%)
West Germany	1,217·5	(18%)	543·8	(7%)
France	294·7	(4·3%)	170·6	(2%)
Italy	243·7	(3·6%)	165·1	(2%)
Netherlands	170·4	(2·5%)	143·6	(2%)
Total EEC	3,111·6	(46% of total)	2,394·4	(30% of total)
Belgium			224·7	(3%)
USA	1,458·2	(21·5%)	526·8	(7%)
Japan	690·5	(10·2%)	521·1	(7%)
Switzerland	142·4	(2%)		
Africa (not specified)	356·3	(5·3%)	543·8	(7%)
Asia (not specified)	133·7	(2%)	113·4	(1%)
Total, including others	6,769·4		7,874·1	

Source: IMF Direction of Trade, cited in Carter and O'Meara (eds), *Southern Africa*, p. 8.

South Africa ranks very high as a producer of crucial minerals for the maintenance of the economies of the Western countries. It accounts for the following percentages of Western mineral production: platinum-group metals, 86 per cent; gold, 75 per cent; chrome ore, 41 per cent; manganese ore, 40 per cent; asbestos, 18 per cent; and uranium, 13 per cent.[6] Also,

Namibia is very rich in mineral deposits: it is particularly rich in diamonds and uranium, and also has other minerals such as oil, tin, copper, and so on.

The prospecting, production and disposition of these minerals and other raw materials in both South Africa and Namibia involve several MNCs based in different countries. For instance, uranium is mined in Namibia by the Rossing Uranium conglomerate owned by British, West German, French and South African companies. When produced, the uranium is processed into fuel elements for nuclear reaction by companies in the USA, West Germany, the UK, France and even the USSR. The sale of the uranium is made through Rio Tinto Zinc Mineral Services, based in Switzerland and overseen at the European end by Euratom, an arm of the European Community. And the EEC itself funds 75 per cent of its exploration costs.

The strategic raw materials which flow from Southern Africa to sustain industries in the EEC member-states include not only uranium, but also diamonds, gold, coal and chromium. Each of them is so important to the industries of West European states, that an attempt to cut off its supply would spell industrial disaster for one European state or the other. Take the last mineral, for instance: it is believed that the interruption of the supply of chrome to West Germany could spell industrial disaster for that country. A recent West German Foreign Office study estimated that a one-third fall in the supply of chrome could reduce German industrial production by a quarter in a few weeks and cost West Germany 7 million jobs! West Germany is also highly dependent on Namibia and South Africa for its uranium, an important source of its energy supply. The West German government receives 30 per cent of its uranium from Namibia (46 per cent of its supplies from South Africa are included).[7] The EEC countries also depend on Southern Africa for coal. In 1979 South Africa alone provided 23 per cent of the EEC's coal imports; France took the lion's share of this, since it finds it more economical to obtain coal from the relatively younger mines in Africa than from the almost-exhausted, high-cost mines of France. Southern Africa is very important to Europe as a major source of two precious minerals: gold and diamonds. Like the USA, the West European states have a crucial interest in maintaining a stable supply of gold from Namibia and South Africa which, as noted above, is the Western world's most important supplier. Gold is of importance, of course, to the

West because of its central role in the Western monetary system.

It is primarily because the present socio-political setup in Southern Africa seems to offer very conducive conditions for the exploitation of these raw materials by the European companies, that their home states do their utmost to forestall or frustrate all attempts to change the status quo in the subregion. Some of the conditions which the West European-based MNCs find attractive are: the apparent political stability which South Africa enjoys, the cheap labour which the apartheid policy creates[8] and the liberal investment incentives which the racist regimes use to attract private foreign investment.

The multinational corporations are also attracted to South Africa by the huge profits which accrue from their investments in the subregions. Before we take a look at the size of the profits from foreign investments in the area, it is necessary to note first that the bulk of foreign private investment in South Africa emanates from the EEC countries.

Table 8.4   *Foreign Private Investment in South Africa, 1967–72 (in US $m.)*

Years	Net total	EEC's share	EEC's share as %age of net total
1967	190·4	162·4	85
1968	467·6	359·8	77
1969	224·0	161·0	72
1970	585·2	424·2	72
1971	716·8	453·6	63
1972	515·2	492·8	96

Source: Compiled from data in table 18 of John Suckling, Ruth Weiss and Duncan Innes, *Foreign Investment in South Africa*, Uppsala, Africa Publication's Trust, 1975, p. 188.

From Tables 8.4 and 8.5 it is clear that during 1967–72 EEC members were the largest investors in South Africa. Two factors should be noted. First, the bulk of foreign investment in South Africa emanates from Western Europe, especially from the EEC. Secondly, private companies, principal among which are the MNCs, have over the years provided the economic foundation for the maintenance of apartheid. The biggest companies are either British- or American-owned. Nevertheless, the two major EEC powers – France and West Germany – also have significant investments in Southern Africa. Of the two, West Germany has the more extensive involvement and its investments have been growing rapidly. In

1966 the value of West German investment in South Africa was \$4·2 million. By 1977 this had risen to \$335·7 million and then to \$345·8 million by 1978.

Table 8.5 *Public (Governmental) Investment in South Africa, 1967–72 (in US \$m.)*

Years	Net total	EEC's share	EEC's share as %age of net total
1967	–110·6	–36·4	33 of net outflow
1968	98	89·6	91
1969	–8·4	–1·4	over 100
1970	145·6	121·8	84
1971	274·4	56	20
1972	127·4	198·8	over 100

Source: As Table 8.4.

Apart from differences in the value of their investments and degree of corporate involvement, French and West German investments can also be contrasted in another respect. While French assets in Southern Africa consist, by and large, of indirect investments, that is, mortgage and short- and long-term loans, West German investments are predominantly direct investments. This means that, given the mode of operation of MNCs and their decision-making structures, it would be easier to bring about a curtailing of French investments in the area than to accomplish the same task with respect to West German investments.

However, one factor that could frustrate attempts to persuade European firms to either withdraw or curtail their investments in South Africa is the unusually large amounts of profits they make in the area. As John Suckling has argued, a very important reason why foreign companies invest in South Africa is that 'the rate of return to investment is high, from 10–15% for British investment and rates around 20% for U.S.A. investment over the decade 1960–1970'.[9] Indeed, in some instances, the South African subsidiaries provide the bulk of the profits for a multinational firm. Take Rio Tinto Zinc (RTZ), for instance: it was its South African subsidiary, the Palabora Mining Co., accounting for only $7·7\frac{1}{2}$ of RTZ's assets that provided 42 per cent of the group's profits in 1970.[10] Similarly, in 1970 the profit made by Leyland Motor Corporation of South Africa (about \$13·5 million) exceeded the total world profits of the British Leyland Group, which amounted to about \$11 million.[11]

Important though it is, the profit motive is no longer a sufficient explanation for the continued operation of a multinational firm in a colonial, semi-colonial, or neo-colonial territory. As Harry Magdoff has convincingly argued, the underlying motive for continued capital export is neither Hobson's notion of surplus capital nor Marx's idea of falling rate of profit; rather, the cause lies in the monopolistic structure of industrial firms based in the advanced capitalist countries. This encourages competition among the MNCs for an exclusive control of sources of raw materials and investment outlets in underdeveloped lands. Investment by multinational corporations in Southern Africa is, therefore, crucial for the survival of giant industries and firms in Europe: there is a felt need to secure control over the key strategic raw materials that are in short supply in the advanced capitalist countries. Not surprisingly, for decades the primary recipient of foreign funds in South Africa was mining, which between the 1930s and 1960s received between 66 and 35 per cent of all foreign funds invested in the country. By 1966 manufacturing had overtaken mining (29 compared with 28 per cent),[12] but this is only because the initial elementary processing of raw materials is now done in the subregion. The critical area of interest for MNCs remains the exploration and production of uranium, diamonds and gold.

To preserve the (socio-economic and political) system which makes the derivation of huge profits by European companies possible while at the same time helping to save jobs, sustain industries through the supply of vital raw materials and strengthen European defence systems by making available strategic raw materials, the West European states provide substantial military support for the governments of racist South Africa. This is a far more important explanation of Western military support for South African racists than the much-talked-about need to protect the Cape route against Soviet interference.

No doubt, the Cape route is important, especially for economic reasons. Its importance as a waterway lies first and foremost in its use as an alternative, longer but safer way through which the highly industrialised societies of the West receive the oil resources of the Persian Gulf, the rubber and tin of Malaysia and even minerals from South Africa and copper from Zambia, using Mozambique and East African ports as points of outlet. But its importance as a strategic trade route for the West does not justify the military and political support extended to South Africa as the route's gatekeeper, unless of course it is accepted that the Soviet Union poses a credible military threat to the West in this area. Since 1968 the USSR has been building up a naval presence in the Indian Ocean. However, the Soviet presence in the Indian Ocean which is hardly adequate to engage the West in a protracted hostile military activity, is more easily explained on political, rather than strategic, grounds. As Professor Spence has noted,[13] the objectives for a Soviet naval presence in the Indian Ocean are: to serve notice on the West that Moscow is no longer willing to allow Washington to go unchallenged on the high seas; to put itself in a position to have the Russian voice heard on issues of contention in the region and to inject an element of uncertainty in the West's strategic thinking concerning ultimate Russian intentions in the area. Even if it is accepted that the Soviet presence is a military threat, Spence argues, the 'most likely trouble spots are in the Persian Gulf, the Arabian Peninsula and the Horn of Africa rather than the coast line of Southern Africa'.[14] Nevertheless, the Western powers have chosen to construe the threat posed by the Soviet Union essentially in military terms. Their actual behaviour, however, shows that in arming the racists, they were thinking less of the external threat from Russia and more of the threat from inside Africa against the racist regimes in Southern Africa.

Countries of Western Europe including the two leading members of the EEC have, indeed, been arming South Africa in particular against the possibility of conventional attack by the armed forces of the African states. In the 1960s following the British Labour government's imposition of an arms embargo against South Africa in line with the December 1963 Security Council resolution, France became South Africa's leading supplier of weaponry. During 1969–73 France delivered arms worth $32 million to South Africa.[15] In June 1971 a French aircraft company, Marcel Dassault, signed an agreement with the Armament Development and Production Corporation of South Africa (ARMSCOR) for the construction, under licence, of Mirage and F-I jet fighters. Licences were also granted by French companies for the manufacture of helicopters, panhard vehicles and land-to-air missiles. By so doing France broke both the letter and spirit of the 1963 UN arms embargo. Even today, long after the UN Security Council imposed a mandatory arms embargo on weapon supplies to South Africa in November 1977, France still supplies South Africa with spare parts for Mirage jet fighters and air-defence rockets.[16]

The Federal Republic of Germany also helps to arm the racist regime. West Germany has provided equipment and made the NATO codification system available to South African naval and other military installations; in fact, the subterranean command centre near the Simonstown naval base, which gathers and analyses data about all subequatorial movements, was designed and furnished by West German firms.[17] Too, West German firms are engaged in the production of helicopters and anti-tank missiles in South Africa, in co-operation with French firms. West Germany has provided nuclear technology to South Africa as well as an isotope analysis system for uranium enrichment. In spite of the 1977 arms embargo, imposed by the UN, West Germany still supplies military trucks to South Africa, and has provided it with an ammunition filling plant for 155-mm cartridges.[18] In addition, missile-carrying South African patrol boats operate on German-built engines. West German companies supplied equipment for the St Lucia missile range in the Indian Ocean; and government-financed research institutes, universities and companies engaged in weapons manufacture and military contracts in West Germany freely make privileged information and technical assistance available to weapon-makers in South Africa.[19]

(4)   The EEC and Decolonisation in Southern Africa: the Political Dimension

In the light of the exposition made above concerning the high level of economic and military co-operation between EEC members (especially France and West Germany) and South Africa it will be interesting to examine their attitude to decolonisation in the region. It has been argued that there is an inverse correlation between the level of advanced capitalist states' economic involvement in Southern Africa and the degree of their support for African liberation. In other words, the more important a country's economic relationship is, the less a state is supportive of political change in the subregion and vice versa. It was on the basis of this premiss that Taapopi and Keenleyside derived the inference that the substantial economic involvement of all the Western capitalist states, except Italy, have negatively affected, at least to some extent, their willingness to support further decolonisation in the subregion. They then recommended that political pressure should be brought to bear on the Western states to curtail their economic ties with racist South Africa.[20]

However, another group of authors have contended that the Western nations have, since 1975, come to accept the need to help produce meaningful change in the subregion 'within a relatively short period'. They argue that, in particular, the nine members of the EEC who now co-ordinate their policies on Southern Africa, have studied contingency plans for 'selective sanctions against the Pretoria regime'.[21] An evidence of this change of policy, they point out, is the Western vote, in which France took part, to make the arms embargo against South Africa mandatory in 1977.[22] If Taapopi and Keenleyside are right, how then may one explain this change of policy? And will this trend continue?

No doubt Taapopi and Keenleyside have amply validated their hypothesis. They have shown that while in 1960–74 Britain ranked first among West European states in the level of its economic involvement in Southern Africa, it ranked last among those supporting measures for decolonisation of the subregion at the UN. Conversely, Denmark ranked last in the economic-tie variable and first in the decolonisation-support variable. The positions of the other EEC member-countries studied are: Belgium, fifth in economic-tie and fourth in decolonisation-support variables, France sixth and fifth and the Netherlands seventh and fifth. The exception is Italy, which is high in both economic involvement and support for decolonisation. Even more interesting, its support for decolonisation has weakened progressively over the years just as its economic ties with the subregion have become stronger.[23] If this trend persists in the 1980s, the European opposition to the institution of coercive measures against the racist and colonialist regime of South Africa will increase, not diminish.

What, then, are we to make of the signs of apparent change of attitude of the West over Southern Africa: the seeming interest of France and Germany (along with the USA, the UK and Canada) in the decolonisation of Namibia, the EEC code of conduct and support of a mandatory arms embargo on South Africa? The point should be underlined that, despite the involvement of the three states in the contact group seeking to work out a transition of a different government in Namibia and the EEC code of conduct for European companies operating in South Africa, and in spite of the apparent change in France's Southern African policy, these European states are not really in support of any fundamental change in Southern Africa: Europe's aim seems to be merely to control the tempo, direction and quality of inevitable change. This point may be illustrated by looking more closely at the three indices of apparent change already mentioned.

First, let us examine the participation of three EEC members in the 'contact group' and their plan for Namibian independence. The Western plan for the independence of Namibia must be seen as an alternative to two other plans: the Turnhalle approach, and the African alternative. While the last will ensure a significant, if not fundamental, change in Namibia, the Turnhalle approach is designed to maintain the status quo. The Western plan is a compromise solution which though not preserving intact the existing situation, will ensure that no radical change occurs in the territory.

The Western plan is based on Security Council Resolution 385 of January 1966 which called on South Africa to permit the UN to supervise and control an election for the transition of Namibia to independence. It was on this basis that five Western powers – among them three EEC member-countries, the UK, France and West Germany, and the USA and Canada – undertook to conduct negotiations between the Republic of South Africa and all political groups inside Namibia, including the South West Africa People's Organisation (SWAPO).

Thus, the Western plan is based on the recognition of the Republic of South Africa as the *de facto* governing authority in Namibia. But SWAPO, though recognised by the General Assembly as the 'sole and authentic representative of the Namibian people', is regarded by the contact group as merely the 'major' of the 'several Namibian political groups'.

More importantly, it is apparent that the aims of West Germany, a member of the group which perhaps commands the greatest influence in Namibia is to ensure the emergence of a moderate coalition of elements drawn from SWAPO and the Democratic Turnhalle Alliance (DTA). The DTA, it is to be noted, is sponsored by the South African government. It is known that the DTA receives between $252,000–$420,000 annually from West German and South African sources.[24] Also the German-speaking section of the business community has already come out in open support of the DTA. All this is in line with the official West German attitude towards the territory. Until 1977 and despite its membership of the Contact Group, West Germany maintained its consulate in Windhoek in defiance of UN Security Council resolutions. It has persistently refused to have any direct relations with SWAPO. Too, as earlier noted, Germany – aided by France, the UK and the USA – has enabled the racist regime in South Africa to exploit the rich uranium resources of Namibia and supplied the racists with the technology capable of producing weapons with grade-enriched uranium. The result is that South Africa now has the technology and knowhow necessary to make and, perhaps, deploy the atom bomb. These actions do not reflect a desire on the part of West Germany and Western Europe to bring about clear and fundamental change in Southern Africa.

Secondly, we may look at the code of conduct established by the European Economic Community. That Western Europe's aim seems to be to moderate the tempo, direction and quality of inevitable change in Southern Africa is further borne out by the conception and manner of implementation of the EEC's code of conduct. Their primary objective seems to be to forestall the emergence of regimes in both Namibia and South Africa that may be hostile to Western economic and strategic stakes in the subregion.

By 1976 the nine members of the EEC had begun to re-evaluate and co-ordinate their policies towards Southern Africa. In 1977 they introduced a code of conduct for European firms operating in South Africa. The code outlined ways in which European companies would enhance the welfare of their South African subsidiaries' black employees through more rapid promotion schemes, training programmes, provision of fringe benefits and social services. This seemed to symbolise 'a hardening of the European Community's attitude toward South Africa'.[25] In reality, however, it represented no significant change of attitude.

The principal motivation of the code was, in fact, not different from that of the recommendations of the Wiehahn Commission set up a year or so later by the South African government. Both the code and the commission recommended the recognition of black trade unions, enabling them to bargain with employers, and an increase in training and apprenticeship facilities for blacks in 'white' areas. The primary objective of both was the 'maintenance of internal security and labour force' in South Africa[26] – to use the words of C. J. Heunis, South Africa's Minister of Economic Affairs.

These measures, added to others such as bringing an end to statutory job reservations which define certain jobs as white only, and the opening of the private business sector to blacks, which are not being pushed, would enable the South African government to make two important breakthroughs. First, it would be able to co-opt and control organised black labour which is becoming increasingly restive, thereby restoring industrial peace. Secondly, the measures would have the effect of polarizing the blacks along class lines by creating a black middle class with a vested interest in perpetuating the status quo. For the South African government, the black middle class will then serve, at best, as an ally in the 'fight' between the whites and the revolution.[27] In this sense the objective of the code and the motive behind the implementation of the report of the Wiehahn Commission by the South African government coincide. That the code is meant merely to complement, rather than counteract, the direction and pace of change which the South African government itself has chosen and charted is supported by the fact that the EEC code of conduct is not mandatory.

The inability of the European Community member-states to enforce the code is often attributed to the need to be faithful to the capitalist ideology of free enterprise, as well as the legal problems involved in the various countries concerned. But the truth is that the European governments have not found it expedient to enforce the code. They are, indeed, not likely to put pressure on the companies either to observe the code or to curtail their investments in South Africa until and unless African states can either apply economic pressure on them or present them with alternative sources of strategic raw materials.

Much has been made of the apparent change of French policy in Southern Africa. In particular, France's decision in 1978 to enforce an arms embargo against South Africa has been mentioned. But a number of points need to be made about France's behaviour in this area. The first is that France, the last Western supplier to abandon its lucrative arms trade with South Africa, did so only after sustained pressure from the black African states and the UN. And it was expedient for France to yield to this pressure because not only had South Africa by then built up its own arms industry with the help of France, but also France made that token concession in order to protect its interest in the rest of Africa, especially of its supply of uranium which it obtains largely from Niger.[28] The second point to note is that in spite of its apparent adherence to the UN prescriptions against arms to Pretoria, France has still not fully cut off South Africa's access to French arms. South Africa still enjoys licensing rights from France for the manufacture of arms, including authorisation to produce F-I fighters, the most advanced fighter in the French arsenal. And thirdly, even in the 1980s, not only does France openly continue to collaborate with South Africa in the nuclear field but it also votes in the UN against resolutions condemning such collaboration. In doing so it receives the support of all other members of the EEC. An example may be drawn from the resolution passed at the 34th regular session of the General Assembly condemning, *inter alia*, the collusion of France, West Germany, Israel and the USA with South Africa in the nuclear field and demanding that all states should cease oil exports to South Africa. Prominent among those countries that opposed the resolution during that 1979–80 session of the General Assembly were: Belgium, France, West Germany, Ireland, Italy, Luxembourg, the Netherlands and the UK – that is, eight out of the nine member-states of the EEC.[29]

The Need for a Change of Strategy in Southern Africa

From the foregoing discussion, a number of points concerning the appropriate – that is, the most effective – strategies to be adopted in the liberation of Southern Africa emerge. The first point to note is that the EEC member-countries, though important underwriters of the racist and colonialist regimes in Southern Africa, will not of their own accord either withdraw their military support or compel private European firms to curtail their investments and other economic transactions with the white minority regimes. Nor will the European governments without any pressure applied upon them, initiate or support action at the UN to bring about fundamental change in colonial Southern Africa.

The second point to note, then, is that more verbal appeals to the West in general or Western Europe in particular, either within or outside the United Nations, to apply economic sanctions on South Africa are an exercise in futility. Indeed, any attempt to place overwhelming reliance on the UN as an instrument of change in Southern Africa is not only unrealistic, given the constitutional as well as real power structure at the UN, but also diversionary. It merely buys the ruling elite in South Africa time to complete their new strategy of building up the buffer of a black middle class. The EEC's approach, as has already been noted, merely complements this strategy. When the strategy comes to fruition, the process of meaningful change will become much more painful and bloody.

Thirdly, given the subordinate role of the European

capitalist states to the USA, both at the strategic and economic levels, the EEC member-states cannot be expected to initiate any meaningful change in Southern Africa unless such a change has the blessing of the USA. Among the Western states generally, it is the USA that provides the policy lead in respect of Southern Africa, although the USA also sometimes defers to the views of Europe. At the strategic level the USA, as the leader of the North Atlantic Treaty Organisation, considers both colonial Namibia and racist South Africa crucial for the defence of the West and is not prepared to accept fundamental change in the political status quo of the subregion. The European members of NATO, many of them members of the EEC, find themselves obliged to merely follow the US lead on this issue. Thus, the USA encourages – and, in particular, the UK and France as well as West Germany agree – to maintain naval facilities and military communications links with South Africa and the surrounding seas. There are, therefore, numerous British and French naval bases and communications stations in the Indian Ocean.

On the economic front US companies are prominent as investors in Southern Africa. By 1976 there were about 350 US companies in South Africa alone. Their investments then totalled $1·7 billion, that is, about 17 per cent of total foreign investment in South Africa. Of these companies, a few dominate the investment scene: General Motors, Mobil, Standard Oil of California, Ford, ITT, General Electric, IBM and Chrysler. These US-based multinational companies are also important in the economies of the West European countries: as a result, their interests in Southern Africa have become inextricably linked with the interests of the European states in the survival of both their own domestic economies and the economy of South Africa and the West in general. Indeed, a recent study conducted by the Centre of Anti-Imperialist Studies asserts that because the French economy is now dominated by US-based companies, the 'role of France [in Africa] has been to maintain order in its traditional sphere of influence on behalf of the imperialist powers'.[30] Thus, the role of the French government in Africa, including Southern Africa, may not necessarily be in the interest of the French state; it is enough if it serves American-French commercial interests.

This brings us to the fourth point concerning the re-evaluation of African strategy in Southern Africa. The point must be stressed that it is the MNCs that, with or without the collaboration of European governments, consolidate the economic links between the West and Southern Africa. As the chairman of the UN Security Council Sanctions Committee observed:

> From the over 400 cases examined by the committee – the Committee's findings show that it is rare for sanctions to be violated by countries at the state level, in other words, by governments . . . directly . . . More commonly, the violations are made . . . by private individuals or companies.[31]

While the implied distinction between Western companies and governments is spurious, the point should be stressed that the multinational corporations are crucial actors not only in Southern Africa, but in the foreign policy-making process of Western countries.[32] Therefore, attention ought to be directed to them.

Africa's strategy must include the following components.

(1) A concerted effort by independent African states, working under the umbrella of the OAU, to apply economic sanctions directly and selectively on those multinational corporations collaborating with the racists in Southern Africa. Tanzania has already blazed the trail in this respect in its actions against Lonrho; and Nigeria has also done so with respect to British Petroleum. Each acted unilaterally; but what is recommended now is a collective approach. This strategy has several advantages: the offender will directly suffer the punishment; it will be less painful to African states than applying economic sanctions generally on either the industrialised states of Western Europe or even one of them; it is within the power of African states to implement, for it does not require passing any resolution in the Security Council of the UN.

This strategy is preferable to the application of economic pressure on European states because the latter will not really work. In the first place, although French and West German investments in the rest of Africa may be of higher monetary value than their investments in Southern Africa, they are not of equal strategic importance, nor do they yield equivalent level of returns, nor are they concentrated in the same geopolitical area. Threats of expropriation of all the assets of one European state cannot, therefore, easily be used by African states who may not readily reach agreement to take such drastic action, for some African countries will be more hurt than the intended victims of sanctions. Collective African effort is also necessary to forestall victimisation by the European firm concerned.

(2) Increased support for the liberation movements in Southern Africa, which should now be encouraged to direct their attacks on the economic assets of the most prominent multinational firms in both Namibia and South Africa. The aim of such attacks should be to make the two territories unsafe for the US-based and Europe-based giant corporations to operate and to drastically reduce the returns on the investments of these companies.

(3) Active encouragement by independent African states of the emergent constellation of anti-imperialist Southern African states which are committed to reducing the commercial, communications and other economic links with racist South Africa. The support to be extended to this group of states comprising nine members should be financial, military and diplomatic. The nine states – Botswana, Mozambique, Tanzania, Zambia, Zimbabwe, Angola, Swaziland, Malawi and Lesotho – should be encouraged to unite with future black-ruled Azania (South Africa) and Namibia into a military bloc one of whose objectives would be to guarantee the freedom of the high seas around the Cape route. At the same time they would work, together with the support and help of OAU member-states, to rid both the South Atlantic and Indian Ocean of the military (naval) presence of the great powers.

(4) Finally, a progressive reduction by African states of their economic ties with the great powers, especially those of the Western bloc. At the diplomatic level efforts should be made by the OAU to win the co-operation of the Soviet bloc in the struggle to put the West on the defensive and bring victory to the liberation movements in Southern Africa. Similarly, the role of multinational corporations in the economic development of African countries should be de-emphasised. Unless this is done, any threat to impose economic sanctions on the MNCs will lack credibility and will therefore be ineffective. There is thus a link between the re-evaluation of the strategy for the decolonisation of Southern Africa and the working out of

a new strategy of economic development for Africa as a whole.

Conclusion

It has been shown that the primary factor determining the behaviour of West European (especially EEC) states in Southern Africa is the security of their sources of raw materials and (to a lesser extent) investment markets. The possibility of losing strategic mineral supplies seems real to them because of the socialist orientation and nationalisation tendencies of some of the already-independent states of the subregion, especially Mozambique, Angola and now Zimbabwe. And retaining these sources of mineral supplies which are crucial for the survival of industries in several West European countries is important for both the MNCs and the European governments. While the former are concerned with obtaining raw materials at cheap prices and expanding areas of the world open to free enterprise, the latter seem committed to maintaining, for their citizens, the prevailing high standards of living: thus, their objectives overlap. As a result, it would seem that all policies which require acceptance, even in the long run, of much less comfort for West European citizens are dismissed by their governments as politically impossible. It is this that gives the African governments room for manoeuvre. Working in concert all or a significant proportion of the economically important African states can threaten to or actually cut off supplies of selected strategic mineral products to selected West European firms; deny them investment and contract opportunities; and threaten to or actually nationalise the assets of a selected few. At the same time they should hold out the carrot of assuring them that the Soviet bloc need not gain any strategic or even economic advantage over the Western bloc in Africa unless the latter remains intransigent on the question of decolonisation. By so doing Africa can force Western Europe to behave differently – that is, reasonably – in Southern Africa.

And of the two EEC member-states whose behaviour in Southern Africa we have examined here, it is on West Germany in particular, that the African 'stick' should fall more heavily. For West Germany is a more intransigent violator of sanctions and collaborator with the racists in Southern Africa than France. West German companies in Black Africa should, therefore, be the first to suffer the collective sanctions to be imposed by African states.

Notes: Chapter 8

1   Gwendolen M. Carter and Patrick O'Meara (eds), *Southern Africa: The Continuing Crisis* (London: Macmillan, 1979), p. 10.

2   See, for example, O. Letelier and M. Moffatt, *The International Economic Order* (Washington, DC: Trans-National Institute, 1977), pp. 15–16; and C. Fred Bergsten (ed.), *The Future of the International Economic Order: An Agenda for Research* (Lexington, Mass.: Lexington, 1973).

3   Harry Magdoff, *The Age of Imperialism* (New York: Monthly Review, 1966), p. 50.

4   *Courier*, no. 48 (March–April 1978), pp. 32–5.

5   See Berhanykun Andemicael, *The OAU and the UN* (New York: Africana, 1976), p. 136.

6   Carter and O'Meara, op. cit., p. 7.

7   *Africa Now*, no. 4 (August 1981), p. 64.

8   For an account of the inhuman conditions and below-subsistence wage rates to which Africans are subjected in Namibia and South Africa, see article by Peter Enahoro, *Africa* (London), no. 8 (April 1972), pp. 21–2.

9   John Suckling, 'The nature of foreign investment in Southern Africa', in John Suckling, Ruth Weiss and Duncan Innes, *Foreign Investment in South Africa* (Uppsala: African Publications Trust, 1975), p. 27.

10   Ruth First, Jonathan Steele and Christabel Gurney, *The South African Connection: Western Investment in Apartheid* (Harmondsworth: Penguin, 1973), p. 163.

11   ibid., p. 168.

12   Suckling, *et al.*, op. cit., p. 18.

13   J. E. Spence, *The Political and Military Framework: Study Project on External Investment in South Africa and Namibia* (Uppsala: Africa Publications Trust, 1975), p. 28.

14   ibid., p. 51.

15   *Afriscope*, vol. 7, no. 7 (1977), p. 38.

16   *New African*, no. 176 (August 1981), p. 20.

17   African National Congress of South Africa, *Conspiracy to Arm Apartheid Continues: FRG-S.A. Collaboration* (Bonn: Progress Dritte Welt/ANC, n.d.), p. 4.

18   *New African*, no. 176 (August 1981), p. 20.

19   ANC, op. cit., p. 5.

20   Leonard Taapopi and T. A. Keenleyside, 'The West and Southern Africa: economic involvement and support for liberation, 1960–1974', *Canadian Journal of African Studies*, vol. 13, no. 3 (1980), p. 370.

21   Carter and O'Meara, op. cit., pp. 10–11.

22   ibid.

23   Taapopi and Keenleyside, op. cit., p. 364.

24   *Africa* (London), no. 87 (November 1978), pp. 50, 53.

25   Carter and O'Meara, op. cit., p. 10.

26   *Africa*, no. 96 (August 1979), p. 48.

27   *Africa*, no. 111 (November 1980), p. 48.

28   Colin Legum (ed.), *Africa Contemporary Record, 1978/79* (London: Rex Collings, 1979), p. B921.

29   *Keesing's Contemporary Archives*, 2 May 1980.

30   Galen Hull, 'The French connection in Africa: Zaire and South Africa',

Journal of Southern African Studies, vol. 5, no. 2 (April 1979), pp. 223–6.

31　*Africa*, no. 93 (May 1979), p. 70.
32　See, for instance, David Horowitz (ed.), *Corporations and the Cold War* (London: Bertrand Russell Peace Foundation, 1969) *passim*; and James Petras and Morris Morley, *The United States and Chile: Imperialism and the Overthrow of the Allende Government* (New York: Monthly Press, 1975), ch. 5.

PART THREE

Change and Continuity in Southern Africa

9
Continuity and Changes in Zimbabwe

BONIFACE OBICHERE

The distinction between continuity and change is elusive. The lines between the defunct and the emergent are often difficult to draw precisely. Social change and societal transformations have always been fascinating subjects of study and will continue to be so in the future. With regard to African societies and cultures, several authors, scholars and even some novices have addressed themselves to the analysis and description of change and continuity with varying degrees of success.[1]

In the colonial period Zimbabwe was ruled by a small clique of white settlers who used coercive and brutal measures to hold down the African majority. The measure of independence now achieved in Zimbabwe has set in motion the political machinery to change the old social and political order. But it remains to be seen whether the black Africans who have now attained political power will constitute just another ruling clique or whether they will transform Zimbabwean society in such a way as to eliminate the odious racial, economic, political and social discrimination that existed before they came to power. Their attitude and policies about these problems will determine the rate and nature of change and continuity in Zimbabwe in the 1980s.

The intriguing question of continuity and change in Africa has given rise to a large body of literature since the retreat of European imperialism from the African continent. The explanation of social change itself has been an abstruse subject since the birth of sociology and before. According to Emile Durkheim, social change 'at each moment of history is itself a result of social causes, some of which are inherent in the society itself, while others depend on interaction between this society and its neighbours'.[2]

Durkheim's views were expressed in a period when the present social phenomenon of rapid change was not fully envisaged, but even so his generalisations are often valid. The contemporary study of social change was elevated to a new level of intellectual activity by the publication of Alvin Schoffler's *Future Shock*. This book injected new dimensions and complexity into the work of present-day social scientists, particularly as regards the enigma of social change and futurology. The problem of causation still has to be sought internally within the societies concerned, but the impact of external influences have assumed more importance than was the case with Durkheim.

Many African scholars, activists and politicians have concerned themselves with the fascinating problem of social change and have bravely waded into the unfathomable waters of futurology with varying results. Osita Agwuna of Nigeria may be considered one of the forerunners because of a number of pamphlets he published in the post Second World War period, the most fascinating of which is *Let's Go with the Masses* (1953). Segun Osoba's letter (November 1980) to *West Africa* is in the same *genre* as this plethora of pamphlets on social change published in Nigeria and Ghana. Mallam Abdallah, Nduka Eze, Fred U. Anyiam, Mokwugo Okoye, Adegoke Adelabu, Olorun Nimbe, Aminu Kano, Samir Amin, Archie Mafeje and Walter Rodney have all been contributors to the abundant literature on equitable social reform and radical social change in Africa.[3] In addition, politicians turned theoreticians and philosophers including Ahmed Sekou Touré, Kwame Nkrumah, Julius Nyerere, Leopold Sedar Senghor, Nnamdi Azikwe, Dennis Osadebe, Obafemi Awolowo, Kenneth Kaunda and Samora Machel have all shown concern for the direction of social change in contemporary Africa.[4]

How can we analyse Zimbabwe in the 1980s in the light of the generalisations that have resulted from the works of these committed scholars and politicians? What are the major factors that will determine the process of continuity and change in Zimbabwe in the 1980s? Are these factors all internal or are some of them external and international? Some of the major factors which we shall examine are: human resources, material resources, reconstruction, education, the UN and the role of international diplomacy, and geopolitics.

(1)   Human resources

Zimbabwe had an estimated population of 7 million in 1980.

Black Africans form the majority of this population and constitute about 96 per cent of the total. Caucasians (whites) make up about 3 per cent, while Asians and coloureds are the smallest minority of 1 per cent. The bulk of the African population is made up of three major ethnic groups: the Shona, the Ndebele and the Karanga, but there are many other ethnic groups besides these.

Black Africans in Zimbabwe have been denied equal access to education by the white minority who have ruled over the country since 1923.[5] The Unilateral Declaration of Independence of Ian Smith in November 1965 tightened the vice of the apartheid system and kept black Africans away from access to education.[6] Only about 30 per cent of the population are literate, and among children of school-age (5–19 years), only about 40 per cent attend schools. The black African share of this percentage is very low indeed. Zimbabwe in the 1980s must tackle the problem of creating a solid core of trained and skilled manpower for her economy and government. There will continue to be the need for agricultural labour both skilled and unskilled; this is especially so if the rural sector is to be activated and brought into the mainstream of Zimbabwean life and the economy.

Therefore, a crucial factor affecting the process of change in Zimbabwe is the place given to manpower development in the 1980s. There should be, too, an increased role for women at all levels of the economy and society. In the past they have been relegated to the factories; nor should they continue to serve as a reservoir for domestics and nannies to the black African elite and bourgeoisie who have now replaced the whites in the political arena. Problems of ethnicity and ethnic rivalries may pose some problems in manpower training and utilisation in Zimbabwe in the 1980s.

The fighting in November 1980 in Entumbane near Bulawayo between ZIPRA and ZANLA guerrillas is symptomatic of how the recrudescence of ethnic rivalries and political feuds can plague the government of Robert Mugabe. That fighting was touched off by acute bitterness and rancour over local government elections and the tough-line speeches of ZANU zealots such as Nathan Shamuyarira, Edgar Tekere and Enos Nkala. Just before the fighting broke out, Josiah Chinamano, vice-president of ZAPU, warned that the invective and criticisms by ZANU Cabinet ministers were not only provocative, but also inflammatory and could lead to violence. The considered opinion of minister Simon Muzenda, a Karanga from Victoria province, was that the government will have 'to cut the tongues of some Cabinet Ministers to silence them', as reported by Richard Carver in December 1980.[7] Victoria province is known to be one of the areas opposed to Edgar Tekere and it is the constituency of Cabinet ministers Eddison Zvobgo and Simon Muzenda.

Finance Minister Nkala is in the vanguard of the constant verbal attacks on Joshua Nkomo's Patriotic Front. It was he who stated at White City Stadium in Bulawayo that if it came to blows, they would throw a few of them. He went further to accuse the Patriotic Front of sabotage and said that ZANU(PF), which commands a majority of fifty-seven out of the 100 seats in the Zimbabwe House of Assembly, would have to think seriously about establishing a one-party state, thus eliminating Nkomo's Patriotic Front altogether from being a thorn in the body politic of ZANU(PF). However, this view is not at present supported by Prime Minister Mugabe, who is of the opinion that such a move would not be in accordance with the Lancaster House Agreement that resulted in the independence of Zimbabwe. In principle, he is enamoured of the idea of a single-party state, even though he is prepared to shelve this problem for the time being. Mugabe stated in November 1980 that

> we believe that it is better to operate under one political umbrella. It is a kind of national unity you create by one party – provided that within the system you have machinery for democratic expression of views.[8]

He has Tanzania in mind as a model, it appears, or perhaps neighbouring Zambia and other new African states that have opted for a one-party system of government. There is a very strong indication here that Zimbabwe will become a one-party state in the 1980s.

(2) Material Resources

Zimbabwe has a small population, comparatively speaking, but it is richly endowed with natural resources, especially minerals and agricultural resources. About 63 per cent of the labourforce are employed in agriculture which is a most vital area of economic activity in Zimbabwe. If due attention is paid to large-scale agricultural development in Zimbabwe in the

1980s, the country could become the breadbasket of the front line states; Tanzania, Mozambique and Zambia all suffer from periodic shortages. What is needed, then, is a serious effort at diversification of the economy and the injection of capital into the rural areas.

The white minority regime of the past decades emphasised urban development at the expense of the rural areas where most of the African population is located. Large-scale commercial farms at present form the backbone of Zimbabwe's agricultural output. In 1979 75 per cent of the total agricultural production came from the large-scale farms, while only 5 per cent came from small-scale farms and 20 per cent from the farmers in the 'tribal' areas of Zimbabwe. Large-scale commercial farms and estates accounted for 90 per cent of traded agricultural products in 1979. In the 1980s Zimbabwean planners will have to address themselves to this imbalance in the agricultural sector.

Furthermore, the imperative need to

> provide a higher standard of living for the rural population and increased job opportunities will require major emphasis on the future development of agriculture. This will require the more intensive settlement of land, training and extension services, the provision of credit and the maintenance of satisfactory producer prices. It will involve the development of irrigation schemes which will make it possible to settle large numbers of people in fairly small blocks of land.[9]

According to E. G. Cross, chief economist of the Agricultural Marketing Authority in Salisbury, this will entail the transformation of the rural farming sector. The prerequisites for this rural transformation are the adoption of land-tenure reform policies together with the provision of inputs, commercial services and the evolution of local government structures. This last factor has already been taken care of by the local government elections of November 1980, leaving the knotty problem of land-tenure reform and commercial services to be tackled sooner or later in response to the swing of the political pendulum of Zimbabwe. These suggested and necessary reforms will definitely result in greatly improved standards of living for the majority of the black Africans in the rural areas. These steps, if implemented in the 1980s, should also curb the flow of migratory labour from the rural population, which in the past has resulted in 'the degradation of the rural economy and the impoverishment of resources'.[10]

The large-scale commercial sector has room for considerable expansion. What is being advocated here is a policy that is people-oriented and not wholly trade-oriented, as was the case during the illegal regime of Smith. Practical policies or rural development along the lines suggested above will do the people of Zimbabwe more good than any amount of sermonising on the virtues of socialism. Continued progress and development in various agricultural spheres in Zimbabwe, in the 1980s, could mean that it would export agricultural technology and extension services to other African states who are struggling to attain self-sufficiency in food production and to feed their own populations.

Zimbabwe has entered the Lomé Convention between the European Economic Community and the African, Caribbean and Pacific states. This commercial agreement will allow Zimbabwe to export 25,000 ton of sugar a year to the EEC. Though this figure is short of the 125,000 ton that Zimbabwe sought in the agreement, it is despite French opposition a step in the right direction. In return, the EEC will provide Zimbabwe with £20 million in financial aid over the next four years. Britain has also promised £30 million in aid to Zimbabwe; Holland and West Germany have promised financial assistance to Zimbabwe, but France has not yet made any move to proffer aid. These disadvantages of the Lomé Convention have been spelled out in *Socialist Forum* in June 1980.[11] The Lomé Convention is seen purely as the 'continuation of an old form of domination' which began with the Treaties of Friendship, Commerce and Protection that followed the Berlin Conference of 1885. This view is in line with the postulate of Mafeje that neo-colonialism is a contractual bondage into which the new states of the Third World enter by their own choice.[12] This is done through the high-pressure salesmanship of the 'hidden persuaders' who function as the agents of the developed countries and arms dealers. I disagree to some extent with Mafeje because there are elements of covert coercion in the conclusion of most, if not all, of the neo-colonial treaties of commerce or defence.[13]

(3) Reconstruction

In historical perspective reconstruction after a civil war is a very difficult problem. We have the abundantly documented case of reconstruction after the American Civil War from 1865 onwards.[14] In recent African history we have seen the cases of Algeria, Angola, Guinea-Bissau, Mozambique, Nigeria and Zaire.[15] In Algeria Ahmed Ben Bella, who was the victor in the infighting that followed the guerrilla war against France, was overthrown by a military *coup d'état* which installed Colonel Houari Boumedienne in power in 1965. In Guinea-Bissau a military coup on 15 November 1980 dethroned Luis Cabral, who took on the mantle of the PAIGC after the assassination of Amilcar Cabral.[16] Nigeria had its third military coup in 1975 during the reconstruction period which followed the civil war in 1967–70. Zimbabwe in the 1980s must walk a tightrope under the leadership of Robert Mugabe if it is to avoid a sudden violent change of government by means of a *coup d'état* by the armed forces of Zimbabwe who are restive and dissatisfied at the present time. The storm caused in 1980 by the statements of Peter Walls about a possible military coup in Zimbabwe should not be regarded as idle talk, or the grunting of a defeated general. Nor the mouthings of what Robert Mugabe has called the 'unintegrated elements' in Zimbabwe; it is an indication of the present malaise in the Zimbabwean military forces and may be interpreted as an omen or portent for the future.

The 1981 Cabinet reshuffle in Salisbury may be a bold stroke of leadership ability on the part of Mugabe. The removal of Manpower, Planning and Development Minister Edgar Tekere from the public searchlight at this time may help ease the tensions that have built up since his trial and acquittal in Salisbury. The removal of Joshua Nkomo from the Home Affairs Ministry may calm the nerves of the zealots and warriors of ZANU(PF) who had accused him of using the police against supporters. One may be tempted to say that the Prime Minister has taken a major step in averting civil war for the time being. He must work hard to find a golden-mean which will assure the success of the ZANU–ZAPU Patriotic Front coalition and minimise the ethnic rivalry and animosity between the Shona and the Ndebele. The arrest of several ZAPU Patriotic Front leaders following the disturbance in Entumbane and the organisation of ZANU(PF) vigilante groups bodes ill for the alliance; Nkomo has complained that it makes him look like 'a china ornament'.

The preaching of doctrinaire socialism is not an issue in the reconstruction of Zimbabwe. The most pressing problem is the dismantling of the structures of racism which had been built up over the years, dating back to 1923. The physical separation of black, white and coloured sections of the various urban areas is a problem that needs to be tackled vigorously and with determination. Already some progress has been made in the enactment of laws to racially integrate the judiciary, the police, the civil service and the military. In addition, some apartheid laws are being repealed and many more will be struck out of the civil and criminal codes of Zimbabwe. For instance, Tekere and his seven bodyguards were acquitted of the murder charge brought against them by the invocation of the Indemnity and Compensation Act passed by the Rhodesia Front Party regime to protect its white officials and ministers.[17] This acquittal left most whites dumbfounded, while Tekere's black supporters and admirers were jubilant. In November 1980 after the trial, the Indemnity and Compensation Act was repealed. Many other laws of this type will have to be repealed in the future in order to ensure justice for all.

Giant steps need to be taken in the 1980s to redress the balance and remove all the handicaps and barriers which the racist rulers of the past have placed in the way of black African education.[18] Blacks should not have to continue their detestable existence in Zimbabwe merely as a reservoir of manpower for servile labour. This is a problem of reconstruction that should not be approached by the type of cautious gradualism that we have seen in the first phase of Mugabe's administration of Zimbabwe.

The rehabilitation of the rural areas destroyed by both sides during the liberation war is another major problem. Not many cattle were lost during the war by the white farmers in the beef export herds. However, the cattle industry was severely affected by the war of liberation. Overall, the nation's herd was reduced from 6·5 million head in 1975 to approximately 5 million in 1979. It has been officially reported that the 'main impact has occurred within the rural sector where beef herds have declined by almost one million head, and cumulative losses now exceed $70 million. In the commercial beef industry herd losses have been somewhat smaller'.[19] These statistics speak for themselves and should be reckoned with in the serious business of reconstruction.

The tobacco industry was hard-hit both by the liberation war and by the sanctions imposed by the UN in 1966 against Smith's Rhodesia. But it has already shown a tremendous recovery rate in both output and prices. The lifting of sanctions should boost the already-recovering tobacco industry and re-establish Zimbabwe as one of the leading exporters of tobacco in the 1980s. The maize industry is at present in a worse shape than the tobacco industry. Maize output has declined since 1973, and by 1979 there was not enough maize produced to meet the domestic requirements of Zimbabwe. Forecasts by experts within Zimbabwe show that maize production in 1980–1 will still fall short of the national requirements. However, the rehabilitation of the rural areas and the end of crop destruction by violence may lead to normalcy in the maize industry by the middle of the 1980s. The production of cotton, sugar, wheat, dairy products, poultry, pigs, tea and coffee are currently in good standing and should expand to the advantage of Zimbabwe in the 1980s.

All the above prognostications and forecasts are posited on a stable government and on a sane and vigorous policy of land reform and rural rehabilitation. For instance, cotton is predominantly produced in the rural areas. Sugar, which is produced in the lowveld region is already the basis of a major ethanol plant. In the 1980s it is hoped that this plant will supply 20–50 per cent of Zimbabwe's petroleum needs. How the implementation of state ownership of the means of production will affect this picture in the 1980s is a problematique that introduces a new factor into the simultaneous equation that has been elaborated in this section on the reconstruction of Zimbabwe; in simple mathematical terms, it indeed becomes a quadratic equation.

The situation with regard to land tenure at the end of the war of liberation was dismally unbalanced. Communal holdings in the erstwhile 'tribal trust lands' constituted 16·5 million hectare. This included most of the worst terrain in the country, and furthermore, it was to serve the needs of about 96 per cent of the population. Small-scale commercial farmers, mostly whites, held freehold titles of 2 million hectare of arable land and numbered about 11,500 in all. Then came the large-scale commercial farmers and enterprises which numbered 3,500 and occupied the lion's share of the best and most fertile lands of about 14 million hectare. Land reform is a matter of pressing urgency in the reconstruction of Zimbabwe.

(4) Party Politics and Reconstruction

The most intractable problem facing Mugabe is not the difficulty of dealing with the ZAPU(PF), but of controlling the factions within his own party – ZANU(PF). Both Nkala and Tekere have recently criticised Mugabe's cautious gradualism.

Tekere used the platform provided by the dock during his trial to elaborate his political testament. He categorically stated that he believed in revolutionary change and expressed 'his impatience at the slow pace of change' in Zimbabwe since April 1980. He also expounded his role in the liberation struggle. Furthermore, Tekere said 'that he believed that the police, civil service and the judiciary in Zimbabwe should be dismantled'.[20]

If Mugabe does not establish firm control over his party, the more militant and less patient faction led by the Tekere–Nkala coalition will take over the government and force him into a secondary position or into retirement. In addition, Mugabe has to reckon with the existence of the Patriotic Front (ZAPU), the White Rhodesia Front Party, ZANU led by Reverend Ndabaningi Sithole, the United African National Congress led by Bishop Abel Muzorewa, and the unpredictable guerrillas of ZIPRA and ZANLA.[21] These are all live political forces that must be reckoned with in the 1980s. All of them, too, have some support among the population. Though Sithole's ZANU and Muzorewa's UANC decided to boycott the local government elections, they still have enough following in Zimbabwe to constitute a 'fifth column' while the Lancaster House Agreement is in force. They may even make it difficult for ZANU(PF) to force a one-party state system down the throats of Zimbabwe without risking a military mutiny or an outright *coup d'etat* led by the whites and blacks who are loyal to Muzorewa. The authorities in South Africa would be willing to destabilise Zimbabwe in order to restore the bishop to power because they believe that he is not in favour of left-wing socialism.

(5)   Education and the New Social Order in Zimbabwe

A critical area in which there is bound to be change is education policy. For many years the black Africans have been relegated to the periphery of the education system. The apartheid regime definitely adopted the racist doctrine of Cecil Rhodes towards the education of the African. It may be recalled that Rhodes stated categorically that there was no need for Africans to acquire literary education, and that if they were to achieve literacy at all, it should be limited to the ability to count, add and subtract at the most elementary level. In the former Southern Rhodesia access to educational opportunity was denied most black African children; in 1975 the literacy rate was 27 per cent. Of the children who were 5–19 years of age, only 37 per cent were in school. If the number of white children in school is subtracted from the total, the percentage of Africans in school will not even approach 20 per cent. Several studies have been made of the problem of apartheid education in Rhodesia and their conclusions all point to the abject neglect of black African children.[22] It is not merely desirable, but essential, to usher in a new social order in Zimbabwe. The old order must perforce change and yield place to a new and more equitable social order. Education can be a very valid tool for making this a reality. There is a great need to counteract and erase the brainwashing of the people by the Rhodesian propaganda machinery, especially the African service of Radio Rhodesia, as well as the Voice of South Africa (RSA). A total revamping of the curriculum, admission policies, teacher training and textbook selection needs to take place without delay. When I stayed at the Great Zimbabwe Hotel in the summer of 1970, one of the books on sale to those of us who came to tour the Great Zimbabwe ruins was *The Arab Builders of Zimbabwe*. The African Literature Bureau with its headquarters on Jamieson Boulevard in Salisbury needs to be restructured: the types of literary works turned out by this Bureau should reflect the new African personality of Zimbabwe. Education at the primary, secondary and university levels should receive adequate attention immediately, *pari passu*, with other areas of reconstruction. Educated Zimbabweans abroad and overseas should be encouraged to return home to teach or to work in any other capacity according to their qualifications. They should be reintegrated into the society like all former exiles and be encouraged to work for the new social order. Education is a crucial area where change is bound to occur in the 1980s. With nearly 25 per cent of Zimbabwe's GNP coming from the industrial sector, it has promising prospects. The steady growth in the industrial sector will call for more skilled and trained technicians. The answer to this need in the 1980s will be the expansion of technical education and higher education generally in Zimbabwe to correct the neglect of past decades and to meet the demands for the future.[23]

(6)   UN Membership

Zimbabwe was unanimously admitted as the 153rd member of the United Nations in August 1980. There were laudatory speeches by Zimbabwe's supporters and even full support by the USA. Zimbabwe's ambassador to the UN, Dr Elleck Mashinguidze, was accompanied by Mr Ken Towsey, who had been Ian Smith's representative in Washington during his illegal regime.

Zimbabwe is no longer an outsider to the United Nations, membership in which is the hallmark of admission into the comity of nations. Zimbabwe will have to transform its status in the UN from that of the perpetual target and beggar to that of a full-fledged member. This means that her stance will be determined not only by her national interests, but also by the vagaries of the Afro-Asian bloc of non-aligned nations.

(7) Zimbabwe and Southern Africa in the 1980s

Zimbabwe will have to deal with the serious problems of being a land-locked country in Southern Africa. It will have to secure suitable international bilateral agreements to guarantee the use of ports and port facilities in Mozambique and South Africa. The railway links to these ports are vital for Zimbabwe's survival and prosperity. The present link with the port of Beira in Mozambique which is in operation on a limited basis must be expanded in the 1980s. The port of Maputo in Mozambique is more suited to the handling of bulk commodities such as sugar, coal, iron ore, chrome ore and maize. The rail link to Maputo must be repaired as a matter of urgency since it was heavily damaged during the war of liberation.[24]

Zimbabwe's heavy dependence on South African rail links should not be allowed to continue unchanged in the 1980s. A drastic reduction in the percentage of Zimbabwe's total traffic carried over South African railways is needed as a matter of priority and pressing urgency. Therefore, the need for the expansion of Zimbabwe's rail facilities to meet the growth and expansion of her economy is a priority and not an option. Geopolitics, and strategic and security considerations, dictate a cutback on the dependence on South African rail links, especially in view of the recent agreement that Zimbabwe signed with Mozambique.

Zimbabwe's new status as a vulnerable member of the front line states in Southern Africa (see Chapter 2) should lead to changes that may defy enumeration at this time. These changes are bound to occur and the most intrepid futurologist will be hard-pressed to offer a blueprint for dealing with them. If the situation in South Africa deteriorates into a full-scale liberation war, Zimbabwe will experience the types of shock treatment and terrorisation which the diehard apostles of apartheid unleased on Angola, Mozambique and Zambia in the 1970s. Zimbabwe's present air links with Zambia, Malawi and Mozambique should be expanded and the predominant Air Zimbabwe flights to Johannesburg and Durban should be curtailed for political and for security reasons. Profit-making motives should be sublimated to these overriding considerations of national survival, self-pride and dignity. Air links with other African countries should be established in the 1980s.

Zimbabwe had much international support for the training and education of high-level manpower in foreign countries during the period of the struggle for black majority rule. These educated Zimbabweans should now be encouraged to return and take on jobs in their country. Former exiles should be reintegrated into the society and government when they return home. The links that some of these people have forged with the leaders and peoples of other African, Caribbean, European and American states should be an asset in the charting and executing of the progressive policies of the 1980s.

(8) Contradictions and Conflicts in Southern Africa

There will continue to be contradictions and conflicts in Southern Africa in the 1980s. The change of leadership in Botswana, and the possible changes of leadership in Zambia, Angola, Namibia, Mozambique, Malawi and even South Africa, may pose diplomatic and military problems: the hidden agenda or future enigma that Zimbabwe must be prepared to deal with.

In conclusion, there will be continuity and change, and some discontinuities, in Zimbabwe internally and internationally in the context of Southern Africa and the world. There definitely will be some continuities. The organisation of local governments, the rehabilitation of the rural sector devastated by war and the integration of the armed forces will pose soluble problems and present serious challenges to the leadership of Prime Minister Robert Mugabe if he can keep the country together and avoid civil war. The 1980s can be forecast as the period when Zimbabwe's growing-pains will be severe, when the expectations of her citizens will be great and when the leadership of the country will be put to the test. I hope they will not be found wanting.

Notes: Chapter 9

1   Ben Magubane, 'A critical look at indices used in the study of social change in colonial Africa', *Current Anthropology*, vol. 12, no. 4–5 (1971), pp. 419–46; Melville J. Herskovitz and William Bascom (eds), *Continuity and Change in African Cultures* (Chicago: University of Chicago Press, 1959); Richard W. Hull, *Modern Africa: Continuity and Change* (New York: Wiley, 1980); Daniel P. Biebuyck (ed.), *Tradition and Creativity in African Tribal Art* (Berkeley, Calif.: University of California Press, 1969); George Peter Murdock, *Africa: Its People and their Culture History* (New York: McGraw-Hill, 1959); and Amatai Etzioni, *Social Change: Sources, Patterns and Consequences* (New York: Basic Books, 1973).

2   Emile Durkheim, *The Rules of Sociological Method*, trans. Sara A. Solovay, John H. Mueller and George E. G. Catlined (Glencoe, Ill.: The Free Press, 1950), pp. 115–21; and George Simpson, *Emile Durkheim* (Glencoe, Ill.: Free Press, 1969), pp. 33–5.

3   Samir Amin, 'The class struggle in Africa', *Revolution*, vol. 1, no. 9 (1964), pp. 23–47; K. W. J. Post and George Jenkins (eds), *The Price of Liberty* (a biography of Adegoke Adelabu) (Cambridge: Cambridge University Press, 1973); and Leopold S. Senghor, *Nationhood and the African Road to Socialism* (Paris: Présence Africaine, 1961).

4   Leopold S. Senghor, 'West Africa in evolution', *Foreign Affairs*, vol. 39, no. 2 (January 1961), pp. 240–6; Kwame Nkrumah, *I Speak of Freedom* (London: Heinemann, 1961); Obafemi Awolowo, *Path to Nigerian Freedom* (London: Faber, 1957); Kenneth Kaunda, *Zambia Shall Be Free* (London: Heinemann, 1962); and Nnamdi Azikiwe, *Political Blueprint of Nigeria* (Lagos: African Book Co., 1943).

5   Philip Mason, *The Birth of a Dilemma* (London: Oxford University Press, 1958).

6   Nathan Shamuyarira, *Crisis in Rhodesia* (New York: Transatlantic Arts, 1966); and Patrick O'Meara, *Rhodesia: Racial Conflict or Co-Existence* (Ithaca, NY: Cornell University Press, 1975).

7   Richard Carver, 'End of a honeymoon', *New African*, no. 168 (December 1980), pp. 35–6.

8   *New African*, no. 169 (January 1981), p. 25; and G. Carter, *African One-Party States* (Ithaca, NY: Cornell University Press, 1962).

9   E. G. Cross, 'Poised for a green revolution', *Africa*, no. 109 (September 1980), pp. 49–51; and Zavaishe Patisai, 'High stakes in mining', *Africa*, no. 109 (September 1980), pp. 51–4.

10 *Africa*, no. 109 (September 1980), p. 51.

11 'From "protection treaties" to the Lomé Convention: domination continues', *Socialist Forum: A Marxist Journal for Social Change*, no. 2 (June 1980), pp. 22–7. See also B. I. Obichere, *West African States and European Expansion* (New Haven, Conn.: Yale University Press, 1971), pp. 226–8; and *African Business* (December 1960), p. 4.

12 Archie Mafeje, 'Neo-colonialism, state capitalism or revolution? from

"The fallacy of dual economies" revisited: a case for East, Central and Southern Africa', in Peter E. C. Gutkind and Peter Waterman (eds), *African Social Studies: A Radical Reader* (London: Heinemann, 1977), pp. 412–22.

13　Boniface I. Obichere, 'American diplomacy in Africa: problems and prospects', *Pan African Journal*, vol. 7, no. 1 (1974), pp. 67–80.

14　W. E. B. Dubois, *Black Reconstruction in America, 1860–1880* (New York: Russell, 1935); Kenneth M. Stamp, *The Era of Reconstruction, 1865–1977* (New York: A. Knopf, 1975); John Hope Franklin, *Reconstruction after the Civil War* (Chicago: University of Chicago Press, 1961); and *Civil War and Reconstruction*, 2nd edn (Boston, Mass.: Little, Brown, 1969).

15　B. I. Obichere, 'Reconstruction in Guinea-Bissau: from revolutionaries and guerrillas to bureaucrats and politicians', *A Current Bibliography on African Affairs*, vol. 8, no. 3 (1975), pp. 204–19.

16　Sennen Andriamirado, 'Le General Joao Bernardo Viera explique son coup d'état: 'Nino: pourquoi j'ai pris le pouvoir', *Jeune Afrique*, 17 December 1980, p. 24; and 'Guinea-Bissau: finding a blueprint for change', *Africa*, no. 113 (January 1981), pp. 25–6.

17　Godwin Matatu, 'The trial of a minister', *Africa*, no. 113 (January 1981), pp. 12–17.

18　Boniface I. Obichere, 'Apartheid education policies and the education of Africans in Rhodesia', paper presented to Conference on Southern Africa, California State University, Northridge, California, USA, March 1975.

19　E. G. Cross, 'Poised for a green revolution', *Africa*, no. 109 (September 1980), p. 49.

20　G. Matatu, 'The trial of a minister', *Africa*, no. 113 (January 1981), p. 17, and 'Monsieur Edgar Tekere: L'aile "dure", coupable et acquitte', *Jeune Afrique*, 17 December 1980, p. 28.

21　'New homes for guerrillas', *Africa*, no. 111 (November 1980), pp. 40–4; and personal communication during interview with Mr Josiah Chinamano, University of California, Los Angeles, California, USA, January 1979.

22　Franklin Parker, 'African education in Rhodesia', in Brian Rose (ed.), *Education in Southern Africa* (London: Collier Macmillan, 1970); Lester K. Weiner, 'African education in Rhodesia since UDI', *Africa Today*, vol. 14, no. 2 (1967), pp. 14–15; W. A. Hospins, 'Burying our talents', *Central African Examiner*, vol. 9, no. 3 (October 1965), pp. 4–5; and K. Good, 'Settler colonialism in Rhodesia', *African Affairs*, vol. 73, no. 290 (1974), pp. 10–36.

23　R. B. Sutcliffe, 'Stagnation and inequality in Rhodesia, 1964–1968', *Bulletin of the Oxford University Institute of Economics and Statistics*, vol. 33, no. 1 (1977), pp. 35–56; and Ian Phimister, 'Peasant production and underdevelopment in Southern Rhodesia', *African Affairs*, vol. 73, no. 292 (1974), pp. 217–28.

24　P. G. H. Lamport-Stokes, Secretary for Transport and Power, 'Revitalizing transport', *Africa*, no. 109 (September 1980), pp. 55–6. See also Zdenek Cervenka (ed.), *Landlocked Countries of Africa* (Uppsala: Scandinavian Institute of African Studies, 1973).

10

Bearing the Burden of War: When People Pay the Piper but Seldom Call the Tune

KENNETH W. GRUNDY

How can you quarrel with Talleyrand when he mused that 'war is much too serious a thing to be left to military men'? Take it out of the hands of the generals, he was in effect saying, and give responsibility for the conduct of war to the politicians. Yet in this modern age of 'total war', whether we are talking about armed struggle and guerrilla tactics or a modern, global war, politicians have sought to involve all segments of society in their war efforts. In this, the South African regime is not alone in perceiving its war against revolutionary opponents as necessitating a 'total strategy'. War and its products are residually 'left' to the people not in the sense that they are empowered to make key military decisions, but in the sense that they bear the ultimate impact of the war. It is the people who supply the combatants and the wherewithal to engage in war. It is the people who reap the whirlwind of social dislocation and physical destruction.

My focus will be on the social impact of the war on the people of Southern Africa. Of course, it is not a single 'war'. The parties to the fighting are not the same from territory to territory. Yet there is, despite intra-alliance animosities and divisions among the two essential sides, a kind of inter-connectedness to the struggle. Though each war can be discussed separately, it cannot be understood in isolation. The forces on the two sides stand for essentially the same things in each territory – their interests coincide. On the one hand there are the forces of the status quo, largely minority regimes or governments propped up by conservative forces, and on the other hand black nationalists, often though not always revolutionary. If the forces from one side do not always co-operate with other kindred forces, that should not hide the fact that Southern Africa is a single cockpit where the outcome in one territory can profoundly affect the conduct of war in another.

It is not possible in this short chapter to deal with all the social ramifications of war. Nor can I discuss the interrelationships that make it impossible to think of these features as discrete analytical or descriptive categories. Instead, I will concentrate on a few generalisable aspects of the war's impact, aspects that exist in all the territories of the region where fighting has occurred, or where fighting is being prepared for in earnest. Section 1 covers the militarisation of societies as a cumulative product of expanding and intensifying the wars. Here will be discussed the widening involvement of the people, from all racial groups, and to some extent the problems of demobilisation once open combat has been concluded. There are also the issues of regime efforts to relocate populations, to create 'no-go areas', the effects of curfews and the impact of the war on social welfare (such as education and public health) and economic life. Related, as well, is the matter of a heightened support for the war effort through a deepening and consciously cultivated 'we–they' mentality on the several sides. Section 2 will touch upon the physical and psychological insecurities brought on by war, the ebb and flow of refugees, the economic dislocations, the deferred developmental goals and the entrapment of neighbouring states' people in the struggles on their own borders. Section 3 analyses the tendency of warfare to spill over borders and to involve foreign powers.

I cannot touch upon all the ramifications of war in Southern Africa. But I can point to the myriad ways in which war, even wars such as were and are being fought in Angola, Mozambique, Zimbabwe and Namibia, can insinuate themselves into and dominate the lives of even the most apolitical citizens.[1] Adaptation becomes a survival technique for participants and bystanders. 'Escape' in an era of total war and protracted conflict is practically impossible.

(1) Gearing Up for Struggle

Throughout the history of settler rule in Southern Africa, direct rule traditionally entailed some form of coercion, especially in rural areas. Even experiments with indirect rule around reconstituted 'traditional' institutions (such as 'homelands' or 'tribal trust lands') have failed to destroy the essential character of military/police rule. Unless one defines military in the broadest sense possible, it seems exaggerated to argue that 'administration of civil affairs has never been clearly differentiated from the administration of military affairs'.[2] Yet agents of the state have often been responsible for para-military tasks as well as civil ones. With the rise of popular national liberation movements, however, what the regime tries to pass off as 'tribal self-government' is usually suspended in favour of military occupation in rural areas. The militarisation of an already-repressive situation has been rendered virtually complete.

One of the first signs that growing unrest had begun to alarm white settlers and their colonial regimes was the institution of compulsory military training for all young white males. From an all-volunteer armed force to a lottery system to a universal military service obligation, it became increasingly difficult to avoid service in the armed forces. This was accompanied by the extension of the initial period for national service and a lengthening of service obligations in various part-time units afterwards. In the various white regimes of Southern Africa the military had been virtually unseen if not non-existent prior to the period of organised insurgency beginning in the 1960s. You were more likely to see the police and the police reserves – albeit para-military formations – charged with maintaining domestic order and even defending the borders.

Not until the revolutionary mobilisation of some of the indigenous peoples for the struggle for independence and/or majority rule were the settler populations and colonial metropoles likely to commence countermobilisation. In Zimbabwe this occurred after the Rhodesian Unilateral Declaration of Independence in 1965, in Angola after the Luanda uprising in 1961, in Mozambique with the thrust into Niassa and Cabo Delgado provinces in 1964 and in Namibia with the SWAPO raids of 1966. The South African military had a significant role to play in the Second World War. But its expansion and increased state of preparation came largely after the Sharpeville massacre (1961) and especially after the Namibian outbreak in 1970–1, and again in 1973–5.

In Ian Smith's Rhodesia virtually every white, Asian and coloured male Rhodesian resident over school age and under 60 and who was medically fit, had undergone some military training. Through the years of insurgency the regime gradually widened call-up obligations to include more categories of Rhodesians. Once registered (within thirty days of one's sixteenth birthday), white boys could not leave Rhodesia without special permission from the authorities. In addition, a system of periodic employer reports to the Directorate of Security Manpower was instituted to make evasion difficult. By January 1979 a service obligation for all non-African males up to the age of 50 years was gazetted and the 50–59 age group had been required to police the April 1979 general elections.

Rhodesian whites, coloureds and Asians found it difficult to evade their service obligations unless they left the country. Deferments and exemptions were ended and administrative loopholes were plugged. In August 1977 the Minister of Combined Operations summarised it tartly: 'We have pretty well scraped the bottom of the barrel as regards European involvement in our security operations.'[3] The upshot was to encourage emigration. Rather than lose their sons in the bush, or have their careers set back by repeated call-ups, many families decided to start anew outside Rhodesia.

The South African situation differs chiefly in that total mobilisation has not yet been instituted. Yet the pattern is evident – the gradual extension of conscription for longer and longer terms of duty. All white males aged 18–25 are conscripted for two years of compulsory service. Yet of the 59,052 men called for National Service in 1977, for example, 32,659 applied for deferment or exemption. Of these requests, only 564 were refused.[4] It is a much different pattern than existed in Salisbury before the 1980 elections. Upon completion of their two years' service these national servicemen are fed into either Citizen Force units where they must serve 240 days of camp for the balance of ten years or into a commando unit. Able-bodied men who have not been national servicemen are expected to volunteer for either the Citizen Force or the commandos.

To supplement – indeed, in the Rhodesian and Portuguese cases to make field-efficient – these thin white ranks all regimes in the region have drawn increasing numbers of black fighting men into their security forces. African troops had been fighting in harness for the Portuguese authorities in Africa for the last 400 years or so. Until 1961 the composition of the colonial armies was usually 50–75 per cent African and the remainder European. During 1961–7 Lisbon took pains to build up the number of white Portuguese troops in Africa.

After 1967 when it was clear that the white troops were not sufficient to contain the festering wars, there was a massive increase in the recruitment, training and deployment of African soldiers in the colonial armies. By 1973 official Portuguese sources claimed that 'at least 60 per cent' of her forces in Africa were black.[5] Unofficial estimates put that percentage higher, especially if one includes all types of forces, such as village militia, commandos, the regular army and various special units.

Increases in absolute numbers and in the percentages of blacks in the armed forces are largely pragmatic and practical responses to political pressures from a white electorate to offset desperate situations. Portugal was determined to make the colonies pay their way. Manpower limitations in metropolitan Portugal and the budgetary constraints of Europe's poorest state led Lisbon to arm blacks from the colonies. By 1974 increasing desertion rates, low officer enlistment, draft-dodging, higher casualties and the overall failure of Portugal's colonisation schemes all required Portugal to look for black African soldiers to replace a dearth of white boys for her armies.

In Rhodesia Africans were first recruited for regular armed service during the First World War. That formation, disbanded after the war, was re-established in 1939 as the Rhodesian African Rifles. Until 1980 it was an all-African regiment staffed by predominantly white officers. Its 4,000 members constituted around 40 per cent of the regular army. Members of RAR troops were posted to other units to compensate for losses due to white emigration.[6] In addition, the Selous Scouts, a reputedly ruthless elite tracker unit consisting of some 1,800 men, included 1,500 blacks. They were active in clandestine para-military operations and intelligence-gathering. About one-third of the Grey's Scouts, a mounted infantry unit, were black, and blacks made up around two-thirds of the British South Africa Police regulars. It was a heavily armed para-military force that played a vital role in counterinsurgency operations.[7]

None the less, the security manpower needs were greater than could be met by 'voluntary' African involvement. Stepped-up recruitment campaigns likewise failed to fill out the establishment. Despite high rates of black unemployment and underemployment, recruitment required increased pressure and coercion. In 1976 the Smith regime began to consider the possibility of conscripting some categories of

Africans into the military. In August 1977 it began by calling up African doctors, and in February 1978 it announced that certain African trade apprentices would be required to register for service. Even though only 220 were to be affected by this move, a large number in fact resigned their apprenticeship rather than be conscripted.

Sensing that they soon would be called into military service protests were registered among African schoolchildren. In September 1978 the Executive Council announced that it intended to conscript blacks for military service on the same basis as whites. Initially this was to be limited only to blacks aged 18–25 who had completed at least three years of secondary school or who had entered into an apprenticeship contract. Some 25,000 men were to be required to register.

Protests were widespread. Students were arrested. When call-up papers were sent out, it became clear where the people stood. Of the 1,544 Africans notified for the January 1979 call-up, only about 250 reported for service. Desertions were common. In addition, Africans refused to enrol in colleges and the university or to take up apprenticeship contracts, for this made them immediately eligible for military service. The result was that the university's 1979 incoming class was the smallest in university history.

Subsequent intakes for Africans (March, July and September 1979) were poorly subscribed. Later, new call-up regulations were announced making all eligible Africans (16–60 years) subject to registration for national service. The authorities had been forced to resort to pressganging to fill ranks. Few Africans had gained NCO or officer rank.[8] Young blacks had refused en masse to participate in an armed force clearly involved in their people's oppression. It was not a matter of the terms of service or the benefits and career opportunities, but one of political principle. In this case black Zimbabweans would rather have fought for the Patriotic Front than against it.

A similar sequence has occurred in South Africa. The major exception is that black military service is still officially voluntary and is altogether on a far smaller scale than in Rhodesia and Portuguese Africa.[9] Blacks made up over 50 per cent of the regular army in Rhodesia (though none of the 58,000-man territorial force). In South Africa, however, blacks (including coloureds and Asians) constitute only 9–10 per cent of the permanent (career) force. This does not include the training and deployment of indigenous Namibian blacks by the SADF in Namibia or the members of the 'homeland' armies.

Despite the use of coloureds in combat roles in the First World War and in auxiliary labour and service roles in the Second World War, and black Africans in both wars as labourers, it was not until 1963 that the South African Coloured Corps was re-established. Its name was changed to the Cape Corps in 1972, and combat training was begun in 1973. In September 1976 the first SACC fighting unit was sent to the 'operational area' in Namibia. Today the unit (with coloured officers as high as major) consists of around 1,000 permanent force members and another 2,900 trainees. The twelve-month initial training period was extended to twenty-four months in 1980. Almost as many coloureds serve in the navy's permanent force, to which around 360 Asians also belong.

In January 1974, a decade after the first coloured South Africans began training, a black African unit was established. It is now into its own base at Lenz outside Johannesburg and has been renamed the 21st Battalion. It began training for operational duty and in 1978 was deployed for combat duty in Namibia. The 21st Battalion today has around 500 PF members, and almost as many trainees. In addition, SADF has created several regional 'ethnic' companies attached to white regional commands and includes both multiethnic and ethnic organisational modes in their black fighting formations.

Even if one adds to these totals the 'homeland' armies in the Transkei, Bophuthatswana and Venda – which are entirely trained and commanded by SADF personnel 'seconded' to the homelands' governments – the use of blacks in South Africa's military is still cautious, experimental, quite limited and manageable. Since blacks make up around 9–10 per cent of the PF, and the PF in turn constitutes only 7 per cent of the total SADF combat force levels, then the employment of blacks (even considering the manpower shortages, especially in the economy) is under 'control'.

In Namibia itself blacks were brought into the security picture in 1974. A number of San (bushmen) were recruited for tracker duties and units strictly because of their extraordinary bush instincts. Today there are around 850 San soldiers in two battalions. Armed black policemen appeared on the border in the late 1960s. And homeland police forces (Ovambo and Kavango) were organised to supplement the South African police.

The first tribal army (this was the original structural mode) was established in 1974 among the Ovambo. A year later a

Kavango Battalion was created. Both approach full battalion strength – perhaps of 500–600 members. A Caprivi battalion has been added. Other ethnic groups were organised into various formations for defence of the status quo.

An all-South West Africa unit, made up of volunteers from groups not possessing their own battalion, was formed in August 1977, drawing in Manas, coloureds, Rehobeth Basters, Hereros, Tswanas and others. This 41 Battalion is proudly referred to by Pretoria as the nucleus of the national army for South West Africa. None the less, the tribal formations are still being retained, and members see their units as very much associated with their people and a tribal territory. Until January 1981 military service for blacks in Namibia was officially voluntary. Since then all Namibian male citizens aged 18–25 are eligible for training in the South West African territorial force. There have reportedly been large numbers of young males fleeing into Angola to avoid the call-up which, so far, has been highly selective and limited, and which has exempted particular northern portions of the territory bordering on Angola and Zambia. Perhaps no more than 1,500–2,000 Namibian blacks are presently under arms and SADF command. Yet efforts by the South African regime to justify such measures by referring to its multiracial defence forces as 'the people's army' or 'a true people's defence force' fools few.[10] The black citizens know who is in command and to what ends these forces are deployed.

The status quo is mobilising both its minority racial groups and selected and carefully screened and indoctrinated segments of the majority communities in order to defend the current, or some negotiated and acceptable new but not revolutionary, order. This has been, by and large, a response to a no less intense mobilisation of the forces committed to regime change. Past years have seen a steady growth in the liberation movements and their cohorts under arms. Although it will be, for some time, difficult to determine precisely how many fighters the liberation movements have prepared to do battle in the targeted territories, numbers mounted steadily as the wars deepened and widened, to such an extent that in areas of Mozambique, Angola and Zimbabwe it was difficult to find able-bodied men of military age among the people. They had been forced, in short, to choose sides. In some cases there was a rapid growth in force levels. In Zimbabwe, in March 1976, it had been officially estimated that there were 700 fighters inside the country. Within a year estimates had risen to 2,350, and by early 1979 the figure of 10,000 was bandied about. The mid-1979 count was 13,000, rising to 15,000 by November.[11] By the time that the post-election monitoring force withdrew, some 22,000 guerrillas had been gathered in assembly camps. Later, 32,000 fighters were estimated to be in the camps.

According to official South African estimates, there were at the end of October 1979 6,000–8,000 SWAPO guerrillas based in Angola and 1,000–2,000 in Zambia. This represents considerable mobilisation, since the black population of Namibia is only around 690,000. Similar levels of recruitment in Zimbabwe would have meant around 90,000 guerrillas under arms. Similar eleventh-hour musterings of the two sides took place in Mozambique and Angola as the struggle for independence raced to a conclusion and as postindependence insecurities and competition prompted parties to be at the ready. Speed and excitement grew as each side scrambled to avoid defeat or to assure victory.

The war's impact also leads to a demobilisation problem, a problem that still exists in Angola where UNITA forces, with South African support, fight on, and in Zimbabwe where the new, integrated Zimbabwean Defence Force cannot hope to absorb all the armed men currently in the country. The Rhodesian security forces consisted of around 102,800 white, Asian and coloured, and 19,400 black soldiers, airmen, conscripts and mercenaries, territorials, members of the guard forces, BSA police regulars and reservists. There were also around 20,000 black security force auxiliaries, quasi-private armies for the factions involved in the Smith–Muzorewa 'internal settlement' since early 1978. Then there were reportedly around 32,000 guerrillas attached to either ZANLA (Mugabe's ZANU Patriotic Front) or ZIPRA (Nkomo's Patriotic Front). These figures represent about 33 per cent of the total white, Asian and coloured population (practically every able-bodied man) and 1 per cent of the African population, approximately 20 per cent of the male 16–25 age group.

These individuals are armed, and small weapons are non-biodegradable. This poses a vexing security issue for the new regime. Thousands of weapons are in circulation, and dissidents are quite prepared to threaten the precarious order that has been inaugurated. Continuing intra-army fighting, especially since November 1980 and reaching its most violent stages in January and February (around 170 killed), plagues the integration effort of the new government. Promises of careers in the new regular army must, of necessity, be limited. The Joint High Command is believed to have considered a plan to form ethnically segregated battalions. Prime Minister Mugabe rejected this idea: 'We are not here to establish Bantustans or tribal states. We are here to establish a nation.'[12] Demobilisation grants might be considered but they are costly. Civilian jobs and training opportunities are not likely to materialise overnight. Yet all are pledged to facilitate the transition to a new peacetime order. Eventually the new regime will be called upon to make good on its undertakings.

Accompanying the direct militarisation of men of fighting age have been governmental and insurgent efforts to justify and glorify the war mentality. The media, the educational system, the songs, stories and even organised religious life is marshalled for the struggle. There is also a large measure of censorship of the media relating to coverage about military affairs. South Africa is a good example, because the practice has been building up through the years, long before the country had been placed entirely on a war footing.

Take, for example, the increasing militarisation of the educational system. Cadet detachments have been set up in the white boys' secondary schools. There, some 150,000–200,000 boys are given para-military drill and training and are prepared for national service or encouraged to join the PF upon graduation. Even before high school, youngsters are urged to attend voluntary *veld* schools where, *inter alia*, political indoctrination to the 'South African way' softens resistance to the next level of training.[13]

In addition, the news and entertainment media, particularly the state-owned and operated radio and television networks and the Publication Control Board, have contributed to a one-sided atmosphere that tends to glorify if not romanticise the military. Intimidation of the press is common, notwithstanding the existence of a vibrant, competitive and often critical press in South Africa.

Minority governments began to realise that maintaining the status quo was as much political as it was a military assignment. The Portuguese, Rhodesian and South African authorities began, too late, to devote efforts in the fields of psychological warfare without instituting the socio-economic and political changes necessary to win over the masses.

South Africa's is, perhaps, the most conscious and systematic programme, especially in the operational area. Features of it have been tried in non-self-governing homelands, too, and even in white 'group areas'. Both the government and SADF refer to a 'winning hearts and minds' (WHAM) philosophy. As part of the practical and propaganda effort undergirding WHAM, the SADF established a division of Burgersake or Civic Action, headed by a specialist in psychological warfare. Despite SADF statements about the need to gain the 'trust and faith' of the local population, it is apparent that the propaganda value of the exercise has been given priority rather than a desire to provide the social changes necessary to dissipate revolutionary discontent. Civic Action has failed to achieve popular black acceptance. Blacks regard it as a military programme designed to bamboozle blacks into co-operating with the authorities against potential dissidents.

For South Africa, this is supposedly a preventive or pre-emptive response to warfare elsewhere in the subcontinent – in Namibia or on South Africa's borders in Zimbabwe, Mozambique and Angola. To be sure, South Africa's military operatives have been in action in all four territories. But their principal concern is the republic itself, so obviously an eventual target. The level of struggle within South Africa has been, so far, limited – sporadic sabotage, uncovered arms caches, infiltration, escape of prospective revolutionary trainees, attacks on police stations and some clandestine political organisation – all in preparation for the eventual large-scale contest. The upward spiral of insurgent activity is at first hidden from public view by censorship and misinformation, yet it mounts none the less. According to a survey published by the Army's Terrorism Research Centre, there have been 100 bomb, fire-bomb and grenade attacks between 15 June 1976 and mid-1979.[14] Since then even more spectacular results have been achieved with the bombing of the massive synthetic fuel complex at Sasolburg.

A pattern of tightening the legal structures in order to inhibit political freedoms and to destroy military opposition has occurred in all embattled territories in the region. Regions under fire were swiftly placed under martial law and emergency regulations were applied, often involving the suspension of constitutional guarantees of civil liberties, where they did exist on paper. By September 1978 around 90 per cent of Rhodesia had been placed under martial law. Definitions of terrorism were expanded to include virtually any criticism of the regime that might lead to direct or organised opposition. The police and security forces were permitted, thereby, to exercise drastic powers of search, seizure and arrest without warrant, to detain without charge or trial, to deny access to legal advice, to prevent or break up gatherings and to enforce controls on the movement of persons. Violent extramural activities by the authorities make ludicrous any reference to the 'protection' of the law. Torture is common. In short, civilians are required to co-operate with the security forces in their search for 'terrorist infiltrators'. Failure to report to the police persons suspected of being in an area unlawfully constitutes a crime. In addition, regulations provide for the forced removal of populations, virtual blanket indemnification of soldiers and police, the creation of 'prohibited areas' or 'no-man's lands' or 'fire-free zones', curfews and other draconian measures. As these provisions are applied to larger and larger segments of the territory, life for the peasants and inhabitants becomes increasingly terrorised at every turn. The least sign of co-operation with the authorities, no matter how much it may be a product of intimidation and coercion, brings swift retribution from the insurgents and their supporters. The pattern existed or exists throughout the region regardless of the legal subtleties and nuances of each regime.

Another common counterinsurgency technique has been to attempt to deny the liberation movements and their fighters access to the people – as a source of recruits, as a supplier of food, as a provider of information and military intelligence. The Portuguese created *aldemeantos*. The Rhodesians called them 'protected' villages. They exist on a smaller scale in Namibia, although the homelands scheme, overall, serves many of the same functions of control. In Rhodesia, in 1976, responsibility for 'population removal' and the administration of the 'protected villages' was transferred from the Ministry of Internal Affairs to the Ministry of Defence. Over half a million peasants, one-seventh of the rural African population, were moved into some 220 such villages. In addition, there were the 'consolidated villages', unfenced but formally planned government villages along main rural roads.[15]

The villages were usually failures. The inhabitants thought of themselves as prisoners. The authorities treated the villages like concentration-camps. Food was rationed and stringent curfews made cultivation of distant fields dangerous. Even before the wars were terminated, some of the villages were abandoned or dismantled and the inhabitants allowed to return to their lands. Yet the Rhodesian Guard Force, a largely black contingent, grew rapidly after its institution in1976. Officially it was to protect the civilians and to isolate the guerrillas. The real reason was to facilitate control of the populace.[16] It alienated the people, the local economies were weakened and the guerrillas still found support, even within the villages and even on occasion among guard force members.

There had been a steady increase in the monetary costs of warfare for the regimes. In Rhodesia after a gradual rise in defence expenditures, in 1964–73, from slightly over R$20 million to a shade over R$40 million, there were several major leaps – R$65 million in 1974, R$77 million in 1975, R$96 million in 1976, R$146 million for 1977 and R$197 million in 1978. These inflated budgets were subsidised, perhaps as high as 50 per cent, by South Africa. Not only could the Rhodesian government not sustain this level of military expenditure, but the administration's ability to collect taxes had deteriorated in contested rural areas. The same trend of higher expenditures, though less precipitous, occurred in the Portuguese and South African defence budgets during their crucial years under fire. From 1971–2 to 1979–80 the defence vote in South Africa was increased by 600 per cent. As a proportion of GNP it doubled – from 2·6 to 5·1 per cent.[17] If we looked at other elements in the budget that have defence ramifications, such as police, internal affairs, roads and transport, this would reflect a deterioration of the security situation.

Other economic indicators point to a territorial expansion of the struggle: the employment situation weakens, and the swelling ranks of the unemployed become the breeding-ground for guerrilla recruits; larger numbers of school-leavers find it difficult to get jobs; tourism, as an earner of foreign exchange, becomes a sensitive barometer of wartime insecurities. This has not yet affected South Africa, but other territories in the region suffered. In Rhodesia, near to the end – that is, since 1975 – there were declines in GNP. In 1975 the growth rate was –1 per cent, in 1976 –3·5 per cent, in 1977 –7 per cent and in 1978 an estimated –4 per cent. During an inflationary period this might well represent a 25 per cent erosion in real per capita income since a 1974 peak.[18] This overall pattern of economic stagnation makes it more and more difficult for the regime to pursue the war. Economic growth goals are deferred and the people most affected, the poorer peasantry, pay the price in economic as well as physical terms.

But most significant for the lives of the citizens of Southern Africa has been the rising curve of casualties. In Rhodesia from the beginning of the sustained guerrilla offensive at the end of 1972 until the start of 1979, total casualties amounted to

14,531. Considerably over half of all those casualties occurred in 1978. Press estimates of the numbers of people killed since late 1972[19] were as in Table 10.1. For black civilians, official casualty figures tended to regard blacks killed as guerrillas or sympathisers. Note that 'insurgent' deaths outnumber 'black civilian' deaths in the accounting. But to ordinary citizens 'civilians killed in crossfire' and 'deaths of "terrorist collaborators"', as reported in the press, are terms devised to mask regime violence. The people obviously were not misled. Wilkinson also speculates that these data almost certainly underestimate the numbers killed in all categories, since they were drawn largely from official security-force communiqués. But they provide a generally reliable guide to the growing intensity of the last months of fighting.[20]

Table 10.1   *Rhodesia: Numbers Killed, 1977–9*

	20 October 1977	23 October 1978	4 January 1979
Insurgents: probably killed outside Rhodesia	?	2,000	2,000
Insurgents killed inside Rhodesia	3,541	5,707	6,309
Security force members	403	724	788
Black civilians	1,860	4,374	5,133
White civilians	113	279	301
	5,917	13,084	14,531

A good deal of the Namibian struggle is taking place in Angola, where the SADF regularly penetrates the border and, indeed, strikes deep into Angola at SWAPO bases and refugee camps, as well as at Angolan villages. Moreover, South African military assistance to UNITA forces engaging Angolan and Cuban forces keeps the Southern African pot at the boil. Although the level of violence within Namibia itself is comparatively low, it is rising. Official reports indicate that SADF contacts with SWAPO have increased from 499 in 1978 to 1,194 in 1980.[21]

Increasing use of sophisticated weaponry, by both sides, adds to casualty figures. The regime uses airpower more effectively and begins to experiment with larger-scale use of chemical weapons. Napalm and defoliants are employed as well as sensitive electronic gear.[22] In return the liberation forces employ portable ground-to-air missiles and the multiple rocket launcher was brought into play during South Africa's 1975–6 invasion of Angola.

(2)   Surviving the Unrest

As with most wars, those in Southern Africa have set in motion a 'demographic upheaval'. Large numbers of displaced persons have been uprooted, moving inside their own countries as well as fleeing them. Life's insecurities in a contested area became too great for many. The simple acts of day-to-day existence – a busride and travel between towns, to school, to a village gathering, and maintaining your cattle – became dangerous undertakings.

Normal administration and services in rural areas become uneven, and even non-existent in places. Almost 1,000 schools for blacks had been closed during the final stages of fighting in Rhodesia. Around a quarter of a million children (around 25 per cent of the total) were thereby kept out of school.[23]

Food supplies were disrupted and health services severely curtailed. Public health specialists feared that malnutrition and starvation might bring on high incidences of mental retardation. It had been government policy to try to deny insurgents access to food supplies. The entire peasantry suffered under this policy. Undernourishment contributes to the spread of a variety of diseases that re-emerge when resistance declines and medical services are reduced or inoperative.

Bus services were cut in half by the war. Buses were targets for bandit and insurgent hold-ups, and were, in addition, vulnerable to mines. White private motorists increasingly travelled by armed convoy in the countryside and black motorists joined for their own safety. Shopkeepers in the bush not only found it difficult to get supplies, but themselves were subject to robbery and harassment. Through large sections of rural Rhodesia, civilian administrators were withdrawn, leaving the military with an administrative free hand. In sum, life for non-combatants becomes intolerable as fighting escalates. A diarchy of sorts emerges and each side tries to assure compliance for its directives by intimidation and coercion. Whom do you obey? The peasantry are prisoners of both sides' inability to control an area uncontestedly. The people know which side they favour, but that doesn't necessarily tell them whom to obey.

People on the run do not plant crops when the hope of harvest is remote. In an effort to undermine government support in rural areas, the Patriotic Front attempted to decimate veterinary services and to force the discontinuance of cattle-dips. They were effective, for the livestock population in the tribal trust lands (TTLs) declined in numbers and quality. Tsetse-fly, screw-worm and various tick-borne diseases have been re-established. In early 1979 it was reported that only 1,500 of the 8,000 cattle-dips were still operating. Some one-third of the cattle owned by TTL blacks had perished, and disease threatens to infect 2·6 million white-owned cattle.[24] Moreover, the military authorities in the combat zones followed a scorched-earth policy in areas where people were herded into 'protected villages'. Existing villages and crops were put to the torch or poisoned. Cattle were summarily confiscated and sold. Marketed African agriculture declined.

Other social stresses that attend warfare have, of course, been reflected in Southern Africa. Marital problems, crime, broken families, unwanted pregnancies, drug and alcohol addiction, and suicide have increased significantly. In both white and black communities physical insecurity has led to psychological disturbances.

A major demographic impact of the wars has been the relocation, presumably temporary, of large numbers of people as refugees. Upwards of 600,000 Angolans, 75,000 Mozambicans and 150,000 Zimbabweans left their home countries during the peak periods of unrest. The precipitous departure of large numbers of whites from Portuguese Africa – 325,000 from Angola and 160,000 from Mozambique – has had a further unsettling effect. These people's flight had an economic influence beyond their numbers, especially in the short run. Zimbabwe is experiencing a similar exodus, although it is taking longer to develop and so far has been contained by the government and by others who want whites to stay. During 1965–75 every year but one (1966) showed a net white immigration gain. After that emigration grew, with losses of 7,072 in 1976, 10,908 in 1977 and 13,709 in 1978.[25] No such white migration has so far hit Namibia or South Africa, although in some border areas farm occupancy has fallen markedly. It is likely that were it not for an increased sense of insecurity in these countries, white immigration would have been far greater.

The data presented above do not include the hundreds of thousands of blacks who have fled fighting in their tribal districts, yet have remained in the country of their domicile, either drifting to the towns and cities, taking up residence elsewhere, or simply living a life on the run. Exact numbers are not known since so many merely drift from place to place and large numbers are unable to find employment.[26] It has been estimated for Rhodesia that since 1972 there were 500,000 internal migrants plus 750,000 in protected and consolidated villages. Add to that the 150,000 refugees abroad and the 32,000 armed fighters and we can see that a quarter of the black population has been directly uprooted by the war.

(3)   The Involvement of External Factors

Such general and extensive warfare has the effect of widening or internationalising the struggles. The ebb and flow of warfare and its inevitable human tragedy tends to make international borders a source of sanctuary and a potential cause for sparking a widened conflict. Take, for example, the case of the refugees.[27]

Homeless and terribly insecure individuals provide a ready source of recruits for the liberation movements, and even for the counterinsurgency forces. Some pressganging of recruits has been reported, especially if two or more movements are competing for support. Zambia had for years been particularly alarmed by the strong-arm methods used by ZAPU and ZANU in securing trainees. In other cases the host government may use refugees as a political lever, as the Portuguese and the MPLA government did with the old Katangan gendarmerie and Zaire with the Angolan/Bakango refugees. South Africa has even created a battalion-strength unit of Portuguese speakers and one of San refugees who fled the MPLA regime in Southern Angola into Namibia.

Refugees and political exiles may be regarded as linkage groups between host and target governments. They pose problems for hosts in terms of maintenance costs, domestic politics, issues of control and as precipitants for conflict with neighbours. In short, they have added to the insecurity and permeability of the borders of Southern African states. Host governments are ready and often vulnerable targets for retaliatory and even pre-emptive action by target regimes. Such regimes have sought to play upon this sense of insecurity of the host governments, and thereby intimidate and persuade them to limit, withhold or withdraw support for nationalist liberation movements. So far, intimidatory politics has not been especially successful. South Africa and Rhodesia continually made subtle and not so subtle threats against neighbouring states that harbour 'terrorists'. They punctuate those threats with military incursions and air strikes into Angola, Zambia and Mozambique. The arrogance of these invasions are illustrated in the 1980 strike by the SADF at ANC havens in the suburbs of Maputo.[28] There is no need to document the many instances of invasion of national territory – they are contained in the documentation accompanying repeated UN complaints and resolutions.[29] Such aggressive strikes easily emerge from an embattled and isolated siege mentality characteristic of white Rhodesians and South Africans (especially Afrikaners).[30] This reality of invasion has, in turn, made black governments feel threatened and imperilled. Invasion occurs, as does support by the white regimes for opposition groups within the black states and economic pressures on transport and communication links. The region has become a chequerboard of competing interests, confused and uncontrolled.

Internationalisation of the struggle also means calling upon forces external to the region – Cuban soldiers and Eastern bloc military instructors, mercenaries and Western great power diplomats frantically trying to piece together 'internal settlements' to attenuate the instability. The region has become a colosseum of great-power competition. The real losers, as always, are the ordinary people who are ill-prepared to weather repeated economic, military and psychological blows.

Conclusions

It is apparent from the foregoing discussion that the Southern African wars, in terms of their social consequences, are expensive. And just as obviously, the peasantry bears the lion's share of the costs. To begin with, there is a growing militarisation of the societies in question. Settler and colonial regimes seem to follow similar patterns of militarisation. There is a progressive widening and tightening of military-service obligations. This leads, eventually, to a large-scale use of recruits from the indigenous majority population. Without these forces, the thin white line could not have held as long as it did. Yet these forces are still not sufficient – the masses will not be denied. As increasing levels of compulsion are required to secure black enlistment and compliance with compulsory-service regulations, protest, defection and overall discontent in the ranks and outside grow. In most of the wars of Southern Africa this was, surprisingly, kept within manageable bounds by the regimes (perhaps least of all in Rhodesia). Yet eventually it raised problems the regimes could not deal with.

The liberation movements are also able to arm and train larger numbers as repressive state policies are enacted and an insensitive apparatus seeks to enforce them. The pace of mobilisation quickens as success appears more and more likely. Yet soldiers once armed and deployed are seldom easy to demobilise, even in the best of times. Victorious Southern African governments have been plagued by a superfluity of fighters, armed, often undisciplined, and sometimes dissatisfied with the political and economic outcome. Neighbouring states may also seek to exploit this vulnerability on the part of unfriendly governments.

Once in train, a mood of acceptance of the garrison state becomes entrenched in the minority community and, more importantly, so does a conviction that such militarisation is necessary and just. The war mentality is injected into the media, the educational institutions and into the popular mystique. Psychological warfare aimed both at supporters and enemies of the contestants confronts the populace with difficult choices. Entrenched regimes, with all the advantages of the superstructure at their bidding, find it impossible to sell their message to the masses disadvantaged by the order of things. Repressive laws dealing with political opposition and leading eventually to emergency regulations and martial law fail to damp down the fires of discontent. Indeed, they add to the growing litany of complaint.

Efforts are made to divorce the people from the insurgents. 'Prohibited areas', 'fire-free zones', 'protected' villages and related schemes are devised, but to little avail. The people know who they prefer to support and they do their best to aid and protect the fighters, even in dangerous and repressive conditions.

Other manifestations of the wars tax the people. Increased military budgets and tax increases, deferred development plans, economic lethargy, unemployment, faltering food production and distribution, disease and malnutrition, rising civilian as well as military casualties, insecure national borders, increased firepower by the combatants, growing numbers of internal and external refugees, declining governmental services, psychological and social upset, and physical insecurity lurks at every turn. This depressing enumeration of conditions leads to a malaise all around as each side scrambles to assure ultimate victory or else to survive. Eventually a rural diarchy prevails, with the impossibility of obeying both claimants and neither. As one or the other party finds itself losing its grip there is a strong tendency and pressure from abroad to call upon outside forces to redress what, to them, is a deteriorating situation. The wars become internationalised – into what had been thought to be sanctuaries for exiles and refugees, and under the gaze of international powers and organisations abroad. It adds up to a tense, dangerous and often tragic environment for ordinary people, people who are ill-equipped to cope with such demands. Each life has become a thread woven into the fabric of warfare.

Notes: Chapter 10

Work on this chapter was supported in part by grants from the Earhart Foundation, Ann Arbor, Michigan, USA, and the Joint Committee on African Studies of the Social Science Research Council. To both I am grateful yet neither bears responsibility for my opinions expressed herein.

1   For background on the wars, see: Basil Davidson, Joe Slovo and Anthony R. Wilkinson, *Southern Africa: The New Politics of Revolution* (Harmondsworth: Penguin, 1976); M. Raeburn, *Black Fire! Accounts of a Guerrilla War in Rhodesia* (London: Julian Friedmann, 1978); and John A. Marcum, *The Angolan Revolution*, 2 vols (Cambridge, Md: MIT Press, 1969, 1978).

2   Michael Bratton, 'Settler state, guerrilla war and rural under-development in Rhodesia', *Issue*, vol. IX, no. 1–2 (Spring–Summer 1979), p. 56.

3   *Herald* (Salisbury), 10 August 1977.

4   *Republic of South Africa House of Assembly Debates* (Hansard), 13 April 1978, Q col. 614: hereafter cited as *HA Debates*; and Muriel Horrell, *Survey of Race Relations in South Africa, 1978* (Johannesburg: South African Institute of Race Relations, 1979), p. 54.

5   Much of the data from this section comes from Douglas L. Wheeler, 'African elements in Portugal's armies in Africa (1961–1974)', *Armed Forces and Society*, vol. II, no. 2 (February 1976), pp. 233–50.

6   *Fire Force Exposed: The Rhodesian Security Forces and their Role in Defending White Supremacy* (London: Anti-Apartheid Movement, 1979), p. 13. See also: P. McLaughlin, 'The thin white line: Rhodesia's armed forces since the Second World War', *Zambezia* (Salisbury), vol. VI, no. 2 (1978), pp. 175–86; and Barry M. Schutz, 'The Rhodesian armed forces: a different kind of animal?', African Studies Association, San Francisco, California, USA, October 1975.

7   *Fire Force Exposed*, op. cit., p. 5.

8   On racism in the security forces, see ibid., pp. 40–2.
9   A more complete coverage of this subject will appear in my forthcoming study on the use of blacks in the South African defence force.
10   See statements by National Party members G. de V. Morrison, R. F. van Heerden and A. J. Vlok in *HA Debates*, 12 March 1979, cols 1720, 1730 and 1752; and Major-General E. A. C. Pienaar, Inspector General of the Air Force, in *Rand Daily Mail* (Johannesburg), 28 January 1979.
11   A. R. Wilkinson, 'The impact of the war', *Journal of Commonwealth and Comparative Politics*, vol. XVIII, no. 1 (March 1980), p. 114.
12   *Observer* (London), 22 February 1981.
13   'The march to militarism', *Financial Mail* (Johannesburg), 23 June 1978, pp. 97–8; and *Star* (Johannesburg) (weekly air edn), 12 April 1980.
14   *Observer*, 13 July 1980; see also *Rand Daily Mail*, 9 April 1980.
15   Bratton, op. cit., p. 60. See also: A. K. H. Weinrich, 'Strategic resettlement in Rhodesia', *Journal of Southern African Studies*, vol. III, no. 2 (April 1977), pp. 207–29; Brendan F. Jundanian, 'Resettlement programs: counterinsurgency in Mozambique', *Comparative Politics*, vol. VI, no. 4 (July 1974), pp. 519–40; and Gerald J. Bender, 'The limits of counterinsurgency: an African case', *Comparative Politics*, vol. IV, no. 3 (April 1972), pp. 331–60, esp. pp. 335–7.
16   For example, the Secretary for Internal Affairs pointed out that his ministry 'always enjoyed a close association with the Police, Army and Air Force [and] the security situation made this association even closer': quoted in Bratton, op. cit., p. 60.
17   Robert S. Jaster, *South Africa's Narrowing Security Options*, Adelphi Paper No. 159 (London: International Institute for Strategic Studies, 1980), p. 16.
18   Wilkinson, 'The impact of the war', op. cit., p. 115.
19   *Survey of Race Relations, 1978*, op. cit., p. 510.
20   Wilkinson, 'The impact of the war', op. cit., p. 114.
21   *Star* (weekly air edn), 28 February 1981.
22   *Fire Force Exposed*, op. cit., p. 39.
23   Wilkinson, 'The impact of the war', op. cit., p. 119; and Bratton, op. cit., p. 61.
24   Wilkinson, 'The impact of the war', op. cit., p. 120. See also the account in the *Star* (daily edn), 2 April 1980.
25   Wilkinson, 'The impact of the war', op. cit., p. 118.
26   For an account of life for one such squatter, see 'Where the grass gets trampled', *Frontline* (Johannesburg), vol. I, no. 2 (February–March 1980), pp. 16–21.
27   See, for example, K. W. Grundy, 'Host countries and the Southern Africa liberation struggle', *Africa Quarterly*, vol. X, no. 1 (April–June 1970), pp. 15–24; and John Marcum, 'The exile condition and revolutionary effectiveness: Southern African liberation movements', in Christian P. Potholm and Richard Dale (eds), *Southern Africa in Perspective: Essays in Regional Politics* (New York: The Free Press, 1972), pp. 262–75.
28   *The Times* (London), 31 January 1981.
29   For just a small picture of one year's activity, see: United Nations Center against Apartheid, 'Acts of aggression perpetrated by South Africa against the People's Republic of Angola (June 1979–July 1980): report of the International Mission of Inquiry', *Notes and Documents*, no. 2

(January 1981). The effects are confirmed by Jonathan Steele in the *Washington Post*, 10 February 1981.

30 See Donald G. Baker, 'Race, power and white siege cultures', *Social Dynamics* (Cape Town), vol. I, no. 2 (December 1975), pp. 143–57.

11

Oil Sanctions and South Africa

OLUSOLA OJO

Introduction

Since the 2nd Conference of Independent African States appealed to Arab oil states in June 1960 'to approach all the petroleum companies with a view to preventing Arab oil from being sold to the Union of South Africa',[1] the pressure to get oil sanctions instituted against the republic has been relentless. African states have brought pressure, with varying degrees of success, on all the international organisations and fora to which they belong, particularly the United Nations (UN), the Commonwealth, the Organisation of Petroleum Exporting Countries (OPEC) and the Non-Aligned Movement – to get energy sanctions imposed on South Africa.

African leaders have assumed that an oil embargo against South Africa would disrupt its economy and cripple its military capability to the extent that its government would be left with no alternative but to reconsider its apartheid policy. On the other hand, a military option for the resolution of the South African problem has not been so attractive to the continent's leaders. This is so for three reasons. First, the Africans are aware of the superiority of the South African military machine. Secondly, they are aware of the formidable political and logistical obstacles they would face in getting a combined African force ready to fight South Africa. And thirdly, they realise that it would take years before South African nationalists could mount an effective armed struggle within the republic.

The theatre of diplomatic pressure to get an oil embargo imposed on South Africa moved from Africa to the UN in 1961: a proposal to that effect was made, but it was rejected as it failed to get the required two-thirds majority. However, in Resolution 1899 (XVIII) of 13 November 1963 on the 'Question of Namibia', the General Assembly agreed to urge all states to refrain from supplying in any form petroleum or petroleum products to South Africa.

Having succeeded in getting the General Assembly to adopt their call for an oil boycott the African states directed their efforts at the Security Council, to take similar action. The reason for this is obvious, since Security Council resolutions unlike General Assembly decisions are mandatory on members. Moreover, the Security Council under article 39 of the UN Charter is the only body empowered to decide on measures to be taken to maintain or restore international peace and security. Such measures may include 'interruption of economic relations' (article 41). If such provisional measures were to be ineffective, the Council is bound under article 42 to take more stringent measures, including force if need be, to get its decisions implemented. The African states' attempt to involve the Security Council was, therefore, tactical: once the Security Council agrees to impose sanctions, theoretically it is bound to take other, more stringent measures if sanctions fail.

In June 1964 the Security Council agreed to set up an expert committee to undertake a technical study as to the feasibility and implications of the measures which could be taken under the Charter. The committee reported in 1965 on the positive role an oil embargo would play in influencing South Africa's apartheid policy. However, no action was taken because of the opposition of Western countries which have extensive economic interests in South Africa.

Thus, the initial moves by the African states to impose an oil embargo on South Africa failed, because neither the UN nor the Arab states were prepared to institute such action. After 1964, no serious attempts were made until the 1970s to get sanctions imposed. This was due, first, to the fact that Africans seemed to have believed then that what was needed was comprehensive economic sanctions and not just selective ones. And secondly, there were serious doubts as to the efficacy of economic sanctions as an effective means of influencing international diplomatic behaviour after the mandatory sanctions imposed on Rhodesia by the Security Council had failed to bring down the illegal regime of Ian Smith. The Rhodesian experience was particularly frustrating from the African point of view.[2]

However, the dramatic success of the Arab oil embargo

against the USA and other Western countries friendly to Israel in October 1973 following the outbreak of the Yom Kippur War has led to a reconsideration of resource manipulation as an effective instrument of foreign policy.[3] The success of the Arab sanctions revived African interest in getting an oil sanction imposed on South Africa. The then secretary-general, Nzo Ekangaki, pointed out that 'countries which are our worst enemies depend considerably on us for their energy supplies'.[4] He said the time was opportune 'for our Arab brothers to use the oil embargo against these countries'. There was an optimism in African circles that an oil embargo would lead to the collapse of South Africa. The Tanzanian *Daily News* opined that an oil boycott would accelerate the African liberation struggle: 'A boycott would completely paralyse the economies of these countries, the regimes would fall and their sinister policies would crumble.'[5] And the *Pioneer* of Ghana noted that an oil embargo would bring Portugal and South Africa to their senses in their 'mad efforts to perpetuate colonialism, racism and oppression in Africa'.[6]

In November 1973 the OAU resolved to put pressure on the Arab states to apply the 'oil weapon' against South Africa. And on 26 November 1973 the Arab League decided to institute an oil boycott against South Africa and Portugal.[7] Efforts were made thereafter by African states to persuade other OPEC nations to take similar action. For instance, in June 1977 the OAU set up a committee of seven – Algeria, Gabon, Ghana, Libya, Nigeria, Sierra Leone and Zambia – specifically for this purpose. The following year the committee was constituted into a Standing Committee on Sanctions with an expounded mandate. This committee was now to follow regularly all matters connected with sanctions against racist regimes in Southern Africa; in doing so it would co-operate with sanctions committees of other international organisations. The OAU further mandated the African Group at the UN to get the Security Council to consider the possibility of imposing an oil embargo against South Africa under the provisions of chapter VII of the UN Charter. In 1979 the Organisation further requested all oil-exporting countries to impose individual and collective penalties against companies which supply oil to South Africa.[8]

The rest of the chapter examines a whole range of issues connected with the question of an oil embargo against South Africa: (1) South Africa's vulnerability to oil sanctions; (2) its sources of oil; (3) attempts by the government to reduce its dependence on imported oil; and (4) measures which could make oil sanctions effective as factors affecting the viability of such a strategy to undermine apartheid.

(1) South Africa's Vulnerability to Oil Sanctions

One of the key factors that determines the effectiveness, or otherwise, of any particular economic sanction is of course the degree to which the target state is vulnerable to it. Vulnerability has an external as well as an internal dimension. The higher the loading the particular import has on important sectors of the economy of the target state, the more vulnerable that state will be to sanctions. Besides this, the absence of an internal as well as an external substitute for the particular import is also vital. In other words, for sanctions to work, the target state should not get substitutes or other sources of supply for the embargoed goods. The application of a sanction must be universal to be effective. To appreciate South Africa's vulnerability to oil it is, therefore, pertinent to examine the republic's sources, as well as the place of oil in its economy.

It is very difficult to obtain accurate data on South Africa's oil industry. This is because the South African government extended the Official Secrets Act to cover the industry in 1973. Since then no official data relating to the industry has been published. And the decision by Iran to cut off oil supplies to South Africa in the wake of the Iranian revolution in late 1978 led to the introduction of a new and more stringent law in June 1979.[9] This law makes it a criminal offence to publish information on the source, manufacture, transportation, destination, storage, quality or stock level of any petroleum acquired or manufactured for or in the republic. Our analysis is, therefore, based on various reports and documents published by the OAU, the UN Center against Apartheid and by the Sanctions Working Group.

Unlike other industrialised countries of the world, oil provides only about 20–25 per cent of all South Africa's energy needs.[10] This is due to a number of factors. First, the republic has an enormous coal reserve which it extracts relatively cheaply due to the very low wages paid to black miners; coal provides about three-quarters of South Africa's energy needs. Secondly, South Africa has no oil of her own. Oil exploration which began in both the republic and Namibia in the 1960s has so far not yielded any worthwhile result. Thirdly, although

South Africa has embarked on a programme of producing oil from coal (SASOL), the total amount so far produced has been negligible – only about 5,000 barrels per day in 1978 or 1 per cent of oil consumption.[11] And fourthly, arising from the above factors, the South African government has done everything possible to reduce the country's foreign oil consumption. Most of the areas in which coal can be substituted for oil have now been exploited.

South Africa imported about 210,000 b/d of crude oil in 1974. By 1978 this had risen to about 400,000 b/d of crude oil and 15,000 b/d of refined oil products[12] such as aviation gasoline, specialised lubricants and solvents which cannot be produced locally. The cut-off of Iranian supplies and the increasing tightening of the oil embargo by a number of OPEC countries may, however, have reduced the total volume of imports.

Of greater importance than the total volume of imports is the use to which oil is put. A sectoral breakdown of oil consumption in 1974[13] shows that it accounted for only 8 per cent of energy consumed by the industrial and commercial sector – the largest energy-consuming sector in the economy, accounting for 62 per cent of consumption. Of the energy provided for the household and agricultural sector, 28 per cent was provided by oil. Mining took only 3 per cent, while transport took a lion's share of 79 per cent. One may, therefore, be tempted to conclude that except for the transport sector, oil does not play any significant role in the economy. However, although the percentage of energy provided by oil for some sectors of the economy may be small, there is no ready substitute for it. In the industrial and commercial sector, for instance, oil is needed for heating and for engines. Besides, a certain amount of oil is required for non-energy requirements. Lubricants are needed for all machinery and the petrochemical industry depends on oil as a basic raw material. The latter provides inputs for industries such as plastics, synthetic fibres and rubber, chemicals and paints. Thus, although South Africa may be less vulnerable than other countries which depend heavily on fuel oil for heating and the generation of electrical power, any substantial cutback of supplies will have a far-reaching and disruptive effect on the economy both directly and indirectly. The agricultural sector is equally highly dependent on oil. The most vulnerable sector, however, is the transport sector. Road vehicles are totally dependent on oil and there is a limit to which oil can be conserved in this sector without seriously disrupting the whole economy.

Equally important is the use of oil by the highly mechanised South African military machine. Oil is basic to the effective mobility of the armed forces and the police whose increasing use of 'mobile warfare' tactics relies on the generous use of Land Rovers, armoured cars, helicopters, aircraft, trucks, gun carriers and ships. The importance of oil to the military in particular and to the transport sector in general was brought home to South Africans in November 1973 when a tanker carrying aviation fuel was delayed for a few weeks in the Middle East. Because of limited available stock, all privately owned aircraft were grounded until the tanker arrived.[14] The South African government has introduced legislation compelling companies to sell oil to the military. If, however, foreign supplies were cut off, the regime would only maintain its military machine at the risk of the whole economy grinding to a halt.

(2)   The Sources of South African Oil

According to a 1973 OAU report, South Africa received about half of its oil from Iran at that time. The other principal sources were Iraq, Qatar and Saudi-Arabia, all Arab states. However, in November 1973 the Arab oil-producing states agreed to embargo oil supplies to South Africa. But the Shah of Iran, because of his close ties with the South African authorities, refused to take a similar action despite appeals by the African states. Iran, in actual fact, stepped up its deliveries to the republic after the Arab boycott decision. According to one UN estimate,[15] Iran supplied 90 per cent of South Africa's oil needs in 1974 and 85 per cent in 1975. These levels were maintained until the fall of the shah. Iranian crude oil was exported to South Africa in two ways. First, through direct export by the government-owned National Iranian Oil Company (NIOC) which had a longstanding contract to supply a refinery near Johannesburg.[16] And secondly, Iranian oil was exported to the republic by the Iranian Consortium – BP, Shell, Mobil, Exxon, Texaco, Gulf, Standard Oil of California and Total.

After the Arabs had officially imposed their oil embargo, it became difficult to know the actual percentage of South Africa's oil originating from them. However, an analysis of the data obtained on tanker movements from Lloyds of London in 1977 shows that oil did continue to flow from the Middle East, particularly from Bahrain, Iraq, Kuwait, Oman, Qatar, the United Arab Emirates (Abu Dhabi and Dubai) and Saudi-Arabia.[17] In June 1979 it was reported that South Africa had exchanged unknown amounts of gold bullion for Saudi-Arabian and Kuwaiti oil.[18] Some quantities of oil also came from Indonesia and Brunei. With OPEC formally instituting an embargo against South Africa and the loss of Iranian supplies, Brunei became the only country openly selling oil to the republic. It now supplies about 8 per cent of South Africa's oil needs.[19]

South Africa receives some of its imported oil from the 'spot market', although at a very high premium. It pays as much as a 60 per cent premium over the already-high crude prices.[20] The oil exporters have no control over this market which operates principally out of Rotterdam, Antwerp and Amsterdam but also from Hamburg, London, Paris, Milan, New York and Singapore. Usually the oil sold in the 'spot market' is not subject to the restrictive terms of sale contracts entered into by oil exporters and oil companies. Purchases on the market are usually done by brokers. Thus, crude oil shipments may pass through a number of intermediaries and the oil itself may not be dispatched directly from the original oil-exporting country to South Africa.

South Africa also obtains some of its oil through 'oil piracy', mainly through the manipulation of tankers. First, a tanker may be deliberately sunk after its cargo has been illegally discharged in South Africa. This was, in fact, what happened to the tanker SS *Salem* (ex-*South Sun*) sunk off the coast of Senegal in January 1980. The *Salem* had loaded 190,000 ton of Kuwaiti crude oil under sales contract between Kuwait and Pontoil, an Italian-based company. Investigation later revealed that the *Salem* headed for Europe with its cargo via the Cape of Good Hope. But while on the high seas Pontoil sold the *Salem*'s cargo to the Shell International Trading Co. for delivery to Europe. *Salem* later changed its name to *Lema* before it approached Durban, where it offloaded its cargo of crude oil and was filled with sea-water. It was deliberately sunk off the coast of Senegal in an attempt to conceal the oil theft.[21] Two other Liberian-registered oil tankers – the *Albahaa B* and *Mycene* – sank off the African coast after the *Salem* incident under similar circumstances.[22] The *Albahaa B*, a 240,000-ton tanker exploded and sank off the coast of Tanzania on its way back to the Middle East after it had offloaded its cargo in Durban. Like the *Albahaa B*, the *Mycene* also a 240,000-ton tanker mysteriously sank off the coast of Senegal with no traces of its oil cargo by the time it sank.

Secondly, there is 'double-loading' of tankers. This is usually done in close collaboration between the oil companies, tanker owners and the South African government. Some tankers load crude oil destined for Europe from the Middle East, but later offload either part or all of the crude in South Africa. The tankers later proceed northwards to load new supplies in one of the loading-points on the west coast of Africa – in Cabinda, Port Harcourt, or Warri. In May 1979 the Nigerian government seized a tanker, *VLCC Kudu*, which called at Port Harcourt to load crude after it was known to have discharged its previous cargo in South Africa. Thirdly, it is not uncommon for a tanker carrying crude oil to feign mechanical breakdown in the vicinity of South Africa. Its contents are offloaded to another vessel which then takes the oil to Durban or Cape Town; the original carrier subsequently proceeds back to the Middle East after 'undergoing repairs'.

Fourthly, international oil companies with the approval of some host governments also swap embargoed oil for non-embargoed oil which is then shipped to South Africa. This arrangement became widely known following the controversy between former British Foreign Minister, Dr David Owen, and Lord Carrington, then Foreign Secretary, in June 1979.[23] Under the arrangement the Conservative government of Margaret Thatcher agreed to pass North Sea oil to Conoco which then sent it to South Africa in exchange for embargoed oil.

Finally, South Africa gets some quantity of its oil from the synthetic production of oil. The first oil-from-coal plant – Sasol I – was opened in Sasolburg near Johannesburg in 1955. Its output of oil products in 1978 was about 5,000 barrels per day. Another oil-from-coal plant – Sasol II – was opened early in 1980. It was to produce about 45,000 b/d of oil products at full production in 1981.[24]

The South African Oil Industry and the Oil Companies
Any consideration of an oil embargo against South Africa must take into account the role of the oil companies in the republic's oil industry, since the implementation of such an embargo would focus on them primarily. Ownership of the companies may also be a vital factor in determining compliance by the companies. The oil industry in South Africa is dominated by five multinational oil companies – BP, Caltex, Mobil, Shell and Total. These companies account for 85 per cent of the

South African oil market and 91 per cent of the service stations.[25] The first four are wholly foreign-owned, while Total-South Africa is 66 per cent owned by the French government and 34 per cent owned by South African interests. It is significant to note that all five companies are subsidiaries of the small group of Western oil companies – the 'oil majors' – which control the world's oil industry. There are four other companies which have smaller operations in South Africa – Esso, Sasol, Sonarep and Trek. Esso, like Caltex and Mobil, is American-owned, while Sonarep is a Portuguese company. Trek is largely owned by South African private interests.

It is pertinent to note that the relationship between the South African government and the oil companies is very close. Because of the profitable nature of the companies' activities in the republic and the fact that their owners share the political beliefs of the government, the oil companies have co-operated willingly with the South African attempts to make the companies serve 'national interests'. In addition, the government had also devised a wide range of methods aimed at controlling these companies' branch plant activities. It is doubtful whether the parent companies would readily have acquiesced to the many obnoxious laws as they have done in South Africa if such legislation had been enacted in some Third World states. For example, it is obligatory since 1967 for all companies to produce the specialised oil products which are needed for strategic purposes irrespective of their commercial potentials.[26] As a result of the extension of the Official Secrets Act to cover information relating to the oil industry, the head offices of the oil companies in Europe and the USA – which are in any case reluctant to impose sanctions – say that it is impossible for them to know what their subsidiaries are doing in South Africa. They have also argued that employees of their wholly owned subsidiaries can refuse to answer questions put to them by the directors of the parent companies on their activities in South Africa.[27]

Furthermore, the managements of some of these companies have frustrated attempts by some of their shareholders to terminate corporate links with South Africa. In 1977, for example, the board of directors of Caltex recommended a vote against such a proposal, arguing among other things that such a step would interfere with US foreign policy 'which under the law is reserved to the Government'.[28]

The active participation of the oil majors has been of great importance to the development of the South African oil industry. It has, for instance, ensured that South Africa has continued to obtain crude oil and oil products despite the OPEC embargo. Sir Eric Drake, chairman of BP, claimed in March 1974[29] that his company and others had intentionally set out to render ineffective all Arab attempts at enforcing oil embargoes on South Africa. Besides, the companies have provided the republic with the vital technical expertise that is needed for oil exploration, petroleum-refining and the petrochemical plants. They also provide some of the huge amounts of capital needed to develop the republic's oil industry. As the *Financial Mail* of Johannesburg acknowledged in its 1971 supplement: 'Without the massive resources of the big international oil companies . . . the oil industry [of South Africa] would not have been built into a R700m. business.'[30]

(3) Moves by the South African Government to Reduce its Vulnerability to Oil Sanctions

The South African government had long recognised its near-absolute dependence on imported oil even before the first call for an oil embargo was made in 1960. The government accordingly took steps to reduce the country's vulnerability, first, by reducing the amount of energy provided by oil, and secondly, by finding internal substitutes for imported oil. Sasol oil-from-coal projects, mentioned earlier, are perhaps the most imaginative and successful attempts to reduce the country's dependence on foreign oil. In February 1979, shortly after the cut-off of Iranian oil supplies, the government announced plans to construct Sasol III, which would have the same capacity as Sasol II, that is, 45,000 b/d when it comes into production in 1983. It is estimated that the various Sasol plants will then provide about one-third of the country's oil needs at current consumption levels.

The government has also been considering the use of additives like methanol or methane alcohol (produced from the distillation of wood or coal) and ethanol (manufactured from sugar or maize). Research is also being conducted into the possibility of using hydrogen as a motor fuel.[31] However, these are still only possibilities at the moment, it will take years before they can make any significant impact on South Africa's dependence on foreign oil.

The government has also spent huge sums of money on oil

exploration within South Africa and Namibia. It established the Southern Oil Exploration Corporation (Soekor) which has had overall responsibility for oil exploration since 1965. The search for oil was intensified thereafter. Leases for oil exploration were also given to foreign firms. However, only minor traces of oil and natural gas have been found and none in a large enough quantity to be commercially exploitable. And by 1977 all onshore exploration drilling had to be terminated and all foreign firms which took leases for oil exploration in the late 1960s have withdrawn.[32] However, offshore exploration has continued, but so far no commercially viable deposits have been found. Moreover, the decline in onshore exploration in South Africa has been matched with the intensification of exploration in Namibia.

South African interests have in recent times been making efforts to have direct control over external oil exploration and production. The Anglo-American Corporation has taken a lead in this direction. Through a change of fortunes of the Hunt brothers – US silver market speculators – the Anglo-American Corporation has secured access to important prospecting rights in the Beaufort Sea, Alaska. In early 1980 the price of silver plunged on the world market and the Hunts found themselves unable to pay for the silver they had pledged to buy at old inflated prices. One such contract was for $665 million with the US company, Engelhard Minerals and Chemicals Corporation, in which Anglo-American had a 29 per cent controlling interest.

Part of the settlement between the Hunts and Engelhard involved the transference to Engelhard of a 20 per cent undivided interest in each of the blocks of permits that they held for exploration in the Beaufort Sea. The concessions cover a total 3·5–3·7 million acres.[33]

This oil-for-silver deal is just one of the means whereby Anglo-American has sought direct control over oil production. It has also acquired a lot of international holdings in oil exploration and producing companies. For example, it has a 62 per cent controlling interest in Canadian Merrill, a company involved in oil and gas exploration and development which is active in Canada and the USA. Francana, in turn, controls Trend International and Trend Exploration which has substantial interests in Canada, Indonesia, Paraguay, the Philippines, the UK and the USA.[34]

The stockpiling of oil is another way in which the government has been trying to blunt the impact of an oil embargo. For over a decade the South African government has been increasing its build-up of stockpiles which are usually held in disused coalmines in the Transvaal. Bailey and Rivers have estimated that 17 per cent of the total amount of oil available to the republic goes into stockpiles.[35] They argue that the country's stock could have lasted about one and a half years had there been a total cut-off of oil supplies in 1978. It is possible, however, that the cut-off of Iranian supplies and the intensification of attempts at enforcing embargoes by some OPEC countries may have reduced the total amount of oil imports and therefore the amount that can be spared for stockpiles.

Finally, the government has taken a number of drastic measures, since the Arab embargo of 1973, to reduce domestic oil consumption. Prices have been increased, partly because of increased cost of imported oil and partly as a result of taxation. A litre of oil which used to cost 12 cents in 1973 had gone up to 54 cents by June 1979.[36] The government has also introduced petrol-rationing, and speed limits have also been lowered. In addition, there is an enforced restriction on the number of hours during which service stations can sell fuel.

(4) Prerequisite for an Effective Oil Embargo against South Africa

From the discussion above, it is apparent that oil is one weapon which, if skilfully deployed, can disrupt the South African economy and force the government to reconsider its apartheid policy. Despite its increasing efforts to be self-sufficient in oil, South Africa will in the foreseeable future depend on vital imported petroleum products as well as for a large percentage of its crude. On the one hand, then, South Africa is very vulnerable. On the other hand, a total ban on the oil export to South Africa will not significantly affect the revenue of any oil-exporting country since none of them is dependent on such exports. Moreover, enforcing an oil embargo against South Africa need not involve the international community in an expensive or controversial naval blockade of the South African coast. A blockade might after all be politically unacceptable to some Western countries, particularly if such an international action involved an increased Soviet naval presence around the Cape.

Furthermore, any disruption in the South African economy

caused by an oil embargo would not have a substantial negative effect on countries outside Southern Africa. It is very unlikely that South Africa would want to retaliate by denying the export of strategic mineral resources with which it is abundantly blessed. Any such retaliatory move would further worsen its economy. It would also not be an attractive option for South Africa to threaten the Western oil lifeline from the Gulf by denying bunkering facilities at South African ports. A vast majority of the passing tankers do not in any case stop for bunkering in South African ports. And to interfere with the international oil trade outside South African territorial waters would be an act of war too risky for the South African government to take.

However, any oil embargo against the republic that was not universally applied and enforced by all oil-producing states would not be effective. It would not be enough for one or even all members of OPEC to enforce an embargo: non-OPEC states would also have to join. This is necessary to ensure that the non-OPEC states do not make up indirectly for losses from OPEC countries. And this is where the problem lies. Most of the non-OPEC oil states are Western countries – for example, Britain, Canada, Norway and the USA – which do not share African sentiments about using economic coercion against South Africa. In the event of all OPEC member-states enforcing sanctions, one or more of these non-OPEC countries could easily switch deliveries to South Africa. The British plan to ship non-embargoed North Sea oil to South Africa and import oil from other sources in return is a typical example of what might happen. It is, therefore, necessary for the African states to continue to press for a mandatory embargo imposed by the Security Council. Although the possibility of Western members of the Security Council allowing this to happen at the moment seems remote, continued South African intransigence over Namibia and the continued unmitigated brutality against the South African non-white population may force a change in Western attitudes. It is to be recognised that it took almost two decades of lobbying by the Africans before the Security Council agreed to a mandatory arms embargo against South Africa.

Moreover, OPEC member-states can still make the oil weapon work even without the co-operation of the Western countries if they are prepared to engage in secondary sanctions, that is, to extend their scope to include South Africa's 'friends', just like the Arabs did against Israel's friends in 1973. This strategy does not, however, appear likely considering the internal dynamics of these states, as well as the political orientation of many of their leaders. Meanwhile, OPEC members can make their embargo more effective by exploring ways and means of reducing the freedom which international oil companies have had in manipulating oil movements. Serious thought should be given to reducing, if not eliminating, the amount of oil that goes to the 'spot market'. The percentage of oil that is usually involved in this market is quite small and the loss of revenue to the oil states would not be unbearable. More attention should also be given to ways and means of detecting illegal supplies to South Africa. OPEC states should consider the possibility of establishing an information centre which will collect, collate, analyse and disseminate information on the world oil trade with particular emphasis on tanker movements to South Africa. Such a centre should liaise with various national and international anti-apartheid organisations, as well as with the national governments of all oil-exporting states.

OPEC member-states should also try to force oil companies to comply with the oil embargo by stiffly penalising known defaulting companies. They should inform all oil companies that any tanker known to have visited South African ports should also be blacklisted and risk possible seizure if found within their territorial waters. The owners, operators, charterers, captains and other sailors of such tankers should also be blacklisted. Non-aligned countries, such as Liberia, Panama and Indonesia, which offer flags of convenience services should withdraw such facilities to any tanker that has delivered oil to South Africa. Without a flag of convenience to fly, such tankers would find normal commercial operations impossible. Other measures such as refusal to sell oil to defaulting companies should also be considered. Tankers belonging to the company can also be prevented from carrying oil from OPEC member-states. In addition, OPEC states could order other companies with whom they transact business not to deal with their blacklisted counterparts. Such a move would prevent oil from reaching the blacklisted companies which could then resell it to South Africa.

Oil-exporting states should monitor what happens to their oil by securing relevant information on all sales contracts, including the identity of buyer, the quantity, port of destination and end-user, as well as transport information. They could also insert very strong end-user and resale clauses in all sales contracts and use these as a means of spotting defaulters, by requiring the initial buyer to supply receipts showing delivery to end-user. They should also prohibit their nationals and companies from engaging in any activity that is related to the South African oil industry. Other non-aligned countries should also be encouraged to take a similar position; the latter should also consider, in particular, making significant inroads into the oiltanker business either on an individual or a collective basis to exercise greater control over the movement and destination of their oil. Other measures which could facilitate the sale of oil directly from oil-exporting countries to end-users should be encouraged.

Any serious thought about oil sanctions against South Africa must give special consideration to its possible effects on South Africa's neighbours which are dependent on oil supplies from or through the republic. Botswana, Lesotho, Namibia and Swaziland are particularly vulnerable to South Africa's retaliatory measures. However, arrangements could be made to get alternative supplies for these countries from neighbouring countries like Angola and Mozambique which already export refined oil products, and also from Zambia. This would involve airlifts of supplies which might be expensive. Such airlifts, though, would not be technically as problematic as the airlift of oil to Zambia immediately after Rhodesia's Unilateral Declaration of Independence.[37] Distances are much shorter and the oil consumption of these countries generally lower.

Notes: Chapter 11

1   *New York Times*, 25 June 1960.
2   For a study of sanctions against Rhodesia, see Johan Galtung, 'On the effects of international economic sanctions, with examples from the case of Rhodesia', *World Politics*, vol. XIX, no. 3 (April 1967), pp. 378–416; and P. Wallensteen, *A Study of Economic Sanctions* (Uppsala: Scandinavian Institute of African Studies, 1968).
3   See, for instance, Richard B. Lillich, *Economic Coercion and the New International Economic Order* (Charlottesville, Va: Michie, 1976); and William Schaneider, *Food, Foreign Policy and Raw Materials Cartels* (New York: Crane, Russak, 1976).
4   *African Research Bulletin (ARB)* (Economic and Financial series), 15 November–14 December 1973, p. 2936.
5   *Daily News* (Dar es Salaam), 23 November 1973.
6   *British Broadcasting Corporation Summary of World Broadcasts*, Pt IV ME/445/B/3, 24 November 1973.

7 *The Resolutions of the Sixth Arab Summit Conference Held in Algeria from 26th to 28th November 1973* (Cairo: Arab League, n.d.).

8 OAU CM/Res. 731 (XXXIII), July 1979.

9 Labour strikes against the late Shah of Iran's rule in December 1978 disrupted the Iranian economy and all oil exports to South Africa were cut. The new revolutionary government banned oil sales to South Africa when production was resumed in February 1979.

10 *The Outlook for Energy in South Africa: A Report for a Subsidiary Committee of the Prime Minister's Planning Advisory Council* (Pretoria: Republic of South Africa Department of Planning and the Environment, 1977), p. 83.

11 'Oil sanctions against South Africa', *Fact Sheet*, Sanctions Working Group (n.d.); mimeo, p. 2.

12 ibid., pp. 1–2.

13 *The Outlook for Energy in South Africa*, op. cit., p. xxxiv. See also 'Oil sanctions against South Africa', op. cit., p. 1. For data on 1975–6, see African National Congress of South Africa (ANC), 'Fueling apartheid', *Notes and Documents*, 13/80 (New York: United Nations Center against Apartheid, April 1980), p. 2.

14 This incident was revealed in a UN Center against Apartheid's commissioned study by Bernard Rivers and Martin Bailey; the main conclusions of the study are provided in *Sunday Times* (London), 11 June 1978.

15 *World Energy Supplies 1971–75* (New York: United Nations Department of Economic and Social Affairs, 1977), p. 39.

16 Fereidun Fesharki, *Development of the Iranian Oil Industry: International and Domestic Aspects* (New York: Praeger, 1976), p. 205.

17 Martin Bailey and Bernard Rivers, 'Oil sanctions against South Africa', *Notes and Documents*, 12/78 (New York: United Nations Center against Apartheid, June 1978), pp. 8b, 8c.

18 *New York Times*, 25 June 1979.

19 Sanctions Working Group, 'Oil – a weapon against apartheid', International Seminar on an Oil Embargo against South Africa, Amsterdam, Holland, March 1980, p. 26.

20 *Journal of Commerce* (New York), 21 March 1979.

21 For further details on Salem, see 'How South Africa obtains illegal supplies of oil. A case study: SS *Salem* (ex-*South Sun*)', Sanctions Working Group, op. cit. (August 1980). See also *Daily Telegraph* (London), 1 February 1980.

22 See 'How South Africa obtains illegal supplies of oil', op. cit., p. 4.

23 For a copy of correspondence between Owen and Carrington, see Sanctions Working Group, op. cit., pp. 72, 74–5.

24 Martin Bailey, 'Oil sanctions: South African's weak-link', *Notes and Documents* 15/80 (New York: United Nations Center against Apartheid, April 1980), p. 6.

25 OAU CM/1042 (XXXV), p. 3.

26 OAU CM/1042 (XXXV), p. 19.

27 OAU CM/1042 (XXXV), p. 21.

28 For details, see 'Oil – a weapon against apartheid', op. cit., pp. 78–9.

29 *Rand Daily Mail* (Johannesburg), 5 March 1974.

30 *Financial Mail* (Johannesburg), 22 July 1977.

31 For details, see ANC, pp. 4–5.

32 Bailey, 'Oil sanctions', op. cit., p. 8.

33 See Sanctions Working Group, 'Implementing an effective oil embargo against South Africa: the current situation' (New York: United Nations Center against Apartheid, August 1980), p. 3.
34 ibid., pp. 1–2.
35 Bailey and Rivers, op. cit., p. 11.
36 Bailey, 'Oil sanctions', op. cit., p. 8.
37 For details, see Martin Bailey, *Oilgate: The Sanctions Scandal* (London: Coronet, 1979), p. 143.

12

South Africa: White Power and the Regional Military-Industrial Complex

TIMOTHY M. SHAW and
EDWARD LEPPAN

The security policy of the present South African regime is inseparable from the question of apartheid and white control over the state. Because the established minority defines the 'national' interests in terms of its own survival and affluence, the threat to its dominance is internal as well as external, with transnational links existing between these twin sources of challenge. The essentially white armed forces have been used, therefore, as a means of domestic oppression as well as regional aggression; they have suppressed internal resistance by the black majority as well as external infiltration on behalf of this majority. Moreover, the armed forces have served to reinforce South Africa's claims to regional dominance in several issue areas: industrial, infrastructural and interactive as well as strategic.

The white regime exists, then, in an antagonistic relationship towards most of its neighbours and towards most of its own population. The (white) South African state seeks to maintain its hegemony over the (largely black) national and regional populations. Containing this antagonism is the primary purpose of its security policy.

The South and Southern African situations are not simply cases of racial conflict; other forms of social inequality reinforce the racial divide. Nevertheless, the racial aspect of the situation is most visible and salient. Both sides have appealed for racial solidarity and support; the (white) South African state to its 'kith and kin' (mainly in Europe and North America) and the (black) South African nation to 'pan-

Africanism' (primarily among the blacks of Africa and the USA). National security has also been simplistically defined in racial terms: the defence of white interests vs black demands.

Given the salience of race as an international issue, the South African situation has implications outside the territory and the region. The relationships and results of the local conflict impact upon race relations in a variety of countries. Any appeal to race as a basis of political support in the region is likely to intensify general racial awareness and divisiveness. This is especially so in the case of South Africa, because of the resources and riches that are at stake.[1]

(1)   South Africa in Comparative Perspective: Semi-Industrialisation in the Semi-Periphery

South Africa's special position as a relatively advantaged part of the semi-periphery has been based on its strategic capabilities, as well as on its economic resources and industrial capacities.[2] Its 'subimperial' role in Southern Africa – a regional 'policeman' on behalf of international, essentially Western, interests – has historic roots; the South African state has long attempted to carve out its own 'sphere of influence'.[3] The determination of its white, especially Afrikaner, settlers to gain a special place in the sun generated a certain ambivalence towards the British Empire, expressed most forcefully by Boer resistance to and desertions from the imperial army in two world wars.

This anti-colonial strand in settler ideology led not only to a successful demand for self-government (in 1923) and for republican status (in 1961) – the political dimension of decolonisation – but also to determination to achieve a high level of economic growth and autonomy. The ability of local capitalism to realise a degree of independence from the British economic empire – an underlying cause according to J. A. Hobson of the Boer War itself – has been reflected in the relative advance of industrialisation in South Africa.[4] This quest has been facilitated, of course, by South Africa's rich reserve of minerals – initially diamonds and gold but then coal, iron ore, copper and a multitude of other ores. But the presence of a national as well as a comprador bourgeoisie meant that these have been increasingly processed locally, rather than externally. Furthermore, the combination of two world wars with an intervening global recession produced appropriate conditions for the rise of South African capitalism within the world system. And after the political victory of the National Party in 1948, the further development of local industrialisation became associated with the advance of Afrikaner as opposed to transnational capitalism; a distinctive aspect of the national military-industrial complex, identified below.

There are two important limits to the industrial (and hence strategic) potential of South Africa, however; hence, the notion of semi-industrialisation within the semi-periphery. The first limit is 'natural', or historical: South Africa has developed outside the industrial metropolitan centres of the world system and so its economic progress and potential are constrained by the rate and mode of production prevailing in these centres. The second limit is 'artificial', but also historical: South Africa's economic growth is restricted by the highly uneven distribution of investment and income based on the tenets of apartheid.[5] And apartheid also limits South Africa's growth by restricting its regional market artificially; a majority-ruled South Africa would not face the political barriers to trade in the continent as these presently exist outside its increasingly narrow 'co-prosperity sphere'. Hence, the present restrictions on South Africa's domination as a semi-peripheral state with semi-industrial characteristics.

(2) Challenges to Regional Co-operation and Conflict

It is at this crucial, regional level that intra- and interstate linkages are so salient. Apartheid not only constrains the success of any outward-looking foreign policy; it also stimulates the interrelated internal and international 'challenges' to which the armed forces are a response. Patterns of interaction, dominance and threat are concentrated at this intermediate level.[6]

South Africa's preoccupations have become increasingly regional in scope: economic integration and strategic defence. But behind the reluctance of neighbouring states to accept its offers of regional exchange and non-aggression lie alternative opportunities for trade and military aid. Southern Africa is the focus of several transnational coalitions of African and extra-African actors, both state and non-state. These have begun to provide alternative forms of regional co-operation – other than dependence on South Africa – based on relations among political and economic equals, as well as strategic support for both guerrilla groups and front line states. They advocated rapid progress towards majority rule, whereas the established status quo grouping centred on South Africa itself is resistant to any such transition. The former is a component of the broader Third World grouping, whereas the latter suffers increasingly from general isolation in world politics.[7]

The challenges to white power's seeming invincibility have intensified from the mid-1970s onwards. The collapse of the Portuguese Empire in 1974 after protracted guerrilla struggles in its African colonies along with the OPEC-induced energy crisis shattered the myths of racist supremacy. The change of government in Mozambique and the civil war in Angola signified the fall of the first tier of 'dominoes' in the region, leaving the second tier of Namibia and Zimbabwe vulnerable. And the transition from Rhodesia to Zimbabwe signified the collapse of the 'unholy alliance'. The rapid rise in the price of oil, combined with recession in the advanced industrialised states, induced stagflation in South Africa as well as elsewhere and revealed the apartheid republic's continuing reliance on external exchange. The only silver-lining for South Africa was the almost simultaneous, rapid rise in the international price of its one inflation hedge: gold.

So the essential assumption under which postwar Western and other policies were framed – namely, the stability of white power in South Africa in particular and Southern Africa in general – was inoperative by the end of the 1970s. South African perceptions and policies were also fundamentally challenged by the Arab oil embargo, by the tightening Western arms embargo, by the Angolan civil war, by the ZANU victory in Zimbabwe and by a growing threat of economic as well as diplomatic isolation and sanctions.

Changes in the international environment as well as in internal society have contributed, then, to a growing re-evaluation of the regime's policy choices and constraints particularly as they relate to security and strategy. From the point of view of South Africa's leadership, the world has become a much less friendly place over the past two decades: the 'wind of change' for decolonisation has generated some 100 new states that are united by few things other than opposition to apartheid.

Moreover, the last five years have seen the political victory of independence in the Third World transformed at times into new forms of economic demand and activism. The consequent economic insistence and instability have been felt intensely in a

South Africa that has coal but no oil and is very vulnerable not only to international economic threats, but also to external economic cycles. And these political and economic challenges have been reinforced by a growing sense of strategic insecurity and isolation.

Hence, the need for South Africa's embattled regime to re-evaluate its military, as well as its political and economic policies. The implications of this re-evaluation have been intensified, moreover, because of their entanglement in a broader, ongoing debate between *verkrampte* and *verligte* fractions over whether to define and defend apartheid in narrow classical or broader revisionist terms respectively. In turn, these choices relate to the very definition of a strategic threat. The former approach tends to view all and any challenges to a restricted old-fashioned definition of apartheid (including the *verlig* one) as verging on treason: blanket declarations of a 'communist' threat serve to legitimise highly repressive responses to any form of disagreement let alone deviance. On the other hand, the latter *verlig* group (that with which the current Prime Minister, P. W. Botha, at times seems to identify) recognises that apartheid produces intolerance on both sides; so it has come to advocate a political rather than a military response to African and other demands.

The intensity of the debate over alternative reactions to black power and protest is reflective of the growing insecurity and uncertainty of the regime. The shocks of the 1970s have undermined the confidence of the white state to a much greater extent than Sharpeville in the 1960s. Indeed, Colin Legum has pointed to 1977 as a significant turning-point: 'the year in which the Republic's façade of internal stability was finally shattered; it marked the beginning of a new and sharper confrontation between entrenched white power and its black challengers; and it shook Western political and economic confidence in the Republic's ability to maintain its existing system.'[8] The 1976–7 risings in Soweto increased support for the Black Consciousness movement. They led to the banning of all major black organisations, leaders and newspapers, and to the assassination by the security forces of Steve Biko: 'The extensive bannings, arrests and other forms of repression predictably served only to widen the racial cleavage, which is the rotting core of South African society.'[9] This cleavage increased further in the subsequent and continuing waves of bannings and arrests, symbolised by the mid-1980 wave of popular uprisings and tactical sabotage.

(3) State Capitalism and White Power: the National Bourgeoisie

The current debate within the South African state about how to reassert and maintain its hegemony is a reflection of the emergence of different factions within the local bourgeoisie as well as of the seriousness of the threat to it. Unlike the situation in the periphery, much of the bourgeoisie in South Africa, as in other parts of the semi-periphery, is increasingly national in form, rather than transnational or comprador. This means that it is more autonomous but also more vulnerable; independent but isolated.

The South African bourgeoisie, especially its Afrikaner component, has always been ambivalent towards transnational, especially British, capital. The postwar development of state capitalism enabled it to maximise its autonomy, but subsequent shocks to South Africa's stability have made external associates increasingly wary of too close an association with apartheid. Afrikanerdom and instability have together made Western disengagement more likely in both financial and institutional terms. The debate over the future of apartheid is increasingly national rather than international, as noted below.

So this *verkrampte–verligte* dispute in South Africa takes place within as well as outside the regime and may even reflect a continuing debate inside the secret confines of the Broederbond, the Afrikaner's own exclusive organisation. Those ministries, institutions and individuals most closely associated with external or internal security tend to advocate a hardline, military response to any apparent challenges to regime authority or the political order. By contrast, those organisations or decision-makers more associated with international affairs, exchange, or image are concerned to respond cautiously and politically to opposition, recognising the legitimacy of some of the resistance to at least the uglier faces of apartheid. They also have come to recognise the impossibility as well as counterproductivity of excessive repression.

In part, the *verkrampte–verligte* divergence over perceptions and policies is related to the alternative definitions of the state and nation already discussed. The *verkramptes* are preoccupied with preserving the identity and integrity of the (white) *volk* against internal (industrialisation, modernisation and secularisation) as well as external threats (decadence and softness as well as 'communism'). By contrast, the *verligtes* have a less exclusive notion of state as nation, recognising that non-Afrikaners of various races have a claim to and interest in South Africa as well as the Afrikaners. They are prepared, therefore, for various forms of coalition or decentralisation to bring more people into the 'nation state' so as to minimise the strategic threats; for them, the issue is not simply one of race. They do not define all extra-Afrikaner pressures as subversive or challenging; rather, they seek to head off such resistance by co-opting elements in other races and classes into the state's orbit.

So while the *verkramptes* are inclined to retreat into the *laager* to defend their nation by military means, the *verligtes* are prepared to deflect opposition by encouraging economic and infrastructural links with neighbouring states – a constellation of countries – as well as by advocating diverse forms of domestic devolution: from confederalism and federalism to grand apartheid and partition. The latter's outward-looking preferences would tend to relegate exclusively strategic threats and responses to a lower priority than the former.

(4) Subimperialism and Interimperialist Rivalries

In part, the *verligte–verkrampte* debate is about different definitions of South Africa's role in the semi-periphery: is its dominance to be expressed in military and/or economic, and/or political terms? The *verligtes* have tended to be products of and to accept the implications of semi-industrialisation; they now seek to maximise the benefits of such a process to South Africa and, perhaps, to themselves. By contrast, the *verkramptes*, because they are worried about modernisation and secularisation, emphasise strategic rather than economic options and display greater confidence in national rather than regional solutions.

The former fraction sees subimperialism in terms of economic outreach and advantage, whereas the latter sees it as military concentration and defence. And whereas both groups are anti-colonial (albeit for different reasons – economic and political respectively), the *verligtes* are prepared to come to terms with and possibly to absorb African nationalist sentiments, whereas the *verkramptes* (despite their own national struggles) are more rigidly anti-nationalist, seeing it as a variant of 'communism'. Decolonisation has, therefore, been accepted and even welcomed by the former but opposed and even feared by the latter.

Despite the strand of anti-imperialism in Afrikanerdom, the postwar period of decolonisation has been seen as one posing a growing threat to the white state. Fearfulness about African nationalism has grown because of its transnational implications – its impact on South Africa's own black population and because of its international associations – its alleged links with communist states. Apprehension has intensified in two ways: (*a*) regionally, with the advent of independent states on South Africa's own borders; and (*b*) globally, with the difficulties of the second half of the 1970s brought about by Third World economic demands.

The global recession of the mid-1970s onwards has increased the vulnerability of the South African economy. Not only is it reliant on the continued flow of high-price oil from the international oil market via Rotterdam; but also it is increasingly dependent (*a*) on the exportation of primary products rather than manufactured goods, and (*b*) on the flow of external loans rather than foreign investment. The mining and export of coal has joined that of gold, diamonds and uranium as a major source of foreign exchange earnings. With continuing price increases for both gold exports and oil imports, South Africa's balance of trade is increasingly dominated by the (indirect) exchange of gold for oil, two essential ingredients in the contemporary global political economy.

Interrelated and unpredictable changes in the global economy have tended to reinforce the *laager* mentality of concentrating on proven resources and tactics and to undermine the 'outward-looking' posture of the *verligtes*.[10] The latter retain confidence in the regional opportunities afforded by semi-industrialisation and decolonisation. On the other hand, the *verkramptes* feel isolated and alienated by contemporary trends. While hitherto they wanted South Africa to keep its distance from the West – and still hint at neutralism and isolationism as strategies – they are now afraid of its pariah status, one that has grown in the second half of the 1970s:

> While increasing pressures on the one hand, the West has steadily distanced itself from South Africa on the other, leaving the white minority feeling abandoned by its traditional friends and isolated at the most difficult hour in its history. This threat

of isolation was acutely felt in 1977 when the possibility of economic sanctions came to be accepted as very real, especially after the Security Council's decision in November 1977 to make the arms embargo mandatory.[11]

While the *verkramptes* have in general neither recognised nor exploited the global trend towards multipolarity because of their paranoia about 'communism', the *verligtes* have been prepared to accept and even to take advantage of it. As revealed by 'Muldergate' and other leaks, some South African leaders have made series of attempts to break out of their enforced isolation by (*a*) developing links with other pariah states (for example, Israel and Taiwan); (*b*) suggesting relations with other semi-peripheral states, particularly in Latin America (for example, Brazil and Argentina); (*c*) forging ties with several African states (for example, Ivory Coast and Zambia); and (*d*) exploiting interimperial rivalries and opening discussions with apparently antagonistic states (for example, tacit alliances with China vs the Soviet Union and trade links with Japan). Perhaps the most bizarre form of adaptation to a changing environment was South Africa's threat, in a fit of pique, to become neutral or non-aligned if the West refused to revive a meaningful military association. But flawed attempts at regional détente and dialogue are nevertheless indicative of the potential for turning contemporary trends to advantage in Africa and elsewhere if flair and creativity were to be applied consistently.

(5) South Africa from a Western Perspective

Despite the West's declaratory intent of distancing itself from South Africa, it has been continually forced back into relying on the subimperial state's services for diplomatic, strategic and resource reasons. And an increasingly isolated and embattled South African state has been eager to exploit the West's need for it. The problematics of Western disengagement have been especially welcome (particularly by the *verligtes*) in a period of international instability and hostility, when sanctions are once again a live issue.[12]

The official Western policy of putting pressure on South Africa to change dates back to Henry Kissinger's Lusaka speech of 1976; but it intensified with the installation of the Carter administration in 1977 and the activities of America's Andy Young and Britain's David Owen. The re-evaluation of

US, EEC and other OECD states' policies towards the region[13] has continued, despite the election of Mrs Thatcher's Tory government to power in Britain, in 1979. However, despite the continued pressures on (and often of) transnationals to disengage, trade between the West and South Africa has continued to grow. Investment and profitability have both tended to decrease but Western banking consortia are once again willing, if not so eager, to lend considerable sums to South Africa's parastatals.

The continued, albeit modified, Western association with apartheid is in part an extension of traditional transnational and intergovernmental patterns. It also reflects the calculations and interests of at least some Western actors over South Africa's diplomatic, strategic and resource capacities; that is, its position within the semi-periphery. First, given South Africa's regional dominance – particularly its military presence and economic interest – its involvement in diplomatic efforts to bring change to Namibia and Zimbabwe was perhaps inevitable, even Africa's front line states have recognised this. However, South Africa has been able to extract a price for its ambiguous role in negotiating with the multilateral five-power 'contact group' (over Namibia) and bilateral Anglo-American team (over Zimbabwe); the price has included no economic sanctions, continued oil and further consultation.

Secondly, given Western concern about the supply and shipment of its oil as well as about the global activities of the Russian navy, the Cape route continues to figure in NATO states' calculations. Most of the oil from the Gulf to Europe comes around the Cape and, with the advent of very large crude carriers, will continue to do so. Furthermore, the growing activities of the Russian navy in the Indian Ocean and elsewhere have revived interest in the strategic importance of the Cape, despite multipolarity and nuclear stalemate.[14]

And thirdly, in an era of apprehension about resource depletion, Western dependence on South Africa's mineral cornucopia has increased. In addition to financially crucial gold, South Africa is a major supplier to the West of uranium and chromium, manganese and platinum. Disruption of supply and/or price would seriously affect Western financial, metal and transportation industries.[15] It is not clear, of course, whether change in South Africa itself would really disturb such Western resource interests; there is no reason to assume that any new regime would collaborate with the USSR to upset Western supplies. But the South African leadership continues to raise this possibility to gain support in Western strategic, resource and financial circles. Nevertheless, despite continued transnational interaction, Western governments have recalculated their interests and have revised regional scenarios and come to distance themselves somewhat from apartheid. Paradoxically, however, this Western response has only served to intensify the apprehensions of the South African state (particularly its *verkrampte* elements), resulting in greater security expenditure, preparedness and repression in the short term.

(6)   White Security and the Military-Industrial Complex

In addition to being isolated internationally, South Africa's armed forces increasingly face a combination of internal as well as external military threats. They have resorted to escalating levels of repression in an attempt to contain the growing activities of nationalist movements within as well as around the country. So aside from the continual arrest of pass-law offenders and the containment of both general and apartheid-based criminality, they now have to deal with guerrilla activities inside South Africa itself. Across the borders South Africa's armed forces have resorted to a variety of tactics to harass the liberation movements and their hosts. Inside its territory they now have to deal with border raids and with urban terrorism.

South Africa is peculiarly vulnerable to both types of attack. Not only because more than three-quarters of its population is alienated by the nature of its regime, but also because its borders are very long and its domestic infrastructure relatively sophisticated and fragile. Furthermore, black workers are particularly central in any developing confrontation: they are urban and exploited yet crucial to the white-run economy. Moreover, the recent recession has increased unemployment levels for blacks dramatically. Given the relatively high level of industrialisation in South Africa, class-consciousness among both black and white workers is considerable. Such workers constitute the revolutionary potential rather than the repressed peasantry with its ethnic identity and rural location.[16] Black workers are most resistant to the Bantustan scheme and were at the core of unrest in Durban, Soweto and other cities during the 1970s.

Urban-guerrilla warfare is particularly threatening to South

Africa's mining and manufacturing industries. The growing military-industrial complex is especially vulnerable to worker sabotage and disruption; and multinational corporate confidence has already worn thin. The attacks on Afrikaner banks, police stations and oil-from-coal plants in 1980 are indicative of the growing sophistication, sensitivity and success of the nationalists inside South Africa. The local police state has never been sufficiently comprehensive to repress successfully all forms of resistance and non-cooperation. Moreover, while the armed forces have considerable reserves, their recruitment potential is limited artificially by apartheid's rules and logic.

South African forces would be unlikely to contain successfully a simultaneous internal as well as external conflict; hence, the attempt to fence, clear and mine border areas, as well as to divide urban and rural African communities. The avoidance of such a threatening situation – of external attack and internal uprising – has been a major feature of the regime's strategic planning and posturing. The demise of the neighbouring Smith regime in such circumstances of sustained cross-border and domestic challenges has served to reinforce the Botha government's determination to avoid a similar circumstance. Soweto took time to contain, despite the regime's apparent omnipresence and invincibility; a simultaneous border incursion might have seriously undermined its ability to contain the unrest. South Africa's dealings with Mugabe's Zimbabwe are reflective of its renewed fear of cross-border and internal threats.

Given the pervasiveness of the challenges to the South African state both domestically and externally, and given the continued danger of a simple race conflict, the regime has belatedly attempted to broaden the basis of its political support and military recruitment somewhat by (a) proposing several complex constitutional structures, and (b) selectively and cautiously opening the military as well as the police to non-white recruits. This dual response has proceeded furthest in the context of the Bantustan scheme under which South African officers have begun to train Africans in the several homeland militia. The related ploys of creating racial 'parliaments' and 'councils' and of recruiting non-whites into the army, especially in South-West Africa/Namibia, represent belated and apparently futile attempts to divide and divert black opinion away from automatic opposition.

Given the overwhelmingly repressive nature of the regime

for most of the population, any threat to it is seen in military as well as in political terms; and any response to such a threat is conceived in strategic as well as constitutional dimensions. In an unrepresentative state structure that is founded essentially on the threat of force any opposition necessarily involves a threat of force too. Moreover, the latter is usually seen to contain such a threat by the regime in question. The issue of potential military response to opposition is pervasive in South African politics and planning, an essential aspect of the defence of white power and privilege. Yet while coercive resources by themselves are not enough, the South African state (perhaps under *verkrampte* rather than *verligte* influences) still seems to rely on and takes comfort from them rather than confront the fundamental cause of opposition – *apartheid*. This rather blind determination continues despite the difficulties of containing Soweto and subsequent uprisings:

The murder of Steve Biko by security police on 12 September 1977 and the total repression of the Black Consciousness movement and its white allies a month later underline two realities about the present situation: the overwhelming physical power still held by the defenders of white supremacy, and the fear felt by these powerful forces of the putative strength of a Black Consciousness movement.[17]

Because South Africa's military has always been racially restricted, only some 4 out of the country's 28 million population have been eligible for recruitment. Military service is compulsory for white males, the period having been gradually extended during the decade to the present twenty-four months requirement. Given the appearance of new external and internal threats, total military expenditure peaked in the mid-1970s; it is currently $2·1 billion out of a GNP of $43·8 billion, or $75 per head. This is 5 per cent of GNP and 20 per cent of government spending. According to Colin Legum, 'rising defence expenditure has put South Africa into the top league of the world's arms spenders: only the US and UK spend more of GNP on defence than South Africa'.[18]

South Africa had the largest and best-equipped military in Africa for many years.[19] But changes in the economic fortune or strategic importance of states like Algeria, Egypt, Libya and Nigeria have eroded its numerical supremacy. Nevertheless, its military capabilities are still considerable although no longer ranked first on the continent, except perhaps in terms of maintenance and preparedness.[20]

Like other newly industrialising countries (NICs), South Africa is developing its own (regional) military-industrial complex;[21] it is particularly advanced in the production of airframes, armoured fighting vehicles and enriched uranium. Its weapons' manufacturing sophistication has increased considerably over the past decade, aided by technical assistance from Italy, France, Britain, West Germany and Israel in particular, the latter pair being especially implicated in the nuclear field.[22] The South African state can now build for itself Mirage jets under licence and local jets (Impala) and turboprops (Bosbok and Kudu), including engines, armaments and avionics. It is also able to manufacture increasingly heavy armoured vehicles (Eland, Hippo and Rhino), including its own version of modern impregnable laminated armour. Furthermore, South Africa has begun to co-produce missiles under French or Israeli licence and to build naval hulls of Israeli Reshef design; together with its nuclear capability, these give it considerable military muscle throughout the region. Its armaments industry is now as sophisticated as that in other NICs like Brazil or India, but it is less autonomous, being dependent still on the continued flow of Western technology and technicians.[23]

This development of a regional military-industrial complex is related, first, to South Africa's perceived defence requirements, and secondly, to the growth of Afrikaner capitalism. After the Second World War, in an increasingly hostile international environment, the South African regime began to recognise the need to deal with conventional as well as guerrilla attack and to enhance its self-reliance in terms of military production and preparedness. In an era of decolonisation and détente, the apartheid republic's 'military preparations aim . . . at providing for counterinsurgency warfare of short and long duration, and for conventional war-making ability'.[24] The realisation of this capability required, however, a more fundamental shift in political economy away from reliance on transnational capitalism and supplies and towards national, especially Afrikaner, capitalism and material.

The growth of state capitalism has had both economic and strategic implications: state support for parastatals and other Afrikaner-dominated institutions helped to rectify the English–Afrikaans imbalance while advancing national security interests. The defence establishment is linked, then, not only to the Nationalist Party and the Broederbond, but also to major state and private enterprises such as the South African

Arms Corporation (ARMSCOR), the steel corporation (ISCOR) and the oil-from-coal plants (SASOL), as well as to the Anglo-American Corporation and Barclays and Standard Banks: 'The republic's military power is thus enhanced by a substantial industrial and logistic infrastructure on a scale that has been attained nowhere else in Africa.'[25]

So this local military-industrial complex has industrial technological and financial implications, as well as serving as a vehicle for Afrikaner economic advancement. In the industrial sector South Africa's iron and steel, chemical transportation and electrical engineering capacities all have military aspects and uses: ISCOR and AECI provide the basic ingredients for arms and ammunition manufacture and the mining and refining industry produces increasingly sophisticated alloys for aircraft and armoured personnel-carrier production. The energy, nuclear and computer fields bridge the gap between industrial and technological capacity. South Africa's oil-from-coal plants (SASOL), uranium-enrichment capability (Uranium Enrichment Corporation, UCOR) and computer branch plants (ICL) all enhance its strategic and bargaining strengths; hence, the symbolism and significance of the ANC attacks on SASOL in mid-1980. Gann and Duignan conclude that:

> The defence complex, including ARMSCOR with its subsidiary arms factories, is one of the country's most advanced technical organisations, one that is engaged in manufacturing, operating and maintaining a wide range of highly sophisticated equipment. About 45% of defence expenditures goes to internal development . . . Defence and defence-related industries thus have a considerable impact on the South African economy . . . South Africa's industrial infrastructure enabled the country to emphasise self-sufficiency in arms production and improvement in its ability to withstand foreign economic pressure.[26]

This military-industrial complex is central, then, to South Africa's quest for economic as well as military security in a hostile environment; and it serves, in addition, to enhance Afrikaner economic power. Some 75 per cent of the state's military requirements can now be produced locally. And just as South Africa's mining houses have achieved a high level of national control and autonomy, so its military-industrial complex is increasingly indigenous in form. The foundations of both, however, were initially laid through co-operation with transnational financial, industrial and technological corporations.[27]

As South Africa's own productive capability has grown and as the arms embargo has become more comprehensive, so the multinational corporation has come to provide technology and finance rather than production or investment; this is particularly so for multinational oil and banking consortia, with their links to parastatals like SASOL, ARMSCOR and ESCOM. As Ann Seidman and Neva Makgetla conclude in a study for the UN:

> Transnational corporations play a key role in providing the hardware and finance for South Africa's military-industrial complex. Their investments in advanced machinery and equipment in South Africa itself creates the industrial infrastructure to enable the South African regime to produce about 75% of its own military needs. In addition, their investments facilitate the import of the parts and materials required to make that production possible. Their international linkages provide the channels through which South Africa continues to import the military machinery and equipment which its own industry cannot produce. Transnational corporate banks provide the essential financial contacts to enable the South African regime to finance its growing domestic and international military purchases.[28]

But even a successful and sophisticated military-industrial complex cannot by itself defend apartheid forever, unless political and economic transformations are envisaged and executed.

(7)   Resources and Reserves: the White Nation's Preparation for War

Given the isolation and opposition that apartheid attracts, the white nation has had to employ all and any support it can (given the limits of its ideology) to defend its power and privilege within the state. While its manpower reserves are artificially limited by racism, its mineral resources are substantial and readily mobilised to blunt threatening external policies. The regime continues to attempt to camouflage its strategic vulnerabilities by emphasising its military strengths.

South Africa's regular armed forces consist of some 125,000 men (more than double the number of five years ago) plus another 135,000 in the commandos, a paramilitary force for local defence and counterinsurgency operations. Its regular reserves consist of a quarter of a million in the Citizen Force, with a total of just under half a million in the potential pool of reserves. The Permanent and Citizen Forces train and serve together, especially on border duty, and are supported by the airforce's considerable logistical and tactical capabilities. The armed forces are now largely Afrikaans-speaking and have problems in keeping trained personnel. Nevertheless, Gann and Duignan still project the orthodox wisdom about the resilience of white power:

> The South African Defence Force reflects the strengths and weaknesses of the country's white society at large. It contains a high proportion of men with developed technical skill. South Africans can thus maintain and deploy sophisticated modern equipment . . . The Army is essentially the white electorate in arms, so the country does not face military coups d'état . . . The army is highly motivated, and is integrated into European society.[29]

As threats to the regime appear within as well as outside the country, so the relationship between the armed and police forces has become closer. The latter is somewhat more multiracial than the military, over a quarter of its 60,000 men being African, reflecting the need to maintain law and order in the black 'locations', as well as in the 'white' cities. Its white members are largely Afrikaners; it exists to implement apartheid, as well as prosecute orthodox crime. Gann and Duignan point to its distinctive role in the apartheid system: 'It is a semimilitary body, and is regarded as the "first line of defence in the event of internal unrest".'[30]

The increase in the incidence and intensity of anti-regime activity in the 1970s has turned South Africa into something of an armed camp. The white minority is increasingly an armed and paranoid one, fearful of and training for more widespread black opposition. The escalating threat of insurgency in both border and urban areas is revealed in the growing numbers of arrests and trials for bomb blasts and other violent attacks: 'There were 45 trials under the 1967 Terrorism Act in 1977 – more than double the all-time record of the previous year.'[31] The combination of continuing internal and external demands has led, belatedly, to marginal reforms in racial, labour, property and other regulations. But white power and privilege remain determined not to abandon their special status easily or before the violence has escalated considerably from its present level.[32]

Given the regime's intransigent advocacy of apartheid and continued white support for its stance – which seems to oppose current *verligte* moves – almost any strategy designed to protect its power and privilege is acceptable to its single constituency. With the intensification of internal and external opposition, defence of apartheid has come to mean 'total war'. The post-Portuguese coup period has been characterised by a reconsideration of South Africa's defence strategy; the forced retreat into the *laager* has been accompanied by a re-evaluation of strategic options and plans.[33]

It has been increasingly recognised by South Africa's political and military leadership that white affluence can only be protected through a 'total national strategy' because the state is already at war. In 1977 the Chief of the Defence Force argued, first, 'that every activity of the state must be seen and understood as a function of total war'; and secondly, that planning has to be based on a 'protracted war of low intensity'.[34] The resultant increased military expenditure and service on, for instance, clearing and patrolling border areas and increasing the period of conscription, has long-term implications for democracy as well as affluence even within the white community.

The choice between racial exclusiveness and democratic values has become finer still in the case of expanding police and security activities.[35] The excesses of 'Muldergate' are only one special instance of growing regime arbitrariness and authoritarianism in its defence of apartheid. However, most whites accept limited freedoms as the price of affluence and stability. Those whites who do not have largely gone into exile already; the blacks have had little choice to date but to accept regime repression. The debate over strategic alternatives is limited, then, to the *verligte–verkrampte* split within the white community[36] (and Vorster's outward-looking policy and Botha's de-apartheid and constellation proposals have cost them white electoral support no matter how marginal the changes proposed). Wider choices are not seriously raised or debated. The white perspective is, indeed, a limited one.

(8)   From Regime Oppression to Black Liberation

If the power as well as the perspective of the white regime is increasingly limited, its intransigence has already foreclosed many options for the multiracial opposition. The liberal solution – the 'parliamentary option' – applied elsewhere on the continent was early excluded by the settlers. Rather, their grim clinging to power and privilege has precluded a parliamentary resolution to South Africa's inequalities. Instead, the nationalist movements have been compelled to match coercion with violence, resulting in an exponentially escalating battle for freedom.[37]

The establishment of apartheid structures since 1948 and the exclusion of African nationalism as well as any party with even moderately radical pretensions has forced the opposition underground and into exile. South African intelligence organisations monitor, subvert and disrupt its activities and constitute the fringe of the South African security machine. This intelligence operation has been active in reporting, misleading and assassinating opposition forces abroad as well as at home. Its preoccupations have lain with the major nationalist parties – the African National Congress (ANC) and the Pan-African Congress (PAC) – as well as with the domestic Black Consciousness Movement – the Black People's Convention (BPC), South African Students' Organisation (SASO) and now the Soweto Civil Association (SCA) and Azanian People's Organisation (AZAPO), as well as Inkatha, the Zulu-based party of Chief Gatsha Buthelezi.

The persistence of black movements despite repeated harassment, bannings and deaths is indicative of continued popular support for their demands and activities: one leadership is identified and contained by the regime only to be replaced by other, usually younger and more radical, cadres. The successes of the liberation movements in neighbouring states – particularly in Mozambique and Zimbabwe – have given courage to South African groups, as well as facilitating their tactical activities. And the difficulties admitted by the South African state in dealing with Soweto and Angola – internal and external security threats – have served to intensify active support for the opposition. With the new fluidity of regional affairs since 1974, the white war machine is no longer invincible; nor is the task of the liberation movements so hopeless.

Instability and black optimism are likely to increase in the 1980s with the advent of independent governments in Zimbabwe and Namibia. The new shape of Southern Africa in the 1980s will require greater flexibility and variety in South African strategic planning. With the advent of black-dominated, and potentially more radical, regimes in

Zimbabwe and Namibia, South Africa has to defend itself from an immediate antagonistic environment. The gradual erosion of white buffer-states through guerrilla struggle and national independence has necessitated a basic reconsideration of defence strategy. Strategic as well as political and economic support for neighbouring white regimes is no longer possible. With the 'fall' of the last white dominoes of the South-West and Rhodesia, South Africa has to defend itself along its own boundary – the Limpopo – not along the more distant Zambezi or Ruvuma rivers. This means not only increased border defence and vigilance, but also covert and airborne strikes into black states; not only into neighbours like Botswana and Mozambique, but also into more distant territories like Angola and Zambia.

A flexible response calls forth tactics such as cross-border raids, strategic bombing operations, subversion, infiltration and support for anti-government guerrillas. Defence of the *laager* involves not only repression and vigilance inside South Africa, but also continued attempts to destabilise, divert and frustrate neighbouring states in their national development and regional liberation.[38] Attacks on roads, railways and bridges in Zambia and Angola, for instance, may be intended to maintain and heighten the dependence of Zambia and Zaire on Southern routes and facilities. The bombing of guerrilla bases is designed to embarrass and humiliate hosts, as well as to eliminate and disorient nationalist fighters.

South Africa's continuing and growing regional militarism may indicate a shift in strategic policy: as it can no longer dominate the subsystem in the political issue area it may attempt to do so in the security sector. This retreat into a strategic, *laager* posture would involve risking its established hegemony over the South African (political) economy. Gutteridge sees this prospect as quite revealing given South Africa's traditional interest in:

> becoming a neo-imperialist power capable of maintaining puppet African governments in the states immediately to the North. Though South Africa might try this if it was really in its interest and power to do so, it is more likely that the strategic rethinking, if that is what it is, is a sign of weakness rather than of strength and that its government would not be running the risks inherent in any steps towards liberalism if they thought there was a practical alternative.[39]

The regime's contradictory postures indicating both

reformist tendencies and reactionary impulses are both indicators of its basic uncertainty and vulnerability. The size of its territory, cost of its defence budget, difficulty in purchasing sophisticated arms, problems in securing a reliable oil supply and sagging morale among white recruits all pose dilemmas for the white nation which a fortress strategy by itself cannot resolve. But Afrikaner nationalism tends to exclude any viable, long-term solution.

The growing prospect of successful resistance to white power has not generated a new realism or pragmatism within the ruling oligarchy thus far. Rather, the debate over strategy has in general been a limited one, about how to resist further black demands, not how to accommodate them. Despite bilateral and multilateral pressures internationally, racial dominance and separateness remain the centrepieces of settler ideology. Most 'reforms' are limited to this restrictive framework – Bantustan 'self-government' for blacks and constitutional consultation for other non-white races. Even the most dramatic internal reforms under consideration – a cantonal arrangement or a spatial partition – do not treat the basic issue of a highly unequal distribution of resources – economic, political and social. And the realignment of white political forces in 1977 making the Progressive Federal Party the official (white) opposition, and proposed reform of trade union and other offensive apartheid legislation in 1979–80, do not really touch such fundamental issues, although they have produced a growing *verkrampte* backlash.[40]

The official doctrine of the South African state is still designed to exclude and exploit the majority of the country's peoples. Given the persistence and intensity of the inequalities, the regime has increasingly had to repress the minority's freedoms as well, in order to safeguard its security and affluence. Liberalism has joined nationalism and communism as a near-treasonable idea. Further intransigence, albeit with improved materiel and strategy, is the dominant response to ANC, ASAPO and Inkatha. The barrenness of the politico-strategic reaction – reflective of continuing *verkrampte* values – is another reason for the inevitability of dramatic change in South Africa.

(9) Beyond the Revolutionary State: Defence in a Post-Apartheid South Africa

South Africa's racial and strategic policies have been intended to prevent revolutionary change whether it be characterised as nationalism or communism. However, repression and industrialisation together form an inflammable mixture. Instead of recognising and responding to the inevitability of change by attempting to co-opt African bourgeois interests in some form of 'neo-colonial' arrangement, the settlers have largely precluded gradualism by opting for separateness and Bantustans rather than assimilation and collaboration.

Now the oft-feared combination of internal explosions and external pressures is all too likely to take place. And the transition when it comes will probably be sudden, violent and fundamental; most black opposition is too well established, sophisticated and radical now to be satisfied with less than a restructuring of South Africa's political economy. And the state's power resources are unlikely to be sufficient to contain such a revolutionary situation. To quote Legum:

> Judged purely in terms of its economic and military strength and the undoubted commitment of white South Africans to using this power to ensure their survival, the Republic's position would seem, if not impregnable, at least fairly secure. But such an evaluation fails to take into account two critical factors: South Africa's long-term dependence on powerful western economic and diplomatic backing, and the system's devastating internal contradictions. Both these factors are likely to be crucial in deciding the Republic's future, the latter in particular.[41]

By contrast, Gann and Duignan restate established myths in overlooking the tensions generated by *apartheid* in a semi-industrial political economy; they concentrate mistakenly on (strategic) capabilities rather than on (societal) contradictions: 'Given the present conditions, hopes for a violent overthrow of the South African system – either by foreign invasion or by internal or external guerrilla assaults – belong in the realm of military fantasy'.[42] The fall of all the region's 'dominoes' other than South Africa makes such apparent 'fantasy' increasingly realistic. Given the inevitability of change, we conclude with a speculative look at military strategy in a post-apartheid state.

Depending on the length and violence of any transition South Africa is likely to remain a semi-industrial country at the semi-periphery after as well as before the realisation of majority rule. Indeed, if income and other resources are redistributed promptly, then the artificial limitations on its economic potential imposed by apartheid will be overcome and its growth facilitated. Moreover, the *raison d'être* of its military-industrial complex would become largely superfluous: white power and privilege would no longer need to be defended and black nationalist movements would no longer need to be suppressed internally or externally. So industrial capacity could be released to satisfy the basic human needs of the majority, rather than protect the super-affluence of the minority. Nevertheless, given the gloominess of trends for most of the continent,[43] South Africa will still have to defend its relative richness and considerable resources against regional demands and external challenges. But these would then be of an 'orthodox' interstate variety, rather than of the pervasive 'transnational' type as at present; they would no longer insist on a fundamental restructuring of the national political economy.

The orientation of a future popular South African government is likely to be Third World rather than Western; it will neither seek association with, nor be rejected by, Western states.[44] Its non-alignment will serve as a partial guarantee of its integrity and its own defence forces will do the rest. It may still play a subimperial role, but this time play it more on behalf of African than of Western interests. And it may come successfully to suggest and sponsor novel forms of regional integration, including a regional defence alliance, of the type long proposed but never consummated by white South African regimes.[45]

A black-ruled South Africa is unlikely to need either a substantial counterinsurgency or a nuclear capability, although internal unrest may continue for some time following the revolution. Rather, its more orthodox defence role and posture will be based on largely traditional defensive resources and reserves, once threats of any white countercoup have been contained. The established military-industrial complex will be restructured to serve a somewhat different purpose, defending the whole state rather than the white state. Then South Africa's view of the world will be transformed as will be its response to any external threat. Popular support for its strategy will be enhanced and new patterns of communication and alliance will be possible, especially at the regional level. And as its definition of military threat will then be largely external rather than transnational, the budget necessary for defence will be reduced. In short, the major problems of opposition, response and resources confronting the present state will be minimised with a change in regime – the possibility of which is the central reason for the contemporary security policy of apartheid. A black-ruled South Africa is likely to have a very different policy compared to that of the present regime, because it will be compatible with rather than opposed to change.[46]

Notes: Chapter 12

An earlier version of this chapter, entitled 'South Africa's security policy in the world system – defence of apartheid', was presented at Symposium on Security Policies of Developing States, University of Illinois, USA, May 1980.

1 See Timothy M. Shaw, 'The military situation and the future of race relations in Southern Africa', in Ali A. Mazrui and Hasu H. Patel (eds), *Africa in World Affairs: The Next Thirty Years* (New York: Third Press, 1973), pp. 37–61, and 'Southern Africa: from detente to deluge?', *Year Book of World Affairs. Vol. 32, 1978* (Boulder, Colo: Westview Press, 1978), pp. 117–38.

2 Indeed, relatively high levels of industrialisation, sophistication and militarisation tend to characterise those states at the semi-periphery like South Africa. See Raimo Vayrynen, 'Economic and military position of the regional power centres', *Journal of Peace Research*, vol. 16, no. 4 (1979), pp. 349–69.

3 See Timothy M. Shaw, 'Kenya and South Africa: "sub-imperialist" states', *Orbis*, vol. 21, no. 2 (Summer 1977), pp. 375–94, and 'International stratification in Africa: sub-imperialism in eastern and southern Africa', *Journal of Southern African Affairs*, vol. 2, no. 2 (April 1977), pp. 145–65.

4 See Kenneth W. Grundy, 'Anti-neo-colonialism in South Africa's foreign policy rhetoric', and Timothy M. Shaw, 'The political economy of technology in Southern Africa', in Timothy M. Shaw and Kenneth A. Heard (eds), *Cooperation and Conflict in Southern Africa: Papers on a Regional Subsystem* (Washington, DC: University Press of America, 1976), pp. 351–79.

5 Moreover, as noted below, apartheid is also uneconomic because it is based on repression; and repression entails considerable 'unproductive' expenditure on the military machine.

6 For useful overviews of relations at this regional level, see Kenneth W. Grundy, 'Regional relations in Southern Africa and the global political economy', in Mark W. DeLancey (ed.), *Aspects of International Relations in Africa* (Bloomington, Ind.: Indiana University African Studies Program, 1979), pp. 90–125, and 'Economic patterns in the new Southern African balance', in Gwendolen M. Carter and Patrick O'Meara (eds), *Southern Africa: The Continuing Crisis* (Bloomington, Ind.: Indiana University Press, 1979), pp. 291–312.

7 See Timothy M. Shaw, 'International organisations and the politics of Southern Africa: towards regional integration or liberation?', *Journal of Southern African Studies*, vol. 3, no. 1 (1976), pp. 1–19.

8 'South Africa', in Colin Legum (ed.), *Africa Contemporary Record:*

Annual Survey and Documents. Vol. 10, 1977–1978 (ACR) (New York: Africana, 1979), p. B860.

9 ibid.

10 See John Seiler, 'South African perspectives and responses to external pressures', *Journal of Modern African Studies*, vol. 13, no. 3 (September 1975), pp. 447–68.

11 Legum, *ACR*, op. cit., 1977–8, p. B861.

12 See, for instance, James Barber and Michael Spicer, 'Sanctions against South Africa – options for the West', *International Affairs*, vol. 55, no. 3 (July 1979), pp. 385–401.

13 See, William J. Foltz, 'US policy toward Southern Africa: economic and strategic constraints', *Political Science Quarterly*, vol. 92, no. 1 (Spring 1977), pp. 47–64; Thomas Karis, 'United States policy toward South Africa', in Carter and O'Meara, op. cit., 313–62; Douglas Anglin, Timothy M. Shaw and Carl Widstrand (eds), *Canada, Scandinavia and Southern Africa* (New York: Africana, 1978); and James H. Mittelman, 'Intervention in Southern Africa: America's investment in apartheid', *Nation*, vol. 228, no. 22 (June 1979), pp. 684–9.

14 For overviews of great power concerns and calculations, see Colin Legum, 'The Soviet Union, China, and the West in Southern Africa', *Foreign Affairs*, vol. 54, no. 4 (July 1976), pp. 745–62, and 'International rivalries in the Southern African conflict', in Carter and O'Meara, op. cit., pp. 3–17. See also Larry W. Bowman, 'Strategic planning in Southern Africa: NATO and the Indian Ocean', Third World Conference, Omaha, Nebraska, USA, November 1978.

15 See Legum, 'International rivalries in the South African conflict', op. cit., p. 7; and L. H. Gann and Peter Duignan, *South Africa: War, Revolution or Peace?* (Stanford, Calif.: Hoover Institution Press, 1978), pp. 15–16.

16 On industrialisation through Western investment as a force for revolutionary change in South Africa, see Ali A. Mazrui, *The African Condition* (New York: Cambridge University Press, 1980), pp. 37–42.

17 Legum, *ACR*, op. cit., 1977–78, p. B864.

18 ibid., p. B915.

19 International Institute for Strategic Studies, *The Military Balance 1979–80* (London: IISS, 1979), pp. 53–4; cf. the somewhat higher figures presented to the US Congress by Sean Gervasi in July 1977, Gann and Duignan, op. cit., pp. 28–9.

20 Gann and Duignan, op. cit., p. 28.

21 See Vayrynen, op. cit.

22 See Abdul S. Minty, 'Military collaboration with South Africa', and Ronald W. Walters, 'Nuclear collaboration with South Africa', *Objective: Justice*, vol. 11, no. 1–2 (Spring–Summer 1979), pp. 28–37; and Zdenek Cervenka and Barbara Rogers, *The Nuclear Axis: Secret Collaboration between West Germany and South Africa* (New York: Times Books, 1978).

23 See Cervenka and Rogers, op. cit.

24 Gann and Duignan, op. cit., p. 42.

25 ibid., p. 25.

26 ibid., p. 26.

27 See Minty, 'Military collaboration with South Africa', and Desaix Myers and David M. Liff, 'South Africa under Botha, the press of business', *Foreign Policy*, 38 (Spring 1980), pp. 143–63.

28 Ann Seidman and Neva Makgetla, 'Transnational corporations and the South Africa military-industrial complex', UN Center against Apartheid, New York, September 1979, 24/79, p. 66.

29 Gann and Duignan, op. cit., p. 32; cf. Mazrui's rejection of Boer distinctiveness: 'there is a lot of foolish romanticism about the Afrikaners' (in *The African Condition*, op. cit., p. 20).

30 Gann and Duignan, op. cit., p. 33.

31 Legum, *ACR*, op. cit., 1977–78, p. B933.

32 Contrast Carter, *Which Way Is South Africa Going?*, with Robert I. Rotberg, *Suffer the Future: Policy Choices in Southern Africa* (Cambridge, Mass.: Harvard University Press, 1980); and Michael Spicer, 'Change in South Africa? Mr. P. W. Botha's strategies and policies', *World Today*, vol. 36, no. 1 (January 1980), pp. 32–40.

33 On this re-evaluation for reasons of resources, setbacks and changes, see William Gutteridge, 'South Africa's defence posture', *World Today*, vol. 36, no. 1 (January 1980), pp. 26–31. South Africa's military commander, General Magnus Malan, now recognises that the struggle 'is only 20% a military struggle; and 80% a struggle for the hearts and minds of the Black population': 'South Africa: Botha's "Brazilian option" or the third phase of apartheid', *Africa*, 105 (May 1980), p. 63.

34 Legum, *ACR*, op. cit., 1977–78, p. B916. On the problems of ensuring the white regime's survival, see Kenneth L. Adelman, 'The strategy of defiance: South Africa', *Comparative Strategy*, vol. 1, no. 1–2 (1978), 33–52.

35 On the origins of the choice, see Albie Sachs, *Justice in South Africa* (Berkeley, Calif.: University of California Press, 1973).

36 Compare Robert I. Rotberg, 'South Africa under Botha, (1): how deep a change?', *Foreign Policy*, 38 (Spring 1980), pp. 126–42; and Spicer, op. cit.

37 See Timothy M. Shaw, 'The international politics of Southern Africa: change or continuity?', *Issue*, vol. 7, no. 1 (Spring 1977), pp. 19–26.

38 See 'The new war', *Africa*, 100 (December 1979), pp. 14–25, and 'Racists wage war in independent Africa', *Anti-Apartheid News* (November 1979), pp. 6–7.

39 Gutteridge, op. cit., p. 31.

40 See Spicer, op. cit.

41 Legum, *ACR*, op. cit., 1977–8, p. B862.

42 Gann and Duignan, op. cit., p. 55.

43 See Timothy M. Shaw, 'On projections, prescriptions and plans: review of literature on the African future', *Quarterly Journal of Administration*, vol. 14, no. 4 (July, 1980), pp. 463–83, 'From dependence to self-reliance: Africa's prospects for the next twenty years', *International Journal*, vol. 35, no. 4 (Autumn 1980), pp. 821–44, and *Alternative Futures for Africa* (Boulder, Colo: Westview Press, 1982).

44 See Thabo Mbeki, 'South Africa: the historical injustice', in Douglas G. Anglin, Timothy M. Shaw and Carl G. Widstrand (eds), *Conflict and Change in Southern Africa* (Washington, DC: University Press of America, 1978), pp. 131–50.

45 Timothy M. Shaw, 'Southern Africa: cooperation and conflict in an international subsystem', *Journal of Modern African Studies*, vol. 12, no. 4 (December 1974), pp. 633–55.

46 See P. Thandika Mkandawire, 'Reflections on some future scenarios for

Southern Africa', *Journal of Southern African Affairs*, vol. 2, no. 4 (October 1977), pp. 391–439. The Freedom Charter of South Africa, agreed among opposition parties in 1955, concludes by reference to South Africa's future world status after liberation: 'South Africa shall be a fully independent state, which respects the rights and sovereignty of nations; South Africa shall strive to maintain world peace and the settlement of all international disputes by negotiation – not war . . . Peace and friendship amongst all our people shall be secured by upholding the equal rights, opportunities and status of all', 'The Freedom Charter of South Africa', United Nations Center against Apartheid, New York, June 1979, pp. 6–7.

PART FOUR

The Future of Southern Africa

13

South Africa's Situation and Strategic Opportunities in Africa

SAM NOLUTSHUNGU

For white South Africa, the rest of the African continent has always had a double fascination – of opportunity and danger – and never more so than in the decade when independent African states emerged, hostile to colonialism and racialism and sworn to aid the overthrow of white rule in South Africa itself. That heady nationalism spelt danger, evoking images of racial retribution of the most brutal kind, but opportunity there was also – in the helplessness of many of those states and their abject dependence on a West of which South Africa knew itself to be a valued member. Under an unchallenged Western hegemony in Africa, South Africa's economic and technological strength could be used to buy off many of the states, and if that failed, its military superiority, yet untested but still seldom questioned, could restrain or subdue the rest. South Africa's first reaction to the prospect of black-ruled African states gaining independence from formal Western control was one of apprehension but that soon gave way to a disdainful self-confidence. An outward-looking policy of enticement and threat, persuasion and subversion, emerged and registered some ambiguous victories; but it was ultimately frustrated by the rigidity of South Africa's domestic policy and the incompatibility of African aspirations and self-images with that racial and colonial world South Africa still continued to represent.[1] Nothing demonstrated South Africa's isolation and, therefore, the failure of its African policy more poignantly than the changes in Southern Africa following the fall of the fascist regime in Portugal. Yet evidently, all was not yet lost to South Africa, and if that great fall was the beginning of the end, the republic's situation and opportunities in Africa might yet help to make that conclusion longer and more complicated.

The accession to power of radical African regimes in Mozambique and Angola profoundly changed South Africa's position in Southern Africa, while it brought important changes in the tenor and direction of its internal politics. The end of the white alliance with Portugal and Rhodesia had begun and the successful completion of the struggle for the liberation of Zimbabwe was to follow shortly. South Africa's policy in Africa had been based on the assumption that political change in these territories would be minimal and slow, while the governments of Rhodesia and Portugal became increasingly dependent on South African economic support. In common with most observers Pretoria's official planners probably anticipated that no serious revolutionary onslaught on the republic itself could be made so long as these two regimes more or less held their ground. Two circumstances sustained this expectation. First, there was the widely shared expectation that armed struggle for South Africa itself would take the form of guerrilla infiltration from outside, while revolutionary activity within the country would only occur as a result and in the degree of success of such 'infiltration'. Otherwise internal discontent could be decisively suppressed or bought off with minor concessions. That being so, the evil day could be put off for quite a while so long as no country adjacent to the republic was controlled by radical African forces. And secondly, South Africa still hoped for a diplomatic breakthrough in Africa, in the early 1970s, while many of South Africa's neighbours seemed ambivalent about the idea of a revolutionary confrontation with her. Despite the failure of the dialogue policy, and South Africa's exclusion from the United Nations General Assembly, by the mid-1970s some of the front line African states were drawn to the view that methods appropriate against Rhodesia and the Portuguese, might not be suitable against South Africa where an armed confrontation might still be averted.[2] This view was reinforced not only by the evident might of the republic, but also by the curious fact that as her allies became more deeply involved in war, South Africa made significant economic gains in the region, expanding her trade with Zambia and Malawi, for example, while progressively acquiring an image of relative moderation compared to the other white regimes. Indeed, successive British governments, and the British media, encouraged the idea that South Africa favoured a liberal solution in Rhodesia and was playing an active role to secure it.[3] South Africa became involved in Anglo-American diplomatic attempts to secure a solution to the problem of UDI and an end to the war.

When, contrary to expectation, the collapse of Portugal's position adduced not a more militant attitude of denunciation of Pretoria, but on Zambia's part an offer of détente, the first indications emerged that liberation in Angola and Mozambique might after all not weaken, but serve to strengthen South Africa's regional influence. The role imputed to Pretoria by London and Washington in ending UDI, African indications of détente – encouraged in some small measure by Vorster's ambiguous promises of internal change – emboldened South Africa to play in the Angolan civil war an interventionary role which (in the form of a lower-key strategy of destabilisation, through periodic raids and continuous material aid to UNITA) has not yet ended.

The Angolan enterprise did, however, fail, and badly so. South Africa did not get the full backing of Western states, African states were mostly hostile or dilatory about the South African role, and those who had encouraged the intervention could not or would not defend it openly and, in general, revised their attitude to MPLA, after independence, rather more readily than South Africa would or could do. The magnitude of the failure lay in the fact that the belief of the NATO powers that South African power was a useful or usable asset for the defence and expansion of Western interests in the region was called into question, and South Africa itself was confronted with the stark reality of the failure of a decade of spirited diplomacy in Africa. Like the Western powers, South Africa had relied on the Portuguese being able to retain their empire against nationalist challenges. South African state corporations had invested in the two Southern colonies while militarily a tacit alliance existed. As buffer-states they fitted into a South African defence doctrine that favoured meeting the 'communist' peril before it reached the republic, and in their expected economic modernisation they would become part of a regional system dominated by South Africa. Thus, when the empire collapsed, it signified a failure for South African as well as Western policy. Subsequent policy towards Angola and Mozambique would amount to no more than desperate, reckless and often bloody attempts to contain the consequences of that failure. The succession of South African raids into the former Portuguese colonies are aimed partly against SWAPO and the African National Congress, and partly against the states themselves. Yet they also bespeak a certain hopelessness:

> I am in blood
> Stepp'd in so far, that, should I wade no more,
> Returning were as tedious as go o'er.

Intervention in the Angolan civil war had seemed to provide an easy opportunity for South Africa to demonstrate its worth to the West and to anti-communist regimes in Africa. But in the event, many African states, including some of the least socialist, had shown a greater disapproval of apartheid South Africa than of 'communism'.[4] Matters were not improved when South Africa became a haven for defeated colonialists, mercenaries, fascists and racists as they retreated from Angola, Mozambique and, later, Zimbabwe.[5] When popular revolt erupted in South Africa's black ghettos and bitter division and recrimination occurred within the ruling group, even domestic policy seemed to be in disarray and unlikely to succeed in the long run.

Radical decolonisation in the rest of the subcontinent had an immediate and dramatic effect on the black population inside South Africa. Revolutionary expectations were aroused, popular attitudes to politics became both more militant and more radical. The spirit of revolt which manifested itself in 1976 proved to be more enduring and widespread than any previous burst of popular resentment and also produced more recruits for the liberation struggle. Latterly, partly in response to the state's concessions to black workers (which were intended to curb their political aspirations and to contain their self-assertion within structures devised and managed by the state), workers have become more political and defiant. Among all sections of the population, support for the ANC has grown, and so has its own activity within the republic.

Among whites, the effects of failure contradicted a widely held belief that crises merely strengthened white unity and resolve. It was as if the state in losing struggles outside its borders had also lost something of its credibility, its mystique and authority at home. The ruling party was involved in a corruption scandal which brought about the downfall of a state president and a former prime ministerial candidate, and was later to suffer a split over racial policy. Class suspicion surfaced between white workers and their leaders as argument raged as to who should bear the burden of adjustment to the changed circumstances: should white workers' privileges be somewhat reduced, or the blacks be repressed even more firmly to preserve the supremacy of all white men? The official response assumes the form of a total strategy which seeks, within South Africa, to manipulate class differences among blacks within a modernised racialist institutional framework, and in relations with African states to place greater emphasis on Southern Africa and on South Africa's coercive power there rather than, as under Vorster, to seek diplomatic influence in Africa as a whole.[6] The aim is to win hearts and minds at home while preparing for a war that will be fought outside South Africa where the republic's superiority in conventional arms can be used decisively.

In practice, however, the winning of hearts has proved a harder task than the military one, for while raids into neighbouring countries have occurred in line with such a strategy, domestic repression and intensive use of physical and psychological torture have in no way been abandoned in a spirit of reform to 'win hearts and minds'. Subversion and sabotage against the alternative economic links that Southern African states establish among themselves to reduce their dependence on South Africa, suggests that military pressure may also serve directly economic aims. Overwhelming technological superiority in arms is an essential aspect of the strategy given that white manpower is limited. The regime's evident project to develop tactical nuclear weapons is the logical outcome of such a situation.

South Africa's opportunities in Africa have always depended heavily on the attitudes and actions of the major Western powers and continue to do so. Typically the colonial powers retained as their spheres of influence the territories they had previously colonised, despite their accession to legal independence. Effectively that amounted to a division of labour among the NATO powers in the preservation of Western dominance in Africa. Portugal, however, was even less able to fulfil such a role than Belgium had been in the Congo a decade and a half earlier, and yet, potentially, the stakes were higher in this much larger empire. There was no easy means of collective Western action and South Africa proved to be of dubious value in that role. The ineffectiveness of American action, contrasted with decisive Soviet and Cuban action gave cause for apprehension and called for a revaluation of the West's options. The United States launched a diplomatic offensive to regain the good-will of African states, publicising its support for human rights in South Africa, Zimbabwe and Namibia, while working more closely with its European allies on African policy generally.[7] The British Labour government worked hard to involve the Nigerian military government in the Anglo-American proposals for an end to the war in Zimbabwe, while the French government for once publicly criticised South Africa and after Shaba proposed the creation of an African intervention force that could, hopefully, preserve the prevailing order in Africa without need of direct European or US involvement. That idea, rejected at the time by most African states, would later be revived when an OAU peace-keeping force was put together under French and US auspices to replace the Libyans in Chad.

In Southern Africa the major capitalist states began to grope for a policy that could secure Western influence and economic dominance more or less independently of and even in competition with South African interests. Thus, a limited improvement of relations with Mozambique and even Angola took place, and the settlement terms pressed by Britain for Zimbabwe – and particularly its attitude to the post-independence regime there – showed little regard for South African anxieties when it appeared that British interests might prosper in spite of the success of a radical nationalist party. It was evident that a negotiated solution to the Namibian problem would consolidate Western influence in the area, while the interests of specifically South African capital were most likely to suffer from majority rule. With the election of Ronald Reagan to the presidency, however, the USA reverted to a policy of affirming the importance of South Africa to the West, and of outright hostility to the socialist movements and states in Southern Africa.

Whether the policy of the Reagan government disrupted a strategy that could have succeeded, or one that could have had any visible impact on South Africa's position in Africa, is open to doubt. For it is not as if the Western governments in the time of President Carter believed that the black states could develop capitalism in isolation from South Africa, or that the socialist ones could remain so without disrupting Western influence in the region. Rather, they believed that their own roles in the economics and politics of the region need no longer depend on an unequivocal subimperial role being conceded to Pretoria. To be sure, for practical as well as ideological reasons, no capitalist development of those states could really occur which did not tie them, through the activity of the international corporations and agencies that would inevitably be involved, more closely to the South African economy and to South Africa's highly advanced systems of communication and transport. The idea was to free, as far as possible, Western capital and political influence from the ideological and political hindrances which their South African counterparts encountered. Where international and South African capital compete, it would be advantageous not to be closely identified with apartheid South Africa.

For economic as well as political reasons, then, international capital might be less eager than before to open doors for specifically South African interests. In so far as foreign capital plays a decisive role within South Africa's own economy – especially in providing advanced technology – the uncoupling of its political representation in the subcontinent from South Africa's local strategic needs and aspirations may *increase* rather than decrease South Africa's responsiveness to the needs of international capital even within its own boundaries. In other words, the more South Africa is isolated, the more willing it may be to make concessions to foreign capitalists and their governments. But this produces a vicious circle. For if Pretoria should be even more accommodating to international capitalists than it already is, then they, for their part, will have every reason to resist disinvestment campaigns and proposals for rapid or disruptive change.

South Africa's response to its crises combines an attitude of suspicion towards the West with a desire to entangle the NATO powers ever more deeply in its own defence. By deploying massive military force and being willing to use it against neighbouring states, South Africa places itself in a position – like Israel – where it can undertake punitive raids and intervene in those states even, if need be, in defiance of the sensitivities of particular Western states in any given conjuncture. Also it ensures that should the burden of defending white domination become too great, at any stage, Pretoria would have the option of internationalising the conflict by provoking black states into military collaboration with the USSR and its allies which would, in turn, challenge the West to defend more actively its very considerable interests in South Africa. There does not appear to be much that the major Western powers are willing or able to do to control this process. For real though the disagreements and mutual suspicion are, they are bounded by common interests represented by trade and investment and by naval and intelligence co-operation.

The advantages which the West derives from South Africa, augmented by the ideological valuation placed upon them by ruling classes that are not only anti-socialist, but who still entertain a certain partiality to whites in conflict with blacks, are too real for competition and disagreements to lead to any decisive change of policy, still less to active attempts by the West to supplant the apartheid regime in the foreseeable future. It is simply not open to any important Western government to 'ditch' Pretoria or to 'sell it down the river' for, say, a prospect of better control over Black Africa, or in preference of an alternative black, subimperial partner elsewhere in Africa. The prospect, therefore, remains real that South Africa might, if the interests of its own state and ruling class should so require, commit Western governments to act, even militarily, in its support against African liberation movements and African states that aid them. By the same token, any attempt to consolidate a Western bloc in Southern Africa – in counterpoise to Marxist-influenced regimes on the one hand, and on the other relatively secured against the possibly disruptive effects of the South African conflict – is unlikely to be conclusive. A measure of freedom of action may be gained for Western interests. So the images of black anti-socialist regimes internationally and, above all, with their own people, may to a degree be protected from the ignominy that would follow from their association with a Western capitalism which was *simply* identified with apartheid. Yet the more deeply such states become economically tied up with the West, the less insistent they will be able to be even about such face-saving distinctions. The nature of their role in South Africa might then depend on the resistances that can be mustered against such capitalist development within the African states themselves.

In this regard one cannot but be sceptical of an argument often heard nowadays that imperialism responding to its imperialist interest in the rest of Africa might be ready to 'ditch' Pretoria, seeking an alternative subimperial outpost, or centre-in-the-periphery. Nigeria, with its oil, large population and armed forces, is often cited as the likely alternative.[8] This argument is based on a superficial appraisal of both countries and their interest for international capital. Western investment is vast and varied in South Africa and so is trade in areas for which Nigeria cannot hope to substitute. Furthermore, the corporations involved in South Africa include some of the most economically powerful in their respective countries of origin and are likely to be influential in the devising of any specifically capitalist policy of assigning roles. Militarily, as well as industrially, it would be no simple and certainly no brief task to create in Nigeria business and military facilities comparable with those in South Africa. Real and important as are Nigeria's resources, they are more limited in range, and given the nature of the overall economy (and particularly Nigeria's heavy dependence on Britain and the West for technology and distribution facilities with regard to oil), those assets themselves secure Lagos only a qualified, and by no means decisive, influence. Moreover, the social development which oil, and the West's use of it, have helped to further within Nigeria argues against any sustained confrontational stance on Nigeria's part on any issue considered important for capitalism.

International capital, then, as is its wont, will choose not one over the other, but both together. Besides, in recent years without any significant modification of Western policy, Western access to African resources and markets and now even military bases has grown rather than lessened. It is callow, indeed, to suppose that any African state that might otherwise stay in capitalism could change course solely out of an aggrieved sense of justice relative to a third country some thousands of miles away. Capitalists have lived long enough with racial oppression. Nor can such a state opt for an independent path of capitalist development untarnished by collaboration with international capitalism and sensitive to black liberation. Such a thing simply does not exist. Those who would develop under 'free enterprise' must, by and large, take it as it comes and learn to live with themselves as best they can.

What is true, all this notwithstanding, is that the genuinely felt abhorrence of racial domination does represent a contradiction, hampering the rationalisation of capitalist domination in the continent. Problems arise in the domestic legitimation of regimes and inconsistencies emerge in their reaction to events, which may sometimes be to the advantage of liberation in Southern Africa.[9] The contradictions at the ideological and political levels may continue, as they do now, to inhibit full and effective assistance to South Africa by the Western regimes leading to a search for a solution through reform and accommodation. South Africa's own responsive attempts to 'accommodate' blacks, in their turn, merely tend to underline the enormity of present wrongs, to emphasise the unreformability of its system of domination and exploitation while, at the margin, they embolden black South Africans in their demands.

If South Africa's African strategic situation highlights issues of capitalist development and its contradictions, the proposals for internal reform are also based on a class strategy. For some time now, elements in the ruling class have favoured the development of a black capitalist stratum that would have a vested interest in the system and be an ally of the whites against radical change. For various reasons this strategy has been pursued haltingly and imperfectly – the greatest inhibitor of progress being the rigidity of the political system and racialist ideology, broadly conceived (that is, not simply as a set of biological beliefs, although these do most assuredly persist in the wider political culture, but also thought habits with regard to social control, and so on). The aim is to use the more privileged blacks not only as a propaganda showpiece to the world, but also as responsible leaders of the African masses. The black resistance movement both within the country and outside is thus challenged to adopt a countervailing class partisanship on behalf of those who are not to be incorporated, while by and large the black population within South Africa is becoming more conscious of 'class', 'capitalism' and 'imperialism' as central elements of their situation.

It will become increasingly difficult to deal meaningfully with the South African problem as a purely racial or national one. Various attempts have been made by South Africa and by the USA to encourage the emergence of 'purely nationalist' leaderships among blacks who might participate in some constitutional solution in the remote future and whose function, in the meantime, is to challenge and discredit the claim of radical nationalist movements like the ANC to represent the black people of South Africa. A similar attempt has been made in Namibia with the creation of the Democratic Turnhalle Alliance and with South Africa's current insistence that United Nations management of a transition to independence is unacceptable so long as SWAPO is regarded by the world body as the sole representative of the Namibian people. African states will be required to take up positions with regard to a struggle that hinges on class relationships that are, in principle, no different from those occurring within their own boundaries. It is not fanciful to argue, in light of the ideological divisions that have plagued the OAU since its creation, that

African responses will become less certain and less united and that there will be a tendency for those who take a radical stance to become isolated. Should that happen, then those states will be more vulnerable to South African retaliation against which, on their own – unaided by a major power (rather than just resolutions of distant fellow-Africans at the UN and the OAU) – they would have no effective counter. They will then either have to disengage, more or less hurriedly from the South African struggle or try to forge alliances with powers outside Africa to give massive support to their own defensive efforts if not to guarantee their very existence. It is difficult to see how they can resist the latter course and still hope to continue to give support to revolutionary forces, especially when these begin to have a major impact on South Africa. That is merely a variant of the problem of African weakness.

African states have simply failed, in the two decades of their independence, to acquire the means of their own collective defence or even the will to secure compliance with the resolutions of their OAU. In their weakness they are dependent on a West that has set its face like a flint against armed revolution in South Africa. Under the influence of the West and in obedience to their own interests as non-revolutionary states, the majority of African states have discountenanced the growth of any countervailing major power involvement in Africa, as by the Soviet Union. Yet unless Western power can be reduced both socially and strategically in Africa, any assault on Western interests in any part of the continent is bound to be both hazardous and at best inconclusive in its outcome.

The emergence of radical socialist states in Southern Africa – Angola and Mozambique – is in this regard an exceedingly hopeful development. Vulnerable and weak though they are, they are so far free from some of the inhibitions of capitalism both as regards their attitude to South Africa and their attitude to external alignment. They give, by their very existence, encouragement to radical forces in the rest of the subcontinent and within South Africa itself. Were Zimbabwe to realise its radical promise, the 'balance of power' both literally and in a figurative-ideological sense would be significantly modified in the region. Should it slide down the path of neo-colonialism, then Mozambique itself would be very hard put to it to sustain a radical policy both as regards internal development and South Africa.

The radicalising effect of the political transformations in neighbouring countries has been felt within South Africa – in the widespread militancy that has erupted in various ways since the mid-1970s and in the diffusion of radical ideas both as to the aims of struggle and its methods. In this lies South Africa's gravest weakness: that popular revolt within its boundaries may deprive it of the Israeli option – of fighting in conventional terms against weaker states outside its own borders. A general situation of militant protest and insurrection by blacks will also make it more difficult to achieve the class structuration of the conflict envisaged in elite accommodation – a problem largely created by the very limitations of South Africa's ability to forge an effective neo-colonial solution.

South Africa's strategy of counterinsurgency will have more difficulty in succeeding if popular resistance to imperialist strategies is sustained and grows in both the Western states and in their dependent semi-colonies: specific resistances to their African policies and general resistance to their class practices even within their own 'independent' domains. It is upon the active involvement of the ordinary people in the struggle against imperialism and its representatives in Africa, a pre-eminently democratic struggle, that the hope for any genuine or lasting liberation can be founded. In this way it will be more difficult for the major Western states to extend effective diplomatic and military support to South Africa, and for African governments to acquiesce in Western and South African attempts to create new and more lasting forms of domination and exploitation in Southern Africa. It is in the absence of that mass involvement that South Africa's chief opportunities in Africa principally lie.

Perhaps all this is as it always was and is no new feature of the 1980s. Yet events have sharpened the outlines, highlighted the issues and confront Africa anew with its weakness and, more hopefully, the challenge to struggle out of that lowly condition.

Notes: Chapter 13

1   See my *South Africa in Africa: A Study in Ideology and Foreign Policy* (Manchester: Manchester University Press, 1975).
2   As, for example, in the Lusaka Manifesto.
3   The opposite was more likely true. See T. Chalcraft, 'Apartheid and white settler rebellion', in *Collected Papers: 5* (York: University of York Centre for Southern African Studies).
4   Some African states were very apprehensive about an MPLA victory backed by Soviet and Cuban power and would, by their approaches to the

US for countervailing support, have encouraged South Africa to believe that it was doing some service to Africa by intervening. There is no clear evidence of direct approaches to South Africa to intervene, even though once Pretoria had acted, some states colluded in various ways. See, *inter alia*, John Stockwell, *In Search of Enemies* (London: Futura, 1976); and A. Klinghoffer, *The Angolan War: A Study in Soviet Policy in the Third World* (Boulder, Colo: Westview Press, 1980).

5   Some of these were subsequently involved in sabotage in Zimbabwe and in Mozambique where the self-styled Mozambique Resistance Movement has been waging a more sustained campaign of sabotage with evident South African support.

6   Some of the features and problems of 'reform' are dealt with more fully in my *Changing South Africa: Political Considerations* (Manchester: Manchester University Press, 1982).

7   See, *inter alia*, 'Briefing', *Review of African Political Economy*, 17 (January–April 1980), pp. 71–82.

8   W. Biermann, 'US Policy towards Southern Africa in the framework of global empire', *Review of African Political Economy*, 17 (January–April 1980), pp. 28–42.

9   Nationalist appeals are made by claimants to power and from time to time, releasing the ever-present though often dormant anti-imperialist feelings among the people.

14

South Africa's Role in Southern Africa in the Year 2000

TIMOTHY M. SHAW

> Very much in the same way as other regional powers, South Africa has ideological doctrines and philosophies for claiming supremacy in Southern Africa. These doctrines were gradually developed after World War II. A great part of South Africa's expansion northwards can be explained by economic factors. (Raimo Vayrynen[1])

South Africa's place in Southern Africa for the rest of this century is likely to be a function of its past, present and prospective political economy, and its inheritance and continuing situation of dependence within the world system. Despite the contrary pressures for fragmentation (through 'separate development') and liberation (through the liberation movements), South Africa's position at the centre of the periphery is unlikely to change dramatically by the year 2000. Kenneth Grundy's comments on the contemporary status of South Africa are relevant, then, to both its history and its future:

> South Africa displays many of the characteristics of an intermediary state. The South African economy . . . [is] located in the middle of the production process, and hence, in between the core and periphery in the global system. This has led to a rather ambiguous combination of foreign and domestic policies, some of which reflect a harmony of interest between South Africa and the imperialist core, and some of which reflect conflicts of interest and competition with the core.[2]

To be sure, the overthrow of the present white minority

regime by the African National Congress (ANC) and its allies may lead eventually to a change of sub- as well as super-structure. But even a non-capitalist South Africa would probably continue to play the role of regional power, albeit on behalf of African rather than Western or transnational interests. However, this chapter is based on the assumption that any change before the twenty-first century is unlikely to produce significant shifts in modes of production, even if certain racially defined relations of production were affected more readily. It proceeds, then, from a consideration of the need to relate 'national', regional and global interactions to an examination of South Africa as a subimperial power at the semi-periphery with semi-industrial characteristics, to an overview of changes at all three levels since 1945, and to an analysis of current challenges to white power both within and around South Africa. It concludes by identifying three alternative futures for South Africa during the present decade – repression, reform, or revolution – and discussing their distinctive but interrelated national, regional and global implications. I turn, first, to an introduction on the levels of analysis debate as it related to the understanding of South Africa.

(1) The Sociology of Knowledge: from 'Subsystem' to 'Subimperialism'

In the late 1960s Larry Bowman argued that 'For far too long, events in Southern Africa have been viewed in a discrete manner, with little consideration given to the interaction of the countries concerned'.[3] He went on to assert that

> Both historical-constitutional approaches and the approaches focusing essentially on racial questions have failed to delineate many of the social, political, and economic links that bind the area. This has led to an under-estimation of some factors which make for stability and unity in Southern Africa.[4]

Subsequent scholarship during the first half of the 1970s – a period characterised by considerable regional continuity until the Portuguese coup of early 1974 – tended to take Bowman's critique seriously and to adopt a subsystemic level of analysis.[5] But this corrective – with its emphasis on regional interaction, co-operation and autonomy – was itself revealed to be deficient (*a*) by revolutionary change and conflict in Mozambique and Angola, and (*b*) by the impact and incidence of the high price and volatile supply of oil. The apparent need to situate regional events in a *global* context and to consider structural issues as well as superficial events led in the second half of the 1970s to another form of analysis, away from a concern for 'subsystem' and towards a focus on 'subimperialism'.

This 'new wave' – reflective as it is of a general trend in the discipline towards a revised and revisionist form of 'international political economy'[6] – does not exclude insights derived from investigations of the regional subsystem. Rather, it seeks to go beyond systems analysis in two ways: (*a*) to examine substructure as well as superstructure, and (*b*) to treat class in addition to race and ethnicity as a salient factor. Moreover, it seeks to go beyond a focus on the subsystem by situating the region in the context of the global order.

This new interest in 'subimperialism' transcends the sometimes controversial debate over degree of autonomy present in the Southern African subsystem. Instead, it assumes that extraregional factors – especially the interests and activities of dominant global actors such as major states and corporations – affect intraregional relations and vice versa. The new mode parts company, then, with the subsystem's *genre* by abandoning the crucial sixth condition originally proposed by students of 'subordinate state systems' such as Michael Brecher; namely, that 'changes in the dominant system should have a greater effect on the subordinate system than the reverse.'[7] Rather, it seeks to identify structural linkages between 'centre' and 'periphery', recognising that while peripheral actors are not powerless, they are both more dependent and more vulnerable than those at the centre.

Finally, in addition to a stress on substructure and on class the new orthodoxy, with its acceptance of centre–periphery distinctions and asymmetries, also draws attention to intermediate actors in the chains of production and command. The notion of 'semi-periphery' serves to relate centre and periphery in both analytic and existential terms. To dichotomise states (and other actors) into centre and periphery is to oversimplify especially in the contemporary period when growth rates outside the advanced industrialised world are so variable. Moreover, in a postcolonial period, the opportunities for leading regional powers to exert a degree of local dominance is enhanced. Therefore, a group of upwardly mobile non-OECD states has become the focus of some attention as constituting a distinctive layer in the world system. As Raimo Vayrynen has indicated in his suggestive comparative analysis of such states at the semi-periphery:

> A regional power centre in the sense of a subimperial country can be defined as an actor which exerts a regional hegemony akin to the global dominance of an imperial power, but at a subsystemic level. It plays an important intermediate role in a sphere of influence by dominating a region, while still being subordinate to major actors at the centre of global feudal networks.[8]

Regional powers like South Africa have increased their share of the global economic product and of global military expenditure over the last ten or twenty years. They have also tended to exhibit higher levels of industrialisation and a greater propensity to regional intervention than countries at the periphery. As Vayrynen concludes himself, especially in reference to the cases of Brazil and South Africa, regional economic expansion along with regional military dominance is a prerequisite of continued growth: 'in the group of regional power centres *economic and military strength coincide and reinforce each other.*'[9] Given these characteristics, states such as South Africa have recently been termed newly influential countries (NICs) (at the superstructural level of diplomacy and strategy) or newly industrialising countries (at the substructural level of production and exchange). This chapter seeks to examine the place of Southern Africa in global and regional affairs by treating it as a subimperial power at the semi-periphery of the world system.

(2) South Africa as a Semi-Peripheral Power

South Africa's place in Southern Africa has been affected by its position in the world system ever since the discovery of diamonds and gold on the rand. The 'mineral revolution' not only disrupted the escapist trek of the Afrikaners away from the moral and industrial revolution in Europe; it also ensured the development of a mining and industrial sector to augment the established agricultural sector. Moreover, it generated a social as well as a structural dualism: mining and industry were initially controlled by transnational, especially British, interests, whereas agriculture remained essentially an

Afrikaner (as well as African) preserve. This particular tension, exacerbated by what he saw as 'Jewish' financial interference, led according to J. Hobson's critical mode of analysis[10] to the Boer War, between agrarian (and 'national') Afrikaner and industrial (and 'transnational') British interests.

This 'ethnic' tension within the white bourgeoisie has remained a central feature of the South African political economy, even if it is less antagonistic than the black–white contradiction. Anglophone hegemony was not simply a function of a colonial connection or industrial development. Rather, English-speaking settlers tended to retain external connections and associations to a much greater extent than the Boer-trekers. And despite South Africa's 'quiet revolution' following the Nationalist Party victory of 1948, the Afrikaners have remained much more 'national' in orientation than other members of the white community. 'Afrikaner nationalism' was not, therefore, another nationalist movement directed against the colonial metropole – the Anglophone community – with its comprador image. Furthermore, Afrikaner nationalism was not socialist in orientation, despite the rural, co-operative strand in Afrikaner ideology. Instead, it advocated use of the state to rectify the historical imbalance between Afrikanerdom and transnational capitalism. It was, at most, an ethnically exclusive form of 'populism'.

As expressed through Afrikaner nationalism, Afrikaner capitalism sought greater national control over the economy in two interrelated ways: (*a*) control over the activities of Anglophone entrepreneurs inside South Africa, and (*b*) control over the transnational orientation of such entrepreneurs ('indigenisation' rather than 'nationalisation'). The use to which the Afrikaner leadership put the state after the Second World War makes a fascinating case of 'state capitalism',[11] especially in terms of the development of a national military-industrial complex. The balance between the national (Afrikaner) fraction of the white bourgeoisie and the transnational (Anglophone) fraction has shifted significantly since 1948 with important implications for South Africa's local and regional autonomy.[12] Given the inheritance of antipathy between the (Afrikaner) state and (Anglophone) business – one that Afrikaner state capitalism has rectified and removed to a considerable extent – the heir to the Anglo-American Corporation, Nicholas Oppenheimer, has called for a 're-creation of the marriage between private enterprise and government', because 'by no stretch of the imagination can business any longer be thought of as the exclusive domain of a particular tribe'.[13] Oppenheimer went on to call for two forms of partnership – integral to the 'reformist' option identified in Section 6, below – to ensure South Africa's place in regional and global systems:

> The partnership required for the 1980s is no longer one simply between state and business leaders, it must be between the state and the free enterprise economic system. Further, if it is to succeed in restoring political acceptability and real and rapid growth it must be an inter-racial partnership between politicians, managers, workers and consumers.[14]

The tension between national and transnational white bourgeois fractions over the definition and orientation of capitalism in South Africa is matched by the continuing debate over whether to defend apartheid in depth or inside the *laager*. With the 'winds of change' of African nationalism blowing after the Second World War, South Africa attempted to create a *cordon sanitaire* around its own borders by encouraging an 'unholy alliance' with the neighbouring white regimes of Rhodesia and Portugal. This strategy was successful for the decade between the mid-1960s and the mid-1970s; that is, between the withdrawal of British and French colonial forces and the demise of the Portuguese empire. During this period South Africa's military hegemony reinforced its economic dominance, a status it continued to have *vis-à-vis* Rhodesia until 1980.

Now defence in depth is no longer an option, although its border and bombing raids continue in a broad band from Angola to Mozambique. Moreover, there is a growing awareness that a retreat into the *laager* by itself is no longer a guarantee of survival for the white 'nation' as during the intervening period non-white interests inside South Africa have been alienated further rather than accommodated. Indeed, the balance between the strategic and economic strands in South Africa's regional dominance has changed considerably over the last two decades, with important implications for explanation and projection (see Section 6, below) as well as for policy.

The importance of 'informal' economic exchange as opposed to 'formal' strategic agreement at both regional and global levels is one reason for focusing on sub- rather than superstructure. Another is that at the level of 'intergovernmental' relations South Africa is an international 'pariah', largely unrecognised and certainly unloved. But at the level of 'transnational' interactions, South Africa remains well integrated into the world system. Corporate links, gold sales, diamond-trading and uranium production are all salient aspects of this external orientation and incorporation. And these transnational and infrastructural arrangements are important at the regional as well as the global level, despite the absence of many formal institutional agreements. South Africa, unlike several other states at the semi-periphery, is not a diplomatic centre; rather, it is a corporate and communications hub. The centrality of such transnational arrangements to South Africa's political economy as well as changes in both global and regional systems reinforce the need to look beyond superstructural phenomenon at underlying substructural features.[15]

(3)　Postwar Change at Three Levels: Global, Regional and National

The position of the South African state – the edifice of white power and privilege – has changed since the Second World War at national, regional and global levels. These levels are, of course, interrelated: apartheid nationally affects South Africa's image and status regionally and globally; likewise the prices of oil and gold globally affect South Africa's growth prospects regionally and nationally. The importance of any one level in defining South Africa's position varies between periods and issue areas. At times of international tension South Africa's strategic location and resources may serve to enhance its political position; at times of international recession South Africa's function as supplier of raw materials may retard its economic prospects. Clearly, the effectiveness of South Africa's military capability has receded over time, whereas the leverage of its economic capacity has tended to increase. Shifts at any one level – for example, its national organisation (separate development), its regional security (independence in neighbouring states), or its global acceptability (arms and oil sanctions) – have implications for all other levels and linkages.

The interrelatedness of issue areas and interactive levels has implications for the ways in which subimperialism is defined and practised in particular cases. For while all states at the semi-periphery have increased their proportion of the world economic product and of global military expenditure, some are more industrialised internally, more technologically autonomous and more dominant regionally than others. South Africa, for instance, is less industrialised than Brazil but more so than Nigeria; it is less autonomous than India but more so than Iran; it is less dominant than India but more so than Venezuela. Nevertheless, South Africa has clearly gone beyond the stage of import substitution in its economic transition but its progress towards the third phase of export-led growth is retarded by (*a*) a very uneven income distribution domestically, and (*b*) resistance to over-reliance on its manufactured products regionally.[16]

South Africa may confront fundamental structural problems based on apartheid in advancing beyond semi-industrialisation because its pattern of 'polarised accumulation' is so accentuated. Paradoxically, therefore, South Africa needs regional markets because its national level of consumption is limited artificially by institutionalised racism; conversely, apartheid is the reason why regional markets are not so large or so stable as they might otherwise be. As Vayrynen notes,

> Patterns of regional expansion vary from one centre to another. Brazil and South Africa have apparently been most vigorous in their economic expansion. This has to be seen in view of the fact that both of these countries are internally deeply divided between haves and have-nots, the latter with very little purchasing power. In these two countries, external economic expansion can be at least partly explained by the economic necessity of exporting goods to create a demand for the domestic industries. Both in Brazil and South Africa the subsidiaries of transnational corporations have also played a major role, in fact actively participating in the export drive.[17]

The relationship between state and corporation in the South African case has been inseparable from the interrelated 'ethnic' issues of who controls the state and who controls the corporation already identified in the previous section. South Africa's postwar industrial development was a function of Afrikaner capitalism nationally, manufactured exports regionally and foreign investment, skills and technology globally. As elsewhere in Africa, corporations were quite prepared to 'indigenise' their South African operations either through local shareholding for the national bourgeoisie or through partnership arrangements within a parastatal framework. Such local participation tends to occur simultaneously with the transition from import substitution towards the stage of export-led growth:

It naturally coincides with the partial indigenisation of the production of technology and capital goods, although the transnational corporations still play a prominent role and may even gain new significance as their activities become more 'internalised' and more closely allied with local capital and public authorities. This *alliance of foreign and domestic capital and the state machinery* in fact forms the backbone for the promotion of manufactured exports as well as for the construction of semi-autonomous military industry.[18]

(4)   South Africa in the World System: from Partner to Pariah

Despite a certain ambivalence inside certain sections of the Afrikaner community about fascism, the South African regime entered the postwar world as an ally of the victors. Its privileged status as a 'self-governing' dominion within the British Commonwealth enabled it to maintain effective control over South West Africa and to participate in the founding of the United Nations. But just as the internationalist Smuts was succeeded by the nationalist Verwoerd, so South Africa became unwelcome in both Commonwealth and the UN. Formal exclusion from the former in 1961 and tacit exclusion from the latter in 1974 signified a dramatic decline in favour as (*a*) the Nationalist Party insisted on institutionalising *apartheid* internally, and (*b*) populist nationalism produced decolonised states throughout the rest of the Third World. Within two decades the partner of the Allies had become a pariah in most global fora.

The struggle between Afrikaner and African nationalisms was situated, therefore, in a world system that had seen the defeat of fascism, the dawn of nationalism and the demise of the Pax Britannica. The white redoubts under the tutelage of South Africa became ever-more anachronistic in a postwar world that contained a substantial and growing 'socialist commonwealth' as well as non-aligned nations. Minority regimes became increasingly anathema in a world in which decolonisation and liberation were central motifs. So to maintain and defend white privilege, the settlers developed their own 'unholy alliance' in the region, which although it had no formal links with either of the Cold War alliances, nevertheless had a range of informal associations with elements within NATO. But under pressure of more progressive leaders and interests, the number of such strategic arrangements declined, although certain transnational linkages appear to have remained intact in the technical and intelligence spheres.[19]

So while at the official intergovernmental level a degree of disengagement has occurred, especially since the mid-1970s among certain Western states, at the less official trans-governmental level considerable communication remains. And the South African regime, unable to gain acceptability within multilateral intergovernmental institutions, has emphasised the continuation of 'functional' linkages in areas such as communications, health, nuclear energy, and so on. Given the regime's fears of further isolation and exclusion, it has gone to considerable lengths to protect its position in, say, international sport or the World Bank. Its neurosis about being an international outcast is revealed also in its brittle response to Western, especially American, demands:[20] South Africa's threat, in a fit of pique, to become neutral or non-aligned is hardly credible given the character of its capitalist political economy and racist culture.

If changes in the international political system have affected South Africa's status at the level of superstructure, then changes in the global economy have affected its prospects at the level of substructure. South Africa's place in the world of international finance was secure under the postwar Bretton Woods structure because of the centrality of its gold. With the interrelated economic crises of the mid-1970s – floating exchange rates, high price for oil, recession and inflation[21] – its position is no longer assured, although its possession of several valuable or strategic non-renewable mineral reserves still serves to enhance its status.[22] In particular, its strategy of semi-industrialisation through import substitution has been endangered by the high price of imported factors, especially oil. But if the value of the rand and the cost (and uncertain supply) of oil have retarded its growth prospects, the escalating price of gold and other minerals (as well as the effects of creating a more autonomous military-industrial complex) have enhanced them.

Moreover, although recession has eroded the price of some South African mineral exports (for example, iron ore and copper), it has increased the price of others (for example, uranium and coal) as fears about energy supplies have grown in countries like Japan.[23] The external Achilles heel of South Africa's political economy – the supply of oil – has become more apparent as OPEC hiked the price and interfered in the supply, especially with the overthrow of the Shah of Iran and the termination of the special Iranian-South African relationship. The internal Achilles heel – the supply of labour – has also become more apparent as worker unrest and the unionisation debate have intensified.

In addition to becoming an economy dependent upon the exchange of two increasingly expensive subterranean products – gold exports for oil imports – South Africa has had to cope with two sets of tensions characteristic of shifts within the global political economy in a period of stagnation. First, it has had to recognise and respond to *'interimperial' rivalries*.[24] In a period of economic expansion relations among the advanced industrialised states tend to be co-operative because the situation is perceived to be 'mixed-sum': all can benefit, even if some more so than others. But in a period of economic recession such relations tend to deteriorate because the situation indeed becomes 'zero-sum': positive growth in one state means negative growth in another state. In such a period – as in 1974–80 – the USA, Japan and the EEC tend to become competitive and protectionist in their intercorporate and intercountry relationships.

This tendency towards neo-mercantilism in the North has profound implications for states like South Africa. On the one hand, given its possession of valuable resources, it can play off one buyer of raw materials against another, so securing a higher price. On the other hand, unemployment in the North means a reduction in overseas investment, so that foreign capital and technology may be both scarcer and more expensive for South Africa than before (this is in addition to the higher interest rates on money for South Africa because of declining investor confidence). One positive product of global economic instability and inflation, to which I turn in Section 5, is that South Africa's regional market has become more secure as extraregional sources become less reliable and less competitive for the most seriously affected and least developed countries of Southern Africa.

Secondly, given shifts in the global hierarchy, South Africa has had to deal with *inter-subimperial rivalries*. Again, during a period of economic expansion, NICs can all grow simultaneously through their respective spheres of influence: the advanced industrialised states provide the financial and technical supports for such growth. However, in a period of recession not only are such supports withdrawn and not only do metropolitan corporations return as regional competitors, but semi-peripheral states attempt to break out of their own traditional regional markets to penetrate the markets of other NICs.

In times of stagnation, then, interests in both the metropole and the semi-periphery tend to redefine and enlarge their respective spheres of influence, on the one hand, generating new forms of competition and conflict. On the other hand, if – as it seems to be so – NICs continue to grow faster than the already-advanced industrialised states, then they may be able to control the degree of inter-subimperial rivalry and expand the level of inter-subimperial exchange, at some cost to OECD members. Table 14.1 suggests that South Africa's trade with countries like Brazil, Taiwan and Israel – other 'pariahs' or NICs – has expanded significantly in the second half of the 1970s. Certainly, formal intergovernmental relations have increased and improved with other pariahs such as Taiwan and Israel, while informal transnational relations have grown with other NICs such as Brazil and Argentina. In particular, the bilateral South African-Israeli linkage has become close and diverse, embracing strategic planning and material as well as technology transfer and energy development,[25] with profound implications for South Africa's links with African and other Third World Countries.

Table 14.1   *Selected South African Export Markets (in US $m.)*

	1970	1973	1976	1979
UK	624	1,010	1,147	1,121
USA	181	232	527	1,908
Argentina	3	4	9	190
Brazil	1	11	31	120
Taiwan	1	25	172*	246*
Israel	5	24	36	125
Venezuela	4	12	69	20
Africa	369	466	521	617

* Data from *South African Digest*, 29 August 1980, p. 2.
Source: International Monetary Fund, *Direction of Trade Yearbook*, 1975 and 1980, Washington, DC, IMF.

Although South Africa continues to industrialise, its exports to OECD countries have contained a decreasing proportion of manufactured goods since the mid-1970s; indeed, it has tended to revert to the role of a 'colony' in trade with the advanced industrialised states – raw materials (especially metals) in exchange for industrial products. By contrast, South African exports to NICs as well as to its own region continue to consist mainly of manufactured goods.[26] In other words, exports to NICs and to Southern Africa are crucial for South Africa's continued industrialisation (as well as for continued white affluence), especially in a period of global recession. Hence, its foreign policy attentiveness towards the semi-periphery globally and the periphery regionally.

(5)   South Africa in Southern Africa: from Dominance to Resistance

Settler, especially Afrikaner, hegemony in South Africa was a major influence on the evolution of the political culture and political economy of the rest of the region. White dominance was reinforced by the mineral revolution and subsequent association with the British Empire in two world wars and in the Commonwealth tariff scheme. As Pax Britannica began to decline, so settler interests became paramount, aided by an increase in autonomy and industry that wars and recession advanced during 1914–45. Cecil Rhodes and other settler activists had always foreseen a special place for South and Southern Africa within the empire, and the expansion of the regional railway network[27] and the establishment of the Southern African Customs Union in 1909 gave form to such dreams.

But the heyday of South African regional dominance was really the years 1960–74, a period of formal decolonisation in which weak and vulnerable political economies were left to the designs of the new subimperial power.[28] To be sure, there were infrastructural and ideological antecedents of South Africa's policies of 'dialogue' and 'détente', notably Malan's Africa Charter, but the combined economic, military and political superiority of the Afrikaner republic was a new phenomenon.[29] Prior to 1960 British, and to a lesser extent Portuguese, colonialism constituted a constraint; and after 1974 radical regimes within (Mozambique and Angola) and without (Russia and Cuba) the subsystem constituted checks. Moreover, the imperative of regional co-operation for the state was reinforced by (*a*) the logic of apartheid and separate development leading to a degree of 'decentralisation' inside South Africa, and (*b*) the opposition to apartheid and separate development outside South Africa. Regional integration provided a political as well as a strategic counter to various international pressures.[30] Not only was it an essential aspect of South Africa's industrialisation strategy, given the artificial restrictions on domestic demand, it also involved external countries and corporations in regional development under South African auspices.[31]

The centrality of South Africa's Southern Africa policy – because of its economic, strategic and political dimensions – is revealed in the almost-continual efforts made by the regime to enhance and embellish it in response to various critiques. Despite earlier setbacks over participation in an Africa Defence Organisation and in the Commission for Technical Co-operation in Africa south of the Sahara, Vorster launched his 'outward-looking' policy of dialogue in 1967 and regional 'détente' in 1974.[32] But while the Customs Union was renegotiated in 1969, the OAU and the front line states (FLS) came to reject such initiatives because (*a*) they never allowed for negotiation over apartheid internally, and (*b*) they were seen to reinforce South African dominance regionally.[33]

Nevertheless, because of the importance of regional interactions to South Africa at the levels of both super- (diplomacy and security) and substructure (economic production and industrialisation), the Botha government has revived and remodelled earlier formulations in its latest designs for a regional 'constellation of states'. These bring together plans for 'multinational' development and devolution domestically with notions of co-operation and alliance regionally. Deon Geldenhuys and Denis Venter put the continuing regional imperative into contemporary perspective:

> The advocacy of a constellation must be seen against the background of South Africa's and Southern Africa's international position. It is . . . clearly linked to the deterioration in the Republic's relations with the West; the escalating conflicts in SWA/Namibia and Zimbabwe/Rhodesia and South Africa's dissatisfaction with Western settlement efforts; South Africa's failure to reach a *modus vivendi* with black states further north; and finally threats to the Republic's own security and prosperity, particularly terrorism and sanctions. The creation of a constellation is therefore part and parcel of Mr. Botha's 'total national strategy' and features in his twelve 'policy principles'.[34]

Given the increasingly unreceptive regional *milieu*, however, the constellation idea, like earlier grandiose expressions, has had to be cut down in scale. First, 'the constellation idea, as initially formulated, sought to extend the frontiers of cooperation to the more contentious political and military spheres';[35] such dreams have largely been abandoned. And secondly, the broader, 'outer' constellation of Southern Africa has been downplayed compared with the narrower 'inner' constellation of a South Africa consisting of 'independent' Bantustans and constitutional 'councils'.[36] So in terms of both range of issue areas and scope of territory, the 'constellation' has already become a more modest proposal. Given the demise of previous grand strategies for the region – from free trade zone to economic community, from *cordon sanitaire* to military alliance, and from confederation to federation[37] – the latest 'package' seems unlikely to be bought by most potential consumers or participants. Given the constellation's antecedents and associations, Wolfgang Thomas has attempted to disaggregate and also forewarn, noting that

> at least three different elements are contained in the concept: economic interaction and cooperation amongst a wide range of fully independent African countries; military nonaggression between South Africa and its more proximate neighbours; and, thirdly, constitutional adjustments within South Africa on its way towards multiracial power sharing. In addressing itself to all three elements the concept is powerful and useful but also deceptive and confusing.[38]

Having been vulnerable to the earlier overtures on dialogue and détente black African leaders, especially following the decisive Mugabe victory in Zimbabwe, are unlikely to be so easily deceived and confused on this occasion. Indeed, the constellation proposal has hardly received any recognition or reaction outside South Africa itself. Instead, the independent states of the region, reinforced and encouraged by change in Zimbabwe, have begun to overcome their inheritance of 'psychological' dependence on South Africa by proposing alternative forms of integration which exclude the erstwhile subimperial power. Building on established linkages such as the FLS nine black leaders agreed at Lusaka in April 1980 on a Southern African 'Declaration toward economic liberation'. Because a degree of political and diplomatic cohesion and consensus already exists within this OAU subgrouping, the emphasis in the African Declaration, by contrast with the competing South African 'constellation' proposal, is on infra-structure and exchange:

> Southern Africa is dependent on the Republic of South Africa as a focus of transport and communications, an exporter of goods and services and as an importer of goods and cheap labour. This dependence is not a natural phenomenon nor is it simply the result of a free market economy. The nine states . . . were . . . deliberately incorporated into the colonial and sub-colonial structures centring in general on the Republic of South Africa.[39]

To reduce dependence on South African communications and industrial facilities the Declaration called for an alternative scheme for transportation and exchange excluding South Africa: 'This we believe is the route to genuine interdependence and represents the best hope for a just and cooperative future for the region as a whole.'

Given the posting of such an alternative to the latest South African proposal it seems highly unlikely that any leader outside of the 'inner' circle of Bantustans is likely to react positively to the constellation concept. Therefore, in addition to facing a growing politico-military threat, South Africa's beleaguered rulers seem destined to watch a gradual erosion in their traditional sphere of influence as it comes to reorient itself away from its inherited economic and infrastructural dependence. The possibility of it being able to use economic leverage to regain influence lost through political decolonisation and military resistance is increasingly unlikely.

(6) White Nation vs Black Power inside the South African State: from Hegemony to Paranoia

South Africa's attempt to re-establish a degree of regional order and stability through the establishment of a constellation of states seems to be a forlorn one. The prospect of external challenge and internal conflict is a particularly alarming one for the isolated white South African nation. It has come to recognise that it cannot easily defeat or deter simultaneous regional and domestic explosions; hence, the attempt to separate the two.[40] This appreciation of vulnerability is a new and unhappy one for the hitherto self-confident possessors of 'white power'; until Sharpeville in 1960 white interests had been ascendant throughout the postwar era. But the Portuguese coup, the defeat in Angola, the uprising in Soweto, disaffection in the 'coloured' community and, most recently, the stunning Mugabe victory have all undermined white assumptions and confidence.

For the first time the white leaders of South Africa are uncertain as the contradictions and constraints of apartheid intensify. Orthodox racial stereotypes and economic theories no longer work; hence, the new scepticism about separate development, confederation and the regional constellation. A further novel feature of the South African political economy is the inability of the white nation to define the state unilaterally in either political or economic terms. Black political leaders and movements and black workers and trade unions now insist on some degree, albeit severely circumscribed, of participation. Because white power and privilege are more problematic than ever, the state has invested considerable sums and hope in the creation of a local military-industrial complex.

This complex is vital not only for the maintenance of white oppression. It is also a reaction (a) to the threat of military sanctions by external arms suppliers, and (b) to the established dominance of Anglophone interests in the internal political economy. Through ARMSCOR and other national and trans-national corporations the South African state has developed a sophisticated and relatively autonomous military-industrial complex. Using British, French and now Israeli technology and skills South Africa has been able since 1945 to learn to build its own fighter jets, armoured vehicles, naval craft, and now missiles and nuclear materials. This capability is important not only for the defence of the state, but also for the advance of Afrikaner capitalism. The Nationalist Party has used the creation of a military-industrial complex to finance Afrikaner entrepreneurs in partnership with state institutions: the parastatal nexus.[41]

But despite the impressive productive capacity and destructive capability of the South African war machine, the white nation is less certain of its control than ever. White power no longer seems to deter expressions of black anger domestically; the regional environment is ever-more threatening; and the global situation provides little hope of new allies or aids. Yet it is the state's fear of black consciousness that is predominant.[42] As Gwendolen Carter notes,

It is commonly said that the Defence Force view of security is that 20 per cent is involved in meeting external dangers but that 80 per cent of South Africa's security problems lie inside its border. The Defence Force feels it can easily handle external dangers, such as they presently are, but that serious internal disruptions would be another and far more dangerous matter.[43]

Ironically, despite the overwhelming electoral dominance of the Afrikaner-based Nationalist Party, its leaders have been unwilling to grasp the nettle of black alienation by offering meaningful changes and concessions. Instead, the party's more reactionary members and regions have been able to undermine any real *verligte* proposals. This situation may change (*a*) if the Botha leadership is determined to enact *verligte* measures; (*b*) if separate-development schemes continue to be rejected by black leaders and peoples; and (*c*) if the military enlarges its role in the political process. One major, perhaps ominous, change under the current regime of ex-Defence Minister Botha is the involvement of the South African Defence Force leadership in decision-making. The inclusion of General Malan as Defence Minister in 1980 and the revival of the State Security Council are symbolic of a growing politico-military alliance, one that has joined the politico-corporate alliance now that the Afrikaner-Anglophone economic competition is rather muted. Following the growth of uncertainty in the 1970s the decade of the 1980s may constitute either a period of repression or a period of experimentation as the South African state attempts to distinguish itself somewhat from the established hegemony of the white South African nation in its dealings with black African countries and communities.

(7)   South Africa in the 1980s

Previous projections on the future of South Africa have been notoriously unreliable.[44] However, in the 1980s the options for the state and its several 'nations' are clearly more limited than before. And if the framework proposed in this chapter is valid – the recognition of sub- as well as superstructure and of global as well as regional and national interactions – then a limited range of plausible scenarios can be identified.

On the one hand, it seems apparent that any return to the status quo ante is now quite unlikely, one indication of the growing power of the Black Consciousness movement. On the other hand, to preserve the present status quo in a situation of growing domestic antagonism and regional and global threat may involve and increase the level of state repression. Alternatively, in a coalition of *verligte*, Bantustan and corporate leaders may devise reforms which are largely acceptable to bourgeois and petit-bourgeois interests throughout the republic. Finally, given class formation internally, radical regimes regionally and intensifying pressures globally, the liberation movements under ANC leadership may yet instigate a revolution in South Africa.[45] In any event all three options – repression, reform and revolution[46] – are plausible because the South African political economy is at a crisis-point. The distinctive national, regional and global implications of each of these scenarios are indicated in Table 14.2.

Table 14.2   *Alternative Futures for South Africa*

Options level	Repression	Reform	Revolution
National	Apartheid	Multinationalism	Socialism
Regional	Subimperialism	Constellation	Collective self-reliance
Global	Pariah	Western	Non-aligned

The mid- to late 1970s constituted, then, an historic conjuncture for South Africa, one in which sub- and super-structural, regional and global features shifted together kaleidoscope-like into a new pattern: a turning-point. At the global level the post-1975 period was characterised by instability in terms of both superstructure (demise of the Pax Americana and superpower détente) and substructure (demise of Bretton Woods and fixed exchange rates based on gold). At the regional level the post-1974 period was characterised by change, especially at the level of superstructure ('revolutions' in Mozambique, Angola and Zimbabwe and resistance to South African initiatives in BLS), even if not at the level of substructure (continued dependence on economic relations with South Africa despite attempts at national self-reliance and socialism). And at the national level the post-1976 period was characterised by an uncertain quest to recover order and direction after the trauma of Soweto, but neither at the level of superstructure (Bantustan 'independence' and 'multinational' councils) nor at the level of substructure (state capitalist mode of production with very unequal distribution of income and property) did the regime attempt or advance fundamental change. Indeed, the debate inside established South African circles is about the repression–reform choice, whereas the issue for black interests inside as well as outside South Africa is about the reform–revolution choice.

The repression scenario is the one preferred by *verkrampte* white interests and a small minority of conservative forces in the advanced industrialised states. By contrast, the reform option has a somewhat broader, and certainly more influential, constituency: *verligtes* inside and outside Afrikanerdom, including the black political and economic bourgeoisie in South Africa, corporate interests inside and outside South Africa, and Western states with some of the more 'moderate' African and other Third World leaders. The revolutionary alternative has by far the widest advocacy: the majority of people in South Africa in particular and in Africa in general, as well as most Third World and socialist states, but they do not necessarily have resources other than 'people's power' to advance such a goal.

However, in the mid-term future the revolutionary scenario seems more likely to occur than either the reformist or repressive options.[47] This is so because of (*a*) the relentless processes of class formation and black resistance inside South Africa; (*b*) the inexorable trend towards political and economic liberation in Southern Africa; and (*c*) changes in the balances of power and values in the world system. Given the continued centrality of South Africa to the region and to the continent – unless partition and implosion occur meanwhile – such a prospect is of considerable importance to Africa's overall development prospects, serving to enhance its returning confidence about the future.[48] Nevertheless, it is important to recognise that the transition towards a new political economy in South Africa will be neither easy nor speedy: advocates of repression and reform will be able to complicate the process, employing white South Africa's remaining links with powerful and conservative external interests.

In conclusion, however, an analysis of sub- as well as super-structure, as well as of South Africa's regional and global connections, points to the likelihood of radical change before the end of the century, with important implications for Africa in particular and for the Third World in general. Steven Langdon and Lynn K. Mytelka conclude their own preview of Africa over the next decade by projecting that:

South–South trade in the African context could be especially useful on a continental basis. But the prospect of such development depends heavily on successful overthrow of the white-run regimes in Southern Africa ... self-reliant black regimes in Namibia, Zimbabwe, and South Africa would make an immense contribution to alternative development strategy for all Africa, but considerable conflict will occur before such regimes finally emerge.

Armed conflict in Southern Africa, though, is likely to be no more than the most dramatic African form of confrontation between dependence and self-reliance in the 1980s.[49]

Given the established interrelationships between South Africa, Southern Africa and the world, such fundamental change within South Africa is pregnant with possibilities for the regional and international systems. For just as change in the world system has affected South Africa in the 1970s, so change in South Africa over the next two decades will impact on regional, continental, and global structures and situations.

In particular, the future of South and Southern Africa has profound implications for the rest of Africa. As Giovanni Arrighi and John Saul remarked prophetically almost twenty years ago, a revolutionary (rather than repressive or reformist) outcome there would affect inherited and continuing patterns of dependence and underdevelopment throughout the continent. They predicted in their own insightful scenario that although political decolonisation may progress northwards from a liberated South Africa,

In the 'centres' of Southern Africa the peasantry has been effectively proletarianised and the social structure ... leaves little, if any, room for a neocolonial solution ... a successful socialist revolution in Southern Africa would radically restructure neocolonialist relationships on the whole continent since, after a necessary (and admittedly difficult) period of reconstruction, it would act as a powerful pole of politico-economic attraction for the less developed and less wealthy nations of tropical Africa.[50]

Notes: Chapter 14

This chapter is a revised version of 'South Africa, Southern Africa and the world system', presented at Conference on South Africa in Southern Africa, Pennsylvania State University, USA, October 1980.

1   Raimo Vayrynen, 'Economic and military position of the regional power centres', *Journal of Peace Research*, vol. 9, no. 4 (1979), p. 356.

2 Kenneth W. Grundy, 'Regional relations in Southern Africa and the global political economy', in Mark W. Delancey (ed.), *Aspects of International Relations in Africa* (Bloomington, Ind.: Indiana University African Studies Program, 1979), pp. 95–6.

3 Larry W. Bowman, 'The subordinate state system of Southern Africa', in Timothy M. Shaw and Kenneth A. Heard (eds), *Cooperation and Conflict in Southern Africa: Papers on a Regional Subsystem* (Washington, DC: University Press of America, 1976), p. 16.

4 ibid., p. 17.

5 See, *inter alia*, Timothy M. Shaw, 'Southern Africa: cooperation and conflict in an international subsystem', *Journal of Modern African Studies*, vol. 12, no. 4 (December 1974), pp. 633–55; and Susan Aurelia Gitelson, 'The transformation of the Southern African subordinate state system', *Journal of African Studies*, vol. 4, no. 4 (Winter 1977–8), pp. 367–90.

6 See Pat McGowan and Felicia Harmer, 'Teaching international political economy: the role of values, history and theory', *Teaching Political Science*, vol. 7, no. 1 (October 1979), pp. 3–32.

7 Bowman, op. cit., p. 19.

8 Vayrynen, op. cit., p. 350. For more on concepts and cases of subimperialism, see Timothy M. Shaw, 'Inequalities and interdependence in Africa and Latin America: subimperialism and semi-industrialism in the semi-periphery', *Cultures et Développement*, vol. 10, no. 2 (1978), pp. 230–63.

9 Vayrynen, op. cit., p. 365.

10 J. A. Hobson, *The War in South Africa: Its Causes and Effects* (New York: Howard Fertig, 1969).

11 See Kenneth W. Grundy, 'Anti-neo-colonialism in South Africa's foreign policy rhetoric', in Shaw and Heard, op. cit., pp. 351–64.

12 See Timothy M. Shaw, 'The political economy of technology in Southern Africa', in ibid., pp. 365–79.

13 Nicolas Oppenheimer, 'Investment in South Africa today and tomorrow', Johannesburg, November 1979, p. 8.

14 ibid.

15 For insightful analysis of South Africa's interrelated regional and global positions, see Kenneth W. Grundy, *Confrontation and Accommodation in Southern Africa: The Limits of Independence* (Berkeley, Calif.: University of California Press, 1973), and 'Intermediary power and global dependency: the case of South Africa', *International Studies Quarterly*, vol. 20, no. 4 (December 1976), pp. 553–80.

16 See Timothy M. Shaw, 'International stratification in Africa: sub-imperialism in Eastern and Southern Africa', *Journal of Southern African Affairs*, vol. 2, no. 2 (April 1977), pp. 145–65. For a general introduction, see Immanuel Wallerstein, 'Semi-peripheral countries and the contemporary world crisis', in his *The Capitalist World-Economy* (Cambridge: Cambridge University Press, 1979), pp. 95–118.

17 Vayrynen, op. cit., pp. 365–6.

18 See Timothy M. Shaw, 'Kenya and South Africa: "sub-imperialist" states', *Orbis*, vol. 21, no. 2 (Summer 1977), pp. 375–94.

19 See, for instance, John Stockwell, *In Search of Enemies: A CIA Story* (London: Futura, 1976), *passim*, and *US Military Involvement in Southern Africa* (Boston, Mass.: South End/WMACAS, 1978); and René Lemarchand (ed.), *American Policy in Southern Africa: The*

Stakes and the Stance (Washington, DC: University Press of America, 1978).

20 On Henry Kissinger's 1976 Lusaka speech and subsequent 'shuttle diplomacy' (over Zimbabwe) and 'contact group' activities (over Namibia), see Donald Rothchild, 'US policy styles in Africa: from minimal engagement to liberal internationalism', in Kenneth A. Oye, Donald Rothchild and Robert Lieber (eds), *Eagle Entangled: US Foreign Policy in a Complex World* (New York: Longman, 1979), pp. 304–35. On the difficulties and dilemmas of effecting policy changes, see David Ottaway, 'Africa: US policy eclipse', in William P. Bundy (ed.), *America and the World 1979* (New York: Pergamon, 1980), pp. 637–58.

21 On these, see Timothy M. Shaw, 'Towards an international political economy for the 1980s: from dependence to (inter)dependence', Centre for Foreign Policy Studies, Halifax, NS, 1980.

22 For a recent illustration of the utility of such resources for South Africa's diplomacy, see the white regime's welcome to the Santini Congressional Subcommittee Report on 'Sub-Saharan Africa: its role in critical mineral needs of the Western world' in 'Information Newsletter Supplement', *South African Digest*, 5 September 1980.

23 See 'Mineral exports – the growth base narrows', *Standard Band Review* (Johannesburg) (August 1980), pp. 1–4.

24 See Mary Kaldor, *The Disintegrating West* (Harmondsworth: Penguin, 1979), esp. pp. 14–28; and Timothy M. Shaw, 'Dependence to (inter)dependence: review of debate on the New International Economic Order', *Alternatives*, vol. 4, no. 4 (March 1979), pp. 557–8.

25 See Timothy M. Shaw, 'Oil, Israel and the OAU: an introduction to the political economy of energy in Southern Africa', *Africa Today*, vol. 23, no. 1 (January–March 1976), pp. 15–26, and 'Inequalities and Interdependence in Africa and Latin America', op. cit., pp. 261–2.

26 See 'Essay: exports just keep on growing', *South African Digest*, 29 August 1980.

27 On the continued place of railways in the Southern African political economy, see Vincent Tickner, 'Southern Africa: the politics of railways', *New African Yearbook, 1980* (London: IPC, 1980), pp. 41–5.

28 On this period, see Timothy M. Shaw, 'Prospects for international order in Southern Africa: conflict and co-operation in a regional subsystem', PhD dissertation, Princeton University, Princeton, New Jersey, USA, 1976.

29 See 'South African international activity has been little more than the extension of its internal conflict – a struggle to make the world safe for apartheid', in Sam C. Nolutshungu, *South Africa in Africa: A Study in Ideology and Foreign Policy* (New York: Africana, 1975), p. 6.

30 On the 'balance of power' between transnational coalitions over Southern Africa, see Timothy M. Shaw, 'International organisations and the politics of Southern Africa: towards regional integration or liberation?', *Journal of Southern African Studies*, vol. 3, no. 1 (1976), pp. 1–9.

31 See Ruth First, Jonathan Steel and Christabel Gurney, *The South Africa Connection: Western Investment in Apartheid* (Harmondsworth: Penguin, 1974); and Barbara Rogers, *White Wealth and Black Poverty: American Investments in Southern Africa* (Westport, Conn.: Greenwood, 1976).

32 See Deon Geldenhuys and Denis Venter, 'A constellation of states:

regional cooperation in Southern Africa', *SAIIA International Affairs Bulletin*, vol. 3, no. 3 (December 1979), pp. 36–50; and Shaw, 'Prospects for International Order in Southern Africa', op. cit.

33 Contrast Douglas G. Anglin, 'Zambia and Southern African "detente" ', *International Journal*, vol. 30, no. 3 (Summer 1975), pp. 471–503; and Timothy M. Shaw and Agrippah T. Mugomba, 'The political economy of regional detente: Zambia and Southern Africa', *Journal of African Studies*, vol. 4, no. 4 (Winter 1977–8), pp. 392–413.

34 Geldenhuys and Venter, op. cit., p. 51.

35 Indeed, according to Nicolas Ashford, 'South Africa's generals in the corridors of power', *The Times*, 1 September 1980: 'Military strategists [were] also responsible for the concept of a "constellation" of Southern African states whereby South Africa plans to use its political, economic and military might to establish a grouping of moderate anti-marxist states in the subcontinent.'

36 See Willie Breytenbach, 'The constellation of states: a consideration', *South Africa International*, vol. 11, no. 1 (July 1980), pp. 54–7.

37 See Wolfgang H. Thomas, 'A Southern African "constellation of states": challenge or myth?', *South Africa International*, vol. 10, no. 3 (January 1980), pp. 113–24; and Geldenhuys and Venter, op. cit., pp. 37–50.

38 Thomas, op. cit., p. 126.

39 'Nine independent states of Southern Africa adopt a declaration toward economic liberation', *Southern Africa*, vol. 8, no. 5 (June 1980), p. 12.

40 See Gwendolen M. Carter, 'Internal and external security: can they be maintained?', in her *Which Way is South Africa Going?* (Bloomington, Ind.: Indiana University Press, 1980), pp. 111–26; and Ashford, op. cit. The latter suggests that the white regime now recognises 'that while the Defence Force, the most powerful conventional force in Africa, has the capacity to resist most forms of external aggression it could not deal with internal unrest as well'.

41 See Timothy M. Shaw and Lee Dowdy, 'South Africa', in Edward A. Kolodziej and Robert Harkavy (eds), *Security Policies of Developing Countries* (Lexington, Mass.: D. C. Heath, 1982), pp. 305–27.

42 For insights into this new form of 'African nationalism', see Gail M. Gerhard, *Black Power in South Africa: The Evolution of an Ideology* (Berkeley, Calif.: University of California Press, 1978).

43 Gwendolen M. Carter, 'Strategies for and against continued white domination', in Carter, op. cit., p. 129.

44 For a review of some of these, see Paul Goulding and Timothy M. Shaw, 'Alternative scenarios for Africa', in Timothy M. Shaw (ed.), *Alternative Futures for Africa* (Boulder, Colo: Westview Press, 1982), pp. 93–130.

45 On ANC policies and projections, see Thabo Mbeki, 'South Africa: the historical injustice', in Douglas G. Anglin, Timothy M. Shaw and Carl G. Widstrand (eds), *Conflict and Change in Southern Africa* (Washington, DC: University Press of America, 1978), pp. 131–50.

46 Compare the apartheid, liberal and revolutionary (nationalist and/or socialist) 'views' identified in Thandika Mkandawire, 'Reflections on some future scenarios for Southern Africa', *Journal of Southern African Affairs*, vol. 2, no. 4 (October 1977), pp. 427–39.

47 Contrast Heribert Adam, 'South Africa: political alternatives and prognosis', in Anglin, *et al.*, op. cit., pp. 214–34, with Timothy M. Shaw, 'Southern Africa: from detente to deluge', *Year Book of World*

Affairs (Boulder, Colo: Institute of World Affairs/Westview Press, 1978), Vol. 32, pp. 117–38. See also Simon Jenkins, 'The great evasion, South Africa: a survey', *The Economist*, 21 June 1980.

48 See Timothy M. Shaw, 'From dependence to self-reliance: Africa's prospects for the next twenty years', *International Journal*, vol. 35, no. 4 (Autumn 1980), pp. 821–44.

49 Steven Langdon and Lynn K. Mytelka, 'Africa in the changing world economy', in Colin Legum, I. William Zartman, Steven Langdon and Lynn K. Mytelka, *Africa in the 1980s: A Continent in Crisis* (New York: McGraw-Hill, for 1980s Project; Council on Foreign Relations, 1979), p. 211.

50 Giovanni Arrighi and John S. Saul, 'Nationalism and revolution in Sub-Saharan Africa', in their *Essays on the Political Economy of Africa* (New York: Monthly Review, 1973), p. 86.

Index

Solodonikov, Vasily 100
  quoted 94
Somalia 99, 140
South Africa:
  apartheid system *see separate entry*
  Bantustans 16, 55, 151, 218, 262, 271, 308
  challenges/threats to, political and economic 254–5, 258, 261, 263, 271, 284–5, 309–11, 312; African states, independence of 254, 281–2, 284, 310; Angolan civil war, intervention in 96, 283–4, 310; communist expansion, fear of 68, 74, 76–7, 125–6, 255, 283; policy re-evaluation resulting from 255–9, 262, 268, 281–2, 285, 287, 312–13; verligte-verkrampte split and 255, 256–9, 268, 311, 313; repressive response 255, 256, 261, 263, 267, 270, 285, 312, 313; *see also* resistance *below*
  constitutional change 262, 271
  defence (SADF) 267; arms sales 12, 181–2 (*see also* arms embargo *under* sanctions); arms (and arms related) industry 264–6, 310; attacks on FLS 229, 261, 270, 283, 285, 287, 299; capability 50, 55, 127–8, 145, 263, 285, 310; nuclear 50–1, 57, 122, 127–8, 185, 264, 285; conscription/ military service 214, 215, 217–18, 228, 262, 263; expenditure 224, 263, 265; manpower 266–7; media coverage, censorship of 221; planning/strategy 137, 264, 270, 283; future scenario 270, 272–4; and police, relationship between 267; politico-military alliance 311; propaganda re 221; psychological warfare 221–2, 285; and state control 251, 253, 261, 263, 268; and terrorism, response to 261, 262
  dependence on 62, 72–3, 79, 208; attempts to lessen xiv, 38–9, 72, 80, 81, 115, 208–9, 253–4, 308–9; sabotage/subversion of 285
  destabilisation policy 56, 206, 270
  détente and dialogue 8–9, 12, 22–3, 27, 34, 54, 66, 74, 80, 114, 283, 307, 308
  education system, militarisation of 221
  economy 51, 298–9, 300–2; exports/ imports 168, 174–6, 177, 258, 304–6; foreign investment 8, 51, 52, 178–80, 188, 256, 260, 266, 287; growth 165, 252–3, 301; military-industrial complex 264–6, 310; state/business alliance 298–9, 301, 311; vulnerability 258; and World

recession 254, 303–6
future scenarios xii, xv–xvi, 153, 269–70, 271–4, 294–5, 311–14
importance of, economic and strategic 120–33 *passim*, 142–3, 145–6, 172–81, 260; arguments against 133–4, 138–40, 146–8, 172
intransigence of 268–9, 271–2
isolation 4–5, 55, 149–52, 163, 189–91, 254, 255, 258–9, 281, 287, 302–3; *see also* sanctions
labour: EEC code of conduct 185–6; militancy of 284; political process, demands for participation in 310; relations 284–5; revolutionary potential 261; Wiehahn Commission recommendations 185–6
media, censorship and control of 221
mineral deposits 51, 129–31, 145–7, 165, 177–8, 246, 252, 260, 266, 297, 300, 303; coal reserves 237, 252; oil from 51, 238, 241, 243
and Namibia 52, 56, 290
oil needs and supplies 237, 238–9, 258, 304; censorship re 237; from coal 51, 238, 241, 243; companies 241–3; exploration 243–4; imports 238, 245, 303; reductions in 238, 243, 245; sources 239–41; stockpiling 244–5
police force 267
policies towards/relations with (and vice versa): African states (in general) 69–70, 81, 253, 281–2, 284, 285, 288, 290; Angola 7, 22, 43, 56, 74–5, 79, 81–2; civil war, intervention in 96, 283–4; *see also* UNITA; Malawi 7–8, 282; Mozambique 7, 22, 74, 283; Nigeria 41–58 *passim*; OAU 10, 11, 14, 15, 16, 114; Rhodesia/ Zimbabwe 7, 22–3, 208, 262, 283; Zaire 62–73, 74, 77–8, 81–2; Zambia 282, 283; Argentina 305; Brazil 305; EEC 149, 171–91; FLS 114–15; France 181, 186, 187; Germany, Federal Republic 182, 187; Great Britain 162–9, 173–6, 252; Iran 239; Israel 187, 264, 305; MNCs 172–3, 178, 188–9, 266; NATO 138, 287; oil companies 242–3; Taiwan 305; USA 8, 39, 56, 121–2, 135–6, 143–5, 150–4, 187, 259–60, 286, 290; USSR 111–17, 147; Western powers (in general) 259–61, 283, 287, 291, 302–3
Portuguese *coup d'état*, effect of 21, 73–4, 254, 268, 281–4, 310
regional dominance 306–9
resistance: liberation movements 10,

foreign policy objectives 93, 97, 103–6 *passim*, 109, 140
in Southern Africa (in general) 89, 93–109 *passim*, 113, 114, 124–5, 141; Angola 91, 96, 97, 99, 101, 102, 105, 106, 124, 140, 285; Mozambique 91, 96, 97, 99, 105, 106, 124, 285; Namibia 102, 109–11; Rhodesia/Zimbabwe 11, 91, 96, 100–1, 102, 106–9, 114, 116, 124; South Africa 111–17
mineral wealth 131
relations with (and vice versa): China xv, 94, 95–6, 99, 113; South Africa 147; Somalia 99; Western powers (in general) 95, 97–8, 101, 102, 104, 105, 106, 111, 116–17; Zaire 80

Vayrynen, Raimo, *quoted* 297, 301
Venter, Denis, *quoted* 307
Verwoerd, Hendrik Frensch 168
Viljoen, Gerrit van Niekerk 163
Vorster, John 14, 22–3, 35, 268, 283, 307 *quoted* 34, 74, 77

Walls, Peter 203
war *see* liberation movements/struggle
West Africa 198
West Germany *see* Germany, Federal Republic of
Western powers (in general) 22
and Southern Africa 89–90, 95, 98, 285–9, 291; Angola 147, 286; Mozambique 286; Namibia 286; Nigeria 288–9; South Africa 259–61, 283, 287, 291, 302–3; apartheid system, attitude to 39, 52, 55, 148–52, 182–3, 288, 289; military ties with 137; sanctions 246; strategic importance of 120–33 *passim*, 142–3, 145–6, 172, 176–7, 178, 260; arguments against 133–4, 138–40, 146–8, 172; Soviet presence in, attitude to 90–1, 95, 96, 103, 123, 124–5, 126, 140, 181
USSR and 95, 97–8, 101, 102, 105, 106, 111, 116–17

see also EEC *and under individual countries*
Wilkinson, A. R. 225
Wilson, Harold (*now* Baron Wilson of Rievaulx) 168

Young, Andrew 134, 144

Zaire 10, 51, 61–82, 203, 228, 270
economy 67–8, 69, 70, 79
foreign policy 78
future scenario 82
ideology 61, 75, 78–9
relations with (and vice versa): African states (in general) 63–4, 78–9, 80–2; Angola 64, 66, 73, 75, 78, 79, 80, 106; Mozambique 81; South Africa 62–8, 68–73, 74, 75, 77–8, 81–2; Tanzania 80; Zambia 78, 80; FLS 81; socialist countries 75, 80; Western powers 62, 64, 65, 75, 77, 78, 79
Shaba invasions, effect of 75–82
transportation, dependence on SA 62, 72–3
Zambia 14, 15, 23, 24, 26–7, 51, 70, 80, 100, 106, 190, 200, 201, 209, 220, 229, 236, 248, 270
ideology 23, 26, 36
and Rhodesia/Zimbabwe: aid links 209; independence, effect of 22; UDI 29, 30
relations with (and vice versa): German Democratic Republic 99; USSR 99; Zaire 78, 80
role in Southern Africa 28, 30, 36–7
SADF raids into 229, 270
and UN 30
ZANU 206
ZANU (later ZANU(PF)) xii, 11, 24, 32, 91, 96, 101, 107, 124, 199, 200, 203, 205, 206, 220, 228
ZAPU 11, 24, 32, 91, 96, 100–1, 107, 108, 114, 199, 203, 206, 220, 228
Zimbabwe *see* Rhodesia/Zimbabwe
Zvobgo, Eddison 200